The Complete Book of
Dreams &
Dreaming

The Complete Book of
Dreams &
Dreaming

Pamela Ball

ARCTURUS

For Hannah, a truly inspirational figure and dreamer
from the past; for Jacob and his generation, the
dreamers of the future; for those in the here and
now, may you enjoy exploring and understanding
your own dream world.

ARCTURUS

This edition published in 2010 by Arcturus Publishing Limited
26/27 Bickels Yard, 151–153 Bermondsey Street,
London SE1 3HA

Design and layout copyright © 2010 Arcturus Publishing Limited
Text copyright © 2010 Pamela Ball

ISBN: 978-1-84837-717-2
AD001603EN

Printed in the UK

Contents

Introduction

The knowledge and information we acquire through our dreams opens up a whole world of creativity and possibility. Dreams tap into a huge database of memory, experience, perception and cultural belief which we might label the past, and they also enable us to form new ideas and concepts – the future. Dreams also give us access to another dimension of our being – spirituality and the use of our inherent power. One definition of spirituality is the awareness of other dimensions of existence beyond that of the purely physical, tangible realms.

Dreams will thus often need to be interpreted from more than one perspective in order to be fully understood. For this reason each entry in the lexicon is divided into three sections. We may simply be looking for an easy explanation for the images in our dream, in which case the section labelled 1 will suffice. We may also choose to look for a more psychological or spiritual interpretation in which case we will consider the second and third interpretations and concepts.

For ease of reference we have also gathered together those common dream images which easily fall into sections all of their own. These are: Animals, Birds, Buildings, Body, Family, Journey, Occupations, People, Religious Iconology and Transport. This means you will only need to look in one place for all images of a certain kind. Do remember that, because we are naturally holistic – that is, the sum of our parts – dream interpretation cannot be an exact science and we must always take into account our understanding of ourselves and our lives.

Dreams also present us with a way of solving problems which may seem impossible on a conscious level. Rather than simply sorting and filing information, which many feel is their only function, dreams become a tool giving us a much wider perspective and fuller appreciation of subtle mental and spiritual skills. Interestingly, many Eastern cultures see sleep itself as a learning experience and also as preparation for when we die.

Free from waking inhibition, our dreaming mind will create scenarios and situations which may apparently defy logical explanation. In looking for explanations we have to become more creative and open to the pursuit of knowledge. We tap into not only our own storehouse of images, but also into an even more subtle level of information that renowned psychoanalyst Carl Jung labelled the Collective Unconscious which is available to everyone.

This is the level that led to his work on the archetypes – which we explore more fully later in the book – and the one which gives us much of the rich imagery of this volume. It is as though there is some kind of internal pendulum which eventually sorts out the opposing concepts of the masculine and feminine into a unified whole. It was Jung who recognised Man's potential for developing symbols as a way of understanding himself and others, and he who first gave a name to the Anima (the feminine within) and to the various parts of the personality.

Nowadays we are aware that the unconscious mind appears to sort information by comparing and contrasting. When we are aware of disharmony within ourselves, whether this is between the inner and the outer selves, the masculine and feminine or whatever, we may dream in pairs (e.g. masculine/feminine, old/young, clever/stupid). Dreams have always been used to make sense of those things which are not understood in everyday terms, and it is perhaps sensible initially to define those aspects of our character which have now been accepted in the modern day to have a validity all of their own.

There are three main aspects of the personality which continually manifest in dreams – the Shadow, the Animus or Anima and the Ego. Most of us become more aware of these facets and the images they create only when we need to deal with them. Sometimes the images are of people we know, sometimes fictitious figures, or those from myths and fairy tales and sometimes images such as animals and birds. We gain a great deal by working with the information presented to us.

Inner development happens when we choose to grasp and bring into harmony each of these aspects of our identity. As each aspect develops, we are able to make use of more and more energy. We need to remember, however, that it is important to manage any initial disharmony which may arise since each separate part of our character has to develop on its own without confusing the others. When disharmony makes itself felt, particularly in dreams, while the effect may be distressing, it does highlight an inner difficulty. When handled properly, this disharmony is ultimately beneficial. We can reach the point where those aspects first seen as separate entities are blended into a harmonious and powerful conscious whole.

The most forbidding entity is called the Shadow and appears frequently in dreams. It epitomises our most basic defects and shortcomings. Because of its shocking and wilful qualities it is the part that we instinctively subdue. It does eventually reveal itself as the same gender as we are. The next entities to be understood are the Anima in man and the Animus in woman – that component of the opposite sex inherent in us. In a man, the Anima is all that is intuitive, feminine and perceptive. In a woman, the Animus is her masculine traits of reason and impartiality.

Our most conscious aspect is the Ego. It tends to be more observant of the hostilities that show up with other aspects. When all of these previous aspects have made their presence felt, the most truly creative part of all, the True Self, becomes apparent. Once it has been allowed the right to express itself, it frequently appears as a guide/mentor or a figure such as the wise old man.

The more ways we have of contemplating our dreams, the greater will be our insights into our own and others' personalities. To make it easier to do this we have included a number of pages at the end of the book to enable you to begin to categorise and work with your own dreams. As time goes on you will begin to build up your own library of images which appear most frequently. Broadly, you will be able to use the entries in this book as a starting point, and gradually you will begin to realise that a particular type of character appears more often or perhaps that an animal or building has significance for you.

It is at this time that dreams become a real tool in your path to self-development. Your inner guru is beginning to make its presence felt, to 'speak' to you through your dreams. You are being encouraged to explore a wider field than just that of your own experience and can begin to make use of what Jung called the Collective Unconscious.

To understand this concept we need to think of it as the deepest levels of the unconscious, beyond our own personal unconscious. It contains the totality of experiences common to all men – our ancestors, right back to the time when man first began to question the whys and wherefores of his own existence. In much simpler shamanic societies, certain chosen individuals were able to journey in this Underworld and bring back information which healed others and enabled them to live their lives more fully.

Today with the help of the use of technology and the work of neuro-physicists we have a much clearer grasp of the way the brain works and, by combining the ancient knowledge with the new, can work with various states of awareness to bring through to consciousness those ideas which have stood the test of time. We are now able to undertake our own personal exploration of our inner space and its many idiosyncrasies.

Dreaming is one such state of awareness and as such is entirely personal. We may need the help of a dream interpreter to unravel the complexities of a dream, just as a shaman needed to unravel the complexities of the Underworld and the demons which existed there. However, ultimately, we must ourselves work with the information we receive and make small and subtle changes in our everyday lives, to accommodate what we learn, whether the dream was good or bad, or – more accurately – disturbing. Just as a matter of interest, in the Jewish community if someone had a bad dream he would say to three different people on waking, 'A good dream I have had'. The reply would be, 'Yes it is good, let it be good', thereby helping the dreamer to turn bad into good. In this way, though the dream itself may have been disturbing, the outcome of working with the dream is of benefit.

Dreaming thus has a dual function and it is this personal aspect of dreaming which makes it the bridge between our own experiences and those of others. First, it allows us to achieve integration between our inner and external being, to make sense of the world in which we live, to quantify who we are. Secondly, it allows us to recognise that we can become part of a greater whole, to understand that we are part of a 'broad brush' approach to life; that we are moving forward to a more integrated, inclusive way of being. We are, if you will, beginning to learn how to fashion a new future and to put in place those habits which will make it a sustainable one for all.

With that knowledge we can live our conscious lives with honesty, integrity and awareness. Then truly, in the words of the poet Arthur O'Shaughnessy,

We are the movers and shakers
Of the world forever, it seems.

Pamela Ball

Abacus

Also see Calculator/Calculations

① As a child's toy the abacus in dreams represents our ability to create order and to quantify information.

② The ability to give a value to something and to use arithmetic and counting shows a degree of psychological maturity.

③ To be able to count was once considered a 'dark art'. An abacus gives tangibility to what once would have seemed magical.

Abandoned

① Similar to the sense of being rejected, this represents a sense of how we experienced not being wanted when we were young. This may not actually be how it was but our feelings give us that perception. For instance, a child having had to go into hospital may have recurring dreams in adulthood of **being abandoned**, and may have problems in forming plans for future success.

② To be abandoned, i.e. **without restraint**, within a dream may mean that we are looking for freedom. This could be emotional freedom, or the freedom to be ourselves.

③ This links with the Dionysian concept of abandoning the serious for fun.

Abdicate/Abdication

① To abdicate is to go back on a promise, so such a dream would suggest that we have given up or are prepared give up an important task or duty.

② When we have a position of responsibility which we feel is beyond our capabilities we may dream of abdication.

③ When we have set out on the path of spirituality there are times when we will wish to abdicate responsibility for our own progress and cease searching. It is at these times that dreams of trying to abdicate can show the way forward. We are being offered choices.

Abnormal

① Abnormality in a dream usually represents something which we instinctively feel is wrong or not balanced properly. If it is abnormal in the sense of extraordinary, such as an **abnormal feeling or sound**, it is the strangeness of it which needs to be explored. We may, for instance, dream of **someone laughing at a funeral** which would indicate that we would need to pay particular attention to the way we feel about that person.

② An awareness of abnormality alerts us to the fact that we should be paying particular attention to areas in life which are not in line with the way we feel they should be. To dream of **a dwarf or a giant** can indicate that our attention is being drawn to particular issues to do with size or deformity. There is something in our life that may be too big to handle.

③ The abnormal or strange usually possesses magical powers, possibilities or opportunities.

Abortion

① There may be a need to reject a feeling, emotion, belief or concept which could be troublesome in some way. A risk has been taken which has not worked, and we now need to put ourselves back to the way we were. We have internalised a new way of thinking or of being which, on further consideration, needs to be rejected.

② The ability to look clearly at what we have undertaken to do or to be in our lives should be utilised. Decisions should be made which will get rid of what is no longer needed.

③ We are in the position of having to abort a previously well-loved concept when circumstances dictate a necessity to move on.

Above
– see Position

Abroad

① To dream about **being or going abroad** gives us an understanding of our feelings towards the widening of our horizons, or making changes in our lives. Such dreams may also be connected with beliefs about the country in the dream *(See Places)*. We are dreaming about personal freedom or the ability to move freely around our universe.

② There is a psychological need to get away from (escape), or leave, a situation. We are perhaps travelling towards something new. Our minds are more than capable of accepting new input and experience and will often do so on a subliminal level. We then become aware through dreams of what we have learnt, or what we have to do.

③ Being aware of **going or being abroad** in a dream indicates we are ready for new spiritual experiences. This may temporarily take us out of our comfort zone, but benefits us in the long run.

Absence

① A dream about someone being absent, or of the absence of something one would expect to find, indicates that the unexpected may happen. We may be looking for something which we have already lost. Our feelings about the absence (e.g. fear or anger) may also be important. A child experiences a strong sense of loss when mother is first absent from his perceived environment, and this can cause extreme distress.

② We are in a situation where we may suffer loss or where we may reject something we need. The type of dream where we are **in a familiar environment, but a much-loved article or person is missing**, suggests we may have a feeling of impermanence .

③ To experience an absence, or a sense of nothingness, suggests the Void or the Abyss.

Absorb

① To be **absorbed in what we are doing** in dreams indicates our ability to be totally focused on our action. We are capable of taking in ideas, concepts or beliefs which then become part of us and the way we function. To **absorb something into ourselves** is to consume it, in the sense of making it our own. A great deal of the process of understanding takes place through absorption of information.

② As we mature and grow we perceive the necessity to belong to social groups. To be **absorbed into something** represents the need to belong to a greater whole, or to make efforts to integrate various parts of our lives.

③ We have the ability to integrate the various parts of our lives. Spiritually our yearning is to go back to Source.

Abstain/Abstention

① We may dream of abstaining from a vote or decision when offered choices in waking life which will force us into a course of action. We may not feel ready to make such a decision.

② Abstention in the psychological sense can suggest either not giving in to temptation of any sort or an act of self-denial.

③ Spiritually, abstention is a deliberate act of asceticism in order to achieve an outcome for the Greater Good.

Abuse

① To be conscious of abuse in a dream is to be aware of mistreatment and the potential to become a victim in some way. To be the abuser shows we are taking advantage of someone else's vulnerability.

② To dream of being abused suggests that we have become aware in waking life that we are being taken beyond our comfort zone. This may be by a part of our own personality – that part that sits in judgement.

③ From a spiritual perspective, abuse is the misuse and misappropriation of our inherent energy and power.

Abyss

① To dream of an abyss indicates we recognise within ourselves the so-called bottomless pit or void. This is an aspect of the unknown which all of us must face at some time or another in our lives. It is a risky action which must be taken without knowledge of what the outcome is going to be.

② There is a fear of losing control, of a loss of identity, or of some type of failure. More positively, it is possible to go beyond our own boundaries or present experience. Also the abyss indicates our coming to terms with opposites such as right or wrong, good and bad.

③ The Underworld, and inferior matters, appears in dreams as the abyss.

Accident

① Dreams of being injured, murdered or killed occur relatively frequently, and attention needs to be paid to the specific circumstances of the dream. We are usually receiving a warning to be careful or to be aware of hidden aggression, either our own or others.

② Dreaming of accidents highlights anxieties we have to do with safety or carelessness – either our own or others. They also indicate or fear of taking responsibility.

③ Since there is no such thing as an accident in spiritual terms, it signifies Divine intervention, or input from an authoritative source.

Accounts
– also see Calculator/Calculations and Invoice

① To dream of accounts or accounting suggests that some kind of reckoning is appropriate. We may need to look at our emotional resources as much as our financial status.

② There is a part in each of us that is continually trying to achieve a balance between our inner resources and the expenditure of energy in our everyday lives. To be working with accounts, particularly a balance sheet, in dreams can both symbolise and clarify this task.

③ In many systems of belief there is the idea of being called to account for our actions. Dreaming of having to deal with accounts may highlight this and enable us to be aware of, and come to terms with, karma - the law of cause and effect.

Acid

① There is a corrosive influence in our life which is usually bad but may be cleansing. There could be the feeling that we are being eaten away by some action or concept. The necessity is to become aware of that which must be used with caution, depending how, and on whom, it is being used.

② Psychologically, there is an awareness that self confidence and our usual sense of well-being is being eroded by outside influences.

③ We should be aware of corrupt behaviour and nastiness and how it can eat away at our Spiritual integrity.

Achieve/Achievement

① To have a sense of achievement in a dream suggests that we have overcome difficulties and problems in waking life and have achieved, or are capable of achieving, an objective.

② The psychological boost we get from achieving an objective in dreams can, with practice, be carried over into our daily lives and symbolise the way we need to act in the future.

③ The achievement of success in a spiritual task can be symbolised in dreams in many ways – climbing a mountain, crossing a river, overcoming a monster and so on.

Acorn

① To dream of acorns indicates that there is a huge growth process beginning to emerge from small beginnings. There is a new potential for strength. Since acorns appear in autumn, there may be the need to harvest or gather up the ideas before they can be stored in order to give them time to work.

② The germ of an idea is present. There is also a need for patience in dealings either with ourselves or others.

③ Life, fertility and immortality are symbolised by the acorn, as is the androgynous. The acorn also represents prosperity.

Acquit/Acquittal
– also see Judgement

① When in waking life we absolve someone from blame, we may dream of an acquittal. We may however have been judgemental and need to justify our decision either to ourselves or others.

② To feel that we have acquitted ourselves well in a trying dream scenario suggests that we have overcome an obstacle within ourselves.

③ Spiritually, to be acquitted of something in dreams is to be found not guilty of a misdemeanour which others may have not recognised in waking life.

Action

① The action within a dream will often inform us of hidden agendas and motivations, since each of us is the producer of our own lives. What we – or others – are doing in a dream often needs to be interpreted, as much as the articles in the dream.

② We should be aware that any particular action which is highlighted needs to be translated from dreams into waking life to enable us to move forward.

③ Being aware if a specific action in a dream can give an indication of our Spiritual abilities.

Activist

① To dream of being an activist for a particular cause suggests a hidden passion for whatever is represented. If the cause is not one for which we have any particular feeling in waking life, we perhaps need to explore our own hidden agendas and decide whether it is simply the idea of participation which needs to be cultivated.

② If one of our dream characters is portrayed as an activist we may need to decide how much we are prepared to take responsibility for our actions.

③ When we undertake a spiritual journey, becoming an activist in a dream can reveal a particular aspect of our progress. A passionately held belief can bring about changes on many levels of existence and such a character appearing demonstrates that we are not powerless.

Actor
– also see Occupations

① To dream of an actor, particularly **a famous one**, is to become aware of the ego in oneself. Very often we become conscious of the roles we play in life and dreaming of such a character recognises that we are perhaps not playing the part we really want to in life.

② We each are actors in our own play, so to see ourselves as actors suggests we may be using an artificial personality or not taking charge of our own destiny. We are being given the opportunity to create a new personality.

③ We each need to take responsibility for our actions and the way we live Life.

Adder
– also see Snake and Serpent in Animals

① A 'slippery' person or situation is present in one form or another. There may be a situation where another person cannot be trusted, or one which we know we cannot control.

② Because any snake is taken to represent matters to do with sex (while more properly being more to do with male sexuality), there are unresolved issues to do with sexuality or fear of sexual activity.

③ The adder as a venomous snake can represent deceitfulness and negativity, particularly when used in a targeted manner.

Addict/Addiction

① To dream of **being addicted** indicates we have to recognise that there is a need and desire to acknowledge obsessive behaviour in ourselves or others. There is anxiety that someone or something is taking us over. To **be addicted to someone** is to have abdicated responsibility for ourselves. To **be addicted to a substance** such as tobacco or alcohol in a dream suggests an inability to relate properly to the world we live in. To dream of an addict is to recognise a part of our personality which chooses to live beyond the norms of everyday society and may be an aspect of self of which we do not approve.

② **The fear of addiction** is an identification of the hold our own passions may have over us. We fear loss of control (that is, control over ourselves), but also our control of other people. To be with a **group of addicts** suggests we do not understand our own behaviour in social situations. Our behaviour in waking life may show a lack of self-respect or discipline. We may discover that we tend to become the victim in everyday life.

③ This is connected with the pleasure-seeking, hedonistic aspect of the Self and a concentration on this, above anything else. We can also be addicted to suffering.

Adjust/Adjustment

① Depending on the circumstances around us in our waking lives we may need to adjust our conduct – dreams can often point the way as to best do this. For example, **adjusting our clothing** in dreams would suggest that we need to make changes in the way we come across to others.

② To find in dreams we are **making adjustments to our surroundings** – such as moving furniture – indicates a dissatisfaction with our present circumstances, and that we have the ability to improve.

③ Any spontaneous adjustment that occurs in our dreams highlights a spiritual shift of which we need to be aware. For instance, being inside and alone and then finding ourselves outside in company may highlight our introversion and extraversion.

Adolescent
– see People

Adopt/Adoption

① Adopting something or someone in dreams acknowledges that what it represents belongs to us – we are aware that we must take possession of, and responsibility for, it. It is this awareness of responsibility which comes across mostly in dreams.

② To dream of adopting a new baby may mean that we are taking responsibility not necessarily for a new life, but a new project or idea which was not ours in the first place.

③ Adoption of the beliefs and tenets of a spiritual way of life often requires forethought, consideration and commitment, before we are able to accept initiation.

Advertisement

① Depending on other aspects of the dream, this indicates those areas in our lives which need to be acknowledged or recognised. For instance, **an advertisement on a hoarding** might mean a way of working in the world, whereas a **television advert** would represent a way of thinking.

② There is a need to put ourselves on the line and to be acknowledged for who we are. If we **ourselves** are the subject of the advertisement, we should expect to be more up-front and open about our activities. If **someone we know** is advertising themselves in our dream, we may have become aware that they have the ability to help us in our activities. Conversely, our subconscious may be alerting us to their need for help.

③ Information received psychically needs acknowledgement so we can move forwards.

Advice

① Receiving advice in a dream means we should consider guidance from within, possibly from a part of ourselves which is unrecognised.

② In dreams **accepting advice** is acknowledging the need to be doing something we don't necessarily want to do. **Giving advice** is recognising that we are aware of information which can be helpful to others.

③ We all have an inner awareness. The Higher Self will often manifest itself as a figure which is giving advice.

Aeroplane
– also see Flight, Flying and Transport

① Dreams of aeroplanes can represent sudden or dramatic life changes. **An aeroplane taking off** represents a leap into the unknown and taking risks. **An aeroplane landing** indicates the success of a new venture or the outcome of a calculated risk.

② An aeroplane denotes a search for psychological freedom; a move towards independent being.

③ By association with the gods' winged chariot, the aeroplane represents a spiritual journey of discovery.

Affair

① We need to come to terms with our own sexual needs and desires for excitement and stimulation. Dreaming of an affair allows us to release such feelings. We may feel the need to do something naughty or something which means we have to take emotional risks.

② We could be actively seeking emotional satisfaction in a way that we usually find unacceptable in our waking lives. It is as though we are, in the dream state, experimenting with our own self-integration.

③ We are seeking an integration of opposite polarities – male/female, drive/receptivity, good/bad and so on. Ultimately, the integration of the duality that is inherent in all of us.

Airport

① In dreaming of an airport we are entering a stage of transition, making decisions to move into new areas of life. It may also indicate we are, or should be, making a fresh assessment of our own identity.

② We are being put in a position where our values may need to be reassessed in the light of our own – or someone else's – authority.

③ An airport, because of its transitory nature, is a place for new experiences. We are ready to consider our spiritual progression.

Alarm

① To **sound an alarm** in a dream shows we are aware of a situation in our everyday lives which is not in our own best interests. To **hear an alarm** is to be alerted to the need to be vigilant. To be fixing an alarm suggests we may mistrust our own intuition in waking life.

② Since an alarm is designed to alert us to danger or difficulty, for one to appear in dreams shows we may become aware of a threat which has not yet consciously registered with us.

③ From a spiritual perspective an alarm may signify some transgression against our own beliefs.

Alcohol
– also see Drunk, Intoxication and Wine

① When alcohol appears in a dream we may need or require a largely pleasurable experience or influence. We have available to us the means of changing perception. We can afford to let go and go 'with the flow' of what is happening to us.

② There is the recognition of the potential for emotional confusion out of which can come clarity. When the normal constraints we put on ourselves in waking life are removed, we can often reach our own truth. The symbol of alcohol can give us permission to do this.

③ Alcohol as 'spirit' is the conjunction of opposites, and is also a means of changing consciousness.

Alien

① There is something unknown and frightening which needs to be faced. We have never encountered the strangeness of the being which appears in our dream, and we must handle what happens.

② There is the potential for experiencing oneself – or a part of oneself – as not belonging. In dreams there is the realisation of being different from others in the way we live our lives.

③ Anything alien is unknown to us and is perhaps therefore to be feared. Only when it is understood can it be accepted unconditionally.

Allergy/Allergic

① In everyday life an allergy is a difficulty with the physical environment, so for one to appear in dreams suggests there is a discomfort around us that is not easily dealt with without help.

② Since the effect of all allergies is a degree of debilitation we need to look at what is sufficiently irritating to sap our energy in ordinary life.

③ An allergy in spiritual terms is a sensitivity to, or awareness of, negativity which requires attention.

Alone

① Dreaming of **being alone** highlights being single, isolated or lonely. More positively, it represents the need for independence. Loneliness can be experienced as a negative state, whereas being alone can be very positive. Often in dreams a feeling is highlighted in order for us to recognise whether it is positive or negative.

② We are recognising the necessity to deal with our own emotional make-up and reactions without the help of others.

③ There is a completeness, a wholeness, an all-oneness within our spiritual make-up. In theory we are our own best friend and have no need of other people.

Altar
– also see Table

① An altar in a dream represents the means or need to give ourselves up to something beyond ourselves that is more important than the immediate situation.

② Psychologically, this depicts being sacrificed either willingly or unwillingly. The act of sacrifice, or of making sacred, needs to be made in public so that it can be properly acknowledged *(See Sacrifice).*

③ In the presence of the Divine, we can give thanks, and be at one. Usually an altar represents religious belief of some sort. It is the table of communion – togetherness – but also it often suggests the division between the physical and the spiritual.

Alternative

① To be offered alternatives in dreams suggests we need to be more aware of the choices we have in waking life and to consider all our options.

② In dreams anything which is alternative – such as an alternative lifestyle or an alternative treatment – highlights our ability to think 'outside the box'. We should not be too narrow minded.

③ Alternatives from a spiritual perspective bring the concept of duality – physical/spiritual, good/bad – into prominence which must be considered before we can progress.

Amateur

① Since to be an amateur suggests a certain ineptness, it is this meaning which will at first be apparent. Such an image would signify a lack of skill in ourselves or others.

② An amateur in dreams, while traditionally a lover of a certain subject, indicates commitment – rather than necessarily skill – to an idea, a principle or a concept.

③ Spiritually an amateur in dreams represents the lover of the Divine or of Divine Power.

Ambulance
– see Transport

Amnesia

① To suffer from amnesia in a dream indicates our attempts to blot out the disliked. It also indicates a fear of change. Losing one's memory in real life can be traumatic, but in dreams it can be even more of a problem since we are not aware how much we actually should remember.

② Psychologically we fear losing access to knowledge, of knowing how to behave. Often we wake up feeling we have dreamt, but cannot remember the dream. This can be because it is too painful to deal with the trauma that lies behind the images created. We are consciously able to forget until such times as we are courageous enough to deal with those images.

③ Amnesia in dreams can suggest death, either past or present. This may not be a physical death, but a time of great change in our life.

Amputation

① When we dream of **amputation of one of our own limbs** we risk or fear losing or cutting off, by repressing, a part of ourselves. There is loss of a facility or something we value. To dream of **amputating someone else's limb** indicates our ability to deny others their right to self expression.

② We have cut short an experience in some way – perhaps in an unnecessarily brutal way. We are suffering from a loss of power or ability.

③ Spiritually we may be disfiguring the perfect, and not appreciating our, or others' abilities.

Amulet
– see Charm/Amulet

Anaesthetic

① To be anaesthetised in a dream highlights the fact that we are trying to avoid painful emotions, and feeling overpowered by external circumstances. It also indicates that we are trying, or being forced, to avoid something.

② We are numbing – or avoiding – something we don't want to face. We may be creating a situation which requires external management. We perhaps need to be quiescent and let events unfold around us.

③ As with amnesia, an anaesthetic can be a possible indication of death, but usually of part of ourselves.

Analyst/Therapist
– also see Occupations

① Whatever kind of analyst we dream about, we have within ourselves a monitor which alerts us to the need to analyse our actions and reactions. We should exercise self awareness and analyse our lives, breaking it down into manageable parts.

② The presence of an analyst can represent the knowledge that we are not acting appropriately in a situation in waking life.

③ We are in contact with the transformative power within.

Anarchy

① Anarchy in the sense of a disordered society is in many ways part of everyone's make-up; it signifies a chaotic part of our being which refuses to accept order. When anarchy appears in dreams we need to understand that part of us which is rebellious and untamed.

② While in everyday life we have to conform to the demands of society, in dreams we are able to protest and this may appear as anarchical acts.

③ Spiritually anarchy can signify the long-held principle that chaos can ultimately be creative and can give rise to necessary change.

Ancestors
– see People

Anchor

① When an anchor appears in a dream it can generally be taken to mean the necessity to remain stable in emotional situations. It shows we need to catch hold of a concept or idea which will give us a point of reference in difficult situations.

② Psychologically, we need encouragement to develop the ability to 'hold fast' during a period of instability. If we can ride out the storm we shall survive. When **an anchor is being dragged** during a dream, the external forces are too great for us.

③ We are in process of achieving hope of a future tranquillity. We become anchored in our own spiritual integrity without it merely being a transitory state.

Androgen
– also see Hermaphrodite/Hermaphrodism

① If we dream of someone and cannot decide if they are male or female, we are making an attempt to reconcile the opposite sides of ourselves. We are searching for completion and wholeness.

② We need the understanding of how our emotional selves can balance our personalities. We often need to reconcile opposing thoughts and feelings within ourselves to achieve a balanced progression.

③ The androgen in dreams can indicate a perfect spiritual balance, a state of autonomy and primordial perfection.

Angels
– also see Religious Iconology

① At its most basic, dreaming of angels indicates either that we are searching for a parental figure which will give unconditional love and support, or that we need to develop these qualities ourselves. We may also be trying to introduce religious concepts into our lives. As more people become conscious of the concept of angelic figures, the awareness of the need for purity becomes more apparent, whether that is purity of thought, emotion or being.

② Psychologically, and perhaps particularly in difficult times, we are in need of a specific kind of support. The angel in dreams is the personification of that kind of support and unconditional love first experienced from mother. To understand the psychic (soul) need for connection with angels and angelic figures, the relationship with the mother or mother figure needs to be looked at as a separate entity to both her and the dreamer. That relationship is believed by some to form a bridge between the physical and spiritual realms.

③ Spiritual development allows us access to different realms of existence, particularly through our dreams. Nowadays with a greater acceptance of the appearance of angelic figures they are once again accepted as messengers of the Gods, bringing heavenly powers and enlightenment. To a certain extent it will depend on which system of belief we subscribe to as to how we classify our angels and whether we choose to work with them and with the Archangels. We may form a relationship through dreams with one particular angel.

Anger/Angry

① Anger in a dream can often represent other passionate emotions. We are struggling with the right to express that which is distressing us. We probably are unable to express emotion appropriately in waking life, but can do so in dreams.

② We can give ourselves permission to feel passion. Often the way we express emotion in dreams can give us information as to appropriate behaviour in everyday life.

③ We are suffering divine displeasure.

Anima/Animus

① When we dream of a figure of the opposite sex we are attempting to give meaning and validity to the attributes and qualities of that particular gender. Thus a man may be trying to access his more sensitive side, while a woman may be attempting to become more logical. Dreams make an attempt to offset unbalanced conscious attitudes. If a man neglects his feminine side the Anima may appear in dreams as vengeful and destructive. If a woman neglects her masculine side, the Animus will appear in dreams as judgmental, competitive and overbearing.

② We are attempting to balance our psychological being through an ability to be objective about ourselves. Only through understanding that we hold within us elements of the opposite sex, can we become whole and properly integrated. The Anima will show herself as a completely unknown woman, aspects of women the dreamer has known or as feminine deities *(see Goddess/Goddesses)*. The Animus will appear as an ideal male figure, aspects of men the woman has known – often based on her perception of her father – or as godlike figures.

③ The polarity of the way we express our own gender is an equally valid part of our personality. Without the development and understanding of the Anima or Animus we do not have access to our fullest potential as human beings. Our relationships may suffer, our perception be skewed and our life's journey be less pleasant. When we make use of the qualities of the Anima or Animus we can develop more fully and achieve much.

Animals

① Most of the time, in dreams, animals represent aspects of our personality which cannot be easily understood except on an instinctive level. Before we look at the animals themselves, there are some basic images and interpretations to consider. For ease of interpretation we have listed them alphabetically.

Animal with a cub This represents motherly qualities, and therefore the mother.

Baby animal We are likely to be trying to understand the child-like side of our personality, or possibly children known to us.

Animals

Cold-blooded animals In dreams, the hostile, heartless aspects of our instincts are often portrayed by reptiles and other cold-blooded animals. They are usually recognised as being ultimately destructive and somewhat alien.

Composite animals To dream of composite animals (perhaps the body of one and the head of another) could indicate difficulty in deciding what qualities we need to use in a particular situation. There are two potentials present in one figure and we need to assimilate and integrate the different characteristics of the animals.

Deformed animals Through such a dream we can come to recognise that some of our impulses may be offensive to others. We understand our own wrong thinking or warped perceptions.

Eating an animal Shamanistic belief systems hold that, through eating the animal, certain aspects of it – such as bravery – can be assimilated. Animals are also often symbols of our lower, more primitive urges. Such a dream could therefore also be about the 'demons' we create which can only be overcome by using them constructively.

Godlike, talking, awe-inspiring or wise animals, or those with human characteristics In both fairy tales and dreams it is important to pay attention to these aspects of animal life, since they are an important part of our make-up. It is the part of us that has an instinctive wisdom and grasp of circumstances, but which is often not listened to in the hurly-burly of everyday life.

Half animal, half man (such as the centaur) We are beginning to recognise our baser animal instincts and to accept that they are a valid part of our personality. This image can also suggest the astrological sign of Sagittarius.

Helpful animals In the practice of modern day shamanism each person develops a relationship with their totem animals. Helpful animals in dreams are an easy way for us to accept assistance from our unconscious side.

Hurt young animal We may perceive a difficulty in becoming mature or facing life. It can be therapeutic to work with dreams as a way of putting ourselves in touch with our inner child, and working through some of the traumas which inevitably occur during childhood. This could be such events as illness or death in the family, a change in location and so on.

Killing the animal This may illustrate the need to come to terms with the energy derived from our baser instincts. We may well be aware that our motives are not necessarily of the purest.

Parts of animals (the limbs, eyes, mouth, etc.) have the same significance as parts of the human body. If the four legs are particularly emphasised, the whole rounded personality with all four functions of the fully developed mind is being highlighted.

Pets Pets represent unconditional love, affection and a mutual appreciation. A dead pet can represent the end of childhood or the loss of innocence.

Prehistoric animals A hidden fear, trauma from the past or from childhood may be causing us some difficulty and needs to be addressed.

Seeking refuge To dream of trying to find some refuge from animals, whether by building defences or perhaps by running away, raises the question as to whether action we take will protect us. We may be fearful of our instincts, and aware that we can lose control and become overwhelmed.

Taming or harnessing an animal shows the efforts we are making to control our instinctual responses and make them productive and useful. Just as a horse can be domesticated, so we can tame our instincts for the Greater Good. When we dream of already domesticated animals we are aware of those parts of ourselves with which we have come to terms. Passions are used in a controlled way, although it may be that those passions were never very formidable in the first place.

Threatening animals Any threat from animals indicates the fears and doubts we have over our ability to cope both with the stirrings of the unconscious and the travails of everyday life.

Transformation of animals We need to give consideration to the process of change as much as to the qualities of the animals in the dream. The transformation of a dreamer or other people into animals and vice-versa shows the potential for change within any situation.

Wild animals Usually wild animals stand for danger, dangerous passions, or dangerous people. There is a destructive force often arising from the unconscious, threatening our safety. Such a dream may also be a way of understanding anxiety.

Wounded animals Most animals have certain specific characteristics and appear in dreams whenever we need some sort of understanding of our own psychological urges. When a wounded animal appears, we ourselves may be suffering either emotional or spiritual wounds.

② Animals have always appeared as dream images and now, as we have a greater understanding of Shamanic belief, it becomes obvious that it is the qualities of the animal which are important in coming to an understanding of ourselves. It was not until the 19th century psychoanalysts began to explore dreams that the connection was made. Animals tend to surface in dreams as messengers from the unconscious. The list below is not exhaustive, but contains the animals which, experience shows, appear most in dreams.

Bear The mother appears in dreams in many guises, the bear among them. The image may be of the all-caring mother (the cuddly bear) or of the possessive, 'devouring' mother. If the bear is masculine then it may represent an overbearing person, or possibly the father or father figure.

Bull In dreams the bull is recognised as sexual passion, creative power and out-and-out masculinity and assertiveness. However, the bull also denotes the negative side of behaviour, such as destructiveness, fear or anger (for example, a bull in a china shop). *Slaying the bull* is a very powerful image, suggesting initiation into the world of the mature adult. This links with ancient festivals such as the slaying of the Minotaur. The bull can also represent the sign of Taurus in the Zodiac.

Cat To dream of cats is to link with the sensuous side in human beings, usually in women. The refined, but also the powerful yet self-reliant, aspect of woman may also be suggested. Goddesses, such as Bast the Egyptian cat goddess, are usually represented as having two sides to their natures, one devious and one helpful, so the cat often denotes the capricious side of the feminine.

Cow The eternal feminine, especially the mother or mother figure, is often depicted by the cow. This is partly because it provides milk and nourishment, but also – because of the herding instinct – the power of the collective.

Deer/Reindeer The deer, particularly the stag, signifies pride, nobility and status. The herd has an organisation, based on rank, so the softer smaller deer can also suggest submission and docility. To be *hunting deer* is pitting oneself against the forces of nature.

Dog (also see individual entry) We may need to recognise either a devoted and loyal companion, a protector or, oddly, somebody who might make trouble or we find bothersome. If the dog is *one that we have owned or known*, there may be memories or associations with that period which have relevance in the here and now. A dream of *a huntress with dogs* connects with one of the feminine archetypes – the Amazon or self-sufficient woman. A dog *guarding gates or being near a cemetery* indicates the Guardian of the Threshold and the potential for an initiation into the Underworld.

Donkey As a beast of burden the donkey symbolises patience or, on the contrary, obstinacy and determination. We may find ourselves being 'put upon' in waking life.

Elephant An elephant appearing in dreams signifies loyalty, memory, patience and strength. In the more esoteric sense it signifies lucid and dazzling wisdom and a grasp of the Collective Unconscious. If you are particularly aware of the elephant's *trunk* it may represent the penis and issues of sexuality. The elephant is also a symbol of Ganesh, the Hindu god of opportunity.

Fox A fox in a dream tells of dissimulation, cunning and crafty behaviour. It may also be a representation of the Trickster *(see Trickster)*, the part that can let us down at the last moment.

Fish Fish generally signify both temporal (worldly) and spiritual power. Dreaming of fish connects not only with our emotional side but also our ability to be wise without being strategic. We can often simply respond instinctively to what is going on, without needing to analyse anything. The Collective Unconscious is becoming available to us. Interestingly, the Celtic myth of the Salmon of Knowledge which ate of the hazel nuts demonstrates this particularly well. To be dreaming of *fishing* suggests we are searching for information. When the image of *two fish swimming in opposite directions* appears, this can be recognised as the astrological sign of Pisces.

Frog A period or act of transformation may be seen as a frog; a frog transforms from a tadpole and moves from water breathing to air breathing. This also represents the change from the unconscious to the conscious self. The symbolism may also be of something repulsive turning into something of value – for example, a frog into a prince.

Goat Dreaming of a goat shows we are aware of creative energy and masculine vigour – the life force. More negatively, it can signify the darker side of human nature, immorality and overt sexuality. Traditionally, the goat may also represent the Devil or Satan. It is also the symbol for Capricorn in the Zodiac.

Hare Because of its affiliation with the moon, the hare can signify the intuitive faculty, spiritual insight and instinctive 'leaps'. It is also the radiant hare (often holding its baby in a cave), and thus the Mother of God. The 'madness' associated with the March hare suggested the renewed energy brought by the changing seasons.

Hedgehog The hedgehog can represent wrong-doing and rudeness or, quite literally, our inability to handle a 'prickly' situation. We become defensive when under pressure. In fairy stories, and therefore sometimes in dreams, the hedgehog can represent a bumbling or somewhat ineffectual character.

Horse/Mare The figure of a horse in dreams represents our intrinsic vitality. Traditionally a *white horse* describes our state of spiritual awareness whereas a *brown* one represents our more rational and sensible side; a *black horse* is our excitable side. A *pale horse* suggests Death, and a *winged horse* depicts the soul's ability to transcend the earthly plane. If the horse is *under strain or dying* we may be having problems with motivation and feel insurmountable pressure in waking life. When the horse is *being harnessed* we may be focusing on thoroughly practical objectives rather than the spiritual. *In a man's dream,* a mare will denote the Anima *(see Anima/Animus),* a woman, or the realm of the feminine. If a woman is *being kicked by a horse* in a dream this may indicate her own Animus *(See Anima/Animus)* or her relationship with the masculine. A horse that can *get through any door* and *batter down all obstacles* is a representation of the collective Shadow – those aspects of the personality which most people attempt to suppress. The horse as *a beast of burden* often signifies the mother, or mother archetype. *Riding a horse* suggests that we have 'harnessed' those drives and motivations which carry us into the future. *Falling off* a horse suggests we have not yet controlled the energy inherent in our more powerful side.

Hyena Because of its scavenging nature, the hyena is taken in dreams to signify imperfection, lack of stability and deviousness. This is something of a stereotype but this animal can represent the darker side of human nature.

Insects Insects in dreams can reflect the feeling that something is irritating or bugging us. They may also indicate a feeling of insignificance and powerlessness in our waking lives. Insects link us to primal instinctive behaviour, that of survival against all odds, and a swarm signifies the effectiveness of a group dynamic which may permit the survival of the species – in this case our own. *Bees* suggest a particular kind of industriousness geared to the common good, it has been said that if the bees die out so, eventually, will humankind. A *wasp* might indicate danger, *flies* a particular kind of negativity, whereas a *beetle* could mean either contamination or – as with the *scarab beetle* – protection from evil.

Jackal/Coyote Esoterically, the jackal is the servant of the 'Transformer', guiding souls from the earth plane into the light. It is often associated with the graveyard, and therefore with death. The coyote also represents a transformer, usually of negative energy into positive. It can signify the Trickster *(see Trickster)* part of the personality. These particular dream images are interesting examples of geographically and culturally specific symbolism.

Jaguar The jaguar's main qualities are its speed and balance. In dreams it therefore suggests the balance of power between the dark and light forces. It is often met in dreams as the totem animal.

Kangaroo This animal often stands for motherhood, protection and also strength. Interestingly, it can also represent archetypal Destructive Mother because of its vicious kick.

Lamb The lamb is the innocent side of man's nature. It is said that evil cannot withstand such innocence, hence the Christian representation of Jesus Christ as the Lamb of God. In some dreams the lamb represents new life or a new way of living.

Leopard The leopard represents oppression and aggression and traditionally the underhandedness of power wrongly used. If it is the *leopard's spots* which are noticeable, there may be a situation in our lives which cannot be changed.

Lion The lion stands for dignity, strength and courage. It can also represent the developing ego and the feelings and emotions associated with this development. A *lion lying with a lamb* suggests that there is a union, or compatibility of opposites; instinct and spirit going hand in hand. If we are *struggling with the lion* there should be a successful development in waking life as long as we are not overpowered or the lion killed. The lion also represents the astrological sign of Leo.

Lynx In dreams the lynx suggests objectivity and clarity of vision, since it is well known for its keen eyesight. The lynx also has the same significances as the cat.

Mole The mole is often taken to represent the powers of darkness, but can signify the heedless perseverance and tenacity which enables us to succeed. We move shortsightedly forward, ignoring any undermining influences.

Monkey The qualities of mischief, impudence and inquisitiveness all belong to the monkey and characterise the immature, childish and undeveloped side of our personality. While these are often seen as regressive tendencies, that of lively curiosity maintains a necessary lightness of spirit.

Mouse The qualities of shyness and reticence seen in a mouse can often be addressed in us through dreams of that animal. Additionally, there may be an aspect of chaos 'gnawing' at us until we gain full understanding of a problem in waking life.

Otter The otter in dreams often suggests the ability to exist in an environment which is highly emotionally charged. We are able to see beneath the surface and look at the deeper picture.

Ox/Buffalo The ox depicts the ability to be untiring, and to make sacrifices for others. Similar to the bull, it suggests hard work and the rewards accrued through this. Interestingly, the buffalo can represent the same qualities and is another geographically significant image. It can sometimes represent the sign of Taurus in the Zodiac.

Pig As we learn and grow, our more Spiritual Self may recognise some unattractive qualities. The pig in dreams often indicates the lower qualities of ignorance, selfishness and greed. Without recognition of these lesser qualities we cannot attempt to master or transmute them. The pig also suggests a kind of earthy sensuality and big litters of piglets can represent fertility. Since the sow can also depict the archetype of the Destructive Mother, that fruitfulness can, however, be somewhat tainted.

Rabbit Rabbits have an obvious connection with fertility and sensuality in dreams. A *white rabbit* may also show us the way to the inner spiritual world and, as such, act as a guide. The Trickster aspect of the personality could also be coming to the fore, as opposed to the innocence of the 'fluffy bunny rabbit'.

Ram The ram is a symbol of masculine potency, energy and authority. It also signifies the qualities of leadership necessary within a flock or group and therefore can represent the dedication needed for such a task. *Sacrificing a ram* symbolises the inception of the Abrahamic religions of Judaism, Christianity and Islam. It also represents the astrological the sign of Aries.

Rat Traditional symbolism suggests that we may be experiencing disloyalty from a friend or colleague. The rat can also represent something which is repellent or gnawing away at us in some way. The rat may also signify the 'contaminated' aspect of a situation we are in, or a devious part of our nature. Slightly more positively, in some Chinese belief systems the rat represents prosperity and the best use of resources.

Reptiles To dream of reptiles indicates that we are looking at our more frightening lower attitudes. We may have no control over these, and could therefore be easily overcome by them until we understand them. If our initial reaction to such creatures is fear or revulsion, we must learn to deal with those feelings first. The *crocodile* is a personification of evil whereas the *lizard* appearing in a dream represents instinctive action or 'one-track' thinking. The *chameleon* suggests the changeability of human nature.

Seal The seal can represent our emergence from the instinctive state and can sometimes have the same significance as the mermaid in dreams. It suggests our ability to exist successfully within our created world. We are in touch with the elements in which we live but may not have progressed too far away from an instinctual reaction to circumstances.

Serpent/Snake The *serpent* is a universal symbol which can be male or female. It can signify life and rejuvenation, yet at the same time death or destruction. It is the instinctive nature and is also potential energy which, when understood and harnessed, enables us to come to a full understanding of our sexuality and sensuality and the Life Force. This means we are then able to make use of the higher and more spiritual energies which have become available. In a *man's dream a serpent* may appear if he has not understood his feminine or intuitive part, or when he doubts his own masculinity. In *a woman's dream*, the serpent may manifest if she is fearful of sex, or sometimes of her own ability to seduce others. Equally it may represent the instinctive Life Force.

We must at some point all come to terms with our more instinctive self. On a purely basic level, the snake or serpent has direct connotations with the penis. The serpent is most often taken to signify evil, yet it actually represents uncontrolled passion. Because of its connection with the Garden of Eden the serpent is the symbol of duplicity and trickery, and also of temptation. However, it also signifies the search for the spiritual.

A *snake entwined around the body or limbs* indicates some form of entrapment, possibly being enslaved to the passions. A *snake in the grass* denotes disloyalty, trickery and evil. The image of the *snake with its tail in its mouth*, the ouroboros, is one of the oldest available to man and signifies completion and the union of the spiritual and physical. *Being swallowed by a snake* shows the need and ability to return to the ultimate, and lose our sense of space and time. When *two snakes are twined around a staff* or similar object it is called the caduceus. It signifies the unconscious forces that are released once we reconcile the opposing sides of ourselves to create healing, rebirth and renewal. The double helix, now recognized as the structure of DNA, echoes this entwining. The symbol of the caduceus is used in many of the healing arts.

The image of the snake or serpent as sustained power is the most potent available, since our most primitive urge is sexual. Often this aspect of the personality is suppressed or thwarted and snake and serpent dreams occur usually when there is an aspect of sexuality or emotional passion that has not been understood.

Sheep The sheep is renowned for its flock instinct, and it is this meaning – the need to belong to a group – which is most usually accepted in dreams. The helplessness and the apparent lack of intelligence of the sheep when off-balance signifies our inability to put right a situation in which we find ourselves. The god-fearing, 'good sheep' and also the passive and 'sheepish' may have relevance within the context of the dream. To dream of *sheep and wolves*, or of *sheep and goats* is to register the conflict between good and evil.

Spider (also see individual entry) The spider represents the Great Mother in her role as the Weaver who weaves destiny from the body of her self, and is therefore the Creator. We become weavers of our own destiny when we recognize the ability to create a perfect pattern which both nurtures and protects us at the same time. On a very mundane level, there is a great deal of ambivalence in the image of the spider. It is disliked perhaps because of its scuttling movement but also because of its unfair association with lack of cleanliness and with dirty *cobwebs*.

Squirrel Because in waking life the squirrel is a hoarder, in dreams it represents the possessive aspect of our personalities. It may also suggest our ability to guard for the future. As an agile climber it reflects the ability for impulsive behaviour.

Tiger The tiger signifies royalty, dignity and power and has a dual aspect, that of both creator and destroyer. Like many of the cat family, the tiger represents femininity at its most powerful and protective.

Toad Implicit in the ugliness of the toad is the power of mutation and growth into something beautiful. To dream of toads is to connect with whatever we may consider ugly in life, yet also to recognise the power of transformation. For a *toad and an eagle* to appear together is to note the difference between earthly and spiritual values.

Vermin In the sense that they are unwanted and invade others' space, any vermin represents a negativity that needs to be got rid of. Often, if it the sheer overwhelming quantity that is noticeable in dreams, for instance, a plague of mice, rats etc.

Whale The whale – a mammal which lives within water – indicates the power of resurrection and rebirth. It signifies the primordial life force and our ability to 'come back from the dead' and to handle more than one set of circumstances at a time. The medium in which the whale lives represents deep emotion and therefore signifies our ability to deal with our own deepest self. Interestingly, the whale can also represent in its sheer size the Collective Unconscious.

Weasel/Stoat/Ferret All of these animals, because of their sinuous body shape, tend to represent a somewhat 'slippery' character. The *weasel* traditionally highlights the devious, more immoral side of ourselves. The *stoat,* while being of the same family, has a different connotation in that in winter it becomes the ermine – a symbol of royalty. In dreams it can therefore represent a transformative energy. The *ferret,* being something of a burrowing animal, can have the same significance as the mole or that of digging out necessary facts.

Wild Boar The wild boar depicts the archetypal untamed masculine principle, and therefore often represents the negative Animus in a woman's dream. Being *pursued by a wild boar* suggests we may be trying to escape from an issue that should be confronted.

Wolf Dreaming of wolves may indicate that we are being threatened by others, whether singly or in a pack. The She-wolf represents not only the hussy but also the carer of orphans and rejected young. There may be an element of cruelty in our lives which has gone unnoticed until the wolf appears in dreams.

Zebra This animal has the same significance as the horse, but with the additional meaning of balancing the negative and the positive in a very dynamic way. The zebra is untamed, so therefore in dreams represents the potential for the understanding of the spiritual.

③ By understanding animals and their symbolism, we are able to reapproach life in a simpler and more natural fashion. By returning to, and understanding, instinctive behaviour we are able to realign ourselves with our own basic Life Force.

Ankh

① The symbolism is similar to that of a cross. It represents our concept of the universe, or our religious beliefs.

② The symbolism of the ankh is that of all encircling power and protection throughout the trials and tribulations of physical life.

③ The ankh is a key to the way to knowledge of hidden wisdom. It is the link between the human and Divine and appears at a particular stage of spiritual development.

Anoint
– see Ointment

Antlers
– also see Horns

① The deer is a noble animal, so the interpretation differs if the antlers are **mounted, as in a trophy,** or are seen **on the animal**. If the latter then the interpretation is that of something which is supernormal, and may represent intellectual powers. If the former, then antlers may be interpreted as attempting to achieve high status.

② Psychologically these represent awareness of the potential for conflict between one's nobler self and the baser instincts.

③ Supernatural powers, fertility and nobleness of spirit are represented by antlers.

Anvil

① Depending on the dream circumstances, the anvil can represent the basic force of nature, brute force or a way of creating an initial spark. By creating a situation in our lives where we are going to be tried and tested, we are pitting ourselves against natural forces.

② As an image of the spark of life and of initiation, the anvil was once a very strong symbol. That spark is now more often represented by the spark plugs in a car.

③ The anvil ties in with the Norse Forge Gods. The symbolism is that of forging new life, creating new beginnings and so on.

Apple
– also see Food and Fruit

① In dreams apples can represent fruitfulness, love and temptation.

② **Eating an apple** indicates the wish to be trying to take in information or knowledge. The apple obviously has connections with Eve's temptation of Adam.

③ Apple blossom is a Chinese symbol of peace and beauty. Spiritually an apple suggests a new beginning and a freshness of approach.

Apron

① This can represent a badge of office or family ties. It depends on our gender and the content of the dream whether this image is negative or positive.

② **If worn by us** this may indicate the need for skill. If **worn by someone else** that part of us which is represented by the other person may need protecting.

③ As in Freemasonry, this suggests craftsmanship and sacrificial regalia.

Appointment

① Dreaming of **going to an appointment** indicates we need to have an aim or a goal. The dream is highlighting something our inner self feels we need to deal with. **Missing an appointment** suggests we are not paying enough attention to detail.

② We can perhaps give ourselves a gift or a reward for good work. There is something which has to be accomplished within a certain time limit.

③ We need to keep, or make use of, time in the most spiritually effective way.

Arc

① We need to pay close attention to a particular part or aspect of our lives.

② Psychologically, we are paying attention only to a segment or portion of what we are trying to deal with at the present time.

③ There is a dynamism available which will enhance our growth. A way forward is highlighted.

Arch

① When we dream of arches or doorways, we are often moving into a different environment or way of life. We have to go through some form of initiation, or acceptance ritual in order to succeed.

② The appearance of an arch of any sort in a dream shows that we are in the process of passing a test. We may be being protected by authority.

③ We are experiencing some form of spiritual initiation. We are being born again, given a fresh start.

Archetypes

Archetypes are basic pictures that each of us hold deep within our subconscious. They are in a sense 'psychic' blueprints. These blueprints – while potentially perfect – can become distorted by childhood experiences, socialisation and even parental experience.

C G Jung began studying archetypes and dividing function into thinking, feeling, sensation and intuition. Following various work by his pupils, it became possible to build up a type of 'map' of the interaction between all of these functions and to discover where one's own distortions occur.

① Perfect balance is achievable by using all aspects of the personality. Each function – thinking, feeling, sensing and intuition – has a 'positive' and 'negative' or rather greater or lesser quality. Both the masculine and feminine sides of the personality have these four functions, thus there are 64 (8 x 8) interactions possible.

Where a distortion has occurred, we tend to project onto those around us the archetype with which we have most difficulty. Consequently there will be a tendency to repeat situations over and over (e.g. the woman who continually finds herself in close relationships with a father figure type, or the man who continually finds himself at odds with women executives) until we learn how to cope with – and understand – our distortion. The obverse of this is that, with awareness, and by learning to use our dreams to help us to understand we are able to accept other's projections onto us, recognise them as projections, and not be being affected by them.

Having a very basic understanding of the archetypes shown below, and allowing them to show themselves in dreams, allows us to operate more fully and successfully in the everyday world. Thus, Kindly Father and Mother are by their nature, self-explanatory; Ogre represents masculine anger used negatively and Destructive Mother may be wilfully destructive, or quite simply the smothering type – that is the mother who, purposely or inadvertently, prevents the adequate growth of her children; Youth and Princess are the more gentle, fun loving aspects of the personality while Tramp is the eternal wanderer and Siren is the seductress or overtly sexually active part of femininity; the Hero is the self sufficient Messianic part of the personality, while the Amazon is the overly self sufficient female – the ultra efficient business woman type; Villain is the masculine part of the self who uses power for his own ends, whilst Competitor is the typical strident female who feels that she has no need for men in her life; Priest and Priestess are the powers of intuition used for the Greater Good while the Sorcerer uses inner power totally dispassionately and Witch uses that same power rather more emotionally and, perhaps, negatively.

② As we learn more, it is possible to be more and more in touch with our own archetypes and to find that in dreams they will act out their own scenarios to bring us greater understanding. When we learn to recognise the archetype in dreams we are able to adjust our day to day behaviour.

In more detail the feminine archetypes are:

Kindly Mother – This is the conventional picture of the caring mother figure, forgiving transgression and always understanding. Because much has been made of this side of femininity, until recently it was very easy to overdevelop this aspect at the expense of other areas of the personality.

Destructive Mother – This woman may be the 'smother-mother' type or the frankly destructive, prohibitive mother. Often it is this aspect who either actively prevents or – because of her effect on the dreamer – causes difficulty in other relationships.

Princess – The fun loving, innocent child like aspect of femininity. She is totally spontaneous, but at the same time has a subjective approach to other people.

Siren – This type is the seductress, the sexually and sensually aware woman who still has a sense of her own importance. In dreams she often appears in historic, flowing garments as though to highlight the erotic image.

Amazon – This is the self-sufficient woman who feels she does not need the male; she often becomes the powerful career woman. She enjoys the cut and thrust of intellectual sparring.

Competitor – She is the woman who competes with all and sundry – both men and women – in an effort to prove that she is able to control her own life.

Priestess – This is the highly intuitive woman who has learnt to control the flow of information and use it for the common good. She is totally at home within the inner realms.

Witch – The intuitive woman using her energy to attain her own perceived ends. She is subjective in her judgement and therefore loses her discernment.

The masculine archetypes are:

Kindly Father – This side of the masculine is the conventional kindly father figure who is capable of looking after the child in us, but equally of being firm and fair.

Ogre – This represents the angry, overbearing, aggressive and frightening masculine figure. Often this image has arisen because of the original relationship the dreamer had with their father or father figure.

Youth – The fun loving, curious aspect of the masculine is both sensitive and creative. This is the 'Peter Pan' figure who has never grown up.

Tramp – This is the real freedom lover, the wanderer, the gypsy. He feels he owes no allegiance to anyone and is interested only in what lies around the next corner.

Hero – The hero is the man who has elected to undertake his own journey of exploration. He is able to consider options and decide his next move. Often he appears as the Messianic figure in dreams. He will rescue the damsel in distress, but only as part of his growth process.

Villain – The villain is completely selfishly involved, not caring who he tramples on in his own search. He is often the aspect of masculinity women first meet in everyday relationships, so can remain in dream images as a threatening figure if she has not come to terms with his selfishness.

Priest – The intuitive man is the one who recognises and understands the power of his own intuition, but who usually uses it in the services of his god or gods. He may appear in dreams as the Shaman or Pagan priest.

Sorcerer – This is the man who uses discernment in a totally dispassionate way for neither good nor evil, but simply because he enjoys the use of power. In his more negative aspect he is the Trickster or Master of unexpected change.

③ Spiritually, when we have access to all the archetypes, we are ready to become integrated and whole. We find our inner Self *(see Self)*. Men and women will express this inner self slightly differently and the ideals for us to reach for are the Woman's Self and Man's Self.

Each and every *Woman's Self* is the essence of feminine dynamism. Her prime concern is the intangible quality in life, her own instinct and perceptive abilities. Her skills manifest themselves through that capacity for perception, along with empathy, intelligence and intuition. She recognises the processes of life, death and rebirth. While often perceiving her principle function as being that of procreation, she also understands herself to be ruthlessly destructive of anything she sees as being without perfection.

Each woman attempts to express every facet of her personality as fully as she can and will often highlight areas of deficiency in dreams. She will often try to compensate for her perceived deficiencies by pursuing balance in her relationships with men. These types of relationships will only work if she understands that in doing this she is developing the less versatile side of her personality. Her partner needs to grow and change with her, lest his lack of understanding prevents her from developing her true potential.

A *Man's Self* will express itself much more through intellect, logic and conscious awareness, and the demands of society can mean that he will tend to deny the intuitive function. Each person again matures by developing the functions of thinking or intellect, sensation, emotion and intuition.

For a man the process of separation from the mother is understood as a process of individuation and development, and the need to be separate from – and yet connected with – his unconscious self. If a man loses himself too much on an intellectual, logical level, his dreams will begin to depict the danger he is in. If he does not try to counteract his inner self by deliberately overdeveloping his macho side at the cost of everything else, he will reach a state of equilibrium. This allows him to relate to the rest of the world on his own terms. He will achieve a coherence which allows him to operate properly as a human being. He will not seek to express his inadequacies through his relationships or need to do so through his dreams.

Arena

① Dreaming of being **in an arena either as a player or as a spectator** highlights the fact that we may need to make the decision to move into a specifically created environment, one which gives more room for self expression and creativity or theatricality.

② We are developing a new focus of attention, or an area of conflict. This conflict may need to be brought out into the open, into open forum.

③ Today sport is often used as an energy release. Spiritually, an arena suggests a ritualised conflict.

Argue/Argument
– see Quarrel

Arms

– also see Body and Weapons

① We use our arms in all sorts of different ways, and in dreams it is often significant to note what is actually taking place. We may be defending ourselves, fighting, being held or acknowledging.

② Arms – in the sense of **weapons** – are used to protect and defend. In olden times, there were quite a series of rituals to do with the Page becoming the Knight and making the transit from the arms-bearer to the user.

③ The arm signifies surrender, wisdom, or action.

Armour

① We need to be aware of emotional and intellectual rigidity in either ourselves or others. If **we are wearing armour** we may be overprotecting ourselves, whereas if **others are in armour** we may be overly aware of their defence mechanisms.

② We may be protecting ourselves from something we feel is threatening us. Our way of protecting ourselves may, however, be outdated and inappropriate in the present circumstances.

③ Armour signifies chivalry, protection and the need we all have to protect or be protected.

Arrested

– also see Authority Figures in People

① To dream of **being arrested** suggests the restraint of one's natural self-expression by moral judgements or questions of right or wrong from other people. To dream of **arresting someone else** would indicate our instinctive disapproval of that part of ourselves which is represented by the character in the dream.

② Psychologically, we are unsure of our motives in an action we are contemplating. We should stop and carefully consider our behaviour before we act.

③ There is a need for authority greater and wiser than our own.

Arrive/Arrival

– see Journey

Arrow

① If we dream of **shooting arrows** we are aware of the consequences of actions, either our own or other people's, which cannot be recalled or revoked. Interestingly enough, arrows can also symbolise words in dreams.

② Communications which we make could be damaging to other people. We could either hurt or be hurt by directness. We are being pointed in a particular direction.

③ Arrows as weapons suggest power, energy, expertise and direction.

Artist

① The artist in a dream makes us recognise the artist in us. We are aware of the aspect of ourselves which is in contact with the irrational, creative side of the unconscious.

② We need to make use of our desire or ability to be creative. We may also be linking with that part of ourselves which records events for posterity.

③ The Creator, the Guiding Principle often manifests as the artist in dreams.

Ascending

① We are becoming conscious of being able to exercise control over passion or sexual pleasure.

② The transition from expressing our energy through sex to expressing it in self-awareness is often shown as ascending. If we are **climbing stairs, going up in an elevator or lift** we are making a movement towards waking or becoming more aware; we are making an escape from anxiety or being down to earth and are freeing ourselves from physical constraints.

③ We are searching for spiritual awareness and a more Cosmic perspective.

Ascension

① The act of Ascension is a breakthrough to a new spiritual plane which transcends the state of being human. It is an awareness of different levels of consciousness, which give a different perspective to being human.

② Ascension is an altered state of awareness which can occur as a result of meditation and spiritual practices. In dreams it is seen as acceptable and real, and is often accompanied by symbols of paradise.

③ Ascension frequently follows the experience of a descent into the underworld.

Ascetic/Ascetism

① There is some conflict with natural drives. There may be an avoidance of sex or contact through fear or the need for restraint. In a dream **to meet an ascetic or holy man** is to meet our higher self, and to recognise the part of ourselves which is continually seeking unity with the divine. We may be looking for simplicity.

② Psychologically, we are searching for purity in ourselves or in others. Equally, we may be afraid of that purity within ourselves and need to come to terms with it.

③ There is an attempt to find the spiritual in our lives and also a development of will and self-discipline.

Ashes

① Ashes in a dream often indicate penitence and sorrow. We are aware that we have been over anxious and stupid within a situation, and that there is little left to be done. That situation has outlived its usefulness. After an event or person has gone we may dream of a fire that has burnt out, leaving ashes. These are what remains of our experience which will enable us to make the best of a situation.

② A memory or a learnt wisdom needs to be retained in order for us to use information in the most appropriate way.

③ Ashes represent purification and death, the perishable human body and mortality, that which is left behind

Asylum/Asylum Seeker

① In dreams dealing with everyday life the emphasis has shifted in the meaning of Asylum. Meaning a **secure retreat**, it actually became a place where specialised care was offered for those unable to survive without it. Now it is taken to mean a safe space for foreign nationals or those less fortunate than ourselves. Dreaming of this type of asylum can highlight aspects of our personality which cause us discomfort, need nurturing and a place of safety, or can signify both the safe space itself and the need to understand the penetration of that safe space.

② Dreaming of **seeking asylum** suggests that there is something to be feared in conditions around us. **Offering asylum** indicates that we have compassion for others. **Meeting asylum seekers** highlights awareness of conditions beyond our own environment, and the needs of others.

③ Dreaming of seeking asylum signifies trying to find our own sacred space, though that may initially require experiencing harsh conditions.

Atom Bomb
– also see Nuclear Explosion

① Where anxiety regarding the external world is experienced, we may need to be aware that the end of a particular way of life is imminent in an especially dramatic fashion. Often there is a sense of an explosion of destructive energy before everything must be rebuilt.

② There is a fear of irrationality and of power which could be used in the wrong way. An atom bomb is a deliberately engineered explosion designed to be destructive. We may feel that someone else may destroy and nullify our carefully constructed life.

③ We have become aware of the uncontrollable forces of life and of the unconscious.

Attack

① **Being attacked** in a dream indicates a fear of being under threat from external events or internal emotions. Unknown impulses or ideas force the dreamer into taking a defensive attitude. If we are **being attacked by animals** we are turning our own aggression and/or sexuality inwards; we have fear of our own natural urges.

② **If we are the attacker** we need to defend ourselves by positive self-expression – we are making attempts to destroy some urge or feeling in ourselves or others.

③ There is a Spiritual or psychic threat around us of which we need to be aware.

Audience

① If we are standing **in front of an audience** in a dream we are probably having to deal with an important issue in our lives. If we are **in the audience** we are witnessing an emotion or process of change in ourselves.

② We need to be carefully considering some aspect of our lives, particularly one which takes place in public. We are the creators of our own play and an audience may also represent the various parts of our own personality we have created.

③ The audience tends to be the multiple parts of our personality. To be seeking an audience denotes an approach to Divine power.

Aura
– also see Nimbus

① To perceive an aura in a dream indicates how powerful we consider ourselves – or others – to be.

② The aura is a representation of the power we hold within, the force field with which we repel and attract people.

③ The aura is an energy field which surround the physical body. It is an expression of the Self.

Authority Figures
(Such as teachers etc.) – see Individual Entries, Authority Figures in People, and Officer/Official

Autumn

① We are being made conscious of the sense of something coming to an end. We recognise that the good in a situation can be brought in and made use of but the rest must be given up.

② Psychologically, we need to consider the cycles that occur in our own lives and whether some of these can be brought to an end.

③ The autumn of one's life – with the mellow feelings and all that old age brings – is symbolised by Autumn appearing in a dream.

Avalanche
– also see Ice/Iceberg and Snow

① If we **witness an avalanche** in our dreams we are experiencing a destructive force. If we are **in the middle of an avalanche** we are being overwhelmed by circumstances.

② Psychologically, we need to regain control of forces outside ourselves. We are in a position which puts us in some kind of danger.

③ The power of frozen emotions could overwhelm us. This may be due to the pressure of external circumstances or internal disturbance.

Axe
– also see Weapons

① When we dream of an axe we need to differentiate between whether it is being **used against us** or if **we are using** it. If it is used against us we feel we are being threatened by someone's greater power. To dream of **using an axe** indicates that we need to become aware of the destructive forces within us.

② There are certain difficulties around us which can only be eradicated with skill and expertise. Such expertise suggests that we will not suffer emotionally.

③ The axe represents power, thunder, conquest of error and sacrifice. It has strong associations with the Norse Storm Gods as well as the vengeful Hindu ones.

Baby
– see People

Bachelor

① To dream of **meeting a bachelor** indicates that we are searching for freedom either within our emotions or in our love life. **If the dreamer is male**, he may be wishing for the freedom to achieve something he might find difficult in partnership.

② We need to open up the masculine side of ourselves in order to accomplish our destiny.

③ A bachelor in a dream can highlight the side of us which does not require emotional ties at this particular time.

Backbone
– also see Body

① If the backbone is particularly noticeable in the dream we need to consider our main support structure.

② Intellectually we need to consider our firmness of character.

③ In certain dreams the backbone – because it is the most stable part of our structure – signifies the Self *(see Self)*.

Backwards

① To dream of going backwards indicates that we may be withdrawing from a situation or slow to learn from it. We may need to recognise that to continue in a particular situation will stop our progress.

② Mentally we are not using our best faculties. When she looked backwards, Lot's wife was turned into a pillar of salt. To look back into the past can be detrimental.

③ Regressive tendencies can cause us to move backwards into previous behaviour patterns. We should take note of what is happening in our lives at this time, and determine the reasons for this.

Bacteria
– see Dirt/Dirty

Bad

① When we dream of something being bad we are being made aware that the dream object is now worthless or defective. **Feeling bad** can have two meanings; one in the sense of **being naughty** and the other **not feeling right**. We are off balance in some way.

② Our thought processes are corrupt. **If we dream of food being bad** we are not taking sufficient care of our inner needs. A **bad smell** in dreams could mean that our environment is not supporting us.

③ For something to be bad it must offend against a code, whether that is a code of behaviour, a code of ethics or one of correct spiritual awareness.

Badge

① To have our attention drawn in a dream to a badge makes us aware of our right to belong to a group.

② We have been singled out for particular recognition, possibly because we have certain qualities. A badge can also have the same meaning as a talisman *(See Talisman)*.

③ A badge signifies an emblem of office. Dreaming of one shows our need to be accepted not just as ourselves, but also as part of a greater whole.

Bag

① We may be having problems with the feminine elements in our identity. Any container normally signifies the feminine or feminine attributes such as intuition. We need to develop these to achieve and to cope with whatever life throws at us.

② Depending on the actual bag (e.g. **a handbag, a shopping bag**) we may be hiding certain aspects of ourselves from public consideration. A handbag would represent more private thoughts, whereas a shopping bag might suggest nurturing and self-worth.

③ A bag spiritually signifies the Secret, the Hidden and the Occult. It will be our decision as to whether we 'open the bag' and makes use of its contents.

Baggage

① To be **carrying extra baggage** in a dream shows we may be carrying an extra load, either emotional or practical. We may also be expecting too much of ourselves or of others. We are still carrying past hurt or trauma.

② We are under some psychological stress, and may have to decide which projects or feelings can be left behind in waking life.

③ An indication of the our feelings of sorrow can manifest in dreams as baggage. However, sorrow, like baggage, may be lost as easily as it is taken on board.

Bailiff
– also see Occupations and Authority Figures in People

① When a bailiff appears in our dream we doubt our own ability to manage our resources. We are aware that we have overstepped the mark in a particular way and must be accountable to some type of authority.

② We have put ourselves at risk and have not fulfilled our obligations. Unless we take responsibility for what we have done we could be 'punished' by material loss and loss of status.

③ The bailiff in dreams signifies retribution or Karma of some kind. Spiritually, as times become difficult, the bailiff may signify the passing on of responsibility.

Baker
– also see Occupations and Oven

① We all have within us the ability to alter our approach or attitude to situations in our lives. Dreaming of a baker alerts us to this ability.

② Our creative ability may need to be enhanced or lightened in order for us to achieve success. **If a woman dreams of baking** she will recognise this as her need to nurture.

③ The Creative Urge, which may need to be pacified, can be seen as the baker. The artisan baker signifies the creativity necessary for Spiritual progress.

Balance

① When we dream of trying to **maintain our balance** or of being **balanced in a difficult position** we are searching for equilibrium. To dream of searching for the **balance in a financial account** means we are looking for something which, at present, remains unrecognised and unknown.

② To have the feeling that we are looking for the **balance of a quantity of goods** indicates we have more mental assets that we had first realised and need to start using them.

③ The Zodiac sign of Libra, Justice – and therefore balance – is symbolised by the scales. We may need to look at what our own sense of justice is, and whether or not it is being served.

Balcony

– also see Buildings

① To dream of being **on a balcony** indicates that we are searching for a higher status than we have at present. To dream of being **underneath a balcony** indicates that we are aware of other people's need for status.

② Psychologically we are searching for power within a situation in which we feel powerless.

③ When we dream of being elevated in some way, we are recognising our spiritual competence or progression.

Bald

① To dream of **someone who is bald** indicates we are perhaps being made aware of a degree of dullness in our lives which can be easily remedied.

② To dream of **ourselves being bald** can be somewhat ambiguous. It usually suggests a loss of intellectual prowess, but can also symbolise intelligence.

③ Baldness in a dream is recognition of the attainment of Spirituality with its attendant humility. Priests used to shave their heads to show they had nothing to hide.

Ball

① A ball connects with the playful, childlike side of ourselves and our need to express ourselves with freedom. **Attending a ball** also suggests a need for freedom, but links with the more flamboyant side of ourselves.

② If we are taking part in **games with a ball** *(see Games/Gambling)* we are conscious of our need for both structure and freedom. Psychologically, the human being needs to celebrate special occasions. A ball – as in a **formal party** – allows him to do just this.

③ Solar and Lunar festivals are often symbolised by the ball, as well as a feeling of impenetrable completeness.

Ballet/Ballerina

– see Dance/Dancing

Balloon

① Very often it is the colour of balloons in our dreams which are important *(see Colour)*. However they can also indicate a party mood or a desire for pleasurable experiences.

② Balloons were once made of pig's bladders and were used by the Court Jester to lighten up the atmosphere around the king and to remind him that he was human. In dreams today they may well introduce a note of fun amid seriousness.

③ A balloon is a symbol for joy, often a feeling of 'light spirited' joy, or indeed the spirit rising.

Bamboo

① The pliability of bamboo indicates yielding but enduring strength. Being one of the most graceful but hardy plants, it also represents these qualities in us.

② Intellectually, bamboo represents good breeding, long life and a fulfilling old age. It also represents the ability to yield when under pressure.

③ Perfect, but pliant, man is symbolised by the bamboo. If we recognise these two aspects within ourselves, we can begin to deal with flaws within our character.

Banana
– also see Food and Fruit

① Most dreams about fruit are to do with sexuality or sensuality. Conventionally the banana, because of its shape, signifies the penis. However, it is also considered, because of its yielding nature, to represent the handling of masculine sexuality.

② In conjunction with other fruit, the banana can be taken to mean fertility or sustenance.

③ The banana symbolises fertility, fecundity, potency and prosperity.

Band

① If the image of a band is that of a **stripe** there is some limitation within our circumstances which needs to be recognised. If however the image is that of a **group of musicians**, this would indicate the need for teamwork.

② There is an appreciation of harmony on a psychological level which needs to be made use of.

③ A band suggests harmony within the Self *(see Self)*.

Bandage

① If a **bandage is being applied** in a dream this shows the beginning of a healing process. There may be hurt feelings or emotional injuries which need attention.

② We may have been made sick by some difficulty within our lives and need to pay attention to our ability to be healed. If **the bandage is coming off** we may have overcome the difficulty, or we may have been careless.

③ Bandages signify preservation – as in the bandages of a mummy. Thus, we can analyse what we want to preserve in our life and act accordingly.

Bank/Banker
– also see Debt, Finance, Money, Savings and Wealth

① Our financial, mental or spiritual resources may need careful management. Money and personal resources tend to be what most people find problematic; our sense of security – a somewhat intangible asset – without which it is difficult to venture into the world, needs to be properly managed and monitored. An authority figure to help us deal with problems that arise is symbolised by the banker or bank manager in dreams. In the light of modern day banking practice such a figure, perhaps formerly feared, is now not necessarily to be trusted.

② Our emotional resources, such as self confidence, social ability and wisdom are held in reserve though there may be fear over the actual management of such resources. Our internal resources need to be available to us in such a way that we have a store of energy available. The banker represents the controlling part of ourselves and that part of us that monitors our expenditure of energy.

③ A bank formerly indicated a secure spiritual space; now it is more likely to represent a state of transition. A banker in a dream signifies our right to have management of our own Spiritual assets.

Bankrupt
– also see Debt, Finance, Money, Savings and Wealth

① In today's economic climate, to recognise in dreams that we are bankrupt indicates that we are doubtful of our ability to remain stable with proper access to the resources we need. Bankruptcy no longer carries the stigma it once did and may present in dreams as a way of escape.

② If in a dream we are aware of being bankrupt, it implies we have used up our emotional reserves and resources. We perhaps should consider what is important to us in the long run.

③ Interestingly, bankruptcy in dreams may be seen as a way to return to the beginning – to start over without the trappings of materialism or ego. This entails a degree of humility and courage which we would not have been able to use otherwise.

Banner
– also see Flag

① If the banner in the dream is a **commercial one**, it represents the need to have something which we may previously have ignored or rejected brought to our attention. If the banner is an old fashioned one – as used in **medieval battles** – it indicates a need to consolidate thoughts and actions.

② Psychologically we may adopt – or need to adopt – some kind of crusade. We need to know we have a common cause to fight for which is organised and specific.

③ A certain standard of spiritual behaviour is required of everybody. Therefore, to dream of a banner alerts us to this.

Banquet
– also see Food

① To dream of a banquet could have two meanings. If we are **serving** at one, we should be careful not to deny ourselves the good things in life by being too giving. If we are **attending** one we should recognise our basic need to be nurtured.

② We are not using our mental faculties as well as we might. Intellectually, we are able to put ourselves in touch with a higher quality of mental nourishment than we have at present.

③ The banquet is a symbol of our need for spiritual nourishment and the need to feast on spirituality.

Baptism

① To dream of **being baptised** indicates a new influence entering our life, cleansing away old attitudes and opening up to one's inner possibilities. To dream of **baptising someone** means we are ready to pass on knowledge to other people.

② There is the possibility that we may need some form of initiation to have an appreciation of the greater good.

③ Baptism is symbolic of many things – initiation, death and rebirth, regeneration, renewal. The basic link of all these is the feeling of optimism that it brings.

Bar/Barmaid/Barman
– also see Public House

① When we dream of a bar, such as an **iron bar**, we should look at how rigid or aggressive we are being in our behaviour. We need to handle ourselves with strength of purpose.

② To **stand at a bar** may represent a barrier to our sexual enjoyment particularly in the male. A **barmaid** in a dream signifies the more sensual understanding aspect of femininity. A **barman** has a similar meaning to a waiter, someone who can cater for our needs.

③ The bar is a symbol of our spiritual power, and power in everyday life. It can also represent Spiritual Honour and Justice.

Barb

① To be surrounded by **barbed wire** in a dream indicates that we are being prevented from moving forward by either our own, or others, hurtful remarks.

② Intellectually, we are trying to be too smart. Equally we may be trying to force other people to do something they do not want to do. **A barbed comment** is one which is specifically designed to hurt the recipient.

③ The barb is traditionally the fork that the Devil carried with him, with which to goad us into action.

Barber
– also see Hairdresser/Barber in Occupations

① When we dream of **visiting a barber** we are considering a change of attitude, thought or opinion about ourselves.

② An influence is becoming apparent in our lives which indicates a need for change. That change needs to be dictated by the way we perceive ourselves to be.

③ The old idea that one's spiritual power was held in the head gives rise to the idea that a barber signifies control of spiritual strength.

Bare
– also see Nude

① If we are **bare** it shows we are becoming aware of our vulnerability. If the **landscape is bare** there is a lack of happiness or perhaps of fertility.

② Psychologically, we are in a situation which at present is not be capable of coming to fruition.

③ We are spiritually vulnerable when stripped of material things and living with the 'bare' necessities of life. A return to basics requires some spiritual readjustment.

Barefoot

① Depending on the circumstances of the dream, to be barefoot can indicate either poverty or the recognition of sensual freedom.

② **To be barefoot and not able to find one's shoes** shows a lack of suitability, an awareness of inappropriate behaviour.

③ Being barefoot at one time indicated great humility. When Christ wished to show that he was no different to other men he washed his disciples' feet.

Barrier/Barricade
– also see Defend/Defence

① The presence of a **barrier** in a dream suggests that we are coming up against some kind of restraint in waking life. A **barricade** would suggest that that restraint is imposed by authority, perhaps as a way of controlling aggression or protest, perhaps of forbidding access to necessary information.

② Often barriers are self-imposed, particularly from an emotional perspective. To be **behind a barricade** might suggest that we are protecting ourselves. To be **in front of a barricade** indicates that we need to bring the barrier down in order to understand ourselves.

③ Spiritually a barrier or barricade would indicate that there is a difficulty in progressing, perhaps until we have learned a certain code of conduct or have established a recognised sense of order.

Base

① If our attention is drawn to the **base of an object** we may need to go back to the starting point of a project in which we are involved in waking life. We should consider how stable we are in any situation.

② To dream of **base metal** indicates that we are dealing with something which is somehow inferior and needs refining in some way.

③ Crudeness, unformed material. Our 'basic instincts' may be brought into question.

Basket

① To dream of a basket, particularly a full one, is to dream of full fruition, abundance and the successful use of resources. It can also represent the feminine closing principle.

② To be **attempting to fill a basket** can mean that we are trying to increase our talents and abilities in waking life.

③ If the basket is **full of bread** it can represent the sharing of resources – as in a sacramental meal.

Bat
– also see Vampire

① Because popular belief has it that bats are frightening, to dream of bats indicates that there are thoughts and ideas within the unconscious that may reveal themselves with frightening potential. Dreaming of a **cricket bat** or other such implement will give an indication of our attitude to controlled aggression, or to how we deal with external forces.

② To dream of **bats attacking** us shows the need to confront fears of madness. We are not able to use implements such as cricket or baseball bats without some kind of training. To dream of using such a bat indicates a learnt degree of competence.

③ A flying bat can represent discernment or obscurity of a spiritual kind. The obscurity may also suggest some idiosyncrasy within ourselves.

Bath/Bathing

① When we dream of **being in the bath**, it may well indicate the need for cleansing of some old feelings, the need to relax, to let go. We have an opportunity to contemplate what has occurred in the past and to adopt new attitudes.

② To dream of **bathing someone** shows the need to nurture or to have an intimate connection with that person.

③ **Communal bathing** depicts innocence and sensuality combined, ultimately leading to spiritual awareness.

Baton

① If the dream is of a **baton**, then it can represent authority or male sexuality.

② If however the dream is of a **drum baton** or stick, it may represent the need for self-expression in a more forceful way than normal.

③ Spiritual authority can be symbolised by the baton helping us to find the way we need to progress.

Battle
– also see Fight

① A battle presupposes that there is more than one participant in the conflict. While the essential fight will be between two opposing forces such as good and evil, or right and wrong, in dreams we often use different parts of our personalities to highlight which skills we need to make changes in our everyday lives. This can be experienced as a battle.

② When under emotional or mental stress we may literally 'battle it out' in dreams. Our opponents may represent actual people or the situations themselves. To be battling a monster might signify a circumstance or event over which we have no control.

③ In that a battle is more strategic and ordered than a simple fist fight, it will suggest a more considered way of overcoming spiritual difficulties.

Bay

① **To dream of a seashore and be conscious of a bay** or inlet shows we are aware of a woman's sexuality and receptiveness.

② To be **keeping something at bay** indicates a need to be on our guard.

③ The **wolf baying at the moon** shows the overcoming of basic animal instincts.

Beach

① **To be on a beach** shows our awareness of the boundary between emotion and reality, and our ability to be in touch with the elements.

② Because most of us connect beaches with holidays dreaming of a beach usually means relaxation and creativity.

③ The potential for emotional clarity is available, particularly if the **beach is deserted**.

Beacon

① This can show, variously, a warning, the need for communication or a strongly held principle by which one lives.

② Our emotions may be 'flaring up' and need directness of communication.

③ Beacons may light the way to spiritual enlightenment and on to spiritual sanctuary.

Beads
– also see Necklace

① When we dream of beads – for instance **a rosary** – we are making a connection with continuity of all kinds. **To dream of beads breaking** indicates the failure of a favourite project.

② Psychologically we are looking for perfection. In many religions prayers are counted by using beads. Repeated prayers are marked in order to ensure that the right number are said ro raise the vibration for manifestation.

③ Beads made from semi precious stones are used as spiritual reminders – as in rosaries or votive beads. In dreams they signify connection to the divine.

Bean

① To be **storing beans** in a dream may show a fear of failure, or a lack of confidence in our ability to carry through an objective, and the need to create something in the future. **To be planting beans** would suggest faith in the future, and a wish to create something useful. Traditionally the bean was supposed to be capable of feeding, clothing and providing an object of exchange for barter.

② Psychologically the bean can represent stored potential. We have the ability to use the stored power to achieve whatever we want.

③ The bean can signify immortality and magical power.

Bear

– also see Animals

① To have a **bear appear alive** in a dream indicates aggression, or if it is **dead,** the handling of our deeper negative instincts. To dream of a **toy bear** – i.e. a teddy bear – shows a childlike need for security.

② Psychologically, we have recognised the need to meet the force of our own creativity.

③ The bear symbolises spiritual strength and power, both latent – for example, when a bear hibernates – and also apparent.

Beard

① **Traditionally,** to dream of a man with a beard means we must guard against cover-up and deceit. Today in our more multi-cultural societies a beard may simply represent an intriguing possibility.

② We perhaps need to consider more masculine attributes in ourselves or others.

③ Spiritually there is an ambivalence in the symbol of the beard and the meaning will depend on our own culture and religion. It may mean wisdom and dignity, or alternatively it may mean deceit and deviousness.

Beating

① In dreams the act of **beating something or someone** represents our need for 'power over' by our aggression and brute force.

② To be beaten, either **physically or in a game,** indicates submission on our part to a greater force.

③ Particularly if we are taking a beating, humility, anguish and grief are symbolised.

Bed/Bedding

– also see Furniture/Furnishings and Mattress

① To be **going to bed alone** in a dream can indicate a desire for a return to the safety and security of the womb. To dream of a **bed made up with fresh linen** indicates the need for a fresh approach to those thoughts and ideas that really matter to us. Dreaming of a new duvet shows we have a need for, and appreciation of, comfort in our lives.

② To be **going to bed with someone else** can variously represent either our sexual attraction to that person or indicate that we need have no fear of them – depending on other circumstances within the dream.

③ A bed can represent a form of spiritual sanctuary and a sense of purity.

Bed wetting

① In dreams, we often regress to a former state, and to dream of wetting the bed indicates our anxieties over lack of control. In some cases it may also signify a problem with sex or sexuality.

② We may have worries about correct behaviour in society or of being condemned for improper behaviour.

③ Bed wetting can in dreams suggest a need for freedom of personal expression and what might be considered inappropriate spiritual behaviour.

Bee

① As a symbol of something to be feared, as well as tamed and used, the meaning of bees in dreams can be ambivalent. To be **stung by a bee** is a warning of the possibility of hurt. **Being attacked by a swarm** indicates we are creating a situation which may become uncontrollable.

② To dream of a **queen bee** registers our need to feel, or be, superior in some way. We may possibly feel the need to be served in our chosen purpose by others. We are also aware of the need for hard work and industry.

③ The bee symbolises immortality, rebirth and order. As more people become aware of ecological issues, it is understood how important the bee is for the continuation of life on earth.

Beehive

① Folk-tales, such as the one about telling one's troubles to the bees, can surface in dreams without us necessarily recognising what they mean. The beehive is said to represent an ordered community and therefore the ability to absorb chaos.

② To dream of **tending a beehive** alerts us to the need for good management of our resources.

③ Eloquence and direct speech. Possibly a connection with the Great Mother *(See Great Mother/Mother Earth)*.

Beetle

① Considered by many to be dirty, in a dream the beetle carries the same symbolism as all insects – that is, something which is unclean or not properly attended to.

② The industriousness of the beetle is often taken to represent hard work which needs to be done.

③ By its connection with the scarab beetle, it represents protection from evil. We should look at what, or who, we feel needs to be protected.

Beg/Beggar

① To dream of **being a beggar** represents our own feeling of failure and lack of self esteem. To dream of **someone else as a beggar** indicates we need to become aware of our ability to help others less fortunate than ourselves.

② Emotions, drives and thoughts which have been 'starved' in our waking lives can often appear in dreams personalised as a beggar.

③ A beggar can be a hermit and therefore a spiritual petitioner. He seeks alms in return for his wisdom *(see Hermit)*.

Behaviour

① Our (or others') behaviour in a dream can differ markedly from normal, since the dream state gives us the freedom to highlight aspects of ourselves of which we would not normally be aware.

② Bizarre behaviour in ourselves or others can often give us clues as to our psychological state.

③ We should consider what is appropriate regarding our own behaviour and amend it if necessary.

Behind

① To be behind someone in a dream indicates that on a subconscious level we may consider ourselves to be inferior in some way. If we are aware of someone or something behind us it shows we have moved on from a situation in waking life.

② We may find we have a fear of being left behind and should consider how we can best overcome this fear.

③ We should look at our spiritual standing as we may, quite literally, be behind in our search for wholeness.

Bell

① Traditionally, to **hear a bell tolling** in a dream was to be warned of disaster or of a death. While that meaning is less prevalent now as there are more efficient ways of communication, a bell in a dream (such as a **door bell**) does warn us to be on the alert. It may also indicate that we have a desire to communicate with someone who is distanced or estranged from us.

② Bells can indicate the conscience and also our basic need to seek approval from others.

③ Because it can charm against the powers of destruction, a bell may be lucky for us in the sense that it can forewarn us of approaching danger.

Belt

① To dream of a belt which attracts our attention represents the fact that we are perhaps being bound by old attitudes, duty and so on. An **ornate belt** can represent a symbol of power or office (as in regimental or nurses' belts).

② Intellectually we may be 'hide-bound' through outdated material.

③ A belt may be an insignia of power, and can represent either the power we have, or the power we can obtain.

Bend/Bent

① When an article or line registers in a dream as being bent, it usually infers that something in our lives is off balance or out of kilter. A queue of people which is not straight might suggest a degree of variation from the norm. It might also represent insincerity in our dealings with other people.

② Psychologically there may be a 'kink' in our perceptions. To actually be bending something indicates that we are attempting to manipulate circumstances – perhaps unfairly – to fit our own agenda.

③ Any deviance from correct behaviour or ethics may manifest in dreams as a bend away from the straight line. We are negating our own inherent standards.

Berries
– see Fruit/Berries

Bet
– see Games/Gambling

Bible/Religious Texts
– also see Religious Iconology

① If we dream of a Bible or other religious book it usually means that we are aware of traditional moral standards. We need a code of conduct which helps us to survive.

② We need to look very carefully at our religious beliefs, myths and legends and how they might be relevant to us.

③ The Bible or other religious text in dreams usually indicates some kind of spiritual realisation.

Bicycle
– also see Transport

① To dream of **riding a bicycle** shows the need to pay attention to personal effort or motivation. We may need freedom of movement.

② Psychologically we could be looking for freedom without responsibility.

③ The bicycle signifies duality using both the spiritual and mundane.

Bigamy

① To dream of **being a bigamist** indicates not being able to decide either between two loves or two courses of action. We are being presented with two alternatives both of which have equal validity.

② When we dream we are **married to a bigamist** we need to be aware that we are being two-timed or deceived by someone very close to us.

③ Spiritually, bigamy can represent the choices one has to make, possibly between right and wrong. By association it may represent the astrological sign of Gemini.

Binge

① Any excess in dreams can be seen as a binge – over-eating, drinking too much, obsessive behaviour. It would seem that we have no way of controlling our more wordly vices and, perhaps by becoming aware of the problem through dreams initially, can seek whatever help we need.

② Because bingeing can be taken to be self-indulgent behaviour, its appearance in dreams alerts us to this aspect of ourselves. We should examine our behaviour in waking life and consider whether it is appropriate.

③ A binge, whether our own or someone else's, suggests a loss of control and a giving in to the 'pleasures of the flesh' or excessive behaviour.

Birds

① Birds have over the years come to represent the Soul - both its darker and its enlightened side. They were believed to be vehicles for the soul and to have the ability to carry it to heaven. Ever since the Stone Age, man has been fascinated by birds and by flight. In dreams, birds usually represent self-reliance and imagination. By nature, there are many thoughts and ideas which need a degree of freedom to become evident. Since ancient times birds have been invested with magical and mystical powers. Their behaviour in dreams can symbolize and mirror Mans' aspirations. There is a common symbolism in dreams about birds.

A *caged bird* can indicate some kind of restraint or entrapment usually imposed from an external source.

A *bird flying freely* represents aspirations and desires and possibly the spirit, set free and soaring towards the Divine. Birds can sometimes denote the feminine intuitive side of the being.

A *display of plumage* indicates our facade - the way we see ourselves or project ourselves to the outside world.

A *flock of birds* represents a group purpose or ideal. A flock of birds containing both *winged and plucked* birds indicates some confusion over conflict between mundane everyday considerations and spiritual aspirations.

The golden-winged bird has the same significance as fire and therefore indicates our spiritual, more esoteric aspirations.

A *high-flying bird* signifies spiritual awareness or that part in us which seeks knowledge, and requires objectivity and a wider viewpoint.

In *a man's dream* a bird can represent awareness of the Anima *(see Anima/Animus)*. In *a woman's dream* it is more likely to represent the archetypal Self *(see Self)*. More mundanely, such a bird can represent our aspirations and wish for success.

A *pet bird* A pet bird can denote some dearly loved principle or ideal which we are unable give up. It can also suggest our sense of carefully nurtured happiness, which still is not totally free.

White/Black birds The dual aspects of the Anima or Self may be represented in any dream as two opposites. Thus, the black bird signifies the dark, unheeded, or hidden aspects, the white the open, clear, untrammelled side. White and black birds can represent any polarity in our waking lives.

Birds

② As with animals, birds can suggest various aspects of our personalities which may need to be studied and understood:

Chicken/Hen Traditionally, the *chicken* represents stupidity and cowardice. It may be that we use imagination as a practical tool. There is potential for growth, though this may come about through belonging to a group or flock. The *hen* denotes discretion, mothering and procreation. When a *hen crows* in a dream it is taken to represent feminine domination.

Cock The cock is the symbol of a new day and also of vigilance or watchfulness. It represents the masculine principle and so the need to be more up front and courageous.

Crane In Chinese law, the crane signifies the Spiritual Self. As one of the birds associated with the martial arts, in dreams it represents inner harmony.

Crow/Rook Traditionally, since they are carrion birds, these warn of bad luck and death. They may be the bringers of bad news but may also represent wisdom and deviousness.

Cuckoo The meaning of the cuckoo is ambivalent, since it can represent deviousness but also unrequited love. As the harbinger of spring there is a change from old, stale energy to newness and freshness.

Dove Always taken to mean the bringer of tranquillity after the storm, the peaceful side of man's nature appears in dreams as the dove. As a symbol of peace, the dove can also represent the Anima *(see Anima/Animus),* or inner peace.

Duck In a dream this can often denote some kind of superficiality or childishness. Floating upon the element of water, the duck signifies our ability to handle our own emotions. A *decoy duck* may represent a displacement activity.

Eagle Because the eagle is a bird of prey, in dreams it signifies dominion and superiority. It can also mean keenness and awareness as well as perception and objectivity. Our own wish to dominate is becoming apparent though there may be some difficulty in reconciling other parts of our nature. If we feel threatened somebody else may be threatening the status quo in our waking life.

Falcon or other birds of prey All birds of prey share the attributes of the eagle to a lesser extent. They embody freedom and hope for those who are being restricted in any way. The falcon, or any trained bird, can represent victory over the lower urges thus signifying a degree of personal control.

Game birds In the sense that game birds are available for 'sport', in dreams they will represent a particular target, aim or objective. Most game birds have the ability to conceal themselves when under threat. To dream of *pheasants* generally foretells of prosperity and good fortune to come. The *quail* represents ardent behaviour, sometimes courage and often luck. The *pigeon* can be a symbol of survival against difficult odds.

Goose/Geese The goose in dreams is said to represent circumspection and love. A *flock of geese* is often taken to represent the powers of intuition and to give warning of possible difficulties. Like the swan the goose can represent the dawn or new beginning. The *wild goose* can represent the soul and often depicts the unrestrained wild side of us. Geese were once considered to be witches' familiars.

Kingfisher A kingfisher signifies honour and peacefulness. Because of elusiveness and bright plumage, it can also suggest a brilliant idea or concept that has not yet been fully formulated.

Lark A lark is traditionally represents the transcendence of the worldly self. To hear *larks singing* in a dream signifies the joy of creation and satisfaction of a task achieved.

Magpie/Jackdaw Because of the belief that magpies and jackdaws are thieves, to dream of one may indicate that someone known to you is trying to take away something of value or take credit for your ideas. The magpie can also denote good news.

Ostrich The ostrich, particularly seen with its *head in the sand*, suggests that we are attempting to run away from responsibility, or hide from knowledge. Because it is flightless the ostrich also signifies natural restriction.

Owl The owl is sacred to Athena, the Greek goddess of strategy and wisdom, therefore in a dream can represent the need for those qualities in waking life. It suggests the use of the intuitive senses, arising from the deep unconscious. Because the owl is also associated with the night-time, it can sometimes represent death; *hearing an owl hoot* in a dream traditionally is said to foretell the death of a relative. A more modern interpretation is that there will be massive changes in lifestyle.

Parrot The parrot being brightly coloured may signify a flamboyant personality, but in its 'chatter' is more likely to represent gossip or loose talk. It may also suggest the chatterbox or negative thoughts internalised in childhood.

Peacock To see a peacock in a dream suggests an expansion of understanding from the plain and unadorned to the beauty of the fully plumed bird. Like the phoenix it represents rebirth and resurrection and in some cultures suggests the 'all-seeing eye'.

Pelican The pelican in dreams represents sacrifice of some sort, and perhaps taking on more than we can deal with. It also signifies the devotion of the mother and the ability to care for others.

Penguin The penguin is thought to represent harmony but also possibly stupidity.

Birds

Often seen as a comical figure, it in fact represents stability and the ability to handle difficult situations. As knowledge grows about our association with birds the penguin can also be seen an element of our self-sufficiency.

Phoenix The phoenix is a universal symbol of rebirth, resurrection and immortality. Though the phoenix has actually never been proved to exist, it is nevertheless a symbol of power in many cultures. It can thus share much of the symbolism of Fabulous Beasts *(see Fabulous Beasts)*.

Raven The raven traditionally was a symbol of the old gods and may still have this significance today. If seen to be talking, it represents prophecy. However, its meaning can also be somewhat ambivalent in that it can represent evil and sin, but also wisdom.

Seagull All seagulls are carnivorous birds but latterly have learnt how to live outside their natural element by scavenging inland. In dreams today the seagull is a representation of freedom and power used wisely and well. *A flock of seagulls* can also suggest efficient communication and, interestingly, mob behaviour.

Sparrow The sparrow or any noticeably small bird in a dream denotes business and industry. As we become more conscious of the inter-relatedness of human and bird population, the sparrow in dreams can become a symbol for survival.

Stork/Ibis/Flamingo or any long legged bird The *stork* is a symbol of new life and new beginnings. The *ibis* is the symbol of perseverance and of aspiration whereas a *heron* represents stability, self-reliance and prudent management of resources. The *flamingo,* seen as rather exotic, embraces all of the qualities shown above. It may also suggest careful watchfulness.

Swallow The swallow seen in a dream signifies the coming of Spring and therefore new beginnings. When *swallows are leaving* it may be seen as the ending of a particular project or phase in waking life.

Swan The swan signifies the soul of man and is often taken to be the divine bird or messenger. In this context it can sometimes denote a peaceful death, though actually its real significance is the serenity gained after a period of hard work.

Turkey The turkey is traditionally a food for celebrations and festivals, and denotes that there may be good times ahead. It also suggests the ability to formulate good plans for the future.

Vulture/Buzzard Vultures and buzzards are birds which scavenge for food and make use of all available resources. Thus, in dreams, they can represent that aspect of our personality which creates opportunities out of very little. We may 'pick over' what we have, discarding the useless. They also are associated with the destructive feminine.

Woodpecker The woodpecker is a guardian of both kings and trees in mythology and is said to sound a warning when there is danger around. It is thus reputed to have magical powers. It can symbolise diligence and hard work.

③ Traditionally birds represent the Soul and its quest for freedom. As mankind moves closer to an understanding of spirituality, that symbolism becomes even more valid.

Birth

① We tend to dream of birth at the beginning of a new way of life, a new attitude, new ability, or a new project – also when we become aware of the death of the old.

② Psychologically we are coming to terms with our existence as human beings. Any symbol of new life manifests deep emotion.

③ The urge to care, to love and to give birth are all suggested by dreams of birth. It may be both a spiritual and a physical need.

Bite

① **Being bitten** in a dream may show that we are experiencing aggression from someone else, or conversely that our own aggressive instincts are not under control.

② To be **biting someone or something** such as fruit within a dream indicates that there is literally an idea or a concept which we need to get our teeth into.

③ We should be aware not only of our capacity for venom, but also our capacity to be on the receiving end of a 'venomous' attack, which may or may not be warranted.

Blackbird
– see Birds

Blindfold/Blindfolding

① If we have **been blindfolded** in a dream, it shows a deliberate attempt is being made to deceive us. If we are **blindfolding someone** else we are not being honest in our dealings with other people. This may be through ignorance on our part.

② Psychologically we may need to spend time 'in retreat' – that is cut off from visual contact with the external world.

③ In spiritual terms, blindfolding is a rite of Passage. It is a transition between two states.

Blindness

① If we ourselves are suffering from blindness in a dream there is an unwillingness to 'see' something. We have lost sight of something or we are refusing to see qualities in ourselves that we don't like.

② Intellectually we may be aware of certain facts, but choose not to use that knowledge in the most appropriate way.

③ Spiritually, blindness is a form of ignorance. It can suggest the irrational. It is also a form of initiation.

Block

① In dreams, a block may present itself in many forms. We can experience it as a physical block – that is, something that needs to be climbed over or got round, a mental block – for instance not being able to speak or hear, or a spiritual block such as the figure of an angel or a demon appearing in our dreams.

② Blocks appear in dreams when we need to make a special effort to overcome an obstacle in order to progress.

③ Spiritually, blocks appearing in our dreams are an indication that we should be taking preventative measures over a situation in waking life. That can also serve as a warning that we should behave correctly.

Blood
– also see Body and Menstruation

① From time immemorial blood has represented the life carrier or the life force. To dream of a **violent scene where blood appears** indicates that we are being self destructive in some way. If we are having to **deal with blood** we need to be aware of our own strength, if we have been injured and **someone else is dealing with the blood** we need to look at what help is necessary to overcome hurt.

② Emotional abuse can translate itself in dreams into **bloody wounds,** either self inflicted or being inflicted.

③ Spiritually, being aware of blood circulating through the body can symbolise the rejuvenating force.

Boat/Ship
– also see Transport

① To dream about a boat or a ship very often indicates how we cope with our own emotions and those of others. It may well represent how we navigate our way through life and whether we are in control of our lives.

② To dream of **being alone in a small boat** means we need to consider how we handle isolation and the ability to be alone. To dream of **being on a large ship** alerts us to how we handle group relationships. To dream of **missing a boat** is often the dream of a perfectionist who fears missing chances or opportunities.

③ Boats represent our attitude to death and 'The Final Journey'. They can also represent fertility and adventure.

Body

① The body forms the prime source of information about us, and often highlights problems we may have. The body in dreams signifies the individual and all that he is and additionally often represents the Ego. Those who appreciate knowledge other than the purely scientific will often find information comes to them through dreams about the body. Psychological stress translated into bodily images often becomes a fertile source of symbolism in dreams. When emotions cannot be faced in ordinary everyday life, they very often become distorted body images in dreams. Different aspects of the body can have various meanings in dreams:

To dream of the *upper part* of the body links with the intellect and the spiritual aspects of our character; the *lower part* represents our natural emotional aspects.

An adult's head on an immature body, or a child's head on an adult body, indicates we need to recognise the difference between mature rational thought and emotions.

If there is *conflict between the upper and lower parts* it would suggest that there is disharmony between our mental faculties and our instinctive behaviour.

Dreaming of a *change in body shape,* such as becoming fat or thin, suggests the possibility of a change in our waking personality or in the way we handle trauma.

The *right side or hand being especially noticeable* signifies we should take note of the logical side of our personality, whereas *the left side or left hand* indicates we need to be aware of more our intuitive, creative side.

② The body offers a great deal of material for interpretation. The various systems of the body – skeletal, circulatory, muscular etc. – provide rich imagery and symbolism which is reflected into every life. Thus:

Abdomen/Stomach/Belly When the dream appears to concentrate on the abdomen, there is a need for us to focus on our emotions and repressed feelings and consciously to deal with them. Since the solar plexus is much connected with how we take in and process subtle information from other people, we may need to look at how we protect ourselves from other people's negativity in waking life.

Anus In dreams, the mind returns to the initial child-like gaining of the control of bodily functions. This control is the beginning of self realisation, self reliance and control, yet at the same time of suppression and defence. To dream of the anus therefore highlights an aspect of childish behaviour or egotism. As adults, such a dream may suggest an overly controlling part of the personality.

Arms We use our arms in all sorts of different ways and generally in dreams they signify our ability to love, or to give and take. If in dreams we are *defending ourselves, fighting or being held* it may suggest a feeling of helplessness or loss of confidence. Depending on the position of the arms we may be indicating supplication or showing passionate commitment.

Back/Backbone If the *backbone* is particularly noticeable in a dream, we should consider the main support structure in our lives. Intellectually, we need to consider our firmness of character. Dreaming of *someone turning their back on* us suggests that other people may not at this present time wish to share their thoughts with us, or indeed may suggest contempt or disapproval. We may need to identify the more private elements in our own personality. We may also be exposed to the unexpected in everyday life. If we then dream of *turning our backs* we probably need to walk away from a particular situation in waking life.

Blood For many people blood symbolises the life-force and can thus represent our essential energy. Dreaming about blood highlights the need to handle fear connected with loss of life. This links into the ancient belief that the blood somehow contained the life of the spirit, and therefore spilt blood was considered sacred. Such a dream suggests an element of martyrdom in waking life, and that some kind of sacrifice is being made. Blood can also represent renewal of life through its connection with menstruation.

Bottom When we become conscious of our own or someone else's bottom, this may be a play on words in that we have literally 'reached bottom' or we are aware of issues to do with sex and sexuality.

Breasts Breasts in dreams most frequently indicate our connection with the mother figure and our need for nurturing. Such a dream can also depict a wish to return to being an infant without responsibilities, although of course there is an erotic element here.

Constipation Any evacuation of the bowel highlights our need to be free of worry and responsibility. Suppressing evacuation signifies an inability to let go of the past or of previous patterns of behaviour, and both the inability to, and the fear of, being able to perform adequately. Being conscious of constipation in dreams indicates the need to learn how to be uninhibited. It can also in dreams signify the sexual act.

Excrement (also see individual entry) In waking life, we may not have been able to go beyond the feeling that anything to do with bodily functions is dirty and self-centred. Anxiety about money, as well as a fear of responsibility for it, is represented in dreams by playing with excrement. If the excrement is *transformed into living animals,* maybe rats, we are coming to terms with the fact that we are responsible for managing our own impulses. In its more esoteric meaning excrement belongs to the realm of feelings. We may simply be trying to get rid of bad feelings which can ultimately be turned into something worthwhile. There may also be an element of rebellion in our waking life.

Eye Any dream to do with the eye is to do with observation and our ability to be discriminating. The eye is connected with the power of light and, in ancient times, of the sun-gods. Through its connection with Egyptian symbolism, as with the Eye of Horus *(see Eye of God in Religious Iconology,)* the eye can also be taken to be a talisman *(See Talisman). Loss of eyesight* in dreams suggests loss of clarity in waking life; depending on which eye it can be either the loss of logic (right eye) or loss of intuition (left eye). *Regaining the eyesight* can indicate a return to innocence and clear-sightedness.

Foot/Feet In dreams the foot can have several meanings. It can represent the way we make contact with reality, our sense of pragmatism. It can also suggest our ability to ground ourselves and our sense of stability. In moving forward we use all parts of the foot, so it can suggest our attention to detail, and the foundation or basic beliefs from which we commence any task. When our *feet are not on the ground* we may be being unrealistic or perhaps searching for a different way of working. A *winged foot* suggests a need for a different, more efficient form of expression. A *foot fetish* suggests a difficulty with the sexual and sensual side of our nature. The toes have a similar interpretation to the fingers in dreams. *Playing with the toes* can suggest a need for security and a loving relationship.

Gall Bladder To dream of a gall bladder, or of a *gall bladder operation*, often represents the need to give up some activity that is not doing us any good at all. We are assimilating the wrong information, which is causing us problems and we need to get rid of bitterness, difficulty or even guilt.

Hair (also see Hairdresser) The hair represents strength and virility. To be *having our hair cut* suggests that we are trying to create order in our lives or, like Samson, are not using our available energy efficiently. In dreams, to be *combing or brushing the hair,* either our own or someone else's, is to be attempting to untangle a particular attitude prevalent in our lives. To be *cutting someone else's hair* suggests that we may be curtailing a particular activity. It is also possible that there may be some fear or doubt connected with sexuality. To *be bald* in a dream rather than in waking life shows we are recognising our own innate intelligence or wisdom.

Hands/Fingers The hands are two of the most expressive parts of the body and signify power and creativity. The *right hand* is traditionally the more powerful hand, the one that transmits power and energy, whereas *the left hand* is more passive and receptive. Sometimes in dreams the left hand can represent cheating and duplicity. *Two hands noticeably contrasting with each other, or perhaps those with a different object in each,* show there may be conflict in us between belief and feeling. *Two people's clasped hands* indicate union or friendship, while *clenched fists* suggest a threat of some sort. *Folded hands* suggest a state of rest or of deep peace. Placed together as in prayer, hands signify defencelessness or some sort or an act of supplication. *Two hands placed in someone else's* are an indication of a kind of surrender. *Hands covering the eyes* generally represent shame, fear or horror – something we do not wish to see. When hands are crossed at the wrists in dreams it suggests we are feeling constrained by something in our waking lives. When the *hands are raised towards the sky* it can indicate adoration, prayer or surrender. If the *palms are turned out and downwards* we are transmitting a blessing; held upwards, it shows we are receiving a blessing from the Ultimate. When the *hands are raised to the head* we should give some thought and care to our situation. *Washing our own hands* suggests innocence or rejection of guilt, *washing someone else's* hands suggests that we are aware of someone else's problems. *Wringing hands* signifies grief and distress. A *hand on the breast* signifies submission to a higher authority. The *open hand* represents justice, while the *laying-on of hands*, particularly if placed upon the neck, signifies healing and blessing. A *huge hand, particularly from the sky,* suggests that we have been 'specially chosen' for a particular task. A *pointing finger* can suggest a way forward or, again, a special kind of selection.

Head The head is the principal part of the body – the motivating force. As the seat of intellect, it denotes power and wisdom. Dreaming of the head suggests that we should consider very carefully how we handle both intelligence and foolishness. To dream of the *head being bowed* suggests prayer, invocation or supplication. When the *head is covered* in dreams it shows we may be hiding up our own intelligence or perhaps acknowledging somebody else's superiority. A *blow to the head* in a dream indicates that we should reconsider our actions in a particular situation in waking life.

Heart 'To know in our heart' suggests faith in ourselves and in dreams this faith can be symbolised by the shape of a heart. The heart is the centre of the being and represents 'feeling' wisdom rather than that of the intellect. It is also representative of compassion, understanding and love, hence the use of its symbolism in romantic poetry. Interestingly, the heart can be represented in dreams by a machine (*See Machine/Machinery*).

Heel The heel symbolises that part of ourselves which is strong and supportive but, at the same time, can be vulnerable. To be *grinding the heel into the ground* in dreams suggests determination or anger, though sometimes of an inappropriate kind.

Jaw The jaw depicts our way of expressing ourselves. *Pain in the jaw* in dreams can signify our need to release some kind of tension in our lives, possibly by expressing ourselves more fully. Spiritually, the jaw is also thought to signify the opening to the underworld, hence the symbolism in the story of Jonah and the whale, where he was given time to consider his actions. It may be that we need to do the same in waking life.

Kidneys The kidneys are organs of elimination, working quietly in the background. To dream specifically of kidneys therefore is to be aware of the need for some kind of cleansing in our lives. We may need to eliminate something which is causing us emotional distress. Through dreams the body can alert us to physical problems before we become consciously aware of them in waking life and the kidneys tend to be part of this 'alert mechanism'.

Knees Being aware of the knees in dreams highlights the support we are able to give ourselves. To be *on our knees* is symbolic of the need for prayer and entreaty and perhaps our inability to move forward without help. *Someone else being on their knees* shows a level of emotional commitment, yet at the same time may also represent an act of submission.

Legs In dreams, legs represent our personal means of support. They enable us to move and therefore often signify some kind of psychological shift or change in attitude. They can also represent our ability to take control of a particular situation. If the *right leg* is highlighted, this suggests movement in a logical sense and may represent moving forward of our own volition whereas the *left leg* tends to suggest passive movement, perhaps following someone else's lead.

Limbs In dreams any limb can be taken to suggest the fears associated with gender issues or with an aspect of sexuality. Being *dismembered* can be taken in its literal sense – we are being torn apart. Sometimes this can suggest the need to restructure our lives and begin again. At other times it can indicate that there is a way in which we must question our core values.

Liver (also see individual entry) In Chinese medicine the liver is representative of irritability and suppressed anger. Dreaming of our own liver may highlight the life force or the ability to process and make sense of our lives. If we dream of a *diseased liver*, there is some aspect within our lives which needs clearing or cleansing, lest we manifest this in waking life as actual disease.

Lungs In Chinese medicine any difficulty with the lungs signifies grief. Spiritually, the lungs are the seat of creativity and connect us to our highest Self. Thus, lungs are involved in correct decision making and highlighted in dreams they can represent the Breath of Life – correct action which moves us forward.

Mouth Representing our need to express ourselves, the mouth in dreams will often help us to decide how best to handle a situation in waking life. If the *mouth appears to be shouting* forceful action is required, if *whispering* a more gentle approach is needed. In old style interpretation, the mouth can represent the devouring, demanding part of ourselves.

Nose The nose in dreams can stand for curiosity, and also for intuition. A proportionately *large nose* can indicate that someone is interfering in our lives, whereas a nose which is *too small* may suggest a degree of disinterest. Dreaming of a *bloody nose* suggests some damage to our reputation.

Penis In dreams any appendage of the human body signifies a process of growth. Dreaming of a penis – either one's own or someone else's – usually highlights our ability to be penetrative, whether sexually or emotionally. The penis can also signify our need to protect our own privacy in an appropriate way.

Skin The skin in dreams represents our persona, the part we choose to make visible to other people. It can also represent the protective camouflage we create in order to hide from ourselves. *Damaged skin* can suggest emotional hurt, whereas an itchy skin in dreams quite literally suggests an irritation which needs to be dealt with in waking life. *Skin peeling off* indicates that we may be becoming more vulnerable or no longer have any need for the protective coating we have built up for ourselves.

Teeth Dreams of teeth are perhaps one of the commonest universal dreams. In old style interpretation, teeth in dreams were thought to stand for aggressive sexuality. It is more appropriate to recognise that, as the teeth are the first visible change in a baby, they represent transition periods in our lives. *Teeth falling or coming out easily* mean such a transition is imminent. If we fear our teeth dropping out it suggests there is an anxiety about maturing, perhaps a fear of getting old, undesirable and helpless. *In a woman's dream* if the teeth are swallowed this can sometimes signify pregnancy, or the desire to become pregnant.

Throat When we become aware of the throat in dreams, we are conscious of the need for self-expression and perhaps of our own vulnerability. *A sore throat* may suggest that we have been hurt by someone else's words. *A throat being cut* suggests the loss of an essential link between the spiritual and the physical, or between head and heart.

Thumb It is our opposing thumbs which differentiate us from other animals, so dreaming of a thumb suggests an awareness of how powerful we are. Conventionally, the thumb *pointing upwards* represents beneficial energy, but *pointing downwards* is negative. This meaning can become reversed in dreams, however.

Tongue The tongue in dreams is associated with our understanding of information that we wish to pass on to other people. We may have deeply felt beliefs we wish to share, but need to recognise when to speak and when to remain silent. A *forked tongue* can suggest duplicity.

Vagina Most often, dreams of the vagina are to do with our self image and self esteem. *In a woman's dream,* it highlights her receptivity on all levels. *In a man's dream* it suggests a barrier to be overcome, whether mentally or physically, to enable him to reach his full potential.

Womb We all have need of security and shelter, and freedom from responsibility. The womb represents a return to the beginning of physical existence where we are sheltered and nurtured. Dreams of the womb can signify our need to satisfy such requirements. Dreams of *returning to the womb* suggest a reconnection with the passive, more yielding, side of our nature. On a slightly more esoteric level, the womb represents our connection with the Great Mother or Mother Earth (*See Great Mother/Mother Earth*). We may additionally need a period of self-healing and recuperation.

③ The body is a physical manifestation of our 'will to be' and of our inner spirituality.

Boil/Carbuncle

① To be aware of a boil or carbuncle in a dream is to recognise there is a collection of negative influences around us which is turning unpleasant or perhaps even harmful. If a boil appears on someone else they have been affected by negativity.

② A boil or carbuncle appearing in a dream is a classic indication that something has 'got under our skin' in everyday life. We may be experiencing an eruption of nastiness on some level which will not go away until we have dealt with, and cauterised, it properly.

③ In Biblical times a plague of boils was seen as just punishment for wrongdoing and in dreams may be seen as a warning that we need to temper our behaviour.

Bonds

① There are two meanings for bonds in dreams. One is as in **savings bonds** (promissory notes) and the second as in **bindings and cords**. To dream of **the former** indicates that we have a sense of commitment to a person or a principle, that we are capable of making promises which we can keep. To dream of **the latter** deals with the binding or holding which can occur in situations and relationships. Depending on whether we are being bound or doing the binding it indicates submission to a greater force.

② Depending on whether we are **giving or receiving** such promissory bonds we need to consider our emotional commitment to ourselves and our own concerns. To be aware of being fettered, snared or held fast by chains indicates the possibility that our emotional selves may be out of control.

③ The changing of conflict into law and order, of chaos into cosmic order. The Silver Cord. It is considered to be the bond which unites the Spiritual Self with the physical body.

Bones
– also see Limbs in Body, Skeleton and Skull

① Bones appearing in a dream usually indicate that we need to be aware of that which we consider to be basic material. We need to 'go back to basics'. To dream of a **dog eating a bone** means we need to consider our basic instincts. To dream of **finding bones** indicates that there is something essential we have not considered in a situation.

② To dream of a full skeleton indicates that we need to reconsider the overall structure of our lives.

③ Bones are one of the integral parts of man. As the structure around which our lives are built, spiritually they can represent our ideas about death and resurrection.

Bonfire
– also see Fire

① To be **lighting or tending** a bonfire in a dream indicates a need for cleansing some aspect of our lives. Such a fire can also represent passions that are not confined by rigidity and custom.

② When we are conscious of **feeding a bonfire**, the passionate side of our emotional selves needs to be allowed freedom of expression. Old, outdated concepts and beliefs can be let go in order to create something new.

③ Spiritually, a bonfire reflects the power of the sun and encourages the power of good. It also represents Solar festivals.

Bomb
– also see Explosion

① Bombs appearing in a dream usually indicate some form of explosive situation with which we need to deal. **Exploding** a bomb indicates the need for positive action. while **defusing** a bomb suggests taking care not to make a situation worse.

② Psychologically we need to be aware that our own emotions are likely to get the better of us.

③ A bomb exploding is usually an unexpected event. Dreaming of one would suggest a fear of sudden radical changes or a situation we cannot control.

Book
– also see Novel

① Our search for knowledge and the ability to learn from other people's experience and opinions is symbolised in dreams by books and libraries. To dream of **old books** represents inherited wisdom and spiritual awareness. To dream of **account books** indicates the need or ability to look after our own resources.

② Intellectually we are searching in our dreams for ways which will help us to handle events in our lives.

③ A book, particularly a sacred one such as the Bible or Koran, signifies hidden or sacred knowledge. Dreaming of such a book can represent our need to look into the realms of sacred knowledge for reassurance that we are going in the right direction.

Bouquet

① **To be given** a bouquet in a dream shows that we recognise our own abilities but also expect others to recognise them. To be **giving someone else** a bouquet indicates that we fully recognise their better qualities.

② Very often a bouquet indicates, on a psychological level, that we have many gifts and talents available to us.

③ A bouquet, by virtue of its beauty and attachment to ceremonies, can symbolise a spiritual offering.

Border
– also see Frontier

① A border can appear in many different ways in a dream. To have our attention drawn to the **edge or border of material** can indicate changes we will make in the material world. To be standing on **a border between two countries** would show the need to be making great changes in life; perhaps physically moving our place of residence.

② Psychologically we may need to make decisive changes in the way we think and feel.

③ Meeting a different aspect of the Self *(see Self)* and thus a new experience in life. We need to decide if the time is right to 'cross the border'.

Bottle

① To a certain extent it depends on which type of bottle is perceived in the dream. **To see a baby's feeding bottle** would indicate the need to be successfully nurtured and helped to grow. **A bottle of alcohol** would show the need to celebrate, or to curb an excess, while **a medicine bottle** might symbolise the need to look at one's own health. **A broken bottle** could indicate either aggression or failure.

② **Opening a bottle** could mean making available resources you have, but may have suppressed.

③ A womb symbol; the principle of containing and enclosure.

Bottom
– see Body and Position

Bounce/Bouncing
– see Jumping/Bouncing

Bow

① Since bowing is indicative of giving someone else status, to be **bowing to someone** in a dream would indicate our sense of inferiority. To perceive a bow, as in **Cupid's bow**, within a dream can indicate the need to be loved – the union of masculine and feminine.

② While intellectually we may not need to feel inferior, on an unconscious level we may actually sense someone else's need to feel superior and then acknowledge that in the dream state. To see a **bow made of ribbon** in a dream is making a connection to the feminine principle and beauty.

③ Variously a bow can indicate superiority, the union of masculine and feminine and celebration.

Bowl

① **A bowl of food** in a dream represents our ability to nurture and sustain others. **A bowl of flowers** can represent a gift or a talent, while a **bowl of water** represents our emotional capacity.

② A bowl appearing in a dream has the same significance as a vase *(see Vase)*.

③ **A bowl of water** represents the feminine, fertility and the receptive principle.

Box

① **To feel boxed in** in a dream is to be prevented from expanding in an appropriate way. To dream of **packing things** in a box indicates that we are trying to get rid of feelings or thoughts with which we cannot cope.

② **Various types of boxes** perceived in a dream may represent different aspects of the feminine personality.

③ The feminine containing principle, intuition contained.

Boy
– see People

Boyfriend
– see People

Brain

① When attention is drawn to the brain in a dream, we are expected to consider our own or others' intellect. To dream of the **brain being preserved** indicates the need to take care in intellectual pursuits. We may be pushing ourselves too hard.

② Since the brain is the seat of learning, we may psychologically need to consider our beliefs and ideals in the light of experience.

③ The seat of the soul, the motivating force.

Bread
– also see Baker, Food and Loaf/Loaves

① Dreaming of bread connects us with our need for basic emotional and biological satisfaction. To be **sharing bread** in a dream represents our ability to share basic experience.

② If the bread in a dream is unusual in any way or tastes bad we may be unsure of what we really need out of life. We may be doing the wrong thing in some area of our lives.

③ Bread is symbolic of life itself. It is food of the soul and can also represent the need to share.

Break

① To dream of something being broken symbolises loss or damage. If a **favourite object** is broken we must make changes and break from the past. If a **limb is broken** we may be prevented from moving forward or carrying out a certain action.

② If we actually dream of **breaking something**, appropriate action needs to be taken in order to break a bond or connection in our life.

③ Shattered idealism and faith; the difference between the spiritual and mundane.

Breastplate

① In mythology, the breastplate was always considered to protect the knight. When we experience ourselves as wearing some form of protection around the heart, we are usually protecting our right to love unconditionally.

② Psychologically we are at our most vulnerable where matters of the heart are concerned, and most often need protection in that area. To be aware of **someone else wearing a breastplate** in a dream indicates their capacity to be hurt emotionally.

③ Our need to protect ourselves spiritually, yet also connect with the Divine.

Breasts
– also see Body

① Considered by many to be one of the most frequently dreamed about parts of the body, breasts are symbolic of the nourishment and love belonging to motherhood. For a **man to dream of breasts** usually indicates his unconscious connection with his mother or the nurturing principle.

② While intellectually we deny the need for mothering or 'smother-love', psychologically this need surfaces when we are under stress and usually comes up as the dream image of breasts.

③ Motherhood, protection and love are all symbolised by the breasts.

Breath

① To become aware of **one's own breathing** in a dream indicates a deep connection with the process of life. To be aware of **someone else's breathing** indicates the need for empathy and understanding with that person.

② Our own emotional state can very often have an effect on the rate at which we breathe which then becomes translated in dreams into, for instance, a panic attack. To be **breathing underwater** is an instinctive return to the womb-like state.

③ The Soul: breath is the power of the Spirit and life-giving power. Without it we are nothing.

Breeze

① To dream of a breeze being meaningful indicates a contented state of mind. **Wind** is generally considered to belong to the intellect, so by association a **gentle breeze** indicates love and compassion, while a **stiff breeze** can indicate a degree of abrasiveness.

② Psychologically for most people a breeze indicates happy times.

③ A warm breeze signifies unconditional love and caring, as well as Spiritual Integrity.

Bride
– also see Marriage and Wedding

① When a **woman dreams of being a bride**, she is often trying to reconcile her need for relationship and her need for independence. She needs to have an understanding of the changes in responsibility. **In a man's dream** a bride indicates his understanding of the feminine, innocent part of himself. To dream of **being at a wedding**, especially your own, indicates the integration of inner feeling and outer reality.

② Psychologically, we are seeking union of the unintegrated part of ourselves. We may be looking for the innocent feminine within.

③ As with a nun's commitment to the Divine, a bride symbolises the need for, and recognition of, love and receptivity.

Bridegroom
– also see Marriage and Wedding

① To dream of a bridegroom usually indicates the desire to be married or to find a partner. It often shows the desire to be more responsible or to take on responsibility for someone else. It is a connection with, and an understanding of, the 'romantic' side of one's nature and indicates the need for integration of the intellect and the real world.

② The need for partnership may be more intellectual than emotional, and we may need to make a connection with the drive of the masculine.

③ A bridegroom can represent our need to take care of somebody or something, and maybe to exert a degree of control.

Bridge

① The bridge is one of the most commonly found images in dreams and almost invariably indicates the crossing from one phase of life to another. The bridge may be depicted as weak or strong, sturdy or otherwise which gives an indication of the strength of connection necessary to make changes in our life.

② The symbol of a bridge in a dream signifies the emotional connection between us and other people or various parts of our life.

③ A transitional state, such as crossing the River of Life or the River Styx.

Bridle

① To be **bridled in a dream,** as in **being yoked to something,** indicates the need for restraint and control. If the **bridle is made of flowers** it indicates a more feminine way of imposing control. If the bridle is harsher – such as **one of metal and/or leather** – we perhaps need to be harder on ourselves or on someone we love.

② The bridle in dreams can indicate the need for focused attention on some aspect of our lives.

③ A degree of spiritual restraint or control may be needed.

Bright

① To experience brightness in a dream means that some part of our life needs illuminating, often by an external source.

② Being aware of brightness indicates that we have the ability to use the brighter, perhaps less serious, side of our personalities.

③ Dreaming of brightness symbolises our move towards spiritual illumination.

Brink

① To be **on the brink of something** in a dream literally means we are on the edge of something. This will have a profound effect on our lives or of those around us.

② We may be having difficulty in sorting out what is rational or irrational behaviour and need to make some careful choices.

③ There is the move towards darkness, and then there is the abyss. We should be careful – and aware – of a downward spiritual spiral.

Broadcast

① When we dream of **taking part in a broadcast** we are aware of needing to reach a wider audience. This may be risky since we have no means of measuring our audience's response. To dream of **listening to a broadcast** means we should be listening to the message that other people are trying to get across.

② Psychologically, the performer in us needs some form of self-expression. We need to broadcast or share our ideas and concepts.

③ The religious broadcast gives voice to those who feel that systems of belief are worth sharing. In dreams a broadcast may represent widespread spirituality rather than religion *per se*.

Broken
– see Break

Brothel

① If a **woman dreams of being in a brothel**, she has not yet come to terms with the sexually active side of herself. However, if a **man dreams of being in a brothel** it may show a fear of the feminine.

② To dream of a brothel indicates the need one has for sexual liberation and freedom.

③ The darker side of femininity. It may also represent awareness of man's spiritual debt to woman.

Brother
– see Family

Brotherhood

① Dreaming of **belonging to a brotherhood** indicates our need to belong to a group of like-minded people. This could be something in the nature of a trade union, or of the Freemasons. We all need approval from our peers, and such a dream indicates the way we handle ritualised group behaviour.

② Any grouping of the masculine usually alerts us to the many sides and aspects of the masculine personality.

③ The Priesthood is representative of joint responsibility for spirituality.

Brutality

① To experience some form of brutality in a dream can be frightening until we realise that we are connecting into the darker, more animal side of ourselves. We may need to deal with fears associated with that side in order to make progress.

② Unrestrained passion – whether sexual or of any other sort – can appear as brutality and cruelty in our dreams.

③ Brutality can manifest itself in demonic acts of evil. Although rather severe, we should take note of this interpretation.

Bubble

① We may dream of bubbles as part of our need to have fun in a child-like way. We often are aware of the temporary nature of happiness, and our need for illusion.

② Bubbles as beautiful but fragile objects remind us of the transitory nature of human existence, that nothing is permanent.

③ A bubble represents the illusory elements of everyday life and, more specifically, the daydream.

Buckle

① Dreaming of an **ornate buckle** has the same symbolism as that of a belt in that it can represent the holding of high office or status. It can also indicate honour and can be a symbol of loyalty or membership.

② To be **fastening a buckle** in a dream shows that we accept responsibility for what we do.

③ A buckle can have a double meaning in this case. It can represent a protective element against the forces of evil; it can also help us take the strain and not 'buckle' under pressure.

Bud

① To dream of a bud is to recognise the unfolding of a new way of life, new experiences or new emotions. To dream of a **bud dying** or shrivelling up indicates the failure of a project.

② A new idea or way of thinking holds a great deal of potential, as yet untapped.

③ How the world unfolds before us – and how we can influence that – is symbolised by the opening bud.

Buddha/Buddhist
– also see Religious Iconology

① There is a saying that goes 'If you meet the Buddha on the road, kill him.' In dreams the Buddha represents the denial or loss of ego. There needs to be a liberation from thinking and desiring.

② If we dream of **being Buddhist** we need to look at the difference between Western and Eastern religion.

③ Spiritual Clarity and all that this entails is encompassed by the Buddha.

Buffer

① In our dream imagery there may need for symbols which represent barriers and difficulties. To **run into a buffer** may indicate the need for caution.

② In our most vulnerable emotional states we may need some sort of buffer between us and the rest of the world, and this may be experienced in dreams as an actual physical barrier.

③ A buffer in Spiritual terms may be the transition area between the material and Spiritual planes.

Buildings

① Buildings can represent the structure we try to give to our everyday lives. The attitudes and beliefs we have formed built from experience and perception can often appear in dreams as buildings. We even construct edifices from the beliefs and perceptions of others round us such as our families. Buildings can become composite in dreams and therefore somewhat confusing. In understanding a dream, we should interpret the main appearance of the building first, and the secondary appearance as qualities to be recognised.

② In waking life we learn a lot about a person from his personal environment. Dreams reflect our character, hopes and concerns, often by highlighting such things through the environment of the dream itself. The features of the building often mirror aspects of our personality. For example, a house with a door that is difficult to open might signify a natural shyness and difficulty in getting to know people. Various buildings have certain meanings as follows:

Castle/Citadel/Fortress Any defended space may variously represent the feminine nature, or a place of safety and our innermost selves. To *breach the walls* of a castle or citadel as happens in many myths and fairy stories suggests freeing of the essential feminine, giving us a more intuitive approach to life. In dreams, it suggests that we have come to an understanding of our own inner power. If it is particularly noticeable that the castle, citadel or fortress has *four walls* it represents mundane concerns or practical considerations.

Church/Tabernacle/Temple (also see individual entry for Church/Holy Buildings) Any religious building will suggest a place of sanctuary and refuge, where we may be at peace with our beliefs. In dreams, a sacred space or one which has been consecrated, including a consecrated circle or grove, allows us to understand the raising of our own vibration to a more spiritual level. It is often that part of ourselves where we can communicate with our idea of Divine Power.

Hotel/B&B/Boarding house/Motel A hotel or any place of temporary residence indicates a situation in waking life which is of a transient nature. Such a building may show that we are becoming aware of our own insecurities and may not feel particularly grounded.

House (also see individual entry) A house most often refers to the soul and the manner in which we live our lives. If we are initially aware that the *house is not empty* and that there is something in it, for example furnishings, it shows an aspect of our waking lives needs consideration. If there is *someone else in the house* it may mean that we are feeling threatened in some way. If there are *different activities going on* – particularly if they are very different –this suggests rivalry between two parts of our personality, possibly the creative and the intellectual, or perhaps the logical and intuitive. The *front of the house* portrays the facade we present to the outside world. *Going into or coming out of* the house means we can decide whether we need to be more introverted or extroverted in our waking lives. Being *outside the house* depicts our more public side. In a dream of an *impressive, awe-inspiring house* we are conscious of the Self or the Soul, the 'higher' aspects of ourselves. *Moving to a larger house* implies that there is need for a change in our lives, perhaps to achieve a more open way of life, or even for more emotional space. If a *small house* is seen we may be seeking security, or perhaps the safety of childhood, without responsibility. If we find the smallness of the house constricting we may feel trapped by responsibilities, and need to escape. *Making changes to the structure of the house or repairing it* in some way shows that we need to firstly look at how we are constructing our lives then pay attention to health matters and then decide whether relationships of any sort need 'repair'. We may need to appreciate that damage or decay has occurred in some way in our lives.

Igloo (also see individual entry) Because of its geodesic shape, the igloo in dreams represents completeness and sanctuary. By its nature, the igloo is warm on the inside and cold on the outside and therefore signifies the difference between the inner self and the external world.

Pyramid (also see individual entry) As a construction, the pyramid is one of the oldest known to man. There are many ideas in existence as to its purpose. Universally it is considered to be a focus of, and for, power and energy. Thus, for one to appear in a dream is to be concentrating on the power within. Since the triangle often represents body, mind and spirit, the pyramid can symbolise this in a very concrete way; that is, based in reality. The true point of power is considered to in the centre of the pyramid, so to dream of such a situation suggests reaching our own potential.

Tower/Lighthouse/Obelisk/Steeple etc. (also see individual entries) An image of a tower of any sort in a dream represents the personality and the Soul within. While there are obvious connotations that connect it to masculinity and assertiveness, it is perhaps more pertinent to perceive it as the Self within the world in which we live. When thought of in this way, we can then pay attention to other attributes of the tower, such as where windows, doors and staircases are placed within. We might consider whether, for example, in a lighthouse the light is bright or dimmed. Since the building of a tower, particularly the steeple of a church, was initially designed to 'point to the heavens' the symbolism indicates greater understanding of the Spiritual Self. Further meditation on the image of a tower can bring a great deal of personal insight.

Warehouse The warehouse, being initially a place for storage, has the symbolism of being a repository either for spiritual energy or for spiritual detritus. As many such buildings in waking life become used for other purposes, the warehouse can in dreams represent useful personal space and intelligent use of available resources.

The various facets, or aspects, of buildings also have meaning:

Balcony/Ledge/Sill A balcony, particularly with a balustrade, indicates both support and protectiveness. Without any kind of surround, a ledge or sill may suggest danger of some sort. Equally, all of these can also represent the Great Mother *(see Great Mother/Mother Earth)* in her protective aspect.

Chimney (also see individual entry) As a conduit from one state to another and a conductor of heat, in dreams the chimney can indicate how we deal with our inner emotions and warmth. It may also represent our connection with the Divine. In ancient civilizations smoke was considered to be a petition to the gods, so a chimney can symbolize directed and specific prayer.

Doors (also see individual entry) Doors often refer to the openings of the body and therefore, by default, to our approach to our sexuality. The front door and back door may signify the vagina and the anus respectively, but from a psychological perspective can also suggest how we allow people to approach us, and how vulnerable we can become. *Breaking down the door* means that we are now ready to tackle inhibitions and an unwillingness to face the issues. Such an act can also represent attack or abuse, often of a dearly held principle. *Opening and closing the door,* while sometimes taken to stand for intercourse, can often show our attitude to social interplay, and our ability to be open and broad-minded over all sorts of issues. *Refusing to open the door* shows a narrow-minded approach to life and also perhaps an innocent approach to sexuality. *A door between the outer and inner rooms* shows there may be a conflict between the conscious and the unconscious, or the inner private self and the public personality. *Barring the door* denotes our need for self-protection, though if the door is barred to us there is a block to progress. Interpretation will depend on whether the door should open inwards or outwards. If an *animal or person forces his way in and destroys the lock* on the door then our own protective mechanisms have let us down. *Escaping* by another door indicates we need to find an alternative solution to a problem in our waking lives. Someone *knocking on the door* signifies that our attention is being drawn to an external situation.

Lift/Elevator/Escalator Lifts or escalators in dreams usually indicate how we deal with information. For instance, a *lift or elevator going down* would suggest exploring into the subconscious, while a *lift going up* would be moving towards the spiritual. It is believed that in the sleep state we leave our bodies, and this can be reflected in dreams of lifts or elevators. Thus, *descending in a lift and getting stuck* represents the 'entrapment' of the spiritual self by the physical body, whereas *going up in a lift and getting stuck* can suggest that we are too geared towards the material world. A slightly more open-minded approach to such matters is symbolised by an escalator.

Passages Passages represent the transitions between the various stages of our lives such as childhood to puberty. Any passage in a dream can also represent the passages within the body – the intestines and so on. Equally, on a psychological level, they signify how we allow our personal space to be penetrated.

Rooms in a dream can describe various parts of our personalities or levels of understanding, but can also signify either the womb or the mother figure. The different rooms and parts of houses in dreams indicate the diverse aspects of our personality and experience. While the purpose of specific rooms is important in dreams as mentioned in the individual entry for House, rooms in general can have significances in other ways: A *small room with only one door*, or a *basement with water in it* is a direct representation of the womb, and may suggest a need to return to the womb-like state,. It may also signify a consideration of issues to do with pregnancy or of new beginnings. A *series of rooms* refers to the various aspects or archetypes of femininity and so often represents the complete Soul. *Something in an upstairs room* denotes an idea or concept belonging to the spiritual or intellectual realms. *Leaving the room and going into another* suggests leaving some aspect of the past behind in order to bring about change. Such a change need not necessarily be for the better. If a *room is empty*, perhaps we feel comfort or support is lacking in our waking lives.

Stairs Stairs in dreams are often an indication of the steps we must take in order to achieve a goal. *Climbing the stairs* is illustrative of the effort that we must make in order to have access to the more mystical, spiritual side of our being. It can also more simply be the exertion we practise in everyday life, whether we find things difficult or otherwise. To have access to the hidden, unconscious side of ourselves, we need to 'go down' into the unconscious, thus *going downstairs* becomes the dream image. *A golden staircase* is such a basic image, with so many interpretations, that particular attention needs to be paid to other aspects of the dream, and also our spiritual state at that specific time. Largely it represents a new beginning or 'death', though not necessarily a physical one. It is more the realisation that we no longer need to be trapped within the physical, but can move towards a more fulfilling life. It is a way out of the mundane.

Walls A wall signifies a block to progress. The nature of the wall will give some clue as to what the block is: for example, an old *wall* suggests a problem, from the past whereas a glass wall would indicate difficulties with perception. *Construction or deliberate demolition* of a wall or building suggests that we all have the ability within us to construct successful lives, yet equally an ability to self-destruct. How we carry this out symbolises our basic attitude to life. A dream that highlights construction or demolition gives us direct access to such qualities in order to make progress. A dream where *walls close in* could describe the remembered feelings of birth, but is more likely to represent a feeling of being trapped by the way in which we live our lives. A *brick wall, rampart or dividing wall* in a dream all signify the difference between two states of reality, often the inner psychological state and the exterior everyday world.

③ In the same way that the physical body develops in the womb, the spiritual self requires a construct in order to create the circumstances in which it can mature. Those constructs are often shown as buildings in dreams.

Bull
– also see Animals

① In dreams the bull represents the masculine principle and fertility. It also can indicate the way we handle male sexuality.

② The bull appearing in a dream can point to our own stubborn behaviour.

③ The bull is connected with the moon goddesses and also represents Taurus in the Zodiac.

Bullet
– also see Gun

① To dream of bullets is to be aware of aggression and a desire to hurt. If the bullet is **being fired at** us it may be considered to be a warning of danger. If, however, we are **firing the bullet** there is an awareness of one's vulnerability.

② There is a need to understand what ammunition we have available in the sense of resources to be used.

③ A bullet can represent the need for, and control of, sexual impregnation. From a Spiritual perspective, the bullet can represent the inherent energy within the Life Force or need for self expression.

Burglar
– also see Intruder and Stealing

① When we become aware of a burglar or intruder in our dreams we are experiencing some form of violation of our private space. This may be from external sources or from inner fears and difficult emotions.

② A part of our psyche may have been neglected, and intrude on our awareness, thus needing attention. Burglary highlights the idea of vulnerability.

③ Penetration and vulnerability – either physical or material – is the symbolism here.

Burial/Bury

① To have a dream about **being buried** indicates a fear of being overcome, possibly by responsibility, or of repressing parts of our personality in ways which are harmful. To be burying something may be either trying to conceal it, or to be attempting to hide it away and ignore it.

② To be **attending a burial** in our dreams shows the need to come to terms with loss. What we are burying needs consideration. If we are burying bulbs or seeds for instance we might are hoping for new growth or opportunities. If in the dream we are hoping that what we are burying is found, we are looking to share information and knowledge, more in the long term rather than the short term.

③ The obvious spiritual symbols of death, loss and pain are relevant here. This is not necessarily a negative meaning, we should look at the resurrection and the positive elements that it can bring.

Bus
– also see Transport

① If we dream of being **in a bus** we are coming to terms with the way we handle group relationships, and the new directions that we need to take in company with others.

② We may be experiencing the need to be an individual, while at the same time belonging to a group with a common purpose.

③ The Greater Good, or what is best for everyone.

Butcher

– also see Occupations

① We see the butcher as one who mutilates, but provides for us at the same time, and this is reflected in dreams when he appears as someone who separates the good from the bad. He may also be a destroyer.

② We may need to become aware of a destructive streak in ourselves. Such a figure may also represent the ability to use our skills to nurture and provide.

③ The butcher has spiritual connotations with the Grim Reaper and death. The meat cleaver could be taken to represent the scythe.

Butterfly

① On a practical level when seen in dreams, the butterfly represents light-heartedness, freedom and sheer joy in existence.

② Psychologically, the butterfly indicates a lack of ability to settle down or to undertake a protracted task. However, this inability reflects the type of personality which has a profound effect on others.

③ When seen in dreams or meditation, the butterfly represents the freed soul and immortality. It shows that there is no need for the soul to be trapped by the physical body.

Cable

① In today's technological society a cable in dreams will frequently suggest a connection, either between two aspects of our lives or even our personalities. If the plug is particularly significant it may also suggest that a source of energy is available to us.

② Being conscious in dreams of cables, whether electrical or otherwise, can be rather ambivalent. It may mean that we are 'wired up and ready for action' or alternatively that we are being held in one place and are unable to widen our sphere of influence in ways other than intellectually.

③ Cables can represent the 'ties that bind' – those subtle forces which make us aware of our own spirituality. A single cable can signify the Silver Cord which links the physical being to the spiritual realms.

Caduceus

① The Caduceus is the symbol that is used by doctors and medical establishments as the sign of healing. To have this appear in a dream usually highlights health matters, which may be our own or other people's.

② The body recognises and communicates in dream images its need and expectation of good health. On a psychological level, to dream of the Caduceus can mean that we need to create better conditions for achieving this.

③ Power and healing in uniting opposites.

Cage/Cell
– also see Prison

① The cage normally represents some form of trap or jail. To dream of **caging a wild animal** alerts us to our need to restrain our wilder instincts. To dream that we are **in a cage** indicates a sense of frustration and perhaps of being trapped by the past.

② We are being warned that we are enforcing too much restraint on our hidden abilities. We could be allowing others to hold us back in some way.

③ Spiritual restriction is good for the soul, and can be represented in dreams by a cell or perhaps a cage.

Cakes

① When we dream of **celebration cakes** – such as a wedding or birthday cake – we are being shown that there is cause for celebration in our lives. This may be to do with the actual cause for celebration or to mark the passage of time. (**Candles on a cake** – *see Candle and Numbers.*)

② **Making cakes** indicates our need to care for others or to nurture an inner, perhaps hidden, need within ourselves.

③ **Sacrificial cakes, or buns** marked with the cross symbolise the round of the moon and its four quarters and thus the passage of time.

Calculator/Calculations
– also see Abacus

① In its simplest meaning, calculation signifies a tallying process, so suggests our ability to reason. A calculator, however technologically sophisticated in dreams, highlights our ability to reach conclusions.

② As consciousness expands, we as mere mortals need a facility which allows us to calculate and quantify complex ideas and logic. A calculator performs this function in waking life and symbolises the need for such actions in dreams.

③ When logic needs to be applied to some kinds of esoteric thought or spiritual ideas we will dream of making calculations or of a calculator. We should ask ourselves if it 'adds up' for us.

Calendar

① If a calendar appears in a dream there can be more than one meaning. Our attention may be being drawn to the past, present or future and something significant in our lives, or we may be being warned of the passage of time in an important scheme.

② Because time is a self imposed limitation, when anything that marks time appears in a dream we are being warned of the potential for limitation.

③ We should become more aware of the timetable and importance of festivals and celebrations and how they are relevant to us as we progress.

Calf
– see Baby Animals in Animals

Camel

① Depending on the environment in the dream the camel can represent the unusual or bizarre. It also represents wise use of available resources and obedience to a basic principle.

② Psychologically the camel can represent stamina and self sufficiency.

③ As a bearer of royalty and dignity, the camel signifies power.

Camera

① The camera is a recording instrument, thus to be **using a camera** in a dream means we are recording events or occasions which may we need to remember or take note of more fully. **Being filmed** indicates that we need to look more carefully at our actions and reactions to certain situations.

② There is a necessity to retain a mental picture of what is important to us.

③ There is a need to be watchful and aware of our surroundings.

Camping
– see Tent

Canal

① Because a canal is a man-made structure, a dream about a canal usually indicates that we are inclined to be rigid insofar as the control of our emotions is concerned. We may be introducing too much structure into our lives at the expense of our creativity.

② We need to structure our knowledge of ourselves in order to create a workable system.

③ Structure, definition and rigid belief, all created by Man.

Cancer

① Cancer is one of the prime fears that a human being has to deal with, so to dream of a cancer indicates that we are out of harmony with our body. It indicates fear of illness and equally can represent something 'eating away' at us – usually a negative idea or concept.

② Intellectually we may have worked through our fears but still be left with attitudes and beliefs that cannot be cleared away. Very often this appears as cancer in dreams.

③ The Mother, the Moon and the astrological sign of Cancer.

Candle

① In Pagan times, the candle or taper represented the dispersing of darkness and a way of worshipping power. To dream of candles indicates that we are trying to clarify something that we do not understand. **Candles on a birthday cake** can therefore indicate that we are marking a transition from the old to the new. **Lighting a candle** represents using courage and fortitude or asking for something which we need.

② Psychologically candles represent knowledge or wisdom that has not fully crystallised. They can also represent our control of personal magic.

③ Illumination, wisdom, strength and beauty are all spiritual qualities.

Cane

① Because many people associate the cane with some form of punishment or sadism, it can represent self punishment or masochism. It is more likely however that we are trying to come to terms with some form of childhood trauma.

② Because a cane also represents pliability, we may be trying to achieve a correct balance between our willingness and our unwillingness to accept a situation.

③ The cane in dreams signifies a degree of self-flagellation, but may also represent support.

Cannibalism

① To dream of cannibalism usually represents unsophisticated or inappropriate behaviour. To become aware of **eating human flesh** in a dream may well indicate our dislike of unsuitable foods or actions. There is often a part of ourselves we have not 'internalised' which we need to absorb.

② Eating human flesh in a dream can mean that we are taking in wrong information in waking life. We should perhaps be more careful who we listen to.

③ We are absorbing powers or qualities belonging to someone else for our own spiritual aims.

Cannon
– see Weapons

Canoe

① To dream of a canoe would indicate that we are handling our emotions in isolation. We are possibly making efforts to control the flow of our emotion. We are aware that we are capable of making changes but only by our own efforts.

② We may be protected from our emotions, but at the same time are also at risk to some extent. A degree of skill and maturity is necessary to enable us to move forward.

③ In ancient symbology the lunar barque and the crescent moon were both symbolised by the canoe.

Canopy

① When we dream of a canopy we are looking to be protected, sheltered or loved. In olden times a canopy was used to shelter those with special duties or powers, such as kings and queens or priests and priestesses. We still acknowledge on a deep internal level this privilege. If **we ourselves are being sheltered** we recognise our own abilities and potential for greatness.

② A canopy protects the head which is the seat of intellect. We have a need to draw attention to higher ideals or aspirations.

③ Royalty or powerful people often used a canopy with a special symbol either for spiritual protection or to signify their rank. We should consider how important we really find such matters.

Cap
– also see Hat in Clothes

① The cap has the same significance as the hat in dreams and draws attention to status or spiritual powers. If we are **wearing a cap** in a dream we may be covering up our creative abilities.

② The cap shows the need for respect for a person's beliefs and wisdom or knowledge. **Doffing the cap** signifies submission to authority.

③ A cap signifies nobility and freedom.

Capital
– also see Places and Money

① To dream of one's **financial capital** would imply a need to conserve resources. **Dreaming of a country's capital city** indicates we should look at our attitude to the wider issues in that country or our connection with that city. We may also need to consider how we deal with large groups of people, particularly those whose customs and accepted behaviour is unknown.

② To dream of capital letters indicates that we need to pay more attention to important issues in our lives. There is a matter around us which needs sorting out.

③ Spiritually, capital is the result of past actions – gain from good deeds.

Car
– also see Transport

① The car is very often representative of our own personal space, an extension of our being. To dream of **being in a car** usually alerts us to our own motivation, thus **driving the car** can indicate our need to achieve a goal, while **being a passenger** could indicate that we have handed over responsibility for our lives to someone else.

② Dream scenarios involving cars are often more to do with what we are doing to ourselves on a psychological or emotional level. **Being alone in a vehicle** indicates independence, while dreaming of the **brakes** of a car shows our ability to be in control of a situation. **The car engine** indicates the essential drives with which we have to deal. **A crashing vehicle** suggests fear of failure in life, while a **car on fire** denotes stress of some sort, either physically or emotionally. **To be in a car which is driven carelessly**, either by us or someone else, marks a lack of responsibility, while a feeling of being left behind would be shown by your car **being overtaken**. To dream of **reversing a car** registers a feeling that one is slipping backwards or having to reverse a decision.

③ A car stands for spiritual direction and motivation.

Cards (Greeting)

① To dream of **giving or receiving a card** such as a birthday card alerts us to the need for a specific kind of communication with the addressee. We may wish to celebrate our own or others good fortune and luck.

② Our subconscious may be registering concern, either about ourselves or others.

③ Visual communication, the ability to convey a message spiritually.

Cards (Playing)

① In a dream, playing with cards highlights our ability to be open to opportunity or to take chances. The cards that one deals, or is dealt, in a dream may have significance as to number (*see Numbers*) or as to suit: *Hearts* indicate emotion and relationship. *Diamonds* represent material wealth. *Spades* represent conflict, difficulties and obstacles. *Clubs* represent action, work and intelligence. *The King* portrays human success and mastery. *The Queen* indicates emotional depth, sensitivity and understanding. *The Jack* represents impetuousness, creativity or an adolescent energy.

② On a psychological level, card playing in a dream can be seen as taking calculated risks and alerts us to potential danger.

③ There is a theory that modern day playing cards evolved from the Tarot – our

Inner Truth. The Tarot particularly gives many rich images which can be used in dream work.

Career
– also see Employment and Work

① A career in the mundane world is the way we nurture or take care of ourselves – not just materially but also to give ourselves self-esteem. A dream where our career is brought into prominence highlights any of these issues that we may have in everyday life. We can then consciously work these through.

② Psychologically we need to feel useful, and dreaming of a change in career can herald a change in lifestyle or the way we relate to other people. We need to note very carefully what was different in the dream and consider what changes we need to make in waking life.

③ The inference that our career must satisfy our needs, wants and spiritual requirements can be clearly demonstrated in dreams.

Carnival
– see Fairground/Carnival and Festival

Carpet
– see Furniture/Furnishings

Carriage
– also see Transport

① Dreaming of a carriage, such as a **horse-drawn** one, could be suggestive of old fashioned attitudes to modern thinking. **A train carriage** indicates that we are taking a journey that is slightly more public in character than a car journey.

② Any symbol which signifies our being moved in some way draws attention to our ability to make progressive changes in our lives.

③ The carriage is a symbol of majesty and power.

Carried/Carrying

① To be aware of **carrying an object** suggests we need to look at what is being accepted as a burden or difficulty. If we dream of **being carried** we may feel that we are in need of support.

② To dream of **carrying someone** registers the fact that we may be accepting responsibility for someone else and that this responsibility is a burden.

③ When we are prepared to 'carry' something we are taking Spiritual Responsibility.

Cask

① Like most containers, a cask represents the feminine principle. Since a cask is usually hand-made, to dream of one indicates the care taken in dealing with one's own emotional make-up.

② It is more likely to be the content of the cask which has meaning on a psychological level and indicates our ability to be creative with raw materials.

③ **A bottomless cask** represents needless effort.

Castle
– also see Buildings

① Dreaming of a castle links us right back to the feminine principle of the enclosed and defended private space. It can represent the fantastic or perhaps difficulty in obtaining our objectives.

② Before we can be fully open to other people, we normally have to let down our barriers, and being **trapped in a castle** may represent our difficulty in freeing ourselves from old attitudes. **Trying to enter a castle** signifies that we recognise obstacles which have to be overcome.

③ Spiritual testing – the overcoming of obstacles in order to gain a greater understanding.

Castrate
– also see Sex

① In any dream that contains sexual trauma, we are usually being alerted to our inner fears. The violent act of castration in a dream indicates the damage we are doing to ourselves in denying such fears.

② Conventionally, there may be some difficulty in coming to terms with the conflict between the masculine and feminine within oneself.

③ We are prepared to make a life sacrifice, to give up or control the sexual act in favour of celibacy.

Cat
– see Animals

Catacomb/Crypt
– also see Tomb

① Many dreams contain images which are to do with space underground, and to dream of a crypt or a catacomb signifies a need to come to terms with subconscious religious beliefs or training. Sometimes these are hidden from us and must be fully explored.

② Our subconscious fears or feelings connected with death can show in a dream as a catacomb or crypt.

③ As a place of hidden forces and occult power, in dreams the catacomb will represent the unconscious.

Caterpillar

① The caterpillar appearing in a dream usually indicates that we are undergoing some form of major change. We may be being warned that we must undergo a complete metamorphosis. We must change and grow from what we are now into a greater potential.

② To dream of caterpillars would indicate that we need to remain flexible in our attitude to change. Also, because of the caterpillar's association with creeping things, it may represent some type of difficulty.

③ The spiritual potential, largely unrecognised, which must transmute into something more beautiful.

Cauldron
– also see Kettle

① Almost universally the cauldron represents abundance, sustenance and nourishment. By association, the magic cauldron suggests fertility and the feminine power of transformation. To dream of a cauldron, therefore, reconnects us with our basic principles.

② Psychologically, when a cauldron appears in a dream we may need to take note of our intuitive abilities, or of our ability to create new things from simple ingredients.

③ Spiritually the cauldron symbolises renewal and rebirth.

Cave

① As with the catacombs, the cave represents a doorway into the unconscious. While initially the cave may be frightening an exploration can reveal strong contact with our own inner selves.

② Passing through the cave signifies a change of state, and a deeper understanding of our own negative impulses.

③ Spiritual shelter, initiation and rebirth takes form internally.

Cemetery
– also see Coffin, Dead People and Death

① The cemetery and its association with death can have a double meaning in dreams. It can represent the parts of ourselves that we have 'killed off' or stopped using. It can also depict our thoughts and feelings about death and the attitudes and traditions surrounding it.

② In dreams we can often allow our fears to come to the surface in an acceptable way. The cemetery can be a symbol of an appropriate way to handle these fears. In other words, we can legitimately allow ourselves to become frightened.

③ A cemetery is the place of the Dead but also of spiritual regeneration.

Celebrity

① In today's society, when the lives of celebrities, media personalities and football stars are open to much scrutiny, dreaming of such people may suggest that we are attempting to identify what qualities they have that we feel are lacking in us. We have perhaps given them status and without really understanding what pressures are involved.

② Wives and girlfriends of soccer players, colloquially known as Wags, often receive attention by default rather than because of their own skills. When such a figure appears, particularly in a woman's dream, it is useful to make an assessment of what our real skills and talents are. Rather than having those skills occluded by someone else's brilliance, we can make use of them in their own right. There is a part of the human personality which both needs and yet abhors adoration, so such figures appearing in our dreams indicate we may be seeking such adoration for the wrong reasons. In a man's dream such a figure may typify the ideal feminine.

③ From a spiritual perspective, celebrities can personify the chosen ones, those from whom we expect a certain standard of behaviour. When they let us down, rather than perceiving them as 'fallen angels' we can be very unforgiving.

Centaur

① To have a Centaur appear in a dream demonstrates the unification of man's animal nature with his qualities of human virtue and judgement.

② The symbol of a Centaur in a dream represents our ability to unite two complete opposites in an acceptable way. As a fabulous beast *(see Fabulous Beasts)* it was believed to have magical powers.

③ Vision and wisdom. Traditionally, the Centaur was half man and half beast, and is associated with the Zodiac sign of Sagittarius.

Centre
– also see Position

① When we dream of **being at the centre** of something, such as in the centre of a group of people, it highlights our awareness of our ability to be powerful within a situation – that everything revolves around us. To be **moving away** from the centre indicates that part of our lives may be off balance.

② Psychologically, to be at the centre, or in the middle, of a situation shows we need to be aware of both our ability to control that situation and our ability to be flexible. **Moving towards the centre** shows our need for integrity in our day to day life.

③ Totality, wholeness, the origin and sacred space are symbolised.

Ceremony
– also see Religious Iconology and Ritual

① When we dream of taking part in a ceremony or religious ritual we are conscious of a new attitude or skill that is needed or an important change which is taking place in our lives.

② Any major life change has a profound effect on us and this is very often shown in dream form as a ceremony of some kind.

③ Ceremonies and rituals are used for initiation, deeper awareness and to establish new order.

Chain

① To dream of chains in any form indicates a type of restriction or dependency. Just as we need strength to break out of chains it is also needed in supporting chains. In becoming aware of what is holding us back we also become appreciative of how to break free.

② In dreams we can become conscious of beliefs or mental attitudes – both in ourselves and others – which can create problems. The links in a chain can very often symbolise the communication that we need to free ourselves.

③ Bondage and slavery, dignity and unity are all symbolised by chains and highlight their ambiguity.

Chalice
– also see Holy Grail

① In dreams the chalice represents the feminine. Because of its religious significance, the chalice usually represents something that may seem to be unattainable except without a great deal of effort. It can also represent an important event or ceremony *(see Cup)*.

② In religion the chalice is associated with the symbolism of the heart, containing the lifeblood. In the chalice this is represented by wine – wine and blood having the same meaning.

③ The source of inexhaustible sustenance, abundance, the Holy Grail.

Chariot

① In modern times most people will dream about the car or other forms of transport rather than a chariot. To dream of a chariot would possibly imply the necessity for old-fashioned methods of control or ways of behaviour within the situations surrounding us in waking life.

② On a psychological level we may have to explore archetypal images *(see Archetypes)* for an understanding of our own motivations. The chariot may represent basic urges before they have been altered by conditioning.

③ The Sun and the Divine are represented by the chariot in dreams.

Charity

① To dream of **giving or receiving charity** has a lot to do with our ability to give and receive love. **A charity box** appearing in a dream usually indicates an awareness of our own needs.

② Charity has connections with our ability to care about others. To dream of a charitable act often alerts us to the wider issues that are important in our lives.

③ Charity comes from the word 'caritas' which means caring from the heart. Its appearance in dreams shows we care about others and the effect we have on them.

Charm/Amulet
– also see Magic

① Strictly, charms are the words used to bring about a certain magical result and amulets are objects charged to protect the wearer. Today a **charm**, such as those found in pendants and bracelets nowadays, usually represents a 'significant object' for us. An **amulet** appearing in a dream signifies the need for some kind of additional protection in everyday life, perhaps insurance or the learning of an additional skill.

② It will depend on our own belief system whether we believe in the magical properties of charms and amulets. Charms generally suggest a miniaturising (or minimising) of a situation – perhaps the realisation that it can be handled, literally, with charm. An amulet in dreams will mean that we need to draw on our deepest power, of which we are perhaps not yet consciously aware, to resolve a situation.

③ Objects imbued with spiritual power allow us to access realms which have little relevance for the uninitiated. Often we can best receive information as to how to access these realms by dreaming of charms and amulets.

Chase/Chased

① Dreaming of **being chased or of trying to escape** is perhaps one of the most common dreams; usually we are trying to escape responsibility, our own sense of failure, fear or emotions we can't handle. To be **chasing something** suggests the pursuit of success or a desired result.

② **Being chased by shadows** shows the need to escape from something previously repressed, such as past childhood trauma or difficulty. To be **chased by an animal** generally indicates we have not come to terms with our own passion.

③ Spiritually the image of being chased or pursued suggests either fear of one's actions, or is a play on words, as in 'chaste'.

Chasm

① When we dream of a chasm or large hole, we are being made conscious of situations that contain some element of the unknown, or are in some way risky. We are going to have to make decisions one way or another.

② We are being confronted by unknown or perhaps unrecognised negative elements in our own make-up; we have no previous experience by which to judge our actions or reactions.

③ We are faced by the Unconscious, the Void, and should consider whether our current way of behaviour is appropriate.

Chemist/Pharmacist
– also see Occupations

① Dreaming of a chemist links with that part of ourselves that is capable of altering the way we are. We are in touch with the wisdom – which is inherent in us all – of the Self *(see Self)*.

② The chemist on a psychological level is the part of us which looks after health concerns and self-healing. Using the raw material of the body, we learn to create power and energy.

③ The Alchemist is one who changes base material (basic spiritual knowledge) into spiritual gold. This image shows great progress in our spiritual discoveries.

Chess
– also see Games/Gambling

① The game of chess originally signified the 'war' between good and evil. So in dreams it may still express the conflict within. It may also indicate the need for strategy in our lives.

② **Playing chess and losing** indicates that we have undertaken an activity in our waking lives which cannot be successful. We have not got the wherewithal, or perhaps the knowledge, to pit ourselves against greater forces.

③ The conflict between the spiritual powers of light and darkness is highlighted.

Chest
– also see Box

① A chest or box appearing in a dream delineates the way we keep hidden or store our emotions. Our most important ideals and hopes may need to be kept secret. It may also show the best in us; our best insights.

② Emotionally, we need to give some limitation to our feelings and secret desires. In dreams a box – whether plain or otherwise – will show how we handle life.

③ Pandora's Box and the story of how negativity was released into the world is the best example of a box image on a spiritual level. We need to be aware that care must be taken when first exploring the spiritual.

Child/Children
– see People

Chimney
– also see Buildings

① When we dream of chimneys we are linking with a very old concept, that of escape from the mundane and ordinary into freedom. Any opening in a roof of a temple, tepee, tent, etc. represents the awareness of a change of state that may be an important part of growth.

② Psychologically, a chimney and the passage of smoke portrays the channelling of energy in a more productive way than is presently occurring.

③ Dreaming of a chimney indicates that escape to the heavens through the solar gateway is possible. It also shows that we are willing to share our spiritual knowledge.

Chisel

① The meaning of a chisel in a dream would depend on whether or not we are a craftsman in waking life. In such a case it will depict pride in achievement and specialist knowledge. If we have no skill it will depend on other symbolism in the dream, but will probably indicate the need to use force in a situation known to us.

② Intellectual drives may put us in a position of needing to break through a barrier in order to succeed in a favourite project.

③ In sacred architecture the chisel is the active, masculine principle in relationship with the passive and feminine.

Choke

① When we find ourselves choking in a dream we are coming up against our inability to express ourselves appropriately. There is some conflict between our inner and outer selves, perhaps some indecision over whether we should speak out or remain silent.

② We are being stifled by people or circumstances and are not in control of either. We should consider how we can best regain control.

③ Choking can indicate spiritual conflict and restraint. Choking in a dream therefore eventually has us learn when to speak and when to remain silent.

Christ
– see Religious Iconology

Christmas
– see Religious Festivals in Religious Iconology

Christmas Tree

① Because for most people the Christmas tree is associated with a time of celebration, to have one appear in a dream signifies the marking of a particular period of time, perhaps a new beginning. It may also indicate a time of giving, and by association the ability to enjoy the present.

② We may recognise in a Christmas tree the lightening up of a situation which has been either oppressive or depressive.

③ The tree of rebirth and immortality, because of its evergreen qualities.

Chrysalis

① There are two ways in which a chrysalis can be interpreted within a dream. Firstly, as potential for action, which has not yet been realised, and secondly protection in a situation that must wait until the time is right.

② Change is taking place within us, but on a very subtle level which is not immediately recognisable.

③ Metamorphosis and Magical Powers are symbolised by the chrysalis. We change from the base to the beautiful.

Church/Holy Buildings
– also see Church in Buildings and Religious Iconology

① A church or holy building represents our feelings about organised religion. In dreams it can be a place of sanctuary, particularly in the sense that we can have a shared belief with other people. This may be as much to do with a shared moral code as with a code of personal behaviour.

② A church or holy building may or may not be considered to be beautiful, but its image links with our appreciation of beautiful objects which mark and enhance our sense of worship. We link with the forces of life within us which enable us to live life more fully.

③ A church or holy building becomes a 'world centre' since it marks all that is holy and essential in our lives.

Churning

① Most dreams in which there is a liquid being churned, boiled or made to move in some way links back to a very primitive sense of chaos (lack of order). This indicates we may need to reassess our creative abilities to make use of the energy available to us.

② We very often need to become conscious of a very deep-rooted chaos in ourselves in order to become appreciative of our capacity for order.

③ One school of thought is that form arose out of churning the Chaos. Ultimately, chaos in our lives must give way to order.

Cigar/Cigarette
– see Smoking

Circle
– see Shapes/Patterns

Circumambulation

① To be walking around a building or a particular spot in a dream is to be creating a 'universe' in which action can take place. It is to be designating that place as having a particular significance.

② Psychologically we all need to have a place which is ours alone, and to dream of circumambulation signifies taking responsibility for ourselves and our actions.

③ We symbolise creating the centre of our universe by circumambulation.

Circumcision
– see Sex

Circumference

① To be **held within** the circumference of a circle is to be made aware through dream images of the limitations we may have set ourselves. To be **shut out** of the circumference of a circle is to be unworthy, or perhaps unknowing.

② We are on the edge of new knowledge or information and could move in either direction. We have a choice between introversion and extroversion.

③ Spiritual limitation and the world in manifestation and enclosure are all signified by the drawing of a circumference.

Citadel
– see Castle in Buildings

City/Town

① Dreaming of a city, particularly **one known to us** is to be trying to understand our sense of community; of belonging to groups. We will often, through dreams, give ourselves clues as to what we require in the mental and emotional environment in which we live, and a bustling city may show our need for social interaction. **A deserted city** may portray our feelings of having been neglected by others.

② A city usually has a core community, and we sometimes represent the place of work or opportunity in this way.

③ A spiritual community to which we belong can be represented by a city. A city was originally given status because it had a cathedral.

Clean/Cleaner

① Any dream where an object, room or environment needs to be cleaned implies a degree of contamination on some level. What is represented as being needed to be cleaned will be significant as also will be the tools we use. A **vacuum cleaner**, for example, would suggest there is a more efficient way of achieving our objective, while a **duster** might suggest that the soiling or difficulty is somewhat superficial.

② Psychologically, the idea of cleanliness suggests that we have nothing to hide. To be cleaning an antique or much-loved object in dreams indicates that we perhaps need to look at old ideas and concepts in a different way. With today's awareness of pollution issues, the type of cleaner may be significant. An **abrasive cleaner** might signify an abrasiveness in our attitude to others whereas a **chemical** one might show our concerns over a particular issue. Interestingly, being aware of 'green' cleaners is likely to highlight strongly held opinions.

③ Cleanliness in spiritual terms signifies purity, so to be cleaning something can indicate the need to return to essential awareness. A meditation to effect a spiritual cleansing – whether of oneself or an area – can instigate many changes on a spiritual level and thus create a sacred space.

Clamp
– see Tools

Cliff

① To be on **the edge of a cliff** in a dream indicates we are facing danger of some sort. It shows the need to make a decision as to how to deal with a situation, and possibly be open to taking a risk. We are often facing the unknown.

② There may be a step we need to take which will psychologically put us either on edge, or on the edge, in such a way that we must overcome our own fears in order to proceed through our own limitations.

③ The cliff edge denotes a step off into the Unknown.

Climb

① To dream of climbing is to dream of getting away from something, possibly to escape. We may be avoiding trouble.

② We are trying to reach new heights in our lives, possibly having to make greater efforts than before to succeed. Climbing down suggests reaching hidden depths.

③ Ascension, in the sense of climbing to achieve enlightenment, is an often perceived spiritual symbol.

Cloak
– see Coat/Cloak/Shawl in Clothes

Clock
– also see Time

① Largely, when a clock appears in a dream we are being alerted to the passage of time. We may need to pay more attention to our own sense of timing or duty, or may need to recognise that there is a sense of urgency in what we are doing.

② The **clock hands** in a dream may be indicating those numbers that are important to us *(See Numbers)*. When an **alarm clock rings** we are being warned of danger.

③ The Realisation of Age and Time is signified by a clock.

Close

① To **be close** to someone in a dream means we are looking for intimacy, or perhaps protection. **To close a door** acknowledges the fact that we must make a decision to put the past behind us.

② We can indicate to ourselves in dreams the fact that we are emotionally closed within a situation. Closeness suggests an emotional connection.

③ Spiritually to be close to someone is to have empathy with them. Closing off from a spiritual perspective can create problems in life.

Clothes

① The clothes we wear in a dream can often depict the facade, or persona, we create for other people. We have certain roles that we adopt in response to other's reactions. Clothes which others are wearing in our dreams can also set the scene for an acting out of some of the confrontations which take place.

② Clothes can often act as a protection against being touched. This protection may also be against having the real self violated. Clothes can conceal or reveal the persona we show others. In covering up nudity they conceal our perceived imperfections. In revealing certain parts of us our dreams may show in which ways we consider ourselves to be vulnerable.

Getting undressed can suggest the shedding of old beliefs and inhibitions. *Losing one's clothes or being naked* highlights our vulnerability and fears. *Dressing inappropriately,* e.g. wearing formal clothes on a casual occasion and vice versa, if we find ourselves in this position in a dream, we are conscious of our own difficulty in 'fitting in' with other people. It will depend on the dream scenario whether we are surprised or distressed, and it is often the emotion that we experience which gives us the correct interpretation. We may be deliberately not conforming to others' perception of us, or trying to conform too much in adopting a certain role. *The colour of the clothing* is often significant *(see Colour)*. *Clothes being worn by someone to whom they do not belong* There is confusion in our mind as to which roles are appropriate for each character. *A man wearing women's clothing* We need to be more conscious of our feminine side. *A uniform on a woman* We are highlighting the need to be aware of the more disciplined and forthright side of our personality. *Changing clothes* We are attempting to change our image. *Clothes that have been cut short* We may be outgrowing former pleasures and need to look to pastures new for our entertainment. *Pretty clothes* We have much to appreciate in our lives. *Clothes belonging to a particular person* We are being reminded of that person, even though we are aware that they cannot necessarily be with us. Various articles of clothing have certain symbolic meanings which may well vary according to our culture and upbringing:

Boots formerly would represent a workaday attitude, although today they more represent safety and warmth. The strictures of fashion may colour our appreciation of such footwear.

Coat/Cloak/Shawl A coat can suggest warmth and love, but also protection. This protection can be either physical or emotional, and particularly in the case of a *cloak*, can be the spiritual protection of Faith. *A sheepskin coat* may emphasise this significance *(also see Sheep in Animals)*. *Fear of losing the coat* can suggest the fear of losing faith and belief. *The coat may be too short, or not thick enough* We may be fearful that our love, or the protection we have, is not adequate for our needs.

Gloves (also see individual entry) The meaning of gloves can be ambivalent. They can represent covering and protecting oneself, but also 'showing one's hand' and challenging the status quo.

Hat/Cap A hat is a symbol of wisdom and the intellect and also of protection. It can also signify both spirituality and sexuality, depending on the other aspects of the dream.

Pyjamas/Nightclothes Pyjamas, and indeed all forms of nightclothes, suggest relaxation and hence openness.

Raincoat A raincoat again holds the symbolism of protection, but this time against other people's emotional onslaught. Very occasionally it may suggest some kind of wish to return to a womb-like state.

Shirt A shirt can suggest appropriate behaviour, dependant on our circumstances. A *hair shirt* would suggest grief and penitence.

Shoes Shoes signify our ability – or otherwise – to be grounded and in touch with everyday life. Recognising shoes that we, or others, are wearing in a dream are strange alerts us to an adjustment that needs to be made to our attitude to life. *Lacing up shoes* in a dream was formerly supposed to be a well-known symbol of death or bad luck as were *shoes on a table*. Nowadays they are more likely to represent great changes.

Tie A tie can have several significances in dreams. For some it can represent correctness and good behaviour, and for others, presumably because of its shape, it will signify the phallus.

Underclothes When we dream of underclothes – whether our own or other people's – we are considering hidden attitudes to self-image or sexuality.

Veil or veil-like garments (also see individual entry) When we, or others, are wearing a veil we are either trying to hide something, or are only partially accepting knowledge about ourselves or our relationship to others.

③ Clothes can suggest spiritual protection. For instance, certain types of clothes will highlight roles and status.

Clouds

① Dreaming of clouds can have two meanings, depending on the other circumstances in the dream. It can either indicate uplifting or religious feelings, or can show that we are feeling overshadowed by someone or something. It can also warn of the possibility of difficulty or danger to come.

② We may have a hidden depression or difficulty which can be dealt with only after it has been given form in a dream.

③ Clouds have long been thought to be the vehicle for Divine Power.

Clover

① Traditionally the clover plant is considered to be lucky, so to find clover in a dream denotes good fortune is on its way.

② We need to look at our ability to bring the various parts of our personality back into harmony with one another.

③ This is an example of body, soul and spirit, or any representation of the triad of divinity, perhaps Father, Son and Holy Spirit.

Club (People)

① When we dream of being in a club such as a **night-spot or sports club** we are highlighting the right of every human being to belong.

② Psychologically we are not able to be part of a group until we have a certain level of maturity, so to dream of being with a crowd can denote our awareness of ourselves.

③ Organised Ritual is an important part of the progression to spiritual awareness.

Club (Weapon)

① To dream of using a weapon to club someone denotes an inner violence or turmoil that has remained unexpressed. Alternatively it may also depict our violence against ourselves.

② We have great strength at our disposal, for which we need to find a suitable outlet other than aggression.

③ The club signifies masculinity and power, although rather crudely expressed in this instance.

Coach

① In dreams there can be a great deal of wordplay and cross-over of images. A coach, as in a carrier of people, has the same significance as a bus. In the sense of someone who helps us to maximise our potential, a coach has the same meaning as a guide or mentor. These two images can sometimes become confused. Either way, we are being carried forward into new experiences.

② It will depend on the other aspects in the dream as to the most relevant interpretation. A business coach implies the need for change in our workaday world. A personal coach or fitness instructor signifies the need for encouragement in matters close to our hearts. A team coach may mean that we have to consider the way we relate to others.

③ Both a coach as in vehicle and as instructor can signify an introduction to our Higher Self and our Cosmic Responsibility.

Coat
– see Clothes

Cobweb
– see Spider/Cobweb

Cock
– also see Birds

① The cock has always been a symbol of a new day, and of vigilance or watchfulness, so to have one appear in a dream forecasts a new beginning or warning to be vigilant in one's daily work.

② We may need to be more up front and courageous in what we are doing. A degree of arrogance may be required.

③ The Masculine principle, the Bird of Fame and the dawn of a new day or time are all perceived in the symbol of the cock.

Cocoon
– see Chrysalis

Coffin
– also see Cemetery, Dead People and Death

① When we dream of a coffin, we are reminding ourselves of our own mortality. We may also be coming to terms with the death of a relationship and feelings of loss.

② We are perhaps shutting our own feelings away and therefore allowing a part of ourselves to die or atrophy.

③ Redemption, resurrection and salvation are all personified by the coffin.

Cold

① To be conscious of cold in a dream is to be aware of feeling neglected, or of being left out of things.

② We can very often translate our inner feelings or our emotions into a physical feeling in dreams. To feel cold is one such translation.

③ Spiritual loss can be felt in dreams as extreme cold, signifying a lack of energy.

Colour

① Colour plays a vital part in all symbolism. This is partly to do with the vibratory frequency which each individual colour has, and partly to do with tradition. Scientific experiments have now been carried out to ascertain what effect colour has, and have proved what occultists and healers have always known. While there is little agreement as to whether we actually dream in colour or not, it is known that colours in dreams are recognisable and will often have significance. In working consciously with the colours of the rainbow, we discover that the warm, lively colours – which give back light – are yellow, orange and red. Cold passive colours are blue, indigo and violet. Green is a synthesis of both warmth and cold. White light holds all colour within it.

② By working with our own colour spectrum we can learn to optimise wellbeing. Some meanings traditionally attributed to colours are:

Black This colour holds within it the potential for all colours. It suggests manifestation, negativity and judgement. *Blue* This is the colour of the clear blue sky and is the prime healing colour. It suggests relaxation, sleep and peacefulness. *Brown* The colour of the earth, and is also the colour of commitment and death. *Green* This is the colour of balance and harmony. It is also the colour of nature and of plant life. *Grey* There is probably no true grey, only shades of the mixture of black and white. It represents devotion and ministration. *Magenta* This is a colour which links both the physical and the spiritual realms. It signifies relinquishment, selflessness, perfection and meditative practice. *Orange* This is an essentially cheerful uplifting colour. Its associated qualities are happiness and independence. *Red* Vigour, strength, energy, life, sexuality and power are all connected with is colour. A beautiful clear mid-red is the correct one for these qualities; if there is any other red in dreams it may suggest a degree of contamination. *Turquoise* The colour is clear greenish blue. In some religions it is the colour of the freed soul. It suggests calmness and purity. *Violet* This colour, while found by some to be too strong and rather overwhelming, means nobility, respect and hope. Its purpose is to uplift. *White* This colour contains within it all colours. It suggests innocence, spiritual purity and wisdom. *Yellow* This colour is the one which is closest to daylight. Connected with the emotional self, the attributes are thinking, detachment and judgement.

③ Colour affirms the existence of light. In spiritual terms, once the colour spectrum was discovered, the vibrational energy of the colours of the rainbow could be given meaning. Red is the colour of self image and sexuality, orange is relationship – both with ourselves and others. Yellow is the emotional self, green is self awareness, blue is self expression and wisdom. Indigo is the colour of creativity, while violet depicts cosmic responsibility.

Column
– see Pillar and Writing

Comb

① A comb is a many-toothed implement and often emphasises the need to neaten or tidy something up in our lives. We need to tidy up our thoughts. **In a man's dream** it can indicate seduction or sensuality.

② We may be conscious of the fact that we need to work with our self-image. Itself a symbol of feminine vanity, the comb also picks up some of the significance of hair *(see Body)*.

③ Fertility, the rays of the sun, entanglement and music are all represented by the comb.

Comet

① To dream of seeing a comet is to recognise the possibility of circumstances arising very quickly over which we have no control. The outcome may well be unavoidable.

② The answer to a problem may come to us with the speed of light.

③ The coming of calamity, war, fire or danger can be seen in dreams as the comet. It is a portent of radical change.

Committee

① To dream of belonging to, or sitting on, a committee suggests that our motivation is not wholly selfish. We have, or perhaps should have, the good of the community in which we live at heart.

② In dreams the many facets of our personality can come together and be envisioned as a committee to enable a decision to be made about best action for our whole being. A committee which cannot agree denotes that there is a part of us which is causing, or may cause, difficulties if we have decisions to make.

③ In spiritual terms a committee in dreams may represent those helpers and friends in the spirit realm who are tasked with guiding us in the everyday world. Such a gathering may also represent the communion of saints in Christian terms or the brotherhood of Man, the idea that we all belong to one living entity.

Compass

① Dreaming of a compass is often about an attempt to find a direction or activity. We need to be able to understand the differing directions offered to us, and to follow the one that is right for us.

② Often having the same significance as the circle the compass can represent the source of life, or sometimes justice.

③ Spiritually, when we are trying to find direction, and sometimes our own limitations and boundaries, we will dream of a compass.

Computer
– also see Internet

① The computer and other such high technology images are now such a part of people's lives that it very much depends on other circumstances in the dream as to the correct interpretation of this image. Remembering that the computer is a tool, it may appear in dreams to signify simply a means to an end. The more we use computers, whether for leisure or personal use, they signify a widening of the horizons and a reminder of personal potential or abilities.

② As computers become more and more sophisticated we begin to understand both the simplicity and the complexity of developments such the fax machine, and latterly the internet and world wide web. We thus have access to a great deal of stored information. This can give us a myriad of images which allow us to access past memories and archetypes which enable us to grow emotionally and mentally.

③ The computer and its use in dreams can symbolise the Akashic spiritual records and the past, present and future. It can also represent the psychic tools that we use in the subtle connections between family, friends and acquaintances.

Conch
– also see Shells

① The spiral convolutions on a shell have often been associated with perfection and therefore plenty. Dreaming of such an object would link with a primitive understanding of those things we can have.

② The conch shell was, and still is, used as a trumpet in certain societies hence it may be seen as a warning.

③ The conch shell links with the spiral *(see Shapes/Patterns)* and all that it means.

Contraceptive
– see Sex

Contract

① In dreams a contract may appear as legal papers. It denotes a binding promise between two parties, and as a reflection of the mundane world, signifies an agreement which benefits both.

② A contract suggests a promise of loyalty or effort, so emotionally in dreams represents a depth of commitment. To dream of breaking a contract indicates that we no longer feel that commitment. Someone else breaking a contract with us may suggest we have not cared enough about the emotions of the other party.

③ A Spiritual contract suggests total commitment to a belief or ideal – an act of faith.

Convolvulus

① When we feel we are in a position of being hampered or smothered by circumstances or people round about us, we can often dream of being bound in some way. The convolvulus plant is one such symbol.

② Convolvulus can represent uncertainty and difficulty in making decisions. Perhaps we have too many options.

③ Convolvulus is said to stand for humility and devotion.

Cooking

① To be cooking in a dream is to be preparing nourishment or to be satisfying a hunger, whether our own or other people's. This hunger may not be as straightforward as a physical hunger, but something more subtle such as a need to make use of the varied opportunities available to us.

② To be able to move forward in our lives we may need to blend certain parts of our existence in new and original ways in order to succeed. Dreaming of cooking highlights this. We may therefore need to nurture a new ability.

③ Cooking can symbolise creativity of all types. There is a delightful fable which tells how God baked the various ethnic races into being.

Cord

① Within any relationship there are certain restrictions or dependencies that become apparent, and these may be depicted in dreams as cords or ties. These emotional bonds can be both limiting and freedom-giving.

② There is a need for us to be more appreciative of the ties of duty and affection and how they affect us.

③ The Silver Cord – that subtle energy which holds the life force within the body.

Corn

① Most dreams containing images of corn or wheat symbolise fertility or fruitfulness. They may also represent new life – either pregnancy or new developments in other ways.

② To be **harvesting corn** is to be reaping the rewards of hard work. We may also be linking with some very primeval needs and requirements.

③ The Great Mother *(see Great Mother/Mother Earth)* in her nurturing aspect is always shown with corn.

Corner

① To turn a corner in a dream indicates that we have succeeded in moving forward into new experiences, despite what may have seemed to be obstacles in front of us. Turning a **right-handed corner** indicates a logical course of action, to turn a **left-handed** one indicates a more intuitive approach.

② We are making available a hidden or little admitted aspect of ourselves. We no longer need to feel trapped or restricted. We can handle the unexpected or the new experience.

③ To turn the corner spiritually is to gain a new perspective on our own spiritual indecision.

Cornucopia

① Like the conch shell, to dream of a cornucopia can denote abundance, endless bounty, fertility and fruitfulness. It may be more than we are used to or can handle.

② Within ourselves we have unlimited potential to create both an acceptable present and a sustainable future.

③ The Horn of Plenty is an image common in one form or another in all spiritual work. The abundance may be for us or the rest of the world.

Corridor
– also see Passages in Buildings

① When we dream of being in a corridor we are usually in a state of transition; possibly moving from one state of mind to another, or perhaps between two states of being.

② We may be in an unsatisfactory situation, but not be able to make decisions except to accept the inevitable.

③ We are in a state of spiritual limbo and should consider carefully how best wecan move forward.

Cosmetics
– also see Make-Up

① **To be using cosmetics** in a dream can have two meanings. There is a need either to register the fact that we are covering up our features or that conversely we are enhancing our natural beauty. **If we are using cosmetics on someone else** we literally need to 'make up' with that person.

② Psychologically we may feel that we have a problem with our public image, and need to put on some sort of front before we can be accepted by others.

③ Using cosmetics in a dream can symbolise the many facets of our personality that we may need to explore before finding our true selves.

Countryside
– also see Places/Environments

① When we dream of the countryside we are putting ourselves in touch with our own natural spontaneous feelings. We may have memories of the countryside that invoke a particular mood state or way of being. We can return, without feeling guilty, to a very relaxed state.

② There is, in most peoples' minds, a type of freedom and openness about the countryside which is not necessarily available in towns and cities. It may signify a need to clarify our own feelings about our lifestyle.

③ The forces of nature and natural behaviour in all of us can often be symbolised by scenes of the countryside.

Cow
– see Animals

Coyote
– see Wolf/Coyote in Animals

Crab

① A crab appearing in a dream can indicate mothering, particularly of the 'smother love' type, but can also be the qualities of unreliability and self interest. The crab can also, because of the way it moves, denote devious behaviour.

② By word association the crab can represent sickness, or something eating away at us causing us distress.

③ The Astrological sign of Cancer and the Great Mother *(see Great Mother/Mother Earth)* are represented by the crab.

Crack

① Dreaming of an article which is cracked indicates our recognition of something which is flawed in our lives. There may be a weakness or difficulty in the attitudes and defences we use to meet life's problems.

② Psychologically a crack may represent the irrational or the unexpected. It may indicate our inability to hold things together mentally.

③ There may be a spiritual flaw in our make-up. A little thought should reveal it.

Cradle

① To dream of a cradle can represent new life or new beginnings. As a **precognitive dream** a cradle can represent pregnancy, while **in a man's dream** a cradle can represent the need to return to a womblike, protected state.

② **An empty cradle** can represent a woman's fear of childlessness or her fears of motherhood, depending on the other aspects of the dream.

③ The physical as opposed to the spiritual body is sometimes represented as a cradle. The Cosmic Cradle signifies the time before the creation of the world began and also the Spiritual imperitive for physical birth.

Crane

① When we dream of a **building crane** we are often being told of the need to raise our level of awareness in some matter. We need to make an attempt to understand the overall or universal implications of our actions.

② We are capable of gaining control or status within a situation so we can build on it to our advantage. By working with a wider perspective we attain greater control.

③ As a **bird**, the crane is a messenger of the gods. It allows communion with the gods and the ability to enter into higher states of consciousness.

Credit
– see Lend/Lending and Loan

Crescent
– see Shapes/Patterns

Cricket
– see Games/Gambling

Crocodile
– also see Reptiles in Animals

① To dream of crocodiles, or indeed any reptile, indicates we are looking at the frightening lower aspects of our nature. We may feel we have no control over these, and it would therefore be very easy to be devoured by them.

② We are consumed by our fear of death, or the death process. We must, however, go through this process in order to overcome death – in order to be resurrected.

③ Liberation from the world's mundane limitations is symbolised by the crocodile.

Cross
– see Shapes

Crossing

① To dream of **crossing a road** is recognising the possibility of danger, fear or uncertainty. We are perhaps pitting ourselves against the majority, or something that is bigger than us.

② We may encounter something we cannot control, and which may control us. **To be crossing a field** shows we could have a false sense of security, or may need to bring our feelings out into the open.

③ Crossing a river or chasm often depicts death, although not necessarily a physical death but possibly spiritual change.

Crossroads
– also see Intersection

① Dreaming of crossroads indicates that we are going to have to make choices in our lives, often to do with career or life changes. We perhaps need to be aware of where we have come from in order to make intelligent decisions. Often, to **turn left** at crossroads can indicate taking the wrong route, though it can indicate the more intuitive path. To **turn right** can obviously mean taking the correct path, but can also mean making logical decisions.

② We are in a situation where two opposing forces are coming together, not in conflict but in harmony.

③ A magical yet, at the same time, challenging space, since we can go in any direction which seems appropriate.

Crow
– see Birds

Crowd/Mob
– also see People

① Dreaming of being in a crowd could be indicative of the fact that we do not wish to stand out, or that we do not have a sense of direction at present. We may wish to camouflage our feelings from others, to get lost, to lose our individuality or even to hide our opinions.

② We need to retain our anonymity, to create a facade for ourselves or, conversely, to join a group of like-minded people – to belong. A mob, with its slightly more negative connotations, represents group energy which has become uncontrolled or unrestrained.

③ A crowd in spiritual terms suggests popular belief, or common religious feelings.

Crown

① To dream of a crown is to acknowledge one's own success, and to recognise that we have opportunities that will expand our knowledge and awareness. We may be about to receive an honour or reward of some sort.

② The crown can represent victory, and dedication, particularly to duty. We may have striven for something and our greatest victory has been against our own inertia.

③ A crown signifies attainment and victory over death and negativity.

Crucible

① The crucible in a dream links in with receptivity, intuition and the creative side of the dreamer. As a container which is capable of withstanding great heat, it is the aspect which can contain change and make it happen.

② Psychologically we all hold within ourselves great power which, when released, enables us to take responsibility for others as well as ourselves.

③ Manifestation of spiritual or psychic energy can be perceived as a crucible, a transforming receptacle.

Crucifixion
– see Religious Iconology

Crutch

① When we dream of crutches we are experiencing the need for support, although it may also be that we need to support others. We may find others inadequate and need to readjust our thinking.

② We may disapprove of other people's shortcomings or weakness and dislike the idea of being used for emotional support. Conversely we may find ourselves in need of such support.

③ In developing spiritually we become aware of our various dependencies, whether these are alcohol, drugs, patterns of behaviour or people. These can be represented in dreams by crutches.

Cry
– see Weeping

Crystal
– see Jewels

Cube
– also see Square in Shapes

① As a solid object, the cube signifies mundane concerns and stability. In dreams it will appear when we need to be entirely practical and focused in our approach.

② Emotionally, the cube suggests Man's need for constancy and security. In dreams cubes will suggest the building blocks we require to obtain such security.

③ The cube represents the plane of physical manifestation, built on a firm foundation. The *Ka'aba* (Arabic for cube) houses the black stone sacred to Islam.

Cuckoo
– see Birds

Cul-de-sac

① When we find that we are **trapped in a cul-de-sac** it symbolises futile action, but perhaps also a state of inertia. Circumstance may be preventing a forward movement, and it may be necessary to retrace one's steps in order to succeed.

② We are stuck in old patterns of behaviour and may be being or feeling threatened by past mistakes. We can do nothing except go over old ground.

③ A spiritual cul-de-sac represents futility and non-progression, as well as an enforced break.

Cup

① The cup has much of the symbolism of the chalice *(see Chalice)*, indicating a receptive state which accepts intuitive information. An offering is being made which we would do well to identify. Often the feminine is offering an opportunity from the unconscious.

② Intuitively, if we are open to the more feminine side, we are able to both give and receive help and assistance.

③ The cup symbolises the feminine awareness of the Draught of Life, immortality and plenty. This gift needs to be intuitively and sensitively used.

Curse
– see Hex/Curse

Cymbals

① Cymbals are connected with rhythm and sound, so for them to appear in a dream is an indication of the need for and return to a basic vibration. In some cultures, along with the drum and tambourine, they are used to induce an ecstatic state.

② We are reconciling passion and desire. This alerts us to the true power of our emotions.

③ Spiritually cymbals signify two interdependent halves – one cannot operate without the other.

Dagger
– also see Knife

① When a dagger appears in a dream, the meaning can either be aggressive or defensive. If we are **using the dagger** to attack someone then we may be trying to cut out some part of ourselves or trying to get rid of something we do not like. If we are **being stabbed** we are highlighting our vulnerability.

② Psychologically, to be penetrated by any sharp instrument is usually to do with our masculine sid and often refers to aggressive behaviour.

③ The dagger, if it turned on oneself, represents an age-old instrument of sacrifice.

Daisy

① Because of its connection with childhood (as in daisy-chains), to dream of daisies usually represents innocence and purity.

② Often in dreams there can be a play on words and the 'days eye' can, in the sense of being particularly aware of the day's events, represent a psychological awakening.

③ The daisy is a recognisable symbol of spiritual purity and joyfulness.

Dam
– also see Water

① When we dream of a dam its significance may vary. We may be bottling up our own emotions and drive, or conversely we could be trying to stop somebody else's emotional outburst from happening. To be **building a dam** indicates we are likely to be putting up defences, whereas if a **dam is bursting** we may feel we have no control over emotional situations around us.

② While on a conscious level we may need to exercise control over our emotions, in dream sequences we will often allow ourselves a natural expression of difficulty or frustration that can be symbolised by an overflow of water.

③ By word association – to be damned, or to be blocked in our progression.

Dance/Dancing

① Dance has always represented freedom and been symbolic of other actions which were necessary for survival. To be dancing in a dream portrays the creation of happiness, feeling at one with the surroundings and possibly getting closer or more intimate with a partner.

② Psychologically, dance can be a reinforcement of freedom of movement, strength and emotion. However, the discipline required in ballet and the grace required by a ballerina are integral parts of that freedom.

③ Spiritually, dancing has always been taken to represent the Rhythm of Life. The patterns created are reputed to mirror the patterns of creativity. Dance also signifies the transformation of space into time.

Danger

① When we find ourselves in dangerous circumstances in dreams, we are often reflecting the anxieties and dilemmas of everyday life. We may be conscious that our activities could be harmful to us if we carry on in the same way.

② Dreams can often point to a danger in symbolic form, such as conflict, fire or flood. We may need to have pitfalls represented in such a way in order to recognise them on a conscious level.

③ Dreaming of ourselves in a dangerous or precarious position can indicate a Spiritual insecurity.

Dark/Darkness

① To dream of **being in the dark** usually represents a state of confusion or being in unknown and difficult territory. It may a secret part of ourselves or a part that we do not yet know.

② Intellectually, we are in touch with the depressed, hidden side and may need to deal with the darker aspects of ourselves.

③ Spiritually, the dark side of oneself is where chaos may reign, and where ultimately evil will prevail, unless some spiritual understanding can be attained.

Darn
– also see Weaving

① As one of the skills passed on from mother to daughter, darning used to be a symbol of feminine skill. In today's more throw-away society it is more likely on a mundane level to represent our fear of poverty or the necessary repairs we must make to our lives.

② Repairing a worn or damaged fabric implies that the basic structure of our lives needs consideration. We must take what is good and renew or rethink those parts that we no longer consider to be useful.

③ In many ways, darning as an image represents the spiritual self and the bridging of the Void through practical application rather than high-flown ideas. It can also signify healing as an art.

Date (Day)

① When a particular date is highlighted in a dream, we are either being reminded of something particularly significant – or possibly traumatic – in our lives or perhaps to consider the symbolism of the numbers contained in the date itself (see Numbers).

② Often the psyche gives us information in dreams which is precognitive and alerts us to particularly important events in dream form.

③ A certain date or day could point to information about a spiritual festival or celebration and which may have relevance for us as we progress on our spiritual journey.

Date (Fruit)

① Because dates are an exotic fruit, when we dream of dates we are becoming conscious of the need for the rare or exotic in our lives. Equally, we may need sweetness and nurturing.

② We need to be cared for and looked after in a way that is different from normal, perhaps needing a more exotic approach.

③ Fruit, and particularly the date, is very often associated with fertility and fertility rites. In Roman times dates, because of their luscious taste and spiritual connections, where often used as an aphrodisiac during pre-nuptial activities.

Dawn

① To dream of a dawn or a new day represents a new beginning or a new awareness in circumstances around us. We are looking for different ways of dealing with old situations.

② Psychologically we are aware of the passage of time, and perhaps the need to mark or celebrate this in some way.

③ A new dawn can bring a great sense of hope. As the new dawn fades that sense of hope grows stronger. A form of spiritual illumination is quite often felt within this type of dream.

Day

① When we dream of a day passing, or register that time has passed, we are alerting ourselves to the fact that we need to gauge time in some activity, or that action needs to be taken first before a second thing can happen.

② Time has no real meaning in dreams, so to note that time is measurable suggests that we are actually looking at the length of our lives.

③ The old saying of 'a day is a long time in politics' goes some way to helping us understand that a day may also represent a much longer period of time than first thought.

Day and Night

① Dreaming of both day and night indicates the cycle of time or of changes that will inevitably take place. Sometimes indication is given of the nature of an aspect of timing.

② We often differentiate between two states in dreams, and the contrast between day and night highlights this.

③ Day and night can represent opposites, as in black and white, boy and girl, etc. Indeed, any two opposites may have relevance, and it is up to us to decide what opposing forces their are in our lives.

Dead People
– also see Cemetery and Coffin

① Dead people we have known appearing in dreams usually refer back to strong emotions we have had about those people, whether they are negative or positive. For instance, there may be unresolved anger or guilt we still hold and the only way we can deal with it is within a dream sequence.

② Memories can remain buried for years and often when people who have died appear in dreams, we are being reminded of different times, places or relationships which will help us to deal with present situations.

③ To dream of dead people may suggest a link of a spiritual nature to our long forgotten ancestors. We need the help of discarnate beings.

Deaf
– see Hearing/Listening

Death

① Traditionally to dream of death indicated the possibility of a birth or a change in circumstances in our own life or that of people around us. Because in the past death held great fear, it also represented calamity, in the sense that nothing would ever be the same again. It was something that had to be experienced and endured rather than understood. In these present times, as peoples' attitudes change, death in a dream indicates a challenge we must confront. We need to adjust our approach to life and to accept that there can be a new beginning if we have courage.

② On an intellectual level we are becoming conscious of potentials we may have missed or not expressed fully and because of this we are no longer able to make use of them. We need to be sensitive to our ability to resurrect these talents. A change of awareness is taking place, and we may be going through some 'rite of passage' such as puberty to adulthood, maturity to old age and so on.

③ The unseen aspect of life; omniscience, spiritual rebirth; resurrection and reintegration.

Death of oneself

① To dream of our own death is to be exploring our own feelings about death; the retreat from the challenge of life or the split between mind and body.

② While we do not normally dream of our own death, the death process can often be used in dreams to explore other's feelings about us and they way we interact with them.

③ Death in dreams is a transition from an awareness of the gross physical to the more spiritual self. Leaving the body is frequently an expression of this breach between the ego (conscious self) and life processes.

Debt
– also see Bank/Banker, Finance, Lend/Lending, Loan and Money

① Dreaming of debt in times of recession is not so surprising as we come to an understanding of what is called 'day's residue' – that which we have internalised from daily life. It indicates an awareness of lack of resources, but also that our way of handling what resources we do have may be suspect. There may be a deficit also in joint resources which creates a drain on our ability to keep ourselves on an even keel.

② A debt in dreams, if it is **our own**, indicates that we feel beholden to someone either for what they have done for us, or for what they have given us. We have used resources which are not ours. If it is **someone else's** debt which is concerning us, or if **we are owed** a debt, the feeling is that our own resources – whether material or emotional – have been used inappropriately. In the present financial climate, as past actions and profligacy come back to haunt us, it may be that we need to learn not to live beyond our means.

③ In spiritual terms a debt also signifies the misuse of resources. The biblical exhortation 'As ye sow, so shall ye reap' suggests that we should learn to husband these resources and look to the future.

Decision

① To be trying to make a decision in a dream suggests that there are circumstances in everyday life which are confusing us. When we can identify those with the help of the dream content we can make progress.

② Dreams will often demonstrate a course of action which may not previously have consciously occurred to us, but suggests what we can and cannot do.

③ Spiritually, making a decision in dreams is to choose Right Action. We contrast what we instinctively or morally consider right or wrong. We decide to go for that which benefits everyone.

Deep
– also see Position

① When we dream of the deep we are usually considering past family influences of which we may not be consciously mindful.

② We may be trying to understand archetypal patterns which have not been recognisable in the past. There may be information available to us which we can only understand through being able to appreciate our own emotions.

③ The Unknown, and therefore the unfathomable, is often symbolised in dreams by depth in some way – deep water, deep underground etc. This can represent the Abyss or Void.

Defecate
– see Excrement in Body and Excrement

Defend/Defence
– also see Barrier/Barricade

① Trying to defend ourselves or our position in dreams suggests that we are feeling threatened either by some circumstance in waking life or by someone's attitude.

② Building defences of any kind – a barrier, a moat or even a wall – indicates the need to take action to preserve an idea, a concept or even a long-cherished dream. We should not sit back and let events overwhelm us.

③ There is a stage in spiritual development where we must learn to defend ourselves against negativity and evil. This need may first manifest in dreams as us building defences.

Demolition

(1) It rather depends on the circumstances in the dream whether demolition highlights major changes in our life, or a self-inflicted trauma. If we are **carrying out the demolition** we need to be in control but if **someone else** is in charge we may feel powerless in the face of change.

(2) We may be conscious of a build up of emotional energy within ourselves which can only be handled by a complete breakdown of old attitudes and approaches.

(3) Fanaticism and anarchy (the need to breakdown an old order), can be demonstrated by demolition in a dream.

Departing
– also see Journey

(1) To be departing from a known situation such as **leaving home** indicates a breaking away from old or habitual patterns of behaviour. We may need to give ourselves the freedom to be independent.

(2) We may have a strong desire to get away from responsibility or difficulties, but must be careful how we handle it.

(3) Conscious rejection of the past can be represented by departure in a dream.

Derelict

(1) In dreams, when there is anything which is derelict, it suggests that there is no longer enough energy or power around to maintain whatever is represented. A **derelict ship** for instance indicates that our emotions have 'run out of steam' whereas a **derelict building** signifies a lack of security.

(2) There is an idea that the power of thought allows us to create the reality we need. Since anything which is derelict is broken down beyond repair, usually after neglect, it follows that we must create change for ourselves in waking life and not waste energy on something which is no longer of use.

(3) In its original meaning of abandonment, dereliction can mean the deliberate negation of our spiritual duty and in this sense serves as a warning that we should consider our actions carefully.

Descent/Descending

(1) When we dream of a descent, such as **coming down a mountain or steps,** we are often searching for an answer to a particular problem and need to be conscious of past trauma or something we have left behind. What we can learn from such trauma is important.

② We may fear a loss of status in our lives, and yet at the same time be aware of the positive aspects of such loss. Something which is apparently negative may in fact not be so.

③ Going down into the underworld, the quest for mystic wisdom, rebirth and immortality are all shown in dreams by descent.

Desert

① To dream of **being alone in a desert** signifies a lack of emotional satisfaction, loneliness or perhaps isolation. Dreaming of **being in a desert with someone else** may show that particular relationship is sterile, or going nowhere.

② We need to consider a course of action very carefully if we are to 'survive' in our present circumstances and reach a successful outcome.

③ A desert can symbolise desolation and abandonment, but also a place of contemplation, quiet and divine revelation.

Desk
– also see Table

① If the desk we are dreaming about is an old one, such as our old **school desk or an antique one** we perhaps should be returning to old values, habits or disciplines. If it is a **work or office desk** we may need to consider the way in which we are carrying out our everyday life.

② To dream of being at **someone else's desk** could indicate we have a lack of confidence in our own abilities. We are perhaps relying too much on other people.

③ When we use our spiritual selves and our surroundings mindfully, we are creating an Act of Worship. Daily ritual and discipline can be relevant spiritual practices in our everyday lives *(see Altar)*.

Destination
– also see Journey

① It is fairly common to dream of trying to get to a particular destination, and this would normally indicate a conscious ambition and desire. If the **destination is not known to us** we may be moving into unknown territory, or be attempting something new and different.

② Destinations such as **exotic and faraway places** could signify our need for excitement and stimulation, or hopes we may have for the future.

③ A Spiritual goal or aspiration is signified in dreams by knowing what our destination is.

Devil/Demon

– also see Fiend and Religious Iconology

① In previous times, the figure of the Devil was one to be feared and hated. As the wilder, more Pagan side of ourselves the conventional figure with horns and a tale will often appear in dreams. It is almost as though it has been given 'life' by the way that people concentrate on it. Once it is understood as something to be confronted, as something belonging to all of us, the Devil loses it potency.

② As a personification of the evil side of ourselves, we often need to have an object to confront. In dreams, as in fantasies, the Devil allows us to do this. If we fear our own wrongdoing, that fear can also manifest as the Devil.

③ The Devil is the personification of Evil. Demons are more personal.

Devour

– also see Eat/Eating

① When we dream of **being eaten** we are facing our fear of losing our sense of identity; of being consumed by something such as an obsession, an overwhelming emotion or drive, or of having to deal with something we cannot control.

② If **we ourselves are devouring something** we may need to consider the way we nurture ourselves.

③ Clearing evil – or taking in good – is symbolised as devouring it. Kali, as the keeper of the graveyard, symbolises this as do the devouring Gods. It is a way of returning to source.

Dew

① Dew or gentle rain falling in a dream can represent a sense of newness and refreshment we have perhaps not been able to obtain so far, except from an external source.

② We may need to accept that gentle emotion can cleanse us of whatever is troubling us.

③ Spiritual refreshment, benediction and blessing are all symbols connected to dew.

Diadem

① The diadem or tiara in a dream often acknowledges the power of the feminine, or the ability to use the mental or intellectual abilities to obtain supremacy.

② There is always a magical feeling or sense of wonder associated with the diadem, and it can be taken to represent the magical and unknown.

③ The diadem is perceived as an emblem of the Queen of Heaven and the circle of continuity. It often has twelve jewels which are said to represent the Twelve Tribes of Israel.

Dice/Die

① To be **playing with dice** in a dream emphasises the fact that we are playing with fate or taking chances in life which we really ought to be considering more carefully.

② If **someone else is rolling the dice** we are leaving our fate in the hands of other people and must therefore run our lives according to their rules.

③ A dice or die, through the play on words, is a way of taking chances which, in the spiritual sense, may be irrevocable.

Dictator
– see People

Digging/Excavation
– also see Mines

① Often when we begin the process of learning about ourselves we need to uncover those parts we have kept hidden, and this is shown in dreams as excavating a hole or digging up an object.

② On an creative level we may have realisations which are hard to access and must be dug out.

③ Spiritually we need to be aware of, and have access to, the characteristics of the unconscious.

Dinosaur
– also see Fossil and Prehistoric

① When we dream of monsters or prehistoric animals we are touching into very basic images which have the power to frighten and amaze us. Because they are considered to be so large, we need to be aware of whether it is their size or their power which is frightening. Urges as basic as this can threaten our existence, by either their size or power.

② We are in touch with an archaic or outmoded part of ourselves. Remembering that the dinosaur is extinct, and that for most people they are perceived as fossils, such a dream can recognise the part of ourselves that has become set in stone.

③ We all have within us a chaotic past which has been a huge part of our lives. Spiritual progress dictates that we understand that this part can be changed and our present selves can grow from that ability to change. Old standards have to break down.

Dirt/Dirty

① We will dream of **being dirty** when we are not operating within our own principles or when someone else's action has put us in a situation which we find compromises us. Dirt can also represent fertile ground, decomposing matter which will provide a growth medium. In this context, **bacteria or germs** might be seen as dirty, but with a good outcome.

② To be dirty in a dream may indicate that we are not at ease with our own bodily functions. If **someone we know has made us dirty** it is an indication not to trust that person. As we become more knowledgeable, such things as bacteria or germs which cause putrefaction and fermentation take on a more positive meaning. They become cleansing agents.

③ Evil or negative impulses are often shown in dreams as things or people being dirty. At some stages of spiritual development, objects or attitudes are seen as needing to be cleansed.

Disc

① A computer disc in a dream could suggest that a great deal of information and knowledge is available to us. Optical discs, of which there are many variations, can have a similar significance except that their content will vary according to their usage. Some will contain music, others images and so on. If we can identify which kind of content is appearing in our dream we should be able to access the additional information we need for clarity.

② As a flat round object, discs today will most likely be associated with technology, but in its original meaning it signified perhaps the intervertebral disc in the back, or perhaps the blades on agricultural instrument. Dreaming that we have a slipped disc suggests that we are not receiving the correct support in a project.

③ Divinity and power are represented spiritually by the Solar disk, and incidentally also by the Feathered Sun (see Feather/Feathered Sun). This type of disk in a dream has the same significance as the sun, and represents perfection and the renewal of life.

Dismemberment

① Dismemberment of the body, or indeed any dream where some type of fragmentation takes place, is largely to do with being rendered powerless. A situation may be tearing us apart and violent action may be necessary before we can recover our equilibrium.

② Psychologically we need to take our old feelings and ideas apart to make sense of what is going on. This process has to take place before a rebuilding of our life can take place.

③ The death and rebirth symbolism of initiation; the death of the Self before reintegration and rebirth.

Distaff

① This symbol will largely have been replaced in dreams by modern technological symbols, but usually represents the feminine attributes and may also represent the passage of time.

② Most symbols dealing with thread or weaving and spinning are to do with the creation of an intuitive pattern within our lives.

③ Time, creation and fate have always been symbolised by the distaff, the Weaver.

Diving

① To dream of diving can represent the need for freedom within our lives, although we may associate freedom with taking risks. We may need to burrow into our unconscious to find the ability to face anxiety.

② We need to be extremely focused and attentive to dive successfully and must bring these qualities into play in a situation we are in in everyday life.

③ Diving suggests the taking of spiritual risk in confronting the unconscious.

Divorce

① Dreaming of divorce may actually refer to our feelings about a particular dream character, and perhaps our need to be free of responsibilities. It may also indicate the necessity to clarify our own relationship between the various facets of our personality.

② We are becoming conscious of the need to express emotion if we are to maintain our own integrity. We are moving into a new way of life, perhaps without the old support systems we have used.

③ To dream of divorce would suggest a potential difficulty in understanding a loss of integration in our personality.

Doctor
– also see Occupations

① When we dream of a doctor we are aware that we need to give way to a higher authority in health matters. For older people the doctor may also represent the professional classes.

② It will depend what sort of doctor appears in our dream as to the correct interpretation. A **surgeon** would suggest the need to cut something out of our lives. A **physician** would indicate that careful consideration should be given to our general state, whereas a **psychiatrist** signifies the need to look at our mental state. If the doctor is **known to us** he may represent an authority figure.

③ Spiritually, the personality of a doctor in dreams suggests the appearance of the healer within.

Documents

① Since the advent of modern technology a document in dreams is more likely to appear as a mundane **printout** rather than an **old-fashioned manuscript**. The former may signify day to day instructions whereas the latter is more likely to denote the need for an understanding of the past.

② A **legal document** in dreams is likely to suggest the need for accuracy in our proceedings with other people, perhaps from a sense of duty or from our need to take responsibility for ourselves.

③ Documents of whatever sort in dreams imply the rationalisation of spiritual law, making perceived norms and correct behaviour in a system of belief tangible for others as well as ourselves.

Dog
– also see Animals

① Dreaming of a dog depends on whether it is **known** to us (such as a childhood pet), when it then may represent happy memories; if **unknown** it may signify the qualities of loyalty and unconditional love associated with dogs.

② To dream of a **pack of wild dogs** portrays emotions and feelings of which we are afraid. Dreaming of any **trained dog**, such as a greyhound, highlights that we need to remain focussed on a particular goal.

③ Spiritually a dog symbolises the guardian of the underworld. In Egyptian mythology this is depicted by Anubis, the dog-headed god.

Doll

① A doll can depict either how we felt as a child, or a need for comfort. It may also express an undeveloped part of our personality.

② We all tend to learn through play, and so for a doll to appear in a dream usually indicates the need to relearn some childhood lessons which we have forgotten.

③ In Spiritual terms the doll can be taken to be a representation of the soul of a particular person who can be helped, or perhaps harmed, by sympathetic magic. It does not mean that someone is attempting to harm us.

Dolphin

① Dolphins are perceived by sailors as saviours and guides, as having special knowledge and awareness, and this is the image which surfaces in dreams. Coming from the depths – the unconscious – the dolphin represents the hidden side of ourselves which needs to be understood.

② Psychologically the dolphin may portray the more playful side of our personality, but at the same time may make us aware of the trickster. Dreaming of **swimming with dolphins** suggests putting ourselves in touch with, and appreciating, our own basic nature.

③ The dolphin is taken to represent Spiritual sensitivity and safety.

Donkey
– see Horse in Animals

Door
– also see Buildings

① A door in a dream signifies a movement between two states of being. It can represent entry into a new phase of life, such as puberty or middle age. There may be opportunities available to us about which we must make deliberate decisions.

② If the door in the dream is **shut or difficult to open** it indicates we are creating obstacles for ourselves, whereas if the door is **open** we can have the confidence to move forward.

③ Spiritually a door represents the sheltering aspect of the Great Mother *(see Great Mother/Mother Earth)*. It could also represent a Rite of Passage.

Dove
– see Birds

Dragon

① The dragon is a complex and universal symbol. Seen as both frightening and yet manageable, under certain circumstances it will represent in us our own untamed nature. We must come to terms with our own passions and chaotic beliefs. Often we can only achieve this through dreams, in an environment that has been suitably created.

② There is a heroic part in each of us which must face dangerous conflict in order to overcome the lower side of our natures and reach our inner resources. Dreaming of a dragon allows us that conflict.

③ The dragon is traditionally the Guardian of Power. In conquering the dragon, spiritually we become custodians of our own future.

Dragonfly

① To dream of a dragonfly is to appreciate the need for freedom, but equally to recognise that freedom can be short-lived.

② We may be pursuing a dream, but without any real focus as to what we actually want out of life. Our reactions are instinctive rather than logical.

③ Although the dragonfly's physical existence is a short one, spiritually it symbolises immortality and regeneration.

Draughts/Chequers
– see Games/Gambling

Draught

① To **feel a draught** in a dream is to be aware of an external force which could affect us or a situation we are in. To **create a draught** is literally to be attempting to clear the atmosphere.

② Traditionally, a **cold draught** when working psychically indicates a visitation by Spirit. In dreams it suggests a communication from a hidden part of ourselves.

③ The Holy Spirit manifested as a rushing wind to enable the disciples to spread the Gospel. We should consider whether we have information we wish to share.

Drink

① To be drinking in a dream is to be absorbing or taking something in. **What we are drinking** is also important, e.g. fruit juice would indicate we are aware of the need for cleansing and purity. The colour of what is being drunk is also important (*see Alcohol and Colours*).

② Drinking in a dream may indicate our need for comfort and sustenance. As a basic requirement for life, drinking symbolises the interplay between the inner need to sustain life and external availability of nourishment.

③ Spiritually there is a belief that the drinking of wine is, or symbolises, the imbibing of Divine life and power.

Drowning
– also see Swimming

① When we are drowning in a dream this usually indicates we are in danger of being overwhelmed by emotions we cannot handle. We are fearful of allowing our emotions truly free expression. Drowning may also indicate a perceived inability to handle a stressful situation around us at the time of the dream.

② We have allowed ourselves to be put in a situation over which we have no control. We may be 'floundering around' with no way of being able to escape from a difficulty we are in.

③ Drowning symbolises an immersion in the Sea of Life, and therefore a loss of ego.

Drugs
– also see Addict/Addiction and Intoxication

① When drugs appear in a dream – whether self administered or not – this suggests that we may need external help to enable us to change our inner perceptions. **To be taking drugs** suggests we feel we have relinquished control of a situation in our waking lives and are having to rely on external stimuli. **To have an adverse drug reaction** could mean that we fear instability. **To be given drugs against our will** indicates that we are being forced to accept an unpalatable truth.

② We may be attempting to avoid reality and drugs can enable us to do this. They can also be a healing agent in restoring balance. **To be given drugs by a qualified person** signifies that we have accepted someone else's greater knowledge. **To be sold drugs illegally** indicates that we are prepared to take unnecessary risks.

③ Certain drugs can be taken to induce a state of euphoria or a change of consciousness. This can be dangerous, since it is like using a crowbar – rather than a key – to open a door. Such practices can only be valid if done with knowledge and understanding.

Drum
– also see Musical Instruments

① To **hear a drum** in a dream indicates the basic rhythm needed to keep us sane and healthy. We need to be more in touch with our natural rhythms and primitive urges. To be **playing a drum** is to be taking responsibility for the rhythm of our own lives.

② We may be seeking a more natural form of expression than the normal, everyday methods we normally use. Drumming can also bring about a change in consciousness.

③ Sound. Divine truth, revelation and the Rhythm of Life.

Drunk
– also see Alcohol, Binge and Intoxication

① **To be drunk** in a dream indicates that we are abandoning ourselves to irrational forces. We want to be free from responsibility and from having inhibitions. **To make someone else drunk** is to force our irresponsibility onto someone else.

② Being drunk indicates the need to reconnect with a part of ourselves which can tolerate inappropriate behaviour. In previous societies it was an accepted part of life that, at certain times, drunkenness was allowed as a way of celebration or as a release of tension – hence the term a 'Bacchanalian revel'.

③ Ecstasy is reputedly achieved after inhibitions have been removed through getting intoxicated, which is actually a shift in awareness.

Duck
– also see Birds

① As always, other circumstances in the dream may indicate the true relevance of the symbol. A **toy duck** may denote the childlike part of ourselves. To be **feeding the ducks** may show some kind of therapeutic or calming activity is important. To be **eating duck** suggests a treat or celebration in store.

② We need to allow the current of life to let us move rather than taking action ourselves.

③ The duck is said to be a symbol of superficiality, presumably because it floats on the water rather than in it.

Dwarf/Dwarves

① Any representation of stunted growth in a dream indicates a part of our personality which has not been integrated or has been left undeveloped. In a dream a dwarf may denote a part of ourselves which has been left damaged by painful childhood trauma or a lack of emotional nourishment.

② Gnomic figures such as dwarves, elves and fairies *(see Fairy)* may signify a small part of ourselves that needs consideration. This may be a stunted aspect of our personality which does not become apparent until we are prepared to take responsibility for it.

③ A dwarf scan sometimes symbolise the Unconscious and undifferentiated force of nature, but may also represent the microcosm within the macrocosm – the potential for perfection.

Eagle

– also see Birds

① An eagle appearing in a dream signifies inspiration and strength. It may also indicate our need to ascend, in order to release ourselves from old ideas or attitudes. As a bird of prey, the eagle is capable of making use of all the opportunities available to it. Dreaming of one shows we can do likewise.

② From a psychological point of view, we have the ability to use our intellect in order to succeed. We can take authority for our own lives. We may need to become objective and to take a wider viewpoint than we have done previously.

③ The eagle also represents a form of Spiritual victory.

Earth

① To dream of the **planet Earth** is to take account of the supportive network we have in place in our lives and the attitudes and relationships we take for granted. We are searching for some kind of parental love or social order. **Soft earth** particularly links with the need for mothering or tactile contact.

② We have the need to be grounded and practical but need support to be so. If we find ourselves **under or trapped by** earth it shows we need to be more aware of, and understand, our unconscious drives and habits.

③ Earth is the Great Mother *(see Great Mother/Mother Earth)* and is synonymous with fertility.

Earthquake

① Dreaming of an earthquake alerts us to an inner insecurity that we must deal with before it overwhelms us. There is great inner change and growth taking place which could cause upheaval.

② Old opinions, attitudes and relationships may be breaking up and giving us cause for concern, shaking our very foundations.

③ An earthquake, by way of its devastating after-effects, represents Spiritual upheaval.

East
– also see Position

① Specifically dreaming of the East indicates we are looking at the mysterious and religious side of ourselves. We link with instinctual belief as opposed to logical reasoning.

② We may be looking towards new life or a new beginning *(see Dawn)*.

③ The East in Spiritual terms suggests the spring, a time for hope and youth.

Easter Egg

① The Easter egg is a Pagan symbol of renewal and in dreams often takes us back to childhood feelings of promise and wonder. It may also alert us to the passage of time since the mind will often produce symbols of times and seasons rather than actual dates.

② Dreaming of an Easter egg indicates there is a great deal of potential available to us on a mental level that needs releasing.

③ An Easter egg is associated with Spring, rebirth and resurrection.

Eat/Eating
– also see Devour, Food and Nourishment

① **To be eating** in a dream shows that we are attempting to satisfy our needs or hunger. Hunger is a basic drive and we need to realise that only once such a drive is met can we move forward to satisfying our more aesthetic needs.

② Dreaming of eating may denote that we lack some basic nutrient or feedback in our lives. **To not eat or refuse food** indicates an avoidance of growth and change. We may be attempting to isolate ourselves from others or be in conflict with ourselves over our body image. If we are **being eaten** in a dream it signifies we are aware of being attacked by our own – or possibly other people's – emotions and fears or by our internal drives. **Being eaten by a wild animal** shows the likelihood of us being consumed by our more basic, animal nature.

③ We are reputed to become what we eat, so from a spiritual perspective we should eat the best food possible.

Eclipse
– also see Moon and Planets

① Dreaming of an eclipse signifies our fears and doubts about our own success. Others around us seem to be more important or able than we are, which does not allow us to shine or excel at what we are doing.

② We are about to go through a period of difficulty when we could find ourselves unable to maintain our usual positivity and cheerfulness.

③ On a spiritual level, an eclipse can represent a loss of faith. By covering up a source of illumination and enlightenment, it can also represent a darkening of the light through external circumstances.

Ecology

① Ecology is an issue which goes beyond individual responsibility and that of the community. Any dream which has such themes may be as much to do with our opinions about these two things as about ecology itself..

② As more people become aware of ecological issues and children in particular internalise the need for the responsible use of resources, dreams about ecology demonstrate a passion for the survival of the world as we know it, and an emotional response to its misuse.

③ In the spiritual sense dreams around the theme of ecology shows a growing maturity in the understanding of issues which affect mankind as a whole.

Education
– also see School and Teacher

① To dream of a place of education, such as **a school or college** indicates that we should be considering our own need for discipline or disciplined action. We are perhaps inadequately prepared for a task we are to perform, and need to access more knowledge. Attending a lesson in dreams highlights our need to learn from others and experience things for ourselves.

② Since dreaming of education usually takes us back to a former state, we need to apply knowledge from the experiences we have had to enable us to deal with a present situation. A lesson is a previously thought out form of instruction, the best and most efficient way that we can learn and will have this meaning in dreams.

③ Education can be taken as a symbol of Spiritual Awareness. A spiritual lesson has a rather negative connotation presupposing some difficulty or hard-won knowledge. If we are able to perceive these as spiritual experiences, they become easier to accommodate.

Egg

① The egg is the symbol of unrealised potential, of possibilities yet to come, so to dream of an egg indicates that we have not made fully conscious our natural abilities. To be **eating an egg** shows the need to take in certain aspects of newness before we can fully explore a different way of life.

② We have a sense of wonder to do with the miracle of life, and a realisation that there is much to plan before we can enjoy life to the full. We may have to withdraw and contemplate before we can undertake new learning experience.

③ The life principle and the germ of all things is said to be contained in the Cosmic Egg, thus spiritually representing our inner potential and power to be perfect.

Egypt
– also see Places/Environments, Pyramid and Sphinx

① Although perhaps less so now, as travel becomes easier faraway places in dreams usually signify the exotic. Egypt in particular has always seen as being connected with ancient knowledge, though this may depend on our own knowledge of the country.

② We are connecting with our magical, mysterious and enigmatic side, particularly if the Sphinx is noticeable.

③ Egypt is a recognition of the hidden side of Self; that which reveres the Divine. The Sphinx stands for vigilence, power and wisdom.

Ejaculation
– also see Sex

① Our attitude to sex often becomes apparent in dreams through the sexual act, and to ejaculate in a dream may be an effort to understand negative feelings. It could also simply be indicative of the need for release, and the satisfaction of sexual needs.

② The act of ejaculation in a dream may be the giving up of old fears and doubts about ourselves and our sexual prowess.

③ Ejaculation, quite literally, may signify a loss of power or 'the little death'.

Election
– also see Vote

① In dreams an election presupposes the need to choose someone for their special qualities to act on our behalf. To be undertaking an election campaign suggests that we feel passionately about the issues involved.

② If we are to bring about change we must have a spokesperson brave enough to act with integrity on our behalf. In dreams, we are looking for that part of ourselves which will act for the greater good.

③ Theologically, election is the choice by the Divine for some special task; in dreams we may feel particularly blessed or elected, thus removing ourselves from political or internal wrangling.

Electricity
– also see Spark

① Electricity often represents power, and gives an indication in dreams of how we manage our energy levels in everyday life. To dream of **electrical wires** is to be aware of our capabilities, while to dream of **switches** is to be aware of the ability to control.

② If in a dream we receive an **electric shock** it shows we are not protecting ourselves from danger, and need to be more aware of external events.

③ Electricity represents the greater Spiritual Power, allowing the energy for change.

Elephant
– see Animals

Eloping/Elopement

① Dreaming of eloping, particularly **with someone you know**, is trying to escape from a situation that could ultimately be painful. We must maintain a balance between the need for emotional and material security.

② In a dream to be **planning an elopement** is creating circumstances where others do not understand the motives behind our actions. We are aware of our own need for some sort of integration within our personalities but feel we cannot do this without people misunderstanding.

③ Elopement signifies a union – Spiritual or otherwise – particularly in adversity.

Email
– see Letter/Email

Embryo

① To dream of an embryo or foetus is to become aware of an extremely vulnerable part of ourselves. We may also be making ourselves aware of a new situation in our lives, one which has not got beyond a germ of an idea.

② We are linking back to conception, to a point where everything begins. We may need to look at the process of becoming consciously knowledgeable of all that we are or can be.

③ The core of being is the embryo, and therefore the centre of Creation.

Emerald
– see Jewels

Emotions

① Within the framework of a dream our emotions can be very different to those we have in everyday life. They may be more extreme, for instance, almost as though we have given ourselves freedom of expression; we may be able to notice that there are strange swings of mood.

② Occasionally in order to properly understand a dream it is easier to ignore the symbols and simply work with the moods, feelings and emotions that have surfaced. Doing this will very often give us a clearer interpretation of what is going on inside us, rather than confusing ourselves by trying to interpret a myriad of symbols.

③ Our emotional requirement, particularly responsiveness to something which is a more subtle energy, permits us to begin the process of spiritual development.

Employment
– also see Career and Work

① Dreams about employment are often more to do with what we consider our proper work to be. Since employment can also represent the way that other people think and feel about us, such a dream will tend to be about us assessing our own worth.

② When we are fully employed our attention is very focused on what we are doing. To dream of **being employed** can suggest that we need to focus our attention on work that creates satisfaction and gives us the lifestyle that we want.

③ Spiritual employment suggests using our talents and gifts effectively for the Greater Good.

Empty

① To experience emptiness in a dream indicates there is a lack of pleasure and enthusiasm. We could be suffering from a sense of isolation, or perhaps of not having anything to hold on to. We may have had expectations which cannot be realised.

② We may need space to be ourselves in order to come to terms with what is occurring in our lives. To be in an **empty house or building** denotes the fact that we have left behind old attitudes and habits.

③ Spiritually, any sort of experience which brings about a feeling of emptiness signifies the Void.

Enchantress
– also see Siren in Archetypes

① The enchantress is such a strong image within both the masculine and feminine psyches that she can appear in dreams in many guises. She is the feminine principle in its binding and destroying aspect; the evil witch or the beautiful seductress. She has the power to create illusion, and the ability to delude others.

② As the negative aspect of the feminine, the enchantress can appear in dreams as a woman meets her self destructive side. She is to be understood rather than feared.

③ An enchantress epitomises the destructive sexual nature of the Feminine, as represented by Lilith.

Enclosed/Enclosure

① In dreams, the defence mechanisms we put in place to prevent ourselves from deeply feeling the impact of such things as relationships, love, anxiety or pain can often manifest as an enclosed space. Restraints and constraints can appear as actual walls and barriers.

② Aspects of ourselves which are too frightening or powerful to be allowed full expression are often perceived in dreams as enclosed spaces.

③ Spiritually, any enclosure represents the protective aspect of The Great Mother (see Great Mother/Mother Earth).

End

① To dream of there being an end or an ending to something signifies the reaching of a goal, or a point at which things must inevitably change. We need to decide what we can leave behind, and what must be taken forward. We must decide what we value most.

② A situation which may have given us problems or causing us difficulties is coming to a successful conclusion.

③ To be at the end of something can mean the subconscious and death, or change of some kind.

Engine
– also see Car and Piston

① The motivating drive or energy that we need within a situation can be perceived in dreams as an engine (see Car). When the dream seems to concentrate on the mechanical action of the engine we may need to be looking at the more dynamic pragmatic ways of dealing with our lives. To be **removing the engine** could indicate a serious health problem.

② Depending on the type, the piston of the engine can represent the sexual act. To perceive a **diesel or railway engine** may be putting us in touch with our own inner power or principles.

③ An engine is symbolic of our own Spiritual inner motivations and drives.

Engineering
– also see Machine/Machinery

① To dream of engineering is to link with our ability to construct. This is our ability to create a structure which will allow us either to move forward or will make life easier for us. To dream of engineering works – as in **roadworks** – is to recognise the need for some adjustment in part of our lives.

② Engineering suggests being able to use forces which are not normally available to us through techniques and mechanical means. To dream of engineering in this way highlights our ability to take control of power which is external to us. We are able to manipulate in order to achieve.

③ Spiritual engineering signifies gaining control of our own inner power and being able to make use of it.

Enter/Entrance/Entry

① An entrance in a dream has the same significance as a door *(see Door)*, representing a new area of experience, or the new experience itself. Such a dream often signifies the need to make changes, to create new opportunities, perhaps to explore the unknown. An entry as in a **book of accounts or diary** signifies something which is to be remembered or taken into account in any calculations or decisions we have to make in everyday life.

② When we need to be in touch with the hidden side of ourselves, the intuitive or more 'knowing' side, and have the knowledge and ability to experience ourselves in new ways, we will often dream of a secret entrance. An entry or **entranceway which has many doorways** suggests that we have many choices available to us.

③ Because of the symbolism of moving from the external to an inner enclosed space, an entrance signifies the Eternal Feminine. An **entry in a book or ledger** follows the idea of our deeds being assessed for further consideration, or the good and bad being accounted for at the end of life.

Escape

① When we dream of escape we are trying to move beyond – or to avoid – difficult feelings. We may be trying to run away from responsibility or from duty.

② It is possible that anxiety or past trauma puts us in a position where we are unable to do anything other than try to escape from the situation itself.

③ Escape also represents our own need for spiritual freedom.

Evacuation

① For many older people **evacuation** holds within it the terrors of war and loss; the image will often come up in dreams whenever this response is triggered in lifestyle changes. In younger people the idea will hold less terror but will often signify the need to get out of a difficult situation.

② To be **evacuating a room or building** suggests that we sense some danger in waking life, without necessarily being able to quantify what it actually is. It may be that some group belief or ideal is being threatened.

③ Spiritually, evacuation may suggest the presence of negativity or evil and the rejection of these aspects by a concerted effort.

Evaporation

① To be aware of water in a dream and then realise that it has evaporated is to recognise the transformation which can take place once emotion is dealt with properly.

② By raising one's consciousness, the energy within a situation can be changed for the better. We have it within our power to create opportunities for transformation.

③ Fire and water combined is an alchemical symbol for the transformative power of the Spirit.

Evergreens

① Dreaming of evergreen trees can represent the need for vitality and freshness, for youth and vigour and sometimes for cleansing.

② To be **walking in woods of evergreen trees** indicates a need for peace and tranquillity.

③ Evergreens, because of their ability to survive any conditions, signifying longevity, immortality and Everlasting Life.

Evening

① When we are aware of it being evening in a dream we need to recognise the fact that we need time for ourselves – perhaps relaxation and quiet peace.

② The evening can be a synonym for twilight and the boundaries of our conscious mind. There may be apparitions around, of which we do not become aware until we start working with the unconscious.

③ Evening signifies old age and many years of Spiritual experience.

Evil

① To experience evil in a dream is usually to be conscious of our own urges, which we have judged to be wrong. Other aspects of evil, such as inappropriate action by others, may be experienced as dread and disgust.

② Evil is that which cannot be explained away, and any violent action can be interpreted as evil. Any darkness can also be seen as evil.

③ Working spiritually we become more consciously aware of polarities. Evil or malign energy can take on frightening form such as devils and gremlins in dreams.

Exams/Being Examined
– also see Tests

① Dreaming of examinations (particularly educational ones) is usually connected with self-criticism and the need for high achievement. We may be allowing others to set our standards of morality and success for us. **Being examined by a doctor** indicates we may have concerns over our own health.

② We may be in the habit of setting ourselves tests of self-value, or habitually be concerned with our accomplishments. There are many instances recorded of people having been abducted by 'aliens', of having been examined, and then returned to earth. Opinions vary as to whether these were dreams or not.

③ There is the need for constant personal examination when working spiritually in, for instance the healing or teaching fields.

Exclude/Exclusion/Exclusive

① When we dream of being excluded from – for instance – a group of people we must often decide whether it is by an authority or by the will of the majority. If the former it will suggest a lack of approval leading to rejection; if the latter it may signify a lack of understanding either on our part or on that of the group.

② Exclusion from any group indicates that certain privileges or aspects of acceptance are being denied. This can manifest in dreams as a sense of being punished or rejected. Thus a school policy of exclusion in everyday life can lead to a sense of alienation in later life. An exclusive group on the other hand, particularly in dreams, can indicate the possession of particular talents or powers.

③ Spiritually an exclusive group indicates that there is special knowledge or information available only to the initiated.

Excrement
– also see Body and Defecate

① When we dream of faeces or excrement we are returning to an infant level of expression and enjoyment. Experiences we have had may have been relevant at the time but we now need to let them go.

② There are certain aspects of our lives which we have used up and need to expel. The detritus of our experiences can be let go.

③ There used to be an ancient belief that an individual 'lost power' through his excrement; he could be susceptible to witchcraft and malign thoughts. This meaning can still surface in modern dreams.

Exercise

① Exercise in the sense of physical activity is now such an integral part of people's lives that it will often appear in dreams. The scenario in a dream may be a gym or sports field or the main theme might be that of exercise. Such a dream will warn us perhaps to take care of ourselves, perhaps to be aware of a group activity. To be carrying out an exercise in the sporting or military sense suggests the necessity for carefully calibrated movement or progress.

② In dreams, exercise can mean that we need to consider carefully our capabilities in other areas. If our waking attitude to exercise is ambivalent we may have other similar issues which need to be clarified.

③ A spiritual exercise is usually one which requires as much discipline and focus as physical exercise. Creative visualisation or meditation used to enhance dreams would be of this ilk.

Exotic

① When something – an object, a person or a situation – strikes us in dreams as particularly exotic or out of the ordinary, we, somewhat perversely, need to look at the ordinary in our lives and decide what different stimuli are needed for us to make progress.

② Anything excitingly strange will have an effect on our emotions and will act to alert us perhaps to a change in our feelings and responses. An **exotic flower** for instance would intrigue us or bring a sense of peace. A **scenario** which strikes us as exotic might alert us to the need for the more conscious exploration of an idea.

③ Interestingly, though an **exotic dancer** is considered to be sensually arousing, from a spiritual perspective such a figure appearing will symbolise the revealing of Spiritual Truth.

Explosion
– also see Bomb

① An explosion in a dream usually indicates a release of energy in a forceful way which will allow us to make changes in the way we express ourselves. Usually the emotion behind the explosion will be considered negative and we may have suppressed it for some time.

② The forceful explosion of anger, fear or sexual release can accomplish a cleansing. A dream may be a safe space in which to accomplish this.

③ An explosion in a spiritual sense would suggest a revelation of some sort. We gather enough information to break through old patterns of behaviour.

Extinct

① Dreaming of, for instance, an extinct volcano or an animal that we know to be extinct signifies that a situation or emotion in our lives is now over and has outlived its usefulness. A dinosaur would suggest that such a situation has grown too overwhelming for us to handle, and we must decide whether it is the size or the power that we cannot handle.

② Extinct generally means lifeless, without the wherewithal to reproduce and it is often this meaning which occurs in an emotional context. We have gone beyond the point of being able to resurrect a former emotion and we must now move on.

③ Extinction in spiritual terms signifies the deliberate cessation of power and energy – that which is needed to allow us to develop our highest potential.

Eye
– see Body

Fabulous Beasts
such as Griffins, Unicorns, Minotaurs

1. In dream imagery, in order to draw our attention to certain qualities, animals may be shown as having characteristics belonging to other creatures. Archetypally, there are many combinations which are possible and which will give unlimited potential to the creative abilities within us. We are being shown that there is freedom from conventional principles.

2. Given the freedom to create, the mind can produce both the fantastic and the grotesque. Such fabulous beasts are the result of trying to reconcile these two polarities.

3. Fearsome and terrifying powers of nature are represented in this interpretation. We should be aware of our own 'animalistic' powers and whether we have control over them.

Face

1. To concentrate on **somebody else's face** in a dream is an attempt to understand the outward personality. To be **looking at our own face** means that we may be trying to come to terms with the way we express ourselves in the ordinary, everyday world. When the **face is hidden** we are hiding our own power, or refusing to acknowledge our own abilities.

2. We learn most about people from their faces, so we may be seeking knowledge or information not otherwise available to us.

3. Elemental powers and spiritual truth. The face also reflects our own integrity.

Factory

1. Dreams about the workplace frequently occur. If we work in a factory in waking life its appearance in our dreams show that we are attempting to work through some difficulty in that area of life. If we do not it may be that we are becoming aware that life is becoming very 'mechanical'.

2. From an emotional perspective a factory environment will highlight issues we

may have about our own security. It will depend on what sort of factory is represented as to the particular interpretation. A **noisy environment** would suggest that there is too much external input for us to cope with, whereas a **starkly modern** factory might represent the need to be highly creative but in different ways to previously.

③ Interestingly, a factory in spiritual terms can represent our inherent creativity.

Failure

① Failure in a dream may not necessarily be personal. If, for instance, **lights fail or refuse to work** we may need to be aware of a lack of energy or power. **Personal failure** can indicate a degree of competitiveness or can offer alternatives in the way we need to act.

② **The fear of failure** is an almost universal fear, and to dream of failure may give us the opportunity to face that fear in an acceptable way. Dreams will often highlight intrinsic difficulties which we are incapable of consciously sharing with others, but which can be dealt with through understanding our own hidden agendas.

③ Depression or spiritual frustration. The failure we may feel at the hands of a greater power.

Fairy

① Because fairies are representations of elemental forces, for them to appear in a dream signifies our connection with those forces within ourselves. It could be that the lighter side of our nature is being highlighted, or it may be the more malign side as in goblins and elves.

② Fairies are known to be capricious, and on a psychological level they may represent the side of our being that does not wish to be controlled, and wishes to have the freedom to react and be spontaneous.

③ Fairies are reputed to have magical powers and as we develop spiritually we begin to understand that we are capable of controlling and using natural power.

Fairground/Carnival

① To dream of **being in a fairground** may represent a reconnection with the light-hearted childlike side of ourselves. We can afford to be less inhibited in public. To be **attending a carnival or fiesta** means we can drop whatever constraints or restraints we may impose on ourselves or others.

② The fairground has a dreamlike quality of its own. It is a sort of enclosed world, and to dream of one indicates we are becoming aware of the more hedonistic side of our nature. We are becoming more wrapped up in our own pleasures.

③ Life's merry-go-round and its spiritual 'ups and downs' can create Joy.

Falcon
– also see Birds

① To dream of a falcon or any trained bird can represent energy focused on a particular project with freedom to act. Such a dream may allow us to concentrate on our aspirations, hopes and desires.

② The power that we have to succeed must be used in a contained way. A falcon – as a trained bird – can depict this.

③ Ascension and freedom from Spiritual bondage are represented in dreams by the falcon.

Fall/Falling

① A fall in a dream outlines the need to be grounded, to take care within a known situation. We may be harmed by being too pedestrian. To dream of falling shows a lack of confidence in our own ability. We may feel threatened by a lack of security, whether real or imagined. We fear being dropped by friends or colleagues.

② It is said that if we forget who we are or where we come from, we will surely fall. We should acknowledge the assistance we receive from others. Falling has come to be interpreted as surrender (particularly sexual) and with moral failure, of not being as one should.

③ Spiritual fear is symbolised here, particularly the Fall from Grace and its attendant consequences. We may feel we are slipping away from a situation, essentially we are losing our place. This can be because of other's negative influence.

Fame
– also see Celebrity

① Dreaming of **being famous** or of **achieving fame within a chosen field** signifies that we ourselves need to recognise and give ourselves credit for our own abilities. In waking life we may be relatively shy, but in dreams we can often achieve things of which we would not believe we were capable.

② The Ego *(see Introduction)* is a very powerful tool and the human being's need for recognition arises from this. If we are trying to make decisions as to how to move forward within our lives, we have to recognise our potential to stand out in a crowd – or not as the case may be – and to dream of fame allows us to crystallise our attitude to this.

③ Spiritually, fame suggests the need to accept our own integrity.

Family

Images of the family, being the first people we relate to, have a great deal of significance in dreams. Beyond the womb, the family structure is the first secure image that a child latches on to. Sometimes, through circumstances not within the child's control, that image can become distorted, and later dreams will either attempt to put this image right or will confirm the distortion.

① All our future relationships, both intimate and platonic, are influenced by the ones we first develop within the family. Therefore, we may dream of arguing with a family member, but the significance depends on both other aspects of the dream and also our everyday relationship with that person.

Almost all of the problems we come across in life are mirrored within the family, so in times of stress we will often dream of previous problems that the family has experienced. It is as though a pattern is laid down which, until it is broken willingly, will continue to appear. There are numerous variations when it comes to interpreting dreams relating to the family.

We know that generally a man's first close relationship with a woman is with his mother or mother figure. The fairly common dream of *a man's mother being transformed into another woman* signifies a profound change in him. Depending on the particulars of the dream, such a change can be either positive or negative. It is often a sign of growth and maturity, enabling him to realise that he can let mother go. This transformation suggests some deepening of his understanding of women.

Similarly, a woman's first relationship with the masculine is usually with her father or father figure. Therefore in dreams where *a woman's father, brother or even lover turns into someone else* she needs to become more independent. Just as the teenage girl recognises on a conscious level the need to form meaningful relationships with other men, so a woman must learn to 'walk away from' or adjust her relationship with father or father figure towards more rounded relationships.

If in a dream the *images are confused* – for example, a mother's face on a father's body – this suggests that we may be having problems in deciding which parent is more important to us; we probably need to decide if it is even necessary to make such a decision. If *one of the family continually appears in dreams*, or maybe does not appear when expected, then the concept we have of, or the relationship with, that person needs to be better understood.

A *relationship which seems to be incestuous* in a dream may signify that the dreamer has become fixated in some way on the relative's behaviour. It is highly unlikely that such a relationship will be present in waking life, but the dream has occurred in order to highlight the obsessive nature of the relationship with the other person. Family members *suffering from injury*, or appeared to be distorted in some way, reflect our fear for or about that person.

If we dream that our *parents are somehow suffocating us* and thus forcing us to rebel, then we need to break away from childhood behaviour and develop more fully as an individual. Dreaming of *a parent's death* can also have the same symbolism. If a *parent appears in our own present-day environment* it suggests we have learnt to change roles within the parent/child relationship. Roles may be reversed or we can possibly accept our parents as friends. If within a dream it appears that our *parents are behaving inappropriately* in some way, it indicates we need to acknowledge that they are only human, and not as perfect as we first might have imagined.

It is easy to project the negative side of our personalities onto members of the family. If the projection continues, it can cause all sorts of problems with family relationships later on. The solution can often present itself in dreams to enable us to come to terms with our own image. So, when a *man's brother or a woman's sister* appears in a dream, it often symbolises the Shadow – the darker side of our own personality.

The antagonistic patterns of behaviour between family members are fairly distinctive, and it is easier to work these through in dreams rather than in waking life. *Rivalry between siblings,* a common problem in life and in dreams, usually reverts to a feeling of insecurity and doubt, possibly relating to whether we feel we are loved enough within the family set-up. This difficulty may be initiated in childhood.

Very early on his life a child moves through extreme self-involvement and interest to an almost exclusive relationship – usually with mother. It is only later in childhood that they acknowledge the need for another kind of relationship; this relationship can sometimes cause the child to doubt his or her own validity as a person. This question needs to be resolved successfully. When this question is not resolved successfully it can show in dream images in later life as a conflict or rivalry with either one, or both, parents.

Learning how to love outside the family is a necessary sign of maturity. To dream of *a conflict between an object of our affection and a member of our family* shows we have not really differentiated between our needs and desires for each person. The idea of a family member intruding in dreams signifies that family loyalties can obstruct our progression in everyday life.

② Individual members of the family and their status within that framework can symbolise the various archetypes *(see Archetypes)*. The father thus represents the masculine principle and that of authority, while the mother signifies the nurturing, protective principle.

Father If the relationship with father or father figure is a good one in waking life, the image of father in dreams will usually be a positive one. Father also represents authority and all the conventional forms of law and order. In a man's life the father generally becomes a role model. However, it is often only when a man discovers that he is not being true to his own nature that dreams of his father can point the way to a more fulfilling life.

In a woman's life father or a substitute figure is the blueprint on whom she bases all later relationships with the masculine. When she appreciates that she no longer needs to use this standard, she is able to work out, through her dreams, a more suitable way of having a mature relationship. If the relationship with father has been a difficult one, there may be in her some opposition to resolving the various conflicts that have arisen. Often this can be accomplished in dreams.

Mother In the main the child's relationship with mother or mother figure is the first relationship that he develops. Ideally this should be perceived by the child as a loving, caring one. If this does not happen anxiety and mistrust may arise which can result, for instance, in men perpetually having relationships with older women, or in some cases completely denying the right to any fulfilling relationship.

In a woman's life her ability to relate to others will depend to some extent on her relationship with her mother and her sense of self. Perhaps negatively she may feel that she is required to look after the needy male, or perhaps form relationships with both men and women that may not be totally fulfilling for her. In using dreams as therapy we can find many ways of working through relationships with the mother figure if we dare. Both material and spiritual success can be enhanced.

Daughter When the relationship with a daughter is emphasised in dreams, it often symbolises the outcome of the relationship between husband and wife. At various points in a woman's life rivalry and jealousy with her daughter can surface, particularly at transitional times such as puberty and the menopause. This can often be dealt with through dreams. Largely the relationship with a daughter suggests a jointly supportive one. *In a man's dream* a daughter may bring into prominence his fears about his ability to handle his own vulnerability and his fears for her. Dreaming of *a daughter when we do not have one* in waking life can signify the more disparate creative urge.

Son The son appearing in dreams is frequently a projection of our own need for self-expression. Signifying the drives and curiosity of the more innocent masculine, he can also symbolise parental responsibility. *In a father's dream* he can highlight unfulfilled hopes, dreams and desires, perhaps reawakening the qualities in the dreamer suggested by the dream. *In a mother's dream* he may characterise her own ambitions, sense of continuity and sometimes even her disappointment at herself. Dreaming of *a son when there is not one in waking life* is an extension of the idea that dreaming of *a baby* is a new project. A son may represent the urge to create something of value.

Sister The sister in dreams generally represents the sensitive, feeling side of ourselves. Through being able to understand our sister's personality we develop the ability to make connections with our shared inherited patterns of behaviour. If she is the *older sister in a man's dream* she highlights the capacity for persecution, yet at the same time for caring. If she is the *younger sister,* then she will highlight the more vulnerable side of his personality – that part which needs caring for. On the other hand, a *woman dreaming of a younger sister* suggests some kind of sibling rivalry. If she is *older,* the sister stands for aptitude and capability.

Brother A brother appearing in dreams can highlight the opposing feelings of both parity and rivalry. *In a man's dream an older brother* indicates experience coupled with authority, while a *younger, perhaps less knowledgeable* brother suggests vulnerability and possibly immaturity. *In a woman's dream a younger brother* represents a kind of rivalry, but also vulnerability – whether her own or her brother's. *An older brother* can denote her outgoing, confident self.

Grandchildren It might be said that grandparents have no confirmation or otherwise as to whether they have done a good job of raising their children until their sons and daughters have children of their own. Grandchildren appearing in dreams can therefore be an aspect of life affirmation or a promise of better things to come.

Grandparents appearing in dreams denote not only our attitude to them, but also to the traditions, beliefs and inherited characteristics handed down by them, of which there are usually many. As those ancestors with which we are more likely to have contact, they can often represent old-fashioned values.

Extended Family When members of the extended family – cousins, aunts, uncles, nieces, nephews etc. – appear in dreams it typifies the many parts of ourselves that are discernible. Because we all share certain traits and characteristics, it may be easier to deal with these in dreams as a more distant relative.

Husband/Wife relationship Inherent in the husband/wife relationship are the crucial feelings a wife has about her own sexuality, intimacy of body, mind and spirit and her sense of self-approval and commitment. While her view of herself will have initially been formed by her connection with her father or father figure, any ensuing relationship will be coloured by that particular bond. If unresolved doubts about her own validity are not articulated successfully within a committed relationship, they may well appear in dreams as the *loss, or death,* of her husband or partner. These doubts can, on occasion, also be projected onto other women's husbands or partners as a reflection of her own Animus *(see Anima/Animus)*. This is, in fact, the loss of an important part of herself.

Wife/Husband relationship The wife/husband relationship as experienced in dreams is based on how 'good' the man perceives himself to be as a husband in waking life. It will also depend on how well he has come to terms with his more sensitive side. If he has formed a relatively good, if not necessarily entirely successful, relationship with his mother, he will tend to try to prove himself a good husband through his dreams. He may find that as provider, particularly in today's economic climate, he needs to re-evaluate himself. He may also experience in emotional terms the potential loss and death of his partner in the same way as he experienced the severance from his mother.

③ The search for individuality in theory should begin to happen within the relative safety and confines of the family unit in everyday life. This, as we know, does not always happen. In dreams as an adult we are able to 'control' family images in order to work through our difficulties without harming anyone else. It is worth mentioning that one person working on his own dreams can have a profound effect on the interactions and unconscious bonding between other members of the family in waking life.

Famous People/Film Stars
– see Celebrity

Fan

① Dreaming of a fan connects with the feminine side of one's nature and the intuitive forces. Particularly **in a woman's dream** a fan can represent sensuality and sexuality.

② The fan can be used as a symbol for openness to, and a willingness for, new experiences and creativity. **Waving a fan** is reputed to clear away evil forces.

③ Lunar changes and those connected with energy's ebb and flow.

Fare

① To be **paying a fare** in a dream is acknowledging the price that is paid in order to succeed. A **taxi fare** would imply a more private process than a **bus or train fare**.

② Demands may be being made on us and we have to decide on their appropriateness.

③ A fare paying dream often occurs when one feels that past actions have not been paid for, and that we have a need to come to terms with them.

Farm/Farmyard
– also see Animals

① To be in a farmyard in a dream (if it is not a memory) shows us as being in touch with the down-to-earth side of ourselves. There are many facets of behaviour which can be interpreted in animal terms and often this type of dream has more impact than one including people.

② Our natural drives such as a need for physical comfort, herd behaviour and territorial rights are best expressed in a safe, conserving environment.

③ A farmyard is an enclosure in which we may feel safe and looked after. Dreaming of one shows we are within safe Spiritual boundaries.

Fast/Fasting
– also see Speed

① To be fasting in a dream may be an attempt to come to terms with some emotional trauma, or to draw attention to the need for cleansing in some way *(see Eating)*.

② If we have a grievance in dreams, fasting if used as a form of protest may be a way of making it known.

③ Fasting is a way of changing consciousness, and also a move towards realisation through resistance to temptation.

Fat

① To dream of being fat alerts us to the defences we use against inadequacy. Equally, we may also be conscious of the sensual and fun side of ourselves we have not used before, or which we have lost. If we are aware of obesity in dreams, it may be that we need to take back an element of control in our lives. Things have literally become too big for us to handle.

② Depending on how we think of our bodies in the waking state, we can often use the dream image of ourselves to change the way we feel.

③ A choice part of Spiritual knowledge and a sense of completeness.

Father
– see Family

Father Christmas
– see Religious Iconology

Fatigue

① **Feeling fatigue** in a dream may indicate that we should be looking at health matters, or that we are not using our energies in an appropriate way.

② **If others appear fatigued** in a dream we may need to recognise that sometimes we can drive people too hard and expect too much from them.

③ Spiritual inertia. We have got as far as we can on our spiritual journey at the moment and should perhaps allow ourselves to rest and rejuvinate.

Fault/Faulty

① To experience an article in dreams as having a fault or being faulty denotes a negativity or difficulty we may be having in – quite literally – making things work in everyday life. A **faulty plug** would suggest a difficult connection with a colleague or friend; a **fault in the ground** would mean that we have to tread carefully. A fracture will have the same significance as a fault, though is likely to have more personal relevance in meaning.

② Emotionally, when we feel we are at fault – that we can be blamed for our actions or thoughts – this can be represented in dreams by a cracked or broken article.

③ In dreams a fault in spiritual thinking or interpretation will appear as a crack or malformation in our dream content.

Fax/Fax Machine

– also see Computer

(1) Messages from a hidden source or part of ourselves are often brought to us in dreams in a totally logical way. Although now a little old-fashioned, a fax appearing in a dream can represent this. Thus, while the message itself may be unintelligible, how it is initially received is not.

(2) We may be aware that someone is trying to communicate with us but, because we are somewhat distanced from them, the transmission has to be mechanical.

(3) In a dream, a fax machine can have spiritual undertones in that can be a way of transmitting messages from 'beyond'. We need to be open to this and aware that the mind creates the most suitable image for us.

Feather/Feathered Sun

(1) Feathers in a dream could denote softness and lightness, perhaps a more gentle approach to a situation. We may need to look at the truth within the particular situation and to recognise that we need to be calmer in what we are doing. The feathered sun appears in a number of religious images and represents the universe and the centre of ourselves. Its appearance in dreams indicates that we ourselves are the centre of our own universe and must accept responsibility for that.

(2) Feathers often represent flight to other parts of the Self (*see Self*), and because of their connection with the wind and the air, can represent the more spiritual side of ourselves. To see feathers in a dream perhaps means that we have to complete an action before allowing ourselves to rest.

(3) The feather has come to represent the Heavens, the Soul and the Angelic Realms. The feathered sun, in drawing together the symbols of the Sun and the Eagle, represents our ability to move into other areas of perception and knowledge. It also represents the Centre of the Universe and Solar Power.

Feet/Foot

– see Limbs in Body

Fence

(1) When we dream of fences we are dreaming of social or class barriers or perhaps our own need for privacy. We may be aware of boundaries in relationships which can prevent us from achieving the proper type of connection we need. We may have difficulty in expressing ourselves in some way.

(2) When we come up against a fence or a barrier there is extra effort which is needed in order for us to overcome whatever that barrier represents.

③ A fence can represent spiritual boundaries. We need to look at what is restricting us in our spiritual quest.

Fermentation

① To dream of the process of fermentation indicates that events are occurring in the background of which we are aware but we must wait for them to develop.

② A process of fermentation allows us to transform and transmute ordinary aspects of our personality into new and wonderful characteristics.

③ Spiritual transformation and transmutation. We should welcome this alchemical symbol in a dream and be prepared to move forward.

Ferry

① To dream of **being on a ferry** indicates that we are making some movement towards change. Because the ferry carries large numbers of people it may also represent a group to which we belong needing to make changes, to change its way of working and take responsibility for moving as a group rather than as individuals.

② The ferry is one of the oldest symbols that is associated with death. The old idea of being ferried across the River Styx, the boundary between life and death, gives an image of making major change.

③ A spiritual 'death' or change of some kind. We need to be aware that we may, spiritually, be moving on from our present knowledge.

Festivals
– also see Religious Festivals in Religious Iconology

① A Festival was initially a day or series of days specially and publicly set apart for religious observances. Nowadays, more prosaically, it is a time specifically dedicated to one particular aspect of the arts – literary, musical or other. Carnival was even more specifically the time before the strictures of Lent when a good time was had by all. In dreams, such images will surface to highlight a particular memory or emotion or to provide a background to changes in awareness.

② The important aspect of both secular festivals and carnivals is to allow us to drop our inhibitions and to allow us the freedom to express ourselves fully. In dreams we are able to become more aware of our own internal rhythm and joy.

③ Festivals and carnivals were initially a time when the Gods and powers of Nature were thanked and propitiated in order to ensure a good harvest. That focus will often become evident in dreams where the power of many individuals acting in unison is recognised as having an impact on the world in which we live.

Field

① When we dream that we are in a field we are actually looking at our field of activity, what we are doing in everyday life. It may also be a play on words in that it is to do with the feeling state and is to do with the freedom from social pressure.

② We need to be aware of the wider spaces in which we can operate our lives, to be aware of what is more natural to us, and perhaps to get back to basics.

③ The Earth Mother, the Great Provider and quite possibly a 'field of dreams'. We should make use of what is available to us on a practical level to further ourselves spiritually.

Fiend
– also see Devil/Demon

① To dream of a fiend or devil usually means that we have got to come to terms with a part of ourselves which is frightening and unknown. We need to confront this part and make it work for us rather than against us.

② We may be afraid of our own passions, anger and fear overwhelming us.

③ It is said that there is sometimes little difference between 'friend' and 'fiend'. We may well find it worthwhile to look close to home if examining some kind of evil or wrong-doing for the answers to Spiritual problems.

Fight

① If we dream that we are **in a fight**, it usually indicates that we are confronting our need for independence. We may also need to express our anger and frustration and the subconscious desire to hurt a part of ourselves. We also may wish to hurt someone else, although this would be unacceptable in the waking state.

② To fight back is a natural defence mechanism, so when we are feeling threatened in our everyday lives we will often dream of taking that situation one stage further and fighting it out.

③ Quite literally a spiritual conflict. We should try to work out where, and why, there is a conflict and perhaps deal with it in a more subtle way than with 'all guns blazing'.

File

① In modern times to dream of files or filing, and thus to put order into our lives, is to make sense of what we are doing and how we are doing it. To be **filing things away** would perhaps indicate that we no longer need to be aware of a particular situation but need to retain the knowledge that an experience has given us.

② Dreaming of an **abrasive file** – such as a metal file – would indicate that we need to be aware that we can make mistakes in being too harsh with other people.

③ A chaotic situation in our lives can now be dealt with in a more orderly manner. We can create order by careful management.

Film

① To dream of **being at a film** – as in the cinema – indicates we are viewing an aspect of our own past or character which needs to be acknowledged in a different way. We are attempting to view ourselves objectively or perhaps we may be escaping from reality.

② Filming as in recording images is an important part of modern man's make up. To be **viewing film** within a dream is to be creating a different reality from the one we presently have in waking life. If we are **making a film**, when this is not our normal occupation, we may need to question the reality we are creating, but may also be being warned not to try to create too many realities.

③ A **film reel** might represent the past, the Akashic Records.

Finance
– also see Debt, Bank/Banker, Loan, Money, Poverty and Savings

① Because our world is so overshadowed by aspects of finance – money, material goods, possessions and so on –we tend to forget that it is the wherewithal to allow us to live successful lives. Rather than the tangibility of money it is the principle of sufficiency (having enough) and the management of our resources that is important. This is the symbolism which will be most relevant in dreams.

② Management of finance in everyday life is a perpetual worry for most people, rich and poor alike, particularly in times of recession. When we are not sufficiently rewarded for our careful management – either of savings or for the effort put in in such management – we can become distressed and feel devalued. This can result in dreams about money and other resources.

③ From a spiritual perspective we can look at sufficiency as a four step process: Power, Energy, Finance and lastly Money. When any of these aspects is out of kilter we may have dreams to do with finance as a way of balancing our own internal audit.

Find

① If we dream of finding something, such as a precious object, we are becoming aware of some part of ourselves which is or will be of use to us. We are making a discovery or a realisation, which depending on the rest of the dream scenario may be about us or about others.

② The mind has an uncanny knack of drawing our attention to what needs to be done to enable us to achieve our aims. It will use hiding, searching and finding as metaphors for effort we must make in the waking state. So to find something without having to make too much effort would show that events will take place which will reveal what we need to know.

③ We may be close to finding something within our spiritual search which will enable us to move forward. This may be a new way of thinking or being, or new knowledge.

Finger
– see Hand in Body

Fire

① Fire in a dream can suggest passion and desire in its more positive sense, and frustration, anger, resentment and destructiveness in its more negative. It will depend on whether the fire is **controlled** or otherwise on the exact interpretation. To be more conscious of **the flame** of the fire would be to be aware of the energy and strength which is created. Being aware of the **heat** of a fire is to be aware of someone else's strong feelings. Deliberately burning something signifies perhaps cleansing or, if magically inclined, making an offering.

② Psychologically, fire often appears in dreams as a symbol of cleansing and purification. We can use the life-giving and generative power to change our lives. Sometimes fire indicates the need to use our sexual power to good effect. To dream of **being burnt alive** may express our fears of, or about, a new relationship or phase of life. We may also be conscious of the fact that we could suffer for our beliefs.

③ Baptism by fire signifies a new and fresh awareness of spiritual power and transformation. Fire is also a symbol of the Holy Spirit, or a State of Grace.

Fireworks

① Fireworks are generally accepted as belonging to a happy occasion or celebration, though they may also be frightening. When we dream of fireworks we are hoping to be able to celebrate good fortune, although there may be a secondary emotion associated with that celebration.

② Fireworks can have the same significance as an explosion (*see Explosion*). A release of energy or emotion can have quite a spectacular effect on us, or on people around us.

③ There is an excess of spiritual emotion which needs to be channelled properly in order for us to be able to work with it and prevent it shooting off in inappropriate directions.

Fish

① Dreaming of fish connects with the emotional side of ourselves, but more our ability to be wise without being strategic. We can often simply respond instinctively to what is going on, without needing to analyse it.

② The Collective Unconscious as Jung has called it – that part of life everyone shares, the common experience, awareness and knowledge which we all have – is becoming available to us.

③ Fish signify temporal and spiritual power. When pictured as two fish swimming in opposite directions, it is recognised as the sign of Pisces.

Fisherman
– also see Occupations

① Whenever one of our dream figures is carrying out a specific action we need to look at what is represented by that action. Often a fisherman will represent a provider, or perhaps bravery, as with a **deep-sea fisherman** whilst a **fresh water fisherman** may indicate the need for rest and recuperation.

② Within a situation in our lives we may be trying to 'catch' something, such as a job or a partner.

③ Because of its Christian connection, a fisherman can suggest a priest in dreams.

Flag
– also see Banner

① A flag in a dream has the same meaning as a banner – that is, a standard or a place round which people with common aims and beliefs can gather. It may represent old-fashioned principles and beliefs.

② The national flag will signify either a degree of patriotism and belief which may be necessary, or possibly the need to be more militant.

③ Spiritual crusades often require standards of behaviour. These can be represented in dreams by flags.

Flail

① Any instrument used to beat us in dreams is a recognition that someone has power over us, and can use force rather than giving us the power to act for ourselves.

② The flail would reinforce our ideas about authority. In older times the Court Jester would use a pig's bladder to flail the king to remind him of his humility.

③ A flail also sometimes represents spiritual supremacy and Supreme power which may be available to us.

Flame
– see Fire

Fleas

① Fleas are an irritation, and in dreams signify just that. There could be people or situations in our lives which are causing us difficulty, or that we feel are being parasites, and we will need to go through a process of decontamination in order to be free.

② We may be aware that we are not being treated properly and that people who should be our friends are not being fair.

③ Fleas are symbolic of the type of distress which is likely to hurt, rather than destroy – such as gossip. We should be aware that we do have the ability to deal with it.

Fleece

① We may be word-associating as in the sense of being 'fleeced' or cheated. The **fleece of a sheep** also represents security, warmth and comfort and will often signify those creature comforts we are able to give ourselves.

② Dreaming of a fleece, as opposed to the sheep itself, signifies a return to an older set of values. It links with the tasks which are given us when we set out on our own particular life journey. We may fear that what we are about to do is impossible, but our sense of self-preservation will not allow us to give up.

③ We may be in line for a spiritual reward. Our task will bring us success.

Fleur-de-lis

① As a symbol, the fleur-de-lis is very much connected with the French in people's minds, and so may be taken as this in dreams. It also represents the right to power.

② As illustrative of fire and light we may need to look for greater clarity.

③ The right to rule, by association with spiritual power.

Flies

① Flies are always associated with something nasty, which does not allow for the fact that they also devour rotten material. So to dream of flies is to be aware that we have certain negative aspects of our lives which need dealing with. To dream of **a swarm of flies**, which is an entity in itself, is to dream of the sort of purposeful behaviour which occurs when there are large numbers of insects. Where one insect may appear to be moving aimlessly, large numbers do not. Often we can only succeed in changing matters by group behaviour.

② Insects of any sort usually link us to primal instinctive behaviour, that of survival against all odds. Whatever threatens us does so on a very basic level, and we may have no defences, except those of our own nature.

③ Some form of spiritual contamination may have taken place. Hopefully it can be dealt with easily, and steps can then be taken to keep it away.

Flight
– also see Aeroplane and Flying

① Conventionally, to dream of taking flight is to do with sex and sexuality, but it would probably be more accurate to look at it in terms of lack of inhibition and freedom. We are releasing ourselves from limitations which we may impose on ourselves.

② To be **taking flight** is to be moving towards a more spiritual appreciation of our lives, while to be **doing so downwards** is to be making an attempt to understand the sub-conscious and all that it entails.

③ Spiritual Freedom and the right to explore other realms.

Floating

① Floating in a dream was considered by Freud to be connected with sexuality, but it is probable that it is much more to do with the inherent need for freedom. Generally we are opening to power beyond our conscious self; when we are carried along apparently beyond our own volition. We are in a state of extreme relaxation and are simply allowing events to carry us along.

② Because we are not taking charge of our own direction, we are being indecisive and perhaps need to think more carefully about our actions and involvements with other people.

③ Out of Body Experiences. The ability to rise above a situation.

Flock

① To dream of a flock – for instance of **birds or sheep** – is to recognise the need to belong to a group, to have a common aim or way of being.

② When we dream of belonging to a group, our personal behaviour can quite often be different from that of others, and we may be alerted to this by dreaming of a flock.

③ A flock can be symbolic of our spiritual beliefs, and our faith in that what we are following is the correct path.

Flogging

① Any violent act against the person usually indicates some form of punishment. To dream of **being flogged** would indicate that we are aware that someone is driving us beyond our limits, often in an inappropriate manner. **Flogging ourselves** would highlight a type of masochism in our own personality.

② **Flogging someone else** means we have to be careful that we are not attempting to impose our will on that person or indeed others. While painful there is also a degree of encouragement and stimulation present.

③ Atonement of sins and punishment for wrongdoing.

Flood
– also see Water

① Flood dreams are fascinating, because while frightening, they often indicate a release of positive energy. Usually it is an overflow of repressed or unconscious feelings which needs to be got out of the way before progress can be made. To be **in the middle of a flood** indicates we may feel we are being overwhelmed by these feelings, whilst **watching a flood** suggests we are simply watching ourselves. Often a flood dream can indicate depression.

② If we are not good at expressing ourselves verbally, dreaming of a flood may allow us to come to terms with our anxieties and worries in an appropriate way.

③ The end of one cycle and the beginning of another. Old grievances and emotional 'cobwebs' are being washed away, leaving a clear head and a clean way forward.

Flowers

① Flowers in a dream usually give us the opportunity to link to feelings of pleasure and beauty. We are aware that something new, perhaps a feeling or ability is beginning to come into being and that there is a freshness about what we are doing. **To be given a bouquet** means that we are being rewarded for an action – the colour of the flowers may be important *(see Colours)*.

② The feminine principle is often represented in dreams by flowers, as is childhood. The bud represents the potential available, while the opening flower indicates development. In folklore, each individual flower had a meaning in dreams: *Anenome* Your present partner is untrustworthy. *Arum Lily* An unhappy marriage or the death of a relationship. *Bluebell* Your partner will become argumentative. *Buttercup* Your business will increase. *Carnation* A passionate love affair. *Clover* Someone who is in need of finance will try to get in touch. *Crocus* A dark man around you is not to be trusted. *Daffodil* You have been unfair to a friend, look for reconciliation. *Forget-me-not* Your chosen partner cannot give you what you need. *Forsythia* You are glad to be alive. *Geranium* A recent quarrel is not as serious as you thought. *Honeysuckle* You will be upset by domestic quarrels. *Iris* Hopefully, you will receive good news. *Lime/Linden* This suggests feminine grace. *Marigold* There may be business difficulties. *Mistletoe* Be constant to your lover. *Myrtle* This gives joy, peace, tranquillity, happiness and constancy. *Narcissus* Take care not to mistake shadow for substance. *Peony* Excessive self restraint may cause you distress. *Poppy* A message will bring great disappointment. *Primrose* You will find happiness in a new friendship. *Rose* Indicates love, and perhaps a wedding, within a year. *Snowdrop* Confide in someone and do not hide your problems. *Violet* You will marry someone younger than yourself.

③ Spiritually flowers signify love and compassion, both that which we may receive and that which we give to others.

Flute
– also see Musical Instruments

① Many musical instruments – particularly wind instruments – indicate extremes of emotion, enticement and flattery. Because of its shape the flute is often taken as a symbol of masculine virility, but could also be taken to stand for anguish.

② As a way of expressing the sound of the spirit, and therefore harmony, the flute can be used as a symbol of happiness and joy.

③ The flute is said to be a gift from God or the Great Mother *(see Great Mother/Mother Earth)* and can be found in one form or another in most cultures. In dreams it can signify our connection with the Divine.

Flying
– also see Aeroplane and Flight

① To be flying without assistance in dreams suggests a degree of freedom which is not normally feasible in ordinary life. We may have freed ourselves from some constraint which has been holding us back. We have lifted away from mundane concerns and can adopt a wider viewpoint than our usual somewhat pedestrian one.

② Flying dreams can be a precursor to lucid dreaming – where we are aware of the fact that we are dreaming – or to astral travel where we become conscious of the ability to enter other realities and levels of consciousness.

③ Dreams of flying signify a spiritual freedom, possibly the ability to access other realms of existence. When practising voluntary flying rather than spontaneous it is wise to give oneself a reference point, in order to be able to re-orientate oneself in the physical world.

Fog

① To dream of being in a fog marks our confusion and inability to confront, or often even to see, the real issues at stake in our lives. We are often confused by external matters and the impact they may have on us emotionally.

② To be **walking in a fog** is often a warning that matters we consider important can be clouded by other peoples judgement and it may be wiser to sit still and do nothing at this time.

③ A degree of spiritual doubt and a feeling of directionless wandering – which is probably only temporary – is symbolised here.

Follow

① If we are **following someone** or something in a dream we may need a cause or crusade to help give us a a sense of identity. We are looking for leadership or are aware that we can be influenced by other people. It also indicates that, particularly in a work situation, we are perhaps more comfortable in a secondary position rather than out in front.

② When we dream of **being followed** we need to identify if what is following us is negative or positive. If it is negative, we need to deal with past fears, doubts or memories. If positive, we must recognise our need to take the initiative, or to identify what drives us.

③ We are aware of either the need for, or the recognition of, the ability to be a follower or disciple in our life.

Food
– also see Eating and Nourishment

① Food signifies a satisfaction of our needs whether those are physical, mental or spiritual. It is something we might take or are taking into ourselves. Frequent dreams about eating suggest a great hunger for something.

② Our need – or enjoyment – of food fulfils certain psychological needs. The meanings of various foods are as follows; *Bread* We are looking at our experiences and our basic needs. *Cake* This signifies sensual enjoyment. *Fruits* We are representing in dream form the fruits of our experience or effort, and the potential for prosperity. The colour can also be significant *(see Colour)*. *Ham/Cured Meats* Our need for preservation is represented by cured meats. *Jam* will normally signify an additional sweetness in life. In the sense of preserving fruit for future use it also symbolises harvesting with awareness. *Meals* Depending on whether we are eating alone or in a group, meals can indicate acceptance and sociability. *Meat* Physical or worldly satisfaction or needs are shown often in dreams as meat; *raw meat* can supposedly signify impending misfortune. *Milk*

As a basic food, milk will always signify baby needs and giving to oneself. *Onion* The different layers of oneself are often shown as an onion *(also see individual entry)*. *Sweets* These tend to represent sensual pleasure. *Vegetables* Vegetables represent our basic needs and material satisfaction. They also suggest the goodness we can take from the Earth and situations around us. The colour may also be important *(see Colour)*.

③ Spiritual Sustenance – gaining what we need from spiritual nurturing.

Footprints

① To see footprints in a dream indicates that we are needing to follow someone or their way of being. If those footprints are **stretching in front** of us there is help available to us in the future, but if they are **behind us** then perhaps we need to look at the way we have done things in the past. They usually indicate help in one way or another and certainly consideration.

② If we see footprints **going in opposite directions** we need to consider what has happened in the past and what is going to happen in the future. We also need to consider what actions we have initiated in the past to enable us to move into the future. We are, as it were, standing in the present and are considering the confusion of the present and how it may affect our future.

③ We may be aware, on a subconscious level, of a Divine presence.

Foreign Countries
– see Places/Environments

Forest
– also see Trees and Wood

① Dreaming of forests or a group of trees usually means entering the realms of the feminine. A forest is often a place of testing and initiation. It is always to do with coming to terms with our emotional self, of understanding the secrets of our own nature or of our own spiritual world.

② The dark or enchanted forest which very often appears as an image in fairy tales is a threshold symbol. It is the soul entering the areas it has never explored before, and having to work with intuition and with ones own ability to sense and feel what is going on around us. We may find that it has a lot to do with being lost *(see Lose/Lost)* and unable to find direction.

③ The psyche and the mystery of the feminine, that which must be explored.

Fork

① A fork, particularly a three-pronged one, is often considered to be the symbol of the Devil and therefore can therefore sometimes symbolise evil and trickery. In dreams a fork also denotes duality and indecision.

② Psychologically, the fork can signify the same as a barb or a goad – something which is driving us, often to our own detriment.

③ We may have come to a fork on our spiritual path and development and need guidance as to which direction to take.

Forge/Forgery
– also see Fire and Fraud

① When the forge and the blacksmith were a part of normal, everyday life this particular dream would indicate some aspect of hard work or desire to reach a goal. Now it is more likely to mean a ritual action.

② The forge represents the masculine and active force. It also represents the power of transmuting that which is base and unformed into something sacred. To dream of **a forge** indicates that we are changing internally and allowing our finer abilities to be shown. If we dream of **forgery** it indicates we are presenting a false front to others.

③ This represents Sacred Fire, which tempers our souls, and the Forge Gods such as Hephaestus and Thor. Forgery from a spiritual perspective indicates that we are not being true to our ideals.

Fortress
– see Buildings and Castle

Forward
– see Position

Fossil
– also see Museum

① When something is fossilised it is captured in a moment in time. Its dream significance is that a situation or occurrence has stopped progressing and cannot grow any further. Dreaming of fossils may also reveal the intrinsic beauty in a project.

② We may be being too rigid and outdated in our thinking, preventing ourselves from moving forward. We should look to free ourselves from too much rigidity in all areas of our lives.

③ We are being reminded of the sanctity of life and shown that not everything need decay into nothing. Perfection may be captured and preserved at any stage of existence.

Fountain

① To dream of a fountain means that we are aware of the process of life and 'flow' of our own consciousness. Because of its connection with water *(see Water)*, it also represents the surge of our emotions, and often our ability to express this. The fountain can also represent an element of play in our lives and the need to be free flowing and untroubled.

② In dreams the fountain often represents the mother figure or perhaps the source of our emotions.

③ The Fountain of Immortality and Eternal Life.

Fox
– see Animals

Fracture/Fractured
– see Fault/Faulty

Fraud

① When fraud appears in a dream, particularly if we are **being defrauded**, there is the potential to be too trusting of people. If we are the one **committing fraud**, we run the risk of losing a good friend.

② If we accept that the various figures appearing in a dream are parts of our personality, we should guard against being dishonest with ourselves.

③ We should look at our true spiritual aims and be true to them, whilst guarding against complacency and contrived goals.

Friend

① Friends appearing in our dreams can signify one of two things. Firstly we need to look at our relationship with that particular person, and secondly we need to decide what that friend represents for us (for instance security, support and love).

② In dreams friends often highlight a particular part of our own personality that we need to look at, and perhaps understand or come to terms with, in a different way.

③ We can continue on our spiritual search in the knowledge that we are being supported.

Frog
– also see Animals

① Many people associate the frog with a visible growth pattern which mirrors the growth to maturity of the human being. In dreams, to see a frog at a particular stage of its growth depicts the feeling we have about ourselves. For instance, to see it at the stage where it has grown its back legs would suggest that we capable of moving forward in leaps and bounds.

② The frog is a symbol of fertility and eroticism. In dreams it is also representative of an aspect of character that can be changed, something nasty that can be changed into good. This image is seen in myths and legends where the frog becomes a prince.

③ Transmutation and growth, hence spiritual progression.

Front
– see Position

Frontier
– also see Border

① To dream of **crossing a border or frontier** from one place to another represents making great changes in life, actively instigating a change from one state to another, perhaps taking ourselves from the past to the future, or causing other people round us to make those changes.

② Psychologically when we cross from one way of life to another – such as changing from puberty to adulthood or from middle age to old age – we need to depict this by creating an actual marker. In dreams when a frontier appears we are crossing a barrier within ourselves.

③ Spiritually, we have a new experience ahead of us which we can use on our way towards enlightenment.

Fruit/Berries
– also see Food

① To dream of fruit, particularly in a bowl, very often indicates the culmination of actions that we have taken in the past. We have been able to 'harvest' the past and to make a new beginning for ourselves. Berries in dreams will signify the many parts of a project, suggesting that each part must be considered carefully in its own right.

② Psychologically, when we have worked hard we ought to be able to recognise the fruits of our labour. Dreaming of fruit in this way indicates that we have succeeded in what we set out to do. Whereas **fruits with stones** may indicate our gain is through determination, **berries** suggest a gentler, more integrated approach.

③ Creativity and the continuation of life and sustenance. Being aware of the colour of berries in dreams often indicates the need for a more creative approach to life.

Fuel
– also see Oil and Petrol

① Fuel in dreams can range from the simple such as **burning wood** through to energy created by modern day technology. It is the symbolism of energy expenditure which can appear most often in dreams, particularly as we become aware of the misuse of the world's resources. A **fire that will not burn** or **an engine that will not run** can highlight such misuse, both personally and otherwise. **Lack of fuel** will suggest that we are not taking in sufficient nourishment to enable us to function properly.

② While we have tended to ignore the environmental impact of our use of fuel resources, as we adopt a more global perspective dreams will often act as 'way-finders' for future action and we must learn to use what we have wisely and well.

③ Spiritually fuel symbolises the Life force and the joy we have in using it efficiently.

Funeral
– also see Mourning

① To dream of **being at a funeral** indicates that we need to come to terms with our feelings about death. This may not necessarily be our own death but the death of others. It may also indicate a time of mourning for something that has happened in the past; this time of mourning can allow us to move forward into the future. To dream of our **own funeral** can indicate a desire for sympathy. It may also indicate that a part of us is 'dead' and we have to let it go and move on.

② Dreaming of our **parents' funeral** indicates a move towards independence, or of letting go of the past, which may be painful. We may need to let our childhood – or childhood experiences – go and mark that by some ritual or ceremony.

③ Rites of Passage and letting go of the past.

Furniture/Furnishings

① The furniture which appears in our dreams, particularly if it is drawn to our attention, often shows how we feel about our family and home life, and what attitudes or habits we have developed. It also can give an indication as to how we feel about ourselves. For instance, **dark heavy material** would suggest the possibility of unhappiness and depression, whereas **brightly painted objects** could testify to an upbeat mentality.

② Sometimes the furniture which appears in a dream can highlight our need for security or stability, particularly if it is recognisable from the past. Different articles can represent different attitudes:

Bed/Mattress This can show exactly what is happening in the subtle areas of our close relationships. We can get an insight into how we really feel about intimacy and sexual pleasure. For some people the bed is a place of sanctuary and rest, where they can be totally alone. *Carpet* Often when carpets appears in a dream we are looking at our emotional links with finance. The colour of the carpet should also be noted *(see Colour)*. *Chair* A chair can indicate that we need a period of rest and recuperation. We may need to deliberately take time out, to be receptive to other opportunities and openings. *Cupboard/Wardrobe* Cupboards and wardrobes may depict those things we wish to keep hidden, but may also depict how we deal with the different roles we must play in life. *Curtains and soft furnishings* represent comfort and style and in dreams may represent a safe space. *Table* For a table to appear in a dream is often to do with communal activity, and with our social partnerships *(also see individual entry and Altar)*.

③ Revered objects and gifts of attainment.

Future

① There are several aspects to dreaming about the future. We may be aware within the dream itself that the events will take place in the future of our dream, and in which case they are usually to do with actions we need to take in waking life. We also may have precognitive dreams, which is when we dream of events before they take place, and then recognise that we already have the information – we 'knew' about it. The theory behind this is that the past, present and future co-exist side by side, and that it is possible to 'read' these records in the dream state. Our experience of them is subjective, although we are in the position of observers.

② Psychologically, if we are to be in control of our lives, we often need to feel that we must be aware of the future, and dreams can give an insight into how we can or will act in the future. Dreams allow us to play out certain scenarios, to explore possibilities without coming to any harm.

③ Spiritual Manifestation, as in 'all things must pass'. Both past and present combine to create our future. Our actions create potential.

Gag

① A gag in dreams suggests that we are not being permitted to express ourselves properly. If we are **gagging someone else** we do not wish to hear what we are being told. We would do well to consider our circumstances in waking life.

② Oddly, it is worthwhile when interpreting this occurrence to try to remember what was being used as a gag. A **handkerchief** might suggest that there is something available for us to consider, whereas a **bandage** might suggest that we need to keep quiet to effect healing. Interpretation will also differ if we are tied up or constrained in some way.

③ Spiritually, since initiation into selected knowledge requires that we keep quiet, a gag may indicate the need for secrecy and discretion.

Gale

– also see Hurricane and Wind

① Being in a gale indicates that we are being buffeted by circumstances that we feel are beyond our control. We are allowing those outside circumstances to create problems for us when actually we may need to look at what we are doing and either take shelter – to withdraw from the situation – or battle through to some form of sanctuary.

② Since wind in a dream often denotes spiritual matters, we may be taking ourselves too seriously. We are allowing those forces within ourselves, which will lead us forward to something else, to have too much meaning.

③ A gale can be symbolic not only of the spirit we have within us, but also the spiritual side of things, particularly the Spirit.

Gall

– see Gall Bladder in Body

Games/Gambling

① Playing a game in our dream indicates that we are taking note of how we play the game of life. If we are **playing well** we may take it that we are coping well with circumstances in our lives. If we are **playing badly** we may need to reassess our abilities and identify which skills we need to improve in order to do things better. Games and gambling can also represent not taking life seriously. They can show how we work within the competitive field and give us some kind of insight into our own sense of winning or losing.

② Specific games such as **football, baseball, rugby and cricket** which are **team games** represent for many the strong ability to identify with a 'tribe' or a group of people. Because they are mock fights they can be used as expressions of aggression against other people, in the way that wars and tribal localised fights were used previously. They indicate the way in which we gain identity and how we connect with people. In dreams, games which require the power of thought and strategy – such as **chess or draughts** – often give some idea of how we should be taking a situation forward *(see Chess)*. Decisions may need to be made where we have to gauge the result of our action and take into account our opponent's reaction. **Playing golf** can often represent our need to show our prowess, to be able literally to drive as far as we can, and often is used within the context of business acumen. To dream of **gambling** indicates that we may need to look at something in our lives that is figuratively a gamble; we may need to take risks, but in such a way that we have calculated the risks as best we can.

③ Ritualised fighting between two opposing forces. A managed conflict.

Gang
– see Group/Gang

Garage
– also see Workshop

① A garage appearing in a dream may indicate how we store our own personal abilities. It is the workshop from which we need to move out into the world in order to show what we have done. We are looking at our reserves of drive and motivation and possibly at our abilities.

② **A car repair garage** – remembering that a car represents the way we handle our external life – can indicate the need for personal attention and perhaps bodily maintenance.

③ We all have spiritual tools which we can call upon at certain times. A garage is a symbolic reminder that we have these in storage, and they can be utilised at any time.

Garbage/Rubbish/Litter

① Garbage in our dream creates a scenario where we are able to deal with those parts of our experience or our feelings which are like garbage, and need to be sorted in order to decide what is to be kept and what is to be rejected. To be **collecting**

garbage can indicate that we are making wrong assumptions. **Litter** is that which others have discarded as unnecessary. According to our personal attitude it will either demonstrate carelessness for the environment or material to be reused.

② Very often, garbage is the remains of food preparation. Often we are being alerted to what we need to do in order to remain healthy – how we need to treat our bodies and how we need to create space in order to act correctly. To be **recycling** garbage or rubbish highlights our awareness that others can utilise resources for which we no longer have any use. **Litter** is many articles strewn around and therefore represent chaos, however a litter of animals (multiple births) could represent a choice of action or new beginnings.

③ We may need to dispose of spiritual rubbish, and a dream about garbage can alert us that now is the time to do that. Spiritual rubbish or litter might be ideas and concepts which no longer hold any validity for us.

Garden

① Dreaming of a garden can be fascinating, because it may indicate the area of growth in our own lives, or it can be that which we are trying to cultivate in ourselves. It often represents our inner life and what we totally appreciate about our own being.

② The garden is often the symbol of the feminine attributes and the qualities of wildness which need to be cultivated and tamed in order to create order. **Closed gardens** particularly have this significance and can represent virginity.

③ A garden can represent a form of paradise, as in the Garden of Eden. We should look to some spiritual relaxation.

Gardener
– also see Occupations

① Whenever a person appears in our dream in a certain role it is important to look at what he is actually doing. The gardener can represent the insights which we have gathered through our experience in life and can equally represent wisdom, but of a particular sort. Often the gardener indicates someone on whom we can rely, who will take care of those things with which we do not feel capable of dealing.

② If we find ourselves **looking after a garden** within a dream then we are looking after ourselves. We are nurturing those aspects of ourselves that we have carefully cultivated and which we need to keep 'tidy', in order to get the best out of ourselves.

③ A gardener helps us identify with the wiser aspects of ourselves. We need to tend to these gifts of wisdom and not let them become stagnant.

Garland

① Depending on the type of garland in the dream we are recognising some distinction or honour for ourselves. If we are **wearing the garland**, such as a **Hawaiian flower garland**, we are looking at various ways of making ourselves happy. We are looking at dedication, and at some way of setting ourselves apart from others.

② Psychologically, a garland can represent honour and recognition and can link us to the people who have presented us with the garland.

③ A garland is symbolic of the need for dedication, either spiritually or physically. It may also represent an element of our subconscious spirituality, which we will need to acknowledge.

Garlic

① Garlic in olden times had much significance. Because of its shape and its many parts it was often seen as a symbol of fertility; because of its smell it was seen as protection. Dreaming of garlic may therefore link back to either of these meanings.

② Garlic is a psychically protective amulet against evil. Physically it protects the heart area and therefore protects us against fear.

③ Magic, potency and spiritual power are represented by garlic.

Gas

① Gas can have the same significance as air and wind but usually is taken to be slightly more dangerous. So to be dreaming of gas in some way – e.g. **a leak** – indicates we may be looking at some difficulty in controlling our own thoughts, feelings and abilities.

② Gas as a means of assistance or as a tool has the same significance as breath *(See Breath)*. As we become more conscious of world resources and their management, the concept of 'greenhouse gasses' as a danger can appear in dreams, potentially as a warning.

③ The spirit, as an unformed entity, can be symbolised by gas. If it has a smell, it is negative energy.

Gate

① Dreaming of a gate usually signifies some kind of change, often in awareness. We are passing a threshold in our lives, perhaps trying out something different or moving from one phase of life to another.

② Often the awareness of change is highlighted by the type of gate in a dream. For instance, a **farm gate** would tend to indicate a work change, whereas a **garden gate** might represent pleasure.

③ The gate between the physical and spiritual realms has a long established existence As a symbol it is used as a 'gateway' for communication. The 'Pearly Gates' are a symbol of Death and the soul's passage to Eternity and Everlasting Life. Their appearance do not foretell a death.

Gazelle
– see Deer In Animals

Gems
– see Jewels/Gems

Genitals
– also see Body

① To dream of **our own genitals** refers directly to our own sexuality. To dream of **being mutilated** could refer to either past or present abuse, or distress at inappropriate behaviour of some sort.

② Dreaming of **someone else's genitals** either indicates our involvement with that person's issues of privacy, or, if of the opposite sex, our need to understand the hidden side of ourselves.

③ Our awareness of the physical self within a spiritual framework. It is the first area from which a child has a sense of self.

Germs
– see Dirt/Dirty

Ghost

① Actually dreaming of a ghost links us to old habit patterns or buried hopes and longings. We recognise that there is something insubstantial in these, possibly because we have not put enough energy into them.

② We may be resurrecting old memories or feelings in order to understand our own actions. By putting ourselves in touch with what is dead and gone we can take appropriate action in the here and now. To be haunted in dreams usually signifies that we have not come to terms with the past, whether that is old events, patterns of behaviour or concepts.

③ If a ghost appears in a dream we may be alerted to our past states of being – in which case we should try to identify these, and acknowledge that we have moved on.

Giant

① Dreaming about giants may mean that we are coming to terms with some of the repressed feelings we had about adults when we were children. They may have seemed larger than life or frightening in some way; now, as we mature we do not need to be afraid. Titans in dreams appear as huge god-like figures – sometimes overbearing, sometimes large. In this context they represent the forces within us which allow things to manifest, or to happen.

② Giants and ogres often represent the emotion of anger, particularly masculine anger. This can be confronted in dreams where perhaps we cannot do this in waking life. Psychologically we probably use about 10 per cent of our available energy. Those Titanic forces which can arise in dreams are those parts of ourselves that are untamed and untameable. When used properly they are the ability to create a world of our own.

③ Giants tend to represent primordial power and raw, unrestrained energy. Our will and urge to achieve our spiritual goals may be symbolised by the appearance of Titans in a dream.

Gift

– also see Present

① To **receive a gift** within a dream is to recognise our talents and abilities. It also shows that we are acknowledging what we receive from others.

② Each of us has a store of unconscious knowledge which, from time to time, becomes available to us and may appear in dreams as gifts.

③ In a spiritual sense, dreaming of a gift may be pointing us towards our creative talents, of which we may not yet be aware.

Girdle

① **In a woman's dream** the girdle may depict her sense of her own femininity, for instance when she feels bound or constricted by it. **In a man's dream** it is more likely to show his understanding of his power over his own life.

② The girdle can represent the inevitability of life and death. We are bound by the necessity for Life's Experience.

③ A girdle also represents wisdom, strength and power. We should make note of this, as spiritually we are progressing in the right direction.

Girl

– see People

Girlfriend
– see People

Giving

① Giving is all about the internal relationship with oneself or our environment and with others. So to dream of giving somebody something in a dream indicates our need to give and take within a relationship – our need to give of ourselves, perhaps to share with others what we have, and to create an environment that allows for give and take.

② It is one of the fundamental needs of the human being to be able to share with other people. Psychologically this represents our ability to belong to others, to have others belong within our lives and to assume responsibility for other people. So to dream of giving in this way indicates our own innate abilities.

③ We should acknowledge the gifts we have and use them appropriately, perhaps for the Greater Good.

Glacier
– see Ice/Iceberg

Glass

① Dreaming of glass indicates the invisible but very tangible barriers we may erect around ourselves in order to protect ourselves from relationship with other people. It may also represent the barriers that other people put up and also be those aspects of ourselves which we have built up in our own defence.

② To dream of **breaking glass** is to be breaking through those barriers *(see Break)*. We are shattering the emotions that keep us trapped and moving into a clearer space where we do not allow barriers to build. **Frosted or smoked glass** can indicate a desire for privacy or our obscured view of a particular situation within our lives.

③ The barrier between life and the life hereafter.

Glasses/Spectacles
– also see Lens

① For glasses or spectacles to stand out in a dream indicates a connection with our ability to see or to understand. Equally, if **someone is unexpectedly wearing glasses**, it is to do either with our lack of understanding or perhaps their inability to see where we are coming from.

② Psychologically, when we are able to wear glasses we are more able to look at that which is external to ourselves rather than turning inwards and becoming introspective. So, in dreams, glasses can represent the need for extroversion within a situation. Binoculars, being more complex than glasses and allowing a more precise view, signify that the long-term view needs special attention in order to make the best use of resources.

③ Spiritually, a dream of glasses or spectacles may be urging us to take a different viewpoint – on a physical as well as spiritual level.

Globe
– also see World

① To dream of looking at a globe, particularly in the sense of a **world globe**, indicates our appreciation of a wider viewpoint. We can cultivate the ability not only not to be narrow minded but to be more globally aware. If we are looking at, for instance, **a glass globe** we may be looking at a lifestyle that is complete, but which is contained.

② Dreaming of a globe is to dream of power and of dignity. We have certain powers within us that will enable us to create a sustainable future, and for this we need to be able to understand and take a world view.

③ A globe symbolises our need for wholeness or, for someone much further along the spiritual journey, the approach to wholeness. The globe is a representation of the wholeness of life.

Gloom

① If there is gloom around in a dream, it can indicate difficulty in being able to see or comprehend things from an external viewpoint. There may be negativity around of which we have to be aware in order to be able to dispel it – to create light and clarity – so that we can continue with our lives.

② If we find ourselves **enclosed in gloom**, while others appear to be in the light, we may be being warned of a certain type of melancholy that is affecting us, but not affecting them. Conversely if we are **in light while other people are in shadow** we may have information which will help them to enhance their lives.

③ Gloom usually indicates a presence of evil or unpleasantness, which can be lifted with appropriate action.

Gloves
– also see Clothes

① Often in previous times the glove had greater significance than it does nowadays. Because it was so much part of social etiquette it represented honour, purity and evidence of good faith. Now being aware of gloves in a dream often represents some way in which we are hiding our abilities from people around us. To **take off**

the glove signifies respect and an act of sincerity. To dream of **boxing gloves** could indicate that we are trying too hard to succeed in a situation where there is aggression.

② Gloves represent the ability to challenge people, and the ability to hide our own awareness from other people so that we can challenge them in their beliefs and belief system.

③ Spiritually, since hands may be representative of our creativity, gloves can symbolise the need to protect our creative ability. They may also be an impediment to full creative expression.

Goad

① The goad can be shown in many ways. Often if **we are goading somebody** to do something they do not want to do we must take care that we are not creating circumstances which could turn around and control us. We may be trying to force people to take action to move forward but we must also be aware that we need to be in control of that particular movement.

② Psychologically, we are all goaded by our own more aggressive and negative parts. Often a dream can reveal how we are making things difficult for ourselves and can represent which parts of ourselves are taking authority over the other.

③ Power and Spiritual authority often act as a goad so we can improve our knowledge.

Goal

① To dream of **scoring a goal** may indicate that we have set ourselves external targets. In achieving those targets we may also recognise that the goals which we have set ourselves in life are either short or long-term and we may need to adjust them in some way. **To miss a goal** indicates that we have not taken all the circumstances within a situation into account and need, perhaps, to reassess our abilities to achieve.

② **To set life goals** – or to be conscious of doing this in a dream – indicates that we are in touch with our own internal sense of our ability to achieve. The external is often a reflection of the internal and goals can indicate that we instinctively know how much, and what, we are capable of doing.

③ Our spiritual aspirations are being highlighted. If we are aware of our goal, then we can make terrific in-roads towards attainment.

Goat
– *see Animals*

Goblet

① In dreams the goblet has similar significance to the chalice (See Chalice). It represents the feminine, receptive principle and our ability to achieve enjoyment in different ways. We may be able to make a celebration out of something that is quite ordinary. To be **drinking from a goblet** indicates allowing ourselves the freedom to enjoy life to the full.

② To dream of **a set of goblets** as in wine glasses indicates there are several different ways in which we can make our lives more enjoyable and fun.

③ The Feminine Principle, and sometimes the Elixir of Life.

God/Gods
– also see Religious Iconology

① When we dream of God we are acknowledging to ourselves that there is a higher power in charge. We connect with all humanity, and therefore have a right to a certain set of moral beliefs. We all have needs for love and approval which can only be met through our understanding of our childhood. **In a woman's dream**, dreaming of mythical gods will help her to understand various aspects of her own personality. **In a man's dream** he is linking with his own masculinity and his sense of belonging to himself, and therefore to the rest of humanity.

② The powerful emotions we sometimes experience may be connected with our tremendous childhood need for love and parental approval. Often these emotions can be personalised and recognised most easily in the figures of mythical and Classical gods; *Adonis* signifies health, beauty and self adoration. *Apollo* signifies the Sun, and taught *Chiron* the art of healing. It is interesting that although *Heracles/Hercules* was taught the art of healing by Chiron, when he accidentally shot Chiron the latter was not able to accept healing from him. *Jehovah*, in the sense of a vengeful god, alerts us to the negative side of power. *Mars* as the god of war symbolises the drive we require to succeed. *Mercury (or Hermes)* suggests communication, often of a sensitive sort. He is the patron of magic. *Zeus* is the king of the gods and signifies fathering in both its positive and negative forms.

③ Spiritually, we are aware of a greater power. Christian belief holds to one God, although manifesting in three forms – Father, Son and Holy Ghost. Other religions attribute the powers to various Gods. As we grow in understanding, we can appreciate the relevance of both beliefs and can begin to understand God as an all pervading energy.

Goddess/Goddesses
– also see Religious Iconology

① Dreaming of **mythical goddesses** connects us with our archetypal images of femininity (see Archetypes). **In a woman's dream** a goddess will clarify the connection through the unconscious that exists between all women and female creatures. It is the sense of mystery, of a shared secret, which is such an intangible force within the woman's psyche. In the waking state it is that which enables women to create a sisterhood or network among themselves in order to bring about a common aim. To dream about goddesses therefore is to accept our right to initiation into this powerful group. **In a man's dream** the goddess figure signifies all that a man fears in the concept of female power and strength. It usually also gives an insight into his earliest view of femininity through his experience of his mother.

② There are many goddess figures in all cultures. There are those perceived as being destructive such as *Kali, Bast* and *Lilith,* and also beneficent ones such as *Athena* and *Hermia.* The beneficent Classical ones which women most closely relate to are given here: *Aphrodite* is the goddess of love and beauty, who moves women to be both creative and procreative. She governs a woman's enjoyment of love and beauty. *Artemis,* who is the goddess of the moon, personifies the independent feminine spirit whose ultimate goal is achievement. She is often pictured as the hunter. *Athena* is goddess of wisdom and strategy. She is logical and self-assured and is ruled by her mental faculties rather than her emotions. *Demeter* epitomises the maternal archetype and goddess and fertility, she highlights a woman's drive to provide physical and spiritual support for her children. *Hera* as the goddess of marriage denotes the woman who has her essential goal of finding a husband. She sees being married as of paramount importance and any other role as secondary. *Hestia,* goddess of the hearth, manifests the patient woman who finds steadiness in seclusion. She emits a sense of wholeness. *Persephone,* who is ultimately queen of the underworld but only through having rejected her status as Demeter's daughter, gives expression to woman's tendency towards a need to please and be needed by others. Her submissive behaviour and passivity must change to an ability to take responsibility for who she is in order for her to be truly successful.

③ Spiritually, each woman is able to make intuitive links with the essential aspects of her own personality. She then achieves a greater understanding of her own make up, and is able to use all facets of her being within her normal everyday life. As we become more culturally aware, we are able to utilise the qualities from all cultures.

Goggles
– also see Glasses/Spectacles and Mask

① Goggles in a dream can have the same significance as spectacles and also the mask. The meaning can be ambivalent since goggles can be used either to cover up the eyes – often believed to be the seat of the soul – or to enable us to see better. Under most circumstances it can be taken as the latter, but equally we need to be certain that we are not using the dream image of goggles to indicate the protection that we may need in real life. Perhaps we may feel that what we are seeing is going to harm us in some way.

② **For a woman to dream** that she meets a man with goggles generally means that she cannot trust that man to be honest with her.

③ We may be covering up, or denying the existence, of evil. This can only be a negative feeling and should be dealt with appropriately.

Gold

① Gold in dreams suggests the best, most valuable aspects of ourselves. **Finding gold** indicates that we can discover those characteristics in ourselves or others. **Burying gold** shows that we are trying to hide something – perhaps information or knowledge – that we have.

② Gold in dreams can also represent the sacred, dedicated side of ourselves. We can recognise incorruptibility and wisdom, love, patience and care. Interestingly, in this context it seldom stands for material wealth, being more the spiritual assets that one has.

③ The old saying of 'everything that glitters isn't gold' certainly doesn't apply in the spiritual sense. To dream of gold symbolises Spirituality on a supreme level gained after hard work.

Gong

① To **hear the sound of a gong** in a dream is to be aware that some limitation has been reached, or conversely that some permission has been given for further action. **To strike the gong** may represent the need for strength and the need to be able to achieve a particular quality of sound or information within a waking situation.

② In older religions the gong is often used to alert peoples' attention to something that needs recognising. It is this symbolism which is often apparent within the circumstances of the dream.

③ Our awareness to Spirituality is symbolised by a gong. It is literally 'waking us up' on a spiritual level.

Goose
– see Birds

Gossip

① **To be gossiping** in a dream can mean that one is spreading information, but in a way that is not necessarily appropriate. To be in a group of people and **listening to gossip** generally means that we are looking for some kind of information, but perhaps do not have the ability to achieve it for ourselves. We have to use other people to enable us to achieve the correct level of information.

② Within the framework of personal development, there is often what could be called the 'gossip' in the background – the chatterbox – that which is part of our personality but which prevents us from moving away from previously held ideas and behaviour. Thus, to be gossiping in a dream may mean that we have to complete certain actions before moving on.

③ 'Spiritual static', a lack of clarity, and contamination by others' ideas.

Gourd
– also see Vase

① Both as a carrier of water and of sustenance, the gourd appearing in a dream may be a great deal to do with our own view of femininity and our ability to nurture. It is also the ability to link into untapped information and knowledge.

② The gourd is often a symbol of mystery. As something unusual it can denote secret information, sustenance or nurturing. Because it is is used as a carrier after it has fruited, it can often represent the physical body.

③ A gourd can symbolise the mystery surrounding spiritual progression. It is our hidden goodness.

Govern/Government
– see Parliament

Grain

① Dreaming of grains such as wheat, oats, barley, etc. can indicate some kind of a harvest. We have created opportunities for ourselves in the past which now can come to fruition. Provided we look after the outcome of these opportunities, we can take that success forward and create even more abundance.

② To dream of **grain growing in a field** can indicate that we are on the point of success, that we have tended our lives sufficiently to be able to achieve growth.

③ Grain can represent the very seeds of life and our need to discover the hidden truth.

Grandparents
– see Family

Grapes
– also see Fruit/Berries and Vine/Vineyard

① To see grapes in a dream generally indicates that there is a need for celebration. The grape is the fruit most closely associated with Bacchus or, in his Greek form, Dionysus who was the god of conviviality. To dream of grapes indicates the searching for fun, laughter and creativity in our lives.

② Grapes appearing in a dream can represent sacrifice. We need to give something up in order to achieve what we are really looking for. Wine is often taken to represent such sacrifice since it has a close affiliation with blood.

③ Grapes, representative as food of the Gods, can symbolise wisdom and immortality.

Grass
– also see Turf

① Grass is often a symbol of new growth, and of victory over barrenness. In old dream interpretations it could represent pregnancy, but is now more likely to signify new ideas and projects.

② Grass often has the same relevance as 'home turf' and how we feel about our country, which may be either positive or negative. On a more personal level, it can also represent how we feel about our home and immediate surroundings.

③ Changes of Spiritual awareness can be indicated by new grass appearing in a dream.

Grasshopper

① The grasshopper is a symbol of freedom and capriciousness, and in dreams it can often indicate a bid for freedom.

② A grasshopper mind (one which flits all over the place), shows there is an inability to settle to anything and can actually be seen in dreams as a grasshopper.

③ In Chinese history the grasshopper is often associated with enlightenment. Thus, it represents some form of Spiritual freedom.

Grave
– also see Cemetery and Death

① Dreaming of a grave is an indication that we must have regard for our feelings about, or our concept of, death. Such a dream may also be attempting to deal with our feelings about someone who has died.

② Part of our personality may, quite literally, have been killed off, or is dead and buried to the outside world.

③ Spiritually, we may fear not just physical death but also its consequences.

Gravel

① Often our attention is drawn to the size of an article within a dream. Gravel in this context is simply an indication of small particles. Such a dream may also bring back memories of a particular time or place, and remind us of happier times, such as those of childhood.

② **Skidding on gravel** signifies that we should avoid taking risks in everyday life, and be more aware of our surroundings.

③ The microcosm. The need to pay attention to the small details.

Grease/Greasy

① Grease in a dream makes us aware that we perhaps have not taken as much care in a situation as we should have done. We have created circumstances which do not give us an advantage and could be 'slippery' or uncomfortable.

② We should use better judgement before putting ourselves at risk. Grease may also signify making things easier for ourselves.

③ Grease has two spiritual meanings in dreams. It may represent either simplicity and ease, or contamination and difficulty. It will be up to us to decide whether we wish to take the easy route in order to achieve our aims, or the more difficult.

Great Mother/Mother Earth

① The Great Mother or Mother Earth will often appear in dreams as a motherly figure, or a mother goddess such as Demeter *(see Goddess/Goddesses)* or Grandmother Spider. This archetypal figure is not the wholly matriarchal aspect of woman, but is a more enhanced ethereal inner sense of her Self. She is the true epitome of all the attitudes of the feminine, both positive and negative.

② This is the symbol of totality in a woman, and epitomises the aptitude for using all aspects of her character. In aiming for this excellence, a woman must use and promote all the separate functions of her being. She must attempt to use perception, opinion, intelligence and intuition as tools rather than weapons.

③ Great Mother's domain is all life's rich pattern, including an innate perception of the way it works. Her attributes can be cultivated in a totally individualistic fashion in as many ways as there are women.

Group/Gang

① Any group or grouping of articles or people in dreams highlights the energy and power that that grouping creates. It is greater than the sum of its parts. A gang of people has a more negative emphasis. It can appear quite threatening and may mirror a situation in waking life.

② The purpose of a group in dreams may be to draw our attention to the validity of group thought – that we can relate to people who think and feel the same way as we do. If we find ourselves on the outside of a group then we must find common ground. Being on the perimeter of a gang shows we must preserve our own integrity.

③ We should consider the idea of a group purpose from a spiritual perspective. Where there is negativity we can also attempt to change the focus.

Growth

① The changes in us which bring about new and fresh ways of relating to other people, who we ourselves are, or situations around us, are all stages of growth. They are often pictured in dreams as the growth of a plant or something similar.

② Often when we dream of childhood we are able to put ourselves in touch with the growth process. As a child matures he begins to develop a deeper understanding of the world around him and it is this process which is perceived in dreams as growth.

③ Growth in a dream can be the recognition of a new Spiritual maturity, from which we should take heart. A lushness and new growth in vegetation often suggests a fertile source of information.

Guard

① A guard in dreams can have an ambivalent meaning. If we are **guarding something** we may be protecting whatever is represented, perhaps for safety reasons, perhaps because of the intrinsic value. If we are **being guarded by others** we are being prevented from taking specific action.

② Being guarded by another human being suggests the presence of an authority figure in our lives, albeit someone who has been given that authority. In a dream such as this we might consider how our behaviour is inappropriate or offends against the norms of society.

③ From a spiritual perspective a guard may represent the Higher Self, or our Guardian Angel.

Guardian Spirits
– also see Religious Iconology

① Dreams are a way of putting ourselves in touch with other dimensions and to an extent it will depend on your system of belief as to how your particular guardian presents themselves. For some according to shamanism it will be the totem animal, for others the guardian angel and for yet others a beloved deceased family member or what is known as a doorkeeper. Others will also recognise the Higher Self – that part that remains in contact with the Divine.

② As we open ourselves up to the idea that these manifestations are there to help us towards a greater understanding of ourselves and others, they will appear more frequently in dreams as guiding and guarding us, keeping us from harm in everyday life. When we learn to treat them as trusted companions on our inner journey we are beginning to develop a greater spirituality.

③ As cultures intermingle and beliefs synchronise we move towards a time when differences become less important and similarities are recognised. Mankind has always recognised the need for an inner guidance, interdependence and independence. Guardian spirits, particularly in dreams, are a manifestation of our connectedness with the Ultimate.

Guillotine

① A guillotine in a dream indicates something irrational in our personality. We may be afraid of losing our self-control, or perhaps losing our talents through misuse. We could also be aware of an injury to our person or to our dignity.

② There is the potential for us to lose contact with someone we love, or with the part of ourselves which is capable of love.

③ By way of its physical action, a guillotine represents a severance of some kind. We may have become severed from our spiritual yearnings.

Guitar

① Guitar music in a dream can sometimes foretell the possibility of a new romance, but can also indicate the need for caution. **If we are playing the guitar** we are making an attempt to be more creative.

② Any musical instrument characterises our need for rest and relaxation and for harmony in our lives.

③ We may feel the need for harmony in both our spiritual and physical worlds.

Gulls
– see Seagull in Birds

Gun
– also see Weapons

① In dreams the gun has an obvious masculine and sexual connotation. **If a woman is firing** a gun she is aware of the masculine, aggressive side of her personality. **If she is being shot at** she perhaps feels threatened by overt signs of aggression or sexuality.

② There are many different interpretations possible for a gun in a dream, all dependent on other aspects which appear. Perhaps the most common is that we feel there are things which are important to us which need protecting in some way.

③ The spiritual symbolism here reverts to a more base attribute – that of overt masculinity.

Guru

① A guru appearing in a dream is a representation of the wisdom of the unconscious. As that wisdom becomes available we often bring it through to conscious knowledge by the figure of the Wise Old Man (see Wise Old Man).

② Psychologically, we all need a symbol for a father or authority figure and this is one such representation. In searching for knowledge of a specific sort, we need an external figure with whom to relate. In Eastern religions, this is the guru – who performs the same function as the priest in Western religion.

③ For many of us, God is too remote for us to be able to have a personal relationship with him. A guru therefore becomes the personification of all wisdom made available to us through his perception. He will assist us to access our own innate wisdom.

Haggle

① In the sense that haggling is negotiating a fair price, this image may appear in dreams where we feel that we, our skills or attributes are being undervalued. It is worthwhile noting whether we are trying to raise or lower the price in the dream and then applying the same principle in waking life.

② Haggling has a degree of pettiness about it which can be unattractive. In dreams such an action alerts us to such pettiness in ourselves or in others. When we dream of haggling successfully we are overcoming such pettiness.

③ There is a stage in spiritual development where negotiation takes place between the spiritual and material self for a successful outcome. Haggling highlights such negotiation and it will depend on our own awareness of ourselves as to which one gains supremacy.

Hail

① Hail in a dream, because it is frozen water (see Ice/Iceberg), signifies the freezing of our emotions. It would appear that the danger and damage created by these frozen emotions comes from outside influences rather than our internal feelings. In a different context, hailing a cab or a person can signify that we need assistance of some sort, or that we are acknowledging a connection.

② Hail has a particular part to play in the cycle of nature. We need to appreciate that there are times when numbing our emotions may be appropriate. It does not, however, need to be a permanent state of affairs.

③ Emotions connected with spirituality sometimes have to be held in check, and this can be symbolised for us in dreams by hail.

Hair
– see Body

Hairdresser
– also see Occupations

① For many women, her hairdresser is someone with whom she can communicate freely. In dreams the hairdresser may appear as the part of ourselves which deals with self image and the way we feel about ourselves. We perhaps need to consider ways in which we can change our image.

② Psychologically and intellectually, the hairdresser can represent the healer within us. An intimate yet objective relationship can be important within our lives. A hairdresser appearing in dreams would signify this relationship.

③ In terms of spirituality the connection between self image and beauty is obvious. We cannot grow spiritually unless we like ourselves.

Half

① Dreams can often have a very peculiar quality in that our image may only be half there or we perhaps only experience half an action. This usually indicates an incompleteness in us, being a sort of in-between state which means that we have to make decisions. Often it is about either going forward into the future or back into the past: completion or non-completion. For instance, we may have half completed a task and be aware of this, but do not know how to finish it. Often the dream images that appear can show us how to do this. Conversely, if in a dream we have only **partially completed a task** and are left feeling dissatisfied with what has happened, we perhaps need to consider in waking life what needs to be done to enable us to complete the action in the dream. What would we have done had we been able to complete it?

② **To have only half of what we feel we should have** – for instance in quantity – perhaps only to have half of the food or drink we had expected, indicates that we are possibly selling ourselves short. We are not allowing ourselves to have what we need. To dream of being **halfway up a hill or a mountain or halfway down a river** would indicate that there is some indecision. We are not as motivated as we should, or could, be to continue with the task we have in hand. We have made an initial effort but greater effort is needed in order to be where we want to be. This type of dream is very often to do with either motivating ourselves or others. To continually dream of **slipping back**, until we are only halfway through our task, to be repeating it over and over again, would indicate that we do not have the ability to complete it. There is perhaps an extra skill that we need to enable us to achieve success.

③ A degree of spiritual indecision is also indicated here. We should consider where we want to be spiritually and how we can get there.

Hallucinations

① When dreaming, there is an hallucinatory quality about everything that we see. We usually accept what we experience as real and in the actual dream state do not question. Scenes can change as quickly as the blink of an eye, faces can change, we can be looking at one thing then a few seconds later realise we are looking at something completely different. This is totally acceptable within the dream reality. It is only when we consider the dream afterwards that we realise how odd this may be. During dreams, things can take on qualities of other objects and of other feelings. Dreams can create a reality of their own, they do the unexpected – which in normal waking life would be totally illogical and surreal. Within this dream world we need to take a note of what is happening. We do not watch these with amusement, it seems simply that we observe what is going on. Even our own actions can take on an oddness. We may be doing things in a dream which in waking life we would never expect ourselves to do. Freed from the logical quality that mentors our ordinary everyday life, we can be liberated to create a totally different awareness of our own abilities, of our thought patterns and even our own past. We can often dream that we have done things in the past which we have never done, or we can prepare ourselves to do things in the future which again we would never expect to do.

② Psychologically freeing the mind so it can 'roam' under its own speed allows hidden memories, images and thoughts to surface in such a way that we can handle the input when perhaps in real life we may not have been able to do so. We create a reality which suits an action, rather than creating an action which suits the reality. For instance, an abused child may displace the activity into some kind of response that would be acceptable, not allowing the reality of the abuse to come through until such times as he or she was able to come to terms with it.

③ The hallucination-type images that we sometimes experience in dreams can also be direct messages from the unconscious.

Halo
– see Religious Iconology

Halter

① The halter shares the symbolism of bonds, since under normal circumstances it often controls the head. We are dreaming about reigning back on the intellect, instead of allowing the creative energy to flow freely. We are not allowing ourselves the freedom to create to the best of our ability. It usually represents restriction of one form or another, although interestingly enough it may indicate acceptable restriction.

② When we are moving into new areas of growth we sometimes need to be shown the way, and the halter is a symbol of this leading forward into new creativity. We are, as it were, being taken by the head and shown what we need to see.

③ We may be also experiencing some spiritual restraint. If so, we should take time to look at what we want most spiritually.

Ham
– see Food

Hammer

① Dreaming of hammers or blunt instruments highlights the more aggressive and masculine side of our nature. There may be the feeling that there is an aspect of our personality which needs to be crushed or struck for us to be able to function properly.

② Whilst assertiveness may be necessary, often it is the targeted, judicious use of force which will achieve results. In dreams the hammer represents such force.

③ The hammer also has a double-sided symbolism – these are justice and vengeance. Spiritually we need to achieve a balance between the two before passing judgement on others.

Hand
– see Body

Handcuffs

① Dreaming of **being in handcuffs** denotes that we have been restrained in some way, often by an authority figure.

② If we are **putting handcuffs on someone**, we may be attempting to bind that person to us. We may be being overly possessive.

③ Handcuffs are a binding symbol and spiritually would suggest that we are being hampered, probably by our own doubts and fears.

Hanging
– also see Noose and Rope

① Hanging is a violent act against a person, therefore if we are **present at a hanging** we are being party to violence and perhaps need to reconsider our actions. If **we ourselves are being hanged**, we are being warned of some difficulty ahead.

② If we are conscious in our dream of **something hanging up**, there may be word association, in that literally there is a 'hang up' in our lives. If something is **hanging over us**, then we are being threatened by circumstances around us.

③ Spiritual suppression could be at work here. Our ability to communicate may be being hampered.

Harbour
– see Pier

Hare
– see Animals

Harem

① **For a man to dream that he is in a harem** shows that he is struggling to come to terms with the complexities of the feminine nature. **For a woman to have the same dream** shows that she is understanding her own flamboyant and sensual nature. On a different level, she is recognising her need to belong to a group of women – a sisterhood.

② Any group of women appearing in dreams will signify femininity in one form or another. It will depend on whether we relate to a particular person in the scenario for a deeper interpretation.

③ The Great Mother *(See Great Mother/Mother Earth)* in her more playful aspects.

Harness

① Like the halter, the harness indicates some form of control or restraint. It may be that we are actually being restrained by our own limitations, or that we are being controlled by external circumstances. To be **wearing a harness** often takes us back to periods in childhood when we were not allowed the freedom we would have liked.

② Harnessing energy is an important way of using power that we have. To **harness something** is to make it usable in a controlled fashion, so in dreams to be aware of this type of control implies the restraint that is necessary to enable the correct things to happen.

③ Spiritually, we need to harness energy. This means using what we have available in the most efficient way possible. When we have done this, we are then able to control the wilder side of our personality.

Hat
– see Clothes

Harp

① The harp as a musical instrument indicates the correct vibration that we need in order to create harmony within our lives. We ourselves are very much in control of this and since the harp is also a national symbol of music, rhythm and harmony we often link back to our own basic selves.

② To **harp on about something** in a dream – that is, to keep repeating what is going on – is to recognise the need for acknowledgement perhaps in some activity we are undertaking.

③ The ladder to the next world, represented by the harp, is an image which can be used both in dreams and meditation.

Harvest

① To be dreaming about a harvest indicates that we are going to reap the rewards of previous care we have taken. We can create a store for ourselves by, for instance, doing good and then achieving some kind of reward later on. We are able to work hard, and in working hard we take care of the future. So, to dream of a harvest can actually have two meanings. In can mean looking back into the past and reaping the rewards, or it can mean looking towards the future in order to use what has happened previously. The other circumstances in the dream will indicate which interpretation needs to be used.

② To be **taking part in a harvest or perhaps a harvest festival**, indicates that we are celebrating our own life energy – that energy we have available to us – to be used in achieving those dividends we feel are ours by right.

③ Any kind of a harvest represents spiritual fruitfulness and fertility.

Haunt
– see Ghost

Hay
– also see Harvest

① In previous times, for many the hayfield represented fun, relaxation and irresponsibility. Nowadays it is more likely to represent irritation – as in hay fever – and an unknown quality. To dream of hay is probably to be looking at a practical aspect within ourselves. It may be the ability to provide shelter and sustenance for others.

② Happy memories and good feelings may be represented in dreams by stereotyped romantic scenarios where those feelings need to be reproduced.

③ As we progress spiritually, images of summer – such as haymaking and haystacks – and the warmth it generates are likely to appear in our dreams.

Head
– see Body

Hearing/Listening

① While listening and hearing appear to have much the same significance, in dreams they will have slightly different connotations. **Hearing** suggests registering a sound, speech or noise whereas **listening** suggests absorbing the content of what is heard.

② In dreams we may hear something which can only be interpreted later. If we are listening in dreams we are absorbing its importance on more of a subliminal level.

To **be deaf** in a dream suggests that we are deliberately not absorbing the information. If **someone else appears to be deaf** we are not making ourselves clear in some situation in waking life.

③ The faculties of hearing and listening need to be combined, particularly in dreams if we are to reach a full comprehension of our spiritual potential.

Hearse
– also see Death and Funeral

① To dream of a hearse indicates that we are probably recognising that there is a time limit, either on ourselves or on a project we are connected with. Often we need to come to terms with our feelings about death on order to understand ourselves.

② We may be aware that a part of ourselves is no longer 'alive' and it will be better to let it go rather than resurrect it.

③ A hearse, as 'the carriage of death', will always represent death *per se*. However it can also represent the ending of a situation, relationship or even perhaps the conscious letting go of a much loved concept or way of belief.

Heart
– see Body

Hearth

① To dream of a hearth or fireplace is to recognise the need for security. This may be of two different types. One is knowing that the home, our central place of existence, is secure. The other is recognising the security of the inner self, the interior feminine which gives warmth and stability.

② We may be, or need to be, linking with our passionate wilder nature – the seat of our passions, the Fire within. The hearth is still seen by many as the centre of the home.

③ The Anima, and that part of ourselves which is the feminine spirit, can be symbolised by the hearth.

Heaven/Hell
– also see Devil/Demon, Fiend and Religious Iconology

① The dichotomy between Heaven and Hell highlights the polarity between Good and Evil or positive and negative. In dreams, as well as in waking life, we often try to achieve a balance between these two aspects. It will depend to a certain extent on our own personal perception of Heaven and Hell as to how we achieve a new equilibrium.

② Heaven as a state of bliss and Hell as a state of illusion are two states of being which can give rise to a great deal of emotional confusion. They can symbolise happiness and/or depression and may appear in dreams before we recognise such conditions in waking life.

③ The state of heavenly bliss is something to be aspired to in our individual journey towards spirituality. It brings with it joy, peace and tranquillity and a sense of belonging to a Greater Whole. It is often experienced in dreams before we are able to capture the concept in everyday life. By contrast, the concept of Hell, complete with demons, fear and negativity, tends to be more recognisable. When such images appear in dreams we need to have the courage to face our own illusions.

Hedgehog
– see Animals

Heel
– see Body

Heir
– see Inherit/Inheritance

Hell
– see Heaven/Hell and Religious Iconology

Helmet

① In dreams, it will depend on whether the helmet is **being worn by someone else** or by us. If the former, it may have the same symbolism as the mask (see Mask) in that it prevents the wearer being seen. If the latter, then it is a symbol of protection and preservation.

② In olden times, the helmet was the attribute of the warrior or hero. Even today – as with the motorcycle helmet – it is still largely a representation of the masculine.

③ Protection by the Spiritual Self against disaster. The slings and arrows of Fate.

Hen
– see Birds

Hermaphrodite/Hermaphrodism
– also see Sex

① When we dream of a hermaphrodite, we may be having uncertainties about our own gender, or about our ability to adjust to the roles played by our own sex. Interestingly, as we learn more about ourselves, we attempt to achieve a balance between the logical and the sensitive sides of our nature. This can appear as hermaphrodism in a dream.

② As a child grows, he begins to understand that certain behaviour is appropriate or acceptable. This may mean that other natural reactions are suppressed and can surface later on. These may confuse us and be perceived in dreams as hermaphrodism.

③ Spiritually this signifies a perfect balance between the masculine and the feminine – drive and intuition.

Hermit
– also see Occupations

① There is a kind of loneliness within many people which prevents us from making relationships on a one-to-one basis. This may manifest in dreams as the figure of the hermit.

② There are two types of hermit. One withdraws from life in order to live an entirely spiritual existence and knows that others will care for his bodily needs. The other travels throughout the world using his knowledge and expertise to help others. In dreams if **we meet the hermit**, we are discovering the dimension in ourselves which has a spiritual awareness.

③ A holy man, or the Wise Old Man *(see Wise Old Man)* will often appear in dreams as the hermit.

Hero/Heroine
– see People

Hex/Curse

① In magical terms, a hex is a spell usually with malign intent, so dreams can interpret some kind of threat in our working life as a hex. Such a threat can prevent us from progressing in the way we should.

② In its original meaning casting a hex was to be performing witchcraft, so in the dreams of someone without magical knowledge it suggests obtaining an unfair advantage. When there is some magical knowledge it will suggest the use of innate powers in order to succeed. A curse will have the same negative meaning as a hex.

③ In simpler times a hex suggested calling on the power of evil to achieve a negative result. As we accrue more knowledge we become aware that there is inevitably some kind of backlash to such an action.

Hexagram
– also see Shapes/Patterns

① Technically, the hexagram is a figure of six lines and represents the union of two forces, the Yin (feminine) and the Yang (masculine). For this to appear in a dream represents the principle of 'as above, so below'.

② When we attempt to reconcile two forces – the spiritual and the physical – we may experience that union in the form of patterns, one significant group of which are hexagrams.

③ Union of the spiritual and physical worlds is represented by the hexagram.

High
– see Position

Hijack

① Any act of violence in dreams such as hijacking can highlight our perception of the violation of our own personal code. While no physical violence may be apparent in waking life it is the feeling it evokes in us which results in such dreams. Our ideas concepts and principles can often be hijacked.

② Hijacking is, technically, stealing by forcing a vehicle to stop. When a relationship or project fails through someone else's interference and prevents our progress we will feel threatened and violated; hence our dreams will reflect this with images of being hijacked.

③ In spiritual development we can frequently find that our progress is halted by misunderstanding and misapprehensions. There is thus a sense of feeling hijacked or exploited.

Hill
– also see Mound

① To be **on top of a hill** – and therefore high up – indicates we are aware of our own expanded vision. We have made an effort to achieve something and are able to survey the results of what we have done, to assess the effect on our environment and the people around us. We have achieved those things that we previously thought impossible, and are able to undertake further work in the light of knowledge we have attained.

② To be **climbing a hill in the company of others** often indicates that we have a common goal, that a journey we possibly thought was ours alone, is actually connected with other people. We can use their knowledge and comradeship to take us to the heights of our being. To dream that we are **going downhill** would indicate we are feeling as if circumstances are pushing us in a certain direction. We may be moving from a level of attainment and now feel that – with relaxation of effort – we are not so much in control of our own abilities.

③ Effort is needed in order to achieve the clarity necessary for us to continue to progress spiritually.

Historic

– also see Old/Ancient/Antique

① To have a dream which is set in a particular period in history – such as in the Elizabethan or Victorian times – is to link with our past feelings and with that part of ourselves which has passed into history. It links with the person we were at some previous time in our lives and perhaps also with outdated beliefs and ways of living.

② The human being continually assesses both their, and the historic, past. History is perhaps an objective assessment of a subjective way of being. Sometimes to dream in this way is to dream of the person we might have been.

③ Old beliefs and life patterns need to be considered in the light of present knowledge.

Hive

① The hive usually represents an area of work where there is considerable industry and activity going on, and where the best use is made of all possible resources. To dream of **being near a hive** can represent the effort that is needed to be made to create fertility – or fertile situations – for ourselves. The hive can also represent protective motherhood.

② The old belief that one told one's sorrows to the bees *(see Bee)* still manifests in dreams. The hive may represent the activity that is needed to get ourselves out of a situation.

③ The feminine power in Nature is represented by the hive. The symbol of a hollow vessel holding nurture or sustenance links with Mother Earth *(See Great Mother/Mother Earth)*.

Hole

① A hole usually represents a difficult or tricky situation. It can also be a place in which we may hide, or feel protected in. To dream of **falling into a hole** indicates that we are perhaps getting in touch with our unconscious feelings, urges and fears. To **walk round a hole** suggests we may need to get round a tricky situation. We may also need to become aware of the other parts of ourselves that are buried beneath our surface awareness.

② A hole can very often represent the feminine and the emptiness one feels as one moves towards an understanding of the Self *(see Self)*. **A hole in the roof of any sacred building**, or any hole which allows steam or smoke to escape, is the opening upwards to the celestial world and is the door or gateway to other dimensions. It is interesting that, as central heating and living in flats becomes more commonplace, we feel more and more enclosed without recourse to that spiritual awareness.

③ A round hole represents the Heavens, a square hole represents the Earth.

Holiday

① To be on holiday in a dream indicates a sense of relaxation and of satisfying one's own needs without having to take care of others.

② Our need to be independent and to be responsible often comes across in dreams as a holiday. Quite literally, the word means holy-day – a day set apart and we may need to heed the warning that we need time off to create space for ourselves.

③ Spiritual replenishment, rest and relaxation are all part of a holiday.

Hollow

① Dreaming of **feeling hollow** connects with our feelings of emptiness, lack of purpose and inability to find a direction in our lives. To dream of **being in a hollow** would indicate that we need some kind of protection from what is going on around us in our ordinary everyday life.

② Hollowness can come across in a dream in several ways. We can be conscious of our being hollow inside – for instance, 'it felt as though I had hollow legs', or that we are in a hollow state – a state similar to the Void *(see Abyss)*. We are in a position where nothing is happening, where we do not feel in control and need to take control of the space we have been given.

③ A feeling of hollowness can indicate a lack of motivation, particularly on our spiritual journey.

Holy Communion
– see Religious Iconology

Holy Grail
– also see Chalice

① The Holy Grail is such a basic image that in dreams it can appear as something miraculous, something which fulfils our wish and allows us to move forward into our full potential. The grail appearing in a dream would indicate that we can expect some form of satisfaction and change to occur within our lives.

② We are searching for something which we may feel at this particular moment is unattainable, but that by putting ourselves through various tests we may eventually achieve.

③ The Holy Spirit. Mythologically it is the plate or cup used in the Last Supper and is a perpetual source of spiritual nourishment. Often it represents the achievement of spiritual success, but can also represent the cup of happiness.

Home/Homeless

① The human being has certain basic needs such as shelter, warmth and nourishment. The home, and particularly the parental home, can stand for all of these things. To dream of **being at home** signifies a return to the basic standards we learnt as a child.

② Psychologically we all need to integrate our own primary personality traits with learnt behaviour. Dreaming of a safe environment – such as home – allows us to do this. To dream of being homeless means we have lost our point of reference.

③ Sanctuary, that is a place where we can be ourselves without fear of reprisal, is contained in this image. Spiritualists speak of 'going home' when they are approaching death since the physical state is a temporary one. Spiritually, being homeless strikes at our basic security; our system of belief and sense of belonging is compromised.

Honey
– also see Bee

① Honey almost inevitably represents pleasure and sweetness. To dream of honey – and particularly **eating it** – can be to recognise that we are needing to give ourselves pleasure. Equally, it can indicate the essence of our feelings, that we have been through some kind of joyful experience which can now be assimilated as part of ourselves.

② Honey is said to impart fertility and virility. Dreaming of honey would indicate that we are entering a much more actively sexual or fertile time.

③ Immortality and rebirth are two symbols which belong to honey. As a healing substance it has the power to regenerate. It has obvious connotations of plenty, as in 'The Land of Milk and Honey'.

Hood

① A figure wearing a hood in a dream will always appear to be slightly menacing. While not necessarily being evil, there may be a part of us which has been threatened. The hood can also represent part of ourselves which, if we have withdrawn, we are creating a problem. An aspect of our personality may be invisible to us and need to be uncovered in order for us to function in an acceptable fashion.

② Traditionally, **for a woman to be wearing a hood** suggests that she is being deceitful. If a **man is wearing a hood**, it suggests that he is withdrawing from a situation. Equally, in its more advanced sense, the hooded figure of a monk can indicate the more reflective side of us as it begins to become more evident in our everyday lives.

③ Death and invisibility were formerly represented by the hood. It now indicates that certain aspects of knowledge are hidden until the time is right.

Hook

① When we dream of a hook we are are generally understanding that we have the ability to draw things towards us that are either good or bad. It can equally indicate that we are being hooked by someone, and thus not being allowed the freedom to which we feel we have a right.

② In childhood dreams the hook can represent the hold that a parent or authority figure has over us. This symbolism can continue into adulthood, depicting the way that we allow people to take control within our lives.

③ We need to be clear not to get 'hooked' into religious beliefs and practices just for the sake of it.

Horizon

① A dream in which the horizon is significant highlights a change between two states, for instance happiness and sadness, employment and unemployment and so on. Since in theory we do not know what lies beyond the horizon we should perhaps consider what action is necessary to take us forward into unknown territory.

② In many ways, the horizon can represent the boundary of our known world as we understand it. Psychologically we know that we will never actually reach that boundary, yet we must overcome our fears before being able maximise our potential.

③ In understanding that spiritually most boundaries are self imposed, the horizon in dreams is a symbol of how – by having courage – we can widen our perceptions.

Horns
– also see Antlers

① Horns appearing in dreams hark back to the idea of the animal in the human. The god Pan, who represents sexuality as well as life force, wore horns. A horn also represents the penis and masculinity. Because it is penetrative, it can also signify the desire to hurt. Protectiveness is also a quality of horns since the male animal will use his horns to protect his territory. A **musical or hunting horn** suggests a summoning or a warning in dreams.

② Horns in a dream suggest superiority, either earned or conferred. It is interesting that horns are supposed to bestow the powers of the animal on the wearer. In Pagan times, as well as some tribes today, the donning of horns signify a particular senior position within the tribe. In Chinese medicine, **rhinoceros horn** is reputed to be an aphrodisiac. This is possibly because of its association with masculine power.

③ In a spiritual sense, because horns are associated with the head, they represent intellectual as well as supernatural power. Because they rise above the head, they also symbolise Divinity and the power of the soul.

Horse
– see Animals

Horseshoe

① The horseshoe is always taken as a lucky symbol and, traditionally, if it is **turned upwards** it represents the moon and protection from all aspects of evil. When **turned downwards** the power is reputed to 'drain out' and therefore be unlucky. The horseshoe is also connected as a lucky symbol to weddings. Customarily to dream of a horseshoe may indicate that there will shortly be a wedding in your family or peer group.

② In ordinary everyday life, symbols which have a long history become fixed in, and used by, our unconscious – often to represent other happier times or times when there has been more happening.

③ Spiritually, we can link the horseshoe with a talisman or amulet which protects us and our personal space.

Hospital
– also see Operation

① Depending on our attitude to hospitals, when one appears in a dream it can either represent a place of safety, or a place where one's very being is threatened and we become vulnerable. Taken as a **place of healing**, it represents that aspect within ourselves that knows when respite from troubles is necessary – when we can allow ourselves to be cared for and nurtured and put back into one piece. If we find **hospitals threatening**, it may be that we are conscious that we have to 'let go', to put ourselves at the mercy of others in order that a situation can be improved.

② Dreaming of **being in a hospital** may be mentally creating a transition period between something that has not gone well, and an improved attitude where things can get better. To be **visiting someone in hospital** indicates that we are aware that a part of ourselves is perhaps not well, is 'dis-eased' and needs to be attended to in order to give us clarity.

③ A healing environment where things can be brought into a state of balance is signified by a hospital.

Hostility
– also see Emotions

① When we experience **hostility within ourselves** in a dream, it is the direct expression of that feeling. It is safe to express it in a dream whereas we may not dare do this in waking life. If however, someone is being **hostile towards us**, it very often means that we need to be aware that we are not acting appropriately, that others may feel we are putting them in danger.

② Hostility is one of those emotions that can be worked through in a dream. If we can identify what is making us feel hostile in a dream, then we can usually draw a parallel in our waking lives and deal with whatever the problem is. If we can identify the feeling as being appropriate in a particular situation, then we can deal with the feeling.

③ Spiritual opposition – or rather opposition to our spiritual beliefs – can generate a tremendous amount of hostility. We need to be aware that others may not necessarily agree with our spiritual beliefs.

Hot
– also see Warmth

① Pleasurable feelings can be translated in dreams to a physical feeling. To dream of **being hot** indicates warm – or perhaps passionate – feelings. To be conscious of the fact that our **surroundings are hot** indicates that we are loved and cared for.

② Occasionally, extreme emotion can be interpreted as a physical feeling – so anger, jealousy or other such feelings can be experienced as heat. Experiencing **something as hot which should be cold** – e.g. ice – indicates that we are perhaps having difficulty and experiencing some confusion in sorting out our feelings.

③ Spiritual passion is a deeply held feeling. It can be experienced in a dream as heat.

Hotel
– also see Hotel in Buildings

① Dreaming of being in a hotel can mean that we need to escape from a situation in our lives for a short time. Conversely, it can also mean that a situation we are in will only last for a limited amount of time.

② To dream of **being a guest in a hotel** can indicate that we are unsettled and feel we can only settle down temporarily. Being forced into a position of **living in a hotel** signifies a basic restlessness in our character; we may be attempting to escape from ourselves.

③ Temporary sanctuary, or the need for a safe environment, is depicted by a hotel.

Hourglass
– also see Time

① In dreams, time is irrelevant. Dreaming of something which measures time often alerts us to the need for us to measure our thoughts and activities. When such a symbol is old fashioned – as in an hourglass – it is our perception of time and its management which may be old fashioned. It is showing us that we need to learn to use alternative, and more precise, ways of measuring those activities.

② When we are particularly under stress we can be overly aware of the running out of time, that it can become an enemy. This is often symbolised as an hourglass.

③ In former times, the hourglass was frequently taken as a symbol of death. More properly it is now seen as a symbol for the Passage of Life.

House

– also see Buildings

① A house nearly always refers to the soul, and in mundane terms the way that we build our lives from the basic material of our experiences. The external appearance of a house in dreams will offer clues as to how we present ourselves to the rest of the world.

② Rooms in a dream can describe various parts of our personalities or levels of understanding, but can also signify either the womb or the mother figure. The different rooms and parts of houses in dreams indicate the diverse aspects of our personality and experience. For example:

Attic Dreaming of being in an attic is to do with past experiences and old memories. Interestingly, it also can highlight family patterns of behaviour and attitudes which have been handed down. *Basement/cellar* The cellar most often represents the subconscious and those things we may have suppressed through our inability to handle them. A basement can also highlight the power and passion that is available to us in waking life provided we are willing to access, and make use of, it. Additionally, we may not have come to terms with our own sexuality and prefer to keep it hidden. The basement can also represent long-held family beliefs and habits, particularly those that we have internalised without realising. *Bathroom* In dreams our attitude to personal cleanliness and our most private thoughts and actions can be shown as the bathroom or toilet. It being a space where we get rid of unwanted material, the bathroom may also suggest a cleansing away of negativity. *Bedroom* The bedroom portrays a place of safety where we can relax and be as sensual as we wish. As a place of rest and relaxation, we are able to let go of everyday concerns and perhaps return to an inner state of peace. In a dream where both the bathroom and bedroom are portrayed we are preparing to deal with those aspects of our lives which need both privacy and contemplation. *Hall* The hallway in a dream is representative of how we meet and relate to other people. It is also indicative of how we make the transition from the private to the public self and vice versa. A hallway also has the same meaning as any passage. *Kitchen (also see individual entry)* Being the 'heart' of the house, the kitchen is often the place where the family comes together. In dreams, it therefore represents the more complete self – the part from which we nurture and care for others. Finding a hidden cupboard in our dream kitchen suggests finding a particular part of ourselves of which we have not been aware up until now. Having a chaotic kitchen indicates a need to create order, whereas an especially overtidy and clean kitchen suggests an overcontrolling personality. *Library (also see individual entry)* During our lives we take in a great deal of information. Finding ourselves in a library in dreams can suggest that we need to make use of that information or, more spiritually, that we need to access what is known as the Collective Unconscious. *Lounge/Sitting Room/Parlour* would suggest our more relaxed comfortable side which seeks ease and comfort. Such a room may also suggest the 'off duty' fun side of life.

③ A house represents security and safety, and therefore signifies protection and the Great Mother *(see Great Mother/Mother Earth)*. The house is popularly known as the seat of the soul, a safe space, and in spiritual terms is an expression of the way we are in the world.

Hunger
– also see Food

① Experiencing hunger in a dream indicates that our physical, emotional or mental needs are not being properly satisfied. It is also possible that the dreamer is actually hungry, and this is being recognised in the dream.

② Every human being has needs which require satisfaction. While that lack of satisfaction may not be acknowledged in the waking state, it can be translated into dream symbolism and become hunger.

③ Seeking Spiritual satisfaction and fulfilling a need is one aspect of hunger.

Hunt/Huntsman
– also see Occupations

① Dreaming of **being hunted** is frequently taken to be to do with one's sexuality. Its even older meaning is linked with death, particularly a death containing an aspect of ritual killing or sacrifice. By association therefore, to dream of a hunt is to register the necessity for a change of state in everyday life.

② To dream of **being a huntsman** alerts us to the part of ourselves which can be destructive and cruel. We should consider whether such behaviour is appropriate.

③ Death and destruction, but in a ritualised setting is part of the spiritual journey. Interestingly, hounds seen in a dream can represent the rounding up of aspects of life we wish to eradicate.

Hurdle
– also see Barrier/Barricade and Running

① Much the same as any barrier, a hurdle will signify a difficulty to be overcome.

However, by tradition, hurdles are temporary constructions, so the difficulty may only be shortlived. A hurdle race is a potent image of the struggle for promotion at work.

② When we continually create emotional difficulties for ourselves in waking life we may come to realise, through dreams about hurdles or a hurdle race, that we can train ourselves to overcome such difficulties. To be fashioning a hurdle – an intricate way of weaving – suggests that we are creating our own problems.

③ As hurdles are man-made constructs, this would suggest that our blocks to spiritual progress belong to the material world rather than the spiritual or more esoteric.

Hurricane
– also see Gale and Wind

① When we experience a hurricane in a dream, we are sensing the force of an element in our lives which is beyond our control. We may feel we are being swept along by circumstances – or possibly someone's passion – and are powerless to resist.

② A hurricane can represent the power of our own passion, or passionate belief, which picks us up and carries us along. We may not know how to handle the results of that passion, and feel it could be disastrous for others.

③ The intensity of our spiritual belief is depicted here – dependent on the other circumstances in the dream.

Husband
– see Family

Hyena
– see Animals

Ibis
– see Birds

Ice/Iceberg

① When we dream of ice we are usually looking at the emotions. We are aware that perhaps we are colder than we should be, shutting of any display of warmth and compassion. We are thereby enclosing ourselves in a situation from which it may be difficult to free ourselves. As a slow moving heavy mass, a glacier will signify an inexorable movement towards potential disaster or difficulty.

② Ice is also a representation of rigidity, of the brittleness that comes from not understanding what is going on around us, of creating circumstances where people cannot get – or be – in touch with us. Depending on how the ice appears in a dream, it can indicate a state of impermanence. If a glacier or large body of ice such as an iceberg is melting, it will suggest that a new sensation or emotion is changing the status quo for us. There may or may not be an element of danger associated with this.

③ Spiritually, ice symbolises a part of ourselves which has become frozen and needs to thaw out before we can progress. A glacier or an iceberg might well be considered a force of nature.

Ice-cream

① Ice-cream appearing in a dream is a great deal to do with the sensual tastes that one has. Under normal circumstances it is a pleasurable experience and very often reminds us of childhood and happier times. To be **eating ice-cream** indicates that we may be accepting pleasure into our lives in a way that we have not been able to do before. To be **giving other people ice-cream** indicates that we are giving other people pleasure.

② Ice-cream can also depict the state of mind where one has reached conclusions that nothing is permanent – that the pleasure we have can melt away.

③ Ice cream is an image which can be used to signify impermanence, particularly insofar as pleasure is concerned. We need to decide if we wish to go for transitory pleasures or permanence.

Icicles

① Often in dreams icicles can appear to hang in a certain fashion – it is the pattern that is important as much as the icicle itself. We may be aware that we are having problems with our environment and that it is not supporting it in a way we would expect – thereby creating difficulties.

② To see **icicles melting** indicates that the troubles that have been around us will literally disappear within a short space of time. Whether the fault is our own or other people's, it would appear that outside circumstances give the ability to overcome whatever has been troubling us.

③ Spiritual isolation – that is, existing in isolation because of the way our lives have gone – can be symbolised by icicles.

Icon
– also see Religious Iconology

① Dreaming of any religious symbol usually indicates our very deep connection with old ideas and principles. The icon usually symbolises the microcosm within the macrocosm – that is, the small world reflecting the larger world. The human being often needs something tangible to represent what is simply a principle or a concept, and the icon performs this purpose.

② Usually, icons are representations of a belief system and therefore portray the way we feel about a number of other issues. In a dream, when an icon appears to have a religious picture but in actual fact it contains pictures of ones own family, it indicates the ability to idolise the family. When an icon seems to contain a well-known person or personality we are creating an ideal picture – someone who can be revered. In computer parlance, an icon is a small representation of a larger, and can have this meaning in dreams.

③ The icon is a small spiritual picture which symbolises a greater whole. In today's technological, more secular, society the computer icon will have the same significance.

Identify/Identification/Identity

① As we mature, our identity and how we identify ourselves assumes a considerable degree of importance. In times of stress our dreams will reflect these concerns, perhaps resulting in dreams about **losing identity tags or cards** or having to **carry identification papers**.

② Our sense of self or identity is one of our most important possessions. From this basis we can identify our best talents and qualities: dreams will often help us to clarify these. While certain types of identity cards are a bone of contention in waking life, others gain us entry into special places or areas. It is this aspect of exclusivity that is likely to surface in dreams confirming our feelings about ourselves.

③ As we embark on our own individual spiritual journey, some form of inner identification is necessary ('I am this... not that') so that we can progress with honesty and integrity. Identifying the best as opposed to the worst, or right from wrong, often begins on an inner level and surfaces in dreams before such a strong identity is consciously recognised.

Igloo
– also see Buildings

① The igloo is interesting as a symbol in dreams. It can equally represent a cold exterior containing a very warm interior, or the coldness of the construction itself. It can appear as though someone is uncaring and therefore creating an unloving home environment, although in fact there is warmth within that person.

② The igloo can often represent the feminine and the womb. Sometimes it represents frigidity, but at other times the ability of a woman to relax and be herself once her barriers have been overcome.

③ The Feminine Principle, in the sense of sheltering and nurturing, is depicted in the igloo.

Illness
– also see Sick

① Whatever life has to offer, we may be left with painful memories, feelings of anger and difficulties. In a dream these memories and feelings can surface as illness. Sometimes such a dream can foretell real illness, but most of the time it represents the way we deal with things. It means that we are not putting ourselves in touch with a force that can help us to overcome difficulties.

② Often when we are ill in a dream we are grappling with part of our personality. Rather than the whole being ill, part of us is sick and perhaps needs to be dealt with. Often the dream will give the method of dealing with it – perhaps by taking medication, having surgery or a combination of both. It also often represents our fears of not being looked after properly.

③ Lack of spiritual clarity can often be experienced in dreams as illness.

Imitation

① To dream of **being imitated** is ambivalent. It can mean that we are aware that whatever we have done is the correct thing to do and that other people can learn from our example. It can equally mean that other people are seeing us as being leaders, when we ourselves do not necessarily feel that it is the correct role for us.

② If we are **imitating someone else**, we are usually conscious of the fact that we have the ability to be as they are. To be **imitating one's superiors** is to recognise their greater knowledge. However, to be imitating someone in negative action – **mimicking** – may show that we doubt our own integrity and need to look at whether we are happy with our own actions.

③ The microcosm of the macrocosm, the small imitating the large.

Immersion
– also see Baptism and Water

① To dream of being **totally immersed** in water generally indicates the way in which we handle our own emotions, that we are attempting to find the more innocent part of ourselves which does not need to be affected by external circumstances. We are attempting to clarify situations and to cleanse ourselves, perhaps of ideas and attitudes that have been suggested to us by other people.

② To be totally immersed – **totally focused** – on something in a dream indicates we need to be able to concentrate entirely on one particular thought or idea to help us understand ourselves.

③ Transformation and rebirth can only be accomplished by a total immersion in spirituality. This is symbolised by baptism and the cleansing away of the past.

Immobility
– also see Paralysis

① Immobility in a dream can be extremely frightening. This feeling very often occurs as the we are beginning to learn more about ourselves. A feeling of oppression and of not being able to move usually indicates that we need to, quite literally, sit still and be immobile within our ordinary everyday lives. We need to achieve a kind of stillness which is foreign to most people, and therefore initially frightening, while later on it can be a state of peace and tranquillity.

② To be immobilised in a dream usually indicates that we have created circumstances around us which are now beginning to trap us. We need to remain absolutely still until we have decided what the appropriate action needs to be, and then we can move forward in an appropriate way. Often such a dream comes when we are facing the darker side of ourselves – that which could be called evil. A superhuman effort needs to be made to overcome what is holding us down.

③ The Unconditioned State, the Liberated Self. Immobility in this sense is dynamic stillness.

Imp

① An imp appearing in a dream usually foretells disorder and difficulty. The imp often has the same significance as the Devil *(See Devil/Demon)* in its aspect of tormenting one, of creating difficulty and harm within one's life.

② The imp can represent the uncontrolled negative part of ourselves, that part that instinctively creates chaos and takes great joy in doing so. It is perhaps an aspect of loss of control.

③ The Devil as the Tempter can appear in dreams as an imp, or as a manifestation of a particularly irritating type.

Imprisoned
– also see Prison

① Being imprisoned in a dream usually means that we are being trapped by circumstances, often those we have created through our own fear or ignorance. We feel that other people are creating situations which will not allow us to move forward without difficulty. We will often need to negotiate our freedom.

② Imprisonment in a dream shows we are becoming conscious of old attitudes and beliefs which are imprisoning us and preventing us from moving forward.

③ Spiritual imprisonment can suggest that we are too introverted or self involved. We need to 'open ourselves up' to new influences. We may need assistance in doing this – and have to look to an outside influence to release us.

Inauguration

① We have many opportunities to make new beginnings, and inauguration – in that it indicates a change of status – is one such symbol. This may be important to us in terms of either personal growth or within the work situation. To dream that we are being given such an honour means we can receive public acclaim for something that we have done, for our ability to make the transition from the lesser to the greater.

② Often a ceremony is necessary to mark the fact that we have succeeded in one thing and can now move on, putting that knowledge to the test in the outside world. To be dreaming of such a ceremony indicates that we can be pleased with ourselves and what we have achieved, that we have literally inaugurated a different way of being, and can now move forward into the future.

③ A ceremony in a spiritual sense can mark a new beginning. In this case it marks the taking of new spirituality, perhaps Cosmic Responsibility.

Incense
– also see Religious Iconology

① Physically incense is designed to perfume a room. In dreams, it is possible to be aware of the smell of incense, particularly if it has associations for us. For instance, it might hold some childhood memories of church or religious buildings.

② Incense is used in order to raise consciousness or to cleanse atmospheres and sacred spaces. In dreams, when we become aware of it being used in this way, it shows we need to consider how best to improve ourselves or the environment around us.

③ Spiritually incense is used as a vehicle for prayer and as a symbol for the subtle body or soul. In dreams we can become aware of our need to use spiritual symbolism in our work.

Income
– also see Finance, Money and Poverty

① The income we earn is an important part of our support structure, so any dream connected with this will tend to signify our attitude towards our wants and needs. In times of difficulty we have to learn how to tailor our needs to available resources and to make better use of those resources. To dream of an **increased income** shows we feel we have overcome an obstacle in ourselves and can accept that we have value in the world. A **drop in income** signifies our neediness, and perhaps our attitude to poverty.

② In trying to look after ourselves we are aware of what people have to offer us, and also, what we have to do in order to be rewarded for our efforts. Dreaming of receiving a private income – such as **a trust fund** – suggests we perhaps need to look at our relationships with other people.

③ The giving of alms is the belief that what one has one shares, and is a meaningful part of income. It is not important whether this is in the material sense, or in the giving of time and effort.

Indigestion

① To be **suffering from indigestion** in a dream shows that there is something in our lives which is not being tolerated very well. Equally, it may indicate that we are actually suffering from indigestion, and this is recognised in the dream state. There is a belief that certain foods can trigger off lurid dreams.

② If **something is indigestible** in a dream, it may be that we recognise that we have some sort of mental block on our own progress. Perhaps we need to do things in a different way, or perhaps in smaller steps. We need to assimilate information before we move onto something else.

③ Spiritual knowledge that has not been properly assimilated can be represented by indigestion in a dream. Recurring dreams are a type of spiritual indigestion which will re-occur until such times as we have understanding.

Induction

① An induction process introduces us to a new set of rules by which we must operate. In dreams such a process will make us aware of the need for change in some area of our waking life. There does need to be an instructor, or someone who knows what they are doing, available to us.

② Dreaming of some form of induction process may suggest that though we are not consciously aware of a lack of expertise – perhaps in understanding what is necessary for us – there is knowledge available for our use.

③ Spiritually, induction may have the same meaning as initiation, an awareness and acceptance of our own abilities.

Infection

① Dreaming of having an infection suggests that there is the possibility of us having internalised negative attitudes from other people. Depending on where in the body the infection appears, there is information as to the type of 'infection'. For example, an **infection in the leg** may indicate that we feel we are being prevented from moving forward quickly enough in waking life.

② When we are made uncomfortable by external circumstances in waking life, this may appear as an infection in a dream.

③ In spiritual development, and particularly when dealing with outside influences, we can become contaminated – or infected – by ideology and spurious beliefs. We need to be aware of the possibility that we can be 'taken over' by wrong thought and negativity.

Inherit/Inheritance

① From a purely practical perspective a dream about an inheritance or legacy will mean precisely that. We are being given a gift of some sort. More symbolically perhaps it signifies all those traits of character and idiosyncrasies we are heir to and must use to our best advantage.

② Being heir to an inheritance in a dream suggests that we are in a position to recognise our responsibilities, whether that is to our families or the wider world.

③ Spiritually the suggestion is that we 'inherit the earth'. It is ours while we live, but must be passed to those who come after us. Our children and our children's children have a right to a sustainable future.

Initiation
– see Religious Iconology

Injection
– also see Syringe and Vaccination/Vaccine

① To dream of **being given an injection** is to be feeling that our personal space has been penetrated. Other people's opinions, needs or desires may be forced on us leaving us little option but to co-operate. To dream of **giving an injection** suggests that we are attempting to force ourselves on other people. Obviously, this may have sexual connotations.

② An injection may be an attempt to heal, or to make one better. We may feel that we need external help in order to function more successfully. It will depend on our attitude to conventional medicine whether this is seen as co-operation or resistance.

③ Spiritually, to find ourselves accepting an injection indicates that we are prepared to create circumstances within ourselves which will help us to progress. More negatively, an injection can indicate short term pleasure rather than long term gain.

Insects

① Insects in dreams can reflect the feeling that something is irritating or bugging us. It may also indicate our feeling of insignificance and powerlessness. It will depend on the particular insect in the dream as to the interpretation. Thus, a **wasp** might indicate danger, whereas a **beetle** could mean either dirt or protection.

② Psychologically, insects can represent feelings we would rather do without. This could be something niggling at our consciences, or guilt. Insects tend to signify negative feelings.

③ Psychically, insects can appear in dreams as some kind of threat. This is one reason why they are often used in psychological thrillers and science fiction. More positively, insects can also appear in dreams as reminders of instinctive behaviour. A swarm might suggest group behaviour.

Inscription

① Any inscription in a dream is information which will need to be understood. **Reading an inscription** can suggest that something is understood already, whereas **not being able to read an inscription** suggests that more information is required in order to complete a task.

② An **inscription appearing on**, for instance, a rock would suggest old knowledge or wisdom. An **inscription appearing in sand** would suggest that the knowledge either is impermanent, or must be learnt quickly.

③ The image of an inscription often appears in dreams as we reach a certain stage of development. Spiritually, this usually indicates the type of knowledge that can be passed onto other people.

Internet
– also see Computer

① The internet is technologically an idea whose time has come, in that there is a necessity for universal communication. It is this image of a world wide network which is most likely to appear in dreams nowadays when there is need to communicate information. It will often depend on our day to day use of the internet as to what particular meaning it has in dreams. It might be a source of information, a dispenser of information or purely a means of communication.

② In learning to communicate with meaning, Man gave himself an advantage over other species. He must thus take responsibility for the standard of communication and develop it to its highest degree. The internet (a web of communication and connectivity) has become a dream symbol for such development, whether personal or communal.

③ As a universal tool the internet makes tangible the ancient idea that our world is surrounded by lines of power. We move from individual to family concerns, then to community, global and cosmic considerations.

Intersection
– also see Crossroads

① An intersection which appears in a dream – such as a **T junction** – indicates there is a choice of two ways forward. Two opposites may be coming together in our waking lives, and we are able to make changes and move forward in a more focused way.

② If we are conscious of an intersection – perhaps in a pattern which appears in a dream – we are being offered choices, and perhaps have to differentiate between right and wrong.

③ When we come across an intersection in dreams, we are having to make choices which may have a greater impact on others than it does for us.

Intestines
– see Abdomen and Excrement in Body

Intoxication
– also see Alcohol, Drunk and Drugs

① When we are intoxicated in a dream it can be important to decide what has caused us to become intoxicated. **Being drunk** can indicate a loss of control, whereas a **change of state brought about by drugs** can represent a change in awareness.

② The changes that occur in consciousness through intoxication can be mirrored in a dream. Sometimes that change can be depressive – suggesting a need to explode the negative in our lives; sometimes they can be euphoric – showing our ability to reach a state similar to a kind of mania.

③ There is a type of euphoria which is experienced at certain stages of spiritual development. This usually occurs as we move from one level of awareness to another, and is to do with the sudden influx of new energy.

Intruder
– also see Burglar and People

① As human beings, we are very conscious of our own personal space. Dreaming of an intruder indicates that we are are feeling threatened in some way. Often in dreams the **intruder is masculine**, and this generally indicates a need to defend ourselves. If the **intruder is feminine** it may highlight an element of seduction in everyday life.

② To dream of an intruder has an obvious connection with sex and threats to one's sexuality. An intruder in dreams can suggest that we have let our guard down and permitted someone to take advantage of our good nature.

③ Spiritually it is possible to put ourselves in danger of being open to desecration. Our Self *(see Self)* is a sacred space, but until we understand that it is impenentrable, we can be open to challenge. The intruder is that part of ourselves which does not handle our fears and doubts.

Invent/Inventor
– also see Occupations

① Inventing something is quite literally dreaming up a new object or idea. Dreams can be a fertile source of ideas when conscious restraint is removed. Dreaming of in inventor or professor type links us with the more creative sides of ourselves. Usually this is more the thinker rather than the doer; someone who is capable of taking an idea and making it tangible.

② When we dream of an inventor, psychologically we are linking with that side of ourselves which is wiser, but at the same time perhaps more introverted than our waking selves. If, however, we learn in waking life to let the mind idle and play with ideas as it does during sleep, we are often able to invent a solution to a problem.

③ Invent originally meant 'to come upon or discover' and it is this meaning which has spiritual relevance in the joy of discovery. The inventor in us is the part that takes responsibility for our progress. He often signifies our ability to 'create' new ways of being, but needs assistance from us on a conscious level. We need to bring his original thinking into conscious being.

Invisible

① Actually **becoming invisible** in a dream – disappearing – would indicate either that we are not ready to face the knowledge that understanding would bring us, or that there is something we would rather forget.

② When we are conscious that **something is invisible** in a dream, it indicates that we simply need to be aware of the image's presence, without necessarily needing to interpret it immediately. Sometimes a figure (either a man or woman) seeming to be invisible can represent the Shadow *(see Shadow)*.

③ Spiritually, the invisible is the Undefined. Often described as God Unmanifest, it is invisible because it is not experienced by sight alone.

Invoice
– also see Accounts

① An invoice or bill is a request for payment and it will depend on whether we are receiving it or giving it as to the interpretation. In dreams **receiving an invoice** would suggest that we are aware of some kind of debt, whether material or otherwise. **Passing on an invoice** to someone else indicates that we feel we have not yet been properly rewarded for services given.

② An invoice or bill introduces an aspect of formality or conditionality into a transaction. When in waking life we have concerns about money and value, such an object in dreams may highlight our sense of self-worth.

③ In spiritual terms an invoice or bill would indicate that a matter of some concern has been duly considered and given tangibility.

Iris
– see Flowers

Iron

① When the **metal iron** appears in dreams, it usually represents our strengths and determination. It can also signify the rigidity of our emotions or beliefs. We should consider being more flexible.

② When we dream of using a **clothes iron** we are attempting to make ourselves more presentable to the outside world. We may also be trying to 'smooth things over'.

③ Iron in a dream can signify the part of ourselves which requires discipline. Before being tempered by fire and made into hard steel, iron requires protecting against corrosion. It is this quality of protection against spiritual 'corrosion' that needs to be dealt with so we can progress.

Island

① Dreaming of an island signifies the loneliness one can feel through isolation, self imposed or otherwise. We may feel out of touch with others or with situations around us. An island can also represent safety in that, by isolating ourselves, we are not subject to external pressures.

② Occasionally we all need to recharge our batteries, and to dream of an island can help, or warn, us to do this. Dreaming of a **desert or treasure island** indicates there is something to be gained by being alone and exploring our ability to cope with such a situation. We may actually function better in some way.

③ In dreams in island can signify a spiritual retreat – somewhere that is cut off from the world – which will allow us to contemplate our own spiritual Self.

Ivory

① Previously, ivory was a precious and valuable substance. In today's environmentally friendly society however, it is something which must be preserved. Thus, to dream of ivory is to be looking within ourselves to discover what we consider worth preserving.

② Psychologically, the ivory tower symbolises the fact that woman is not easily accessible, unless she herself gives permission. To dream of an ivory tower can signify the way we shut ourselves off from communication.

③ Ivory can symbolise the Feminine Principle. This is in many ways odd, since the most recognisable form of ivory – tusks – are, because of their shape, penetrative in character.

Ivy

① Dreaming of ivy harks back to the old idea of celebration and fun. It can also symbolise the clinging dependence which can develop within some types of relationships.

② Because ivy has the symbolism of constant affection, we can recognise that psychologically we are in need of love and affection.

③ Spiritually, ivy symbolises immortality and Eternal Life. In its twining habit, ivy also symbolises Eternal Love.

Jackal/Coyote
– see Animals

Jackdaw
– see Birds

Jaguar
– see Animals

Jail
– see Prison

Jailer

① To dream of a jailer will indicate we feel we are being restricted in some way, maybe by our own emotions or by somebody else's personality or action. There will be a sense of self-criticism and of alienation which makes it difficult to carry out our ordinary, everyday tasks.

② When we are in a situation we cannot escape from, the personality that appears in our dream often gives us a clue as to how we have got ourselves into that situation. For instance, to experience **ourselves in prison – and at the same time being unfairly treated by our jailer** – would indicate that not only may we have been party to the entrapment, but also that we have become victims of our own circumstances.

③ We may be feeling a degree of spiritual difficulty and that we are being prevented from moving on.

Jam
– see Food and Traffic in Journey

Jar
– also see Vase

① A jar very often represents the feminine principle, perhaps some aspect of mothering or of conservation which we recognise within our lives. It often has the same symbolism as the vase – that is, the receptacle for something beautiful or necessary.

② To be conscious of being jarred – of **being shaken** in some way – indicates that we are not controlling the way we are moving forward. We are putting ourselves in a position where we can be knocked about or hurt.

③ A receptacle for the Soul. This comes from the old idea of the canopic jars which were used in ancient Egypt to preserve the organs of the body so that they could be used in the next life.

Jaw
– see Body

Jesus
– see Christ in Religious Iconology

Jewellery

① Jewellery usually indicates that we have, or can have, something valuable in our lives. **Being given jewellery** suggests that someone else values us; **giving jewellery** signifies that we feel we have something to offer to other people. Those qualities we have learnt to value in ourselves through hard experience are those that we display easiest to other people. Jewellery can also indicate love given or received. For **a woman to be giving a man jewellery** usually indicates that she is attracted to him and perhaps is able to offer him her own sexuality and self-respect.

② Very often, jewellery can represent our own feelings about ourselves. For it to appear in a dream – either as something which is very valuable or as something we know to be false (such as **costume jewellery** which masquerades as something valuable) – gives an indication of our own self-esteem. It may also give an indication as to how others feel about us.

③ Jewellery represents honour and self respect without the usual vanity.

Jewels/Gems

① Jewels appearing in dreams almost invariably symbolise those things which we value. These may be personal qualities, our sense of integrity, our ability to be ourselves, or even our very essential being. When we feel we know what we are looking for, we are aware on some level of its value to us or others. When we simply register that we are **looking for jewels**, sometimes up a mountain, otherwise in a cave, we are attempting to find those parts of ourselves that we know will be of value in the future. **Counting or in some way assessing them** would suggest a time of reflection is needed. If the **jewels are set** – made up into wearable articles – we are aware of some of the uses of whatever the jewel signifies. For instance, to find an **emerald ring** might suggest that we have completed a stage of growth towards immortality.

② There are different interpretations for each gemstone, and opinions do vary as to the most relevant ones. A little consideration will usually tell us what each stone means for us. One system suggests *Amethyst* promotes healing and influences dreams. *Diamond* signifies human greed, hardness of nature and what one values in a cosmic sense. *Emerald* highlights personal growth. *Opal* suggests the inner world of fantasies and dreams; psychic impressions. *Pearl* signifies inner beauty and value. *Ruby* informs on emotions, passion and sympathies. *Sapphire* highlights religious feelings.

Other meanings of some well known jewels and gems which can also be used as sleep aids are, by tradition:

Agate (black) symbolises wealth, courage, assurance and vigour, *red* peace, spiritual love of good; health, prosperity and longevity. *Amber* represents crystallised light and magnetism. *Amethyst* is the healing gem. Connecting us with the spiritual, it represents the influence of dreams. Also humility, peace of mind, faith, self-restraint and resignation. *Aquamarine* embodies the qualities of hope, youth and health. *Beryl* is believed to hold within it happiness, hope and eternal youthfulness. *Bloodstone* holds the qualities of peace and understanding. It is also reputed to grant all wishes. *Carbuncle* Determination, self-assurance and success are retained in this stone. *Carnelian* highlights friendship, courage, self-confidence, health. *Cat's eye* influences longevity, the ability to sustain and the waning moon. *Chrysolite* represents wisdom, discretion, tact, prudence. *Chrysoprase* symbolises gaiety, unconditional happiness, the symbol of joy. *Corundum* influences and helps create a stability of mind. *Crystal* symbolises purity, simplicity, and various magical elements. *Diamond* has a number of influences: light, life, the sun, durability, incorruptibility, invincible constancy, sincerity, innocence. *Emerald* embraces immortality, hope, youth, faithfulness, and also the beauty of Spring. *Garnet* can help energy levels and indicates devotion, loyalty and grace. *Hyacinth* symbolises fidelity and the truth within, but also the gift of second sight. *Jacinth* holds within it humble qualities, verging on modesty. *Jade* 'All that is supremely excellent', the yang power of the heavens, and all its accompanying delights. *Jasper* holds the qualities of joy and happiness. *Jet* Although usually associated with darker emotions such as grief and mourning, jet also controls safety within a journey. *Lapis Lazuli* A favourable stone said to evoke divine favour, success and the ability to show perseverance. *Lodestone* holds within it the qualities of integrity and honesty; also said to influence virility. *Moonstone/Selenite* The moon and its magical qualities, tenderness and the romantic lovers. *Olivine* influences simplicity, modesty and happiness within a humble framework. *Onyx* represents degrees of perspicacity, sincerity, spiritual strength, and conjugal happiness. *Opal* not only represents fidelity, but also religious fervour, prayers and assurance of spiritual beliefs. *Pearl* symbolises the feminine principles of chastity and purity, and also the moon, and waters. *Peridot* represents consolidation of friendships. Also, so to speak, the thunderbolt, with which we may be 'hit' at unlikely times. *Ruby* represents all that is traditionally associated with Royalty; dignity, zeal, power, love, passion, beauty, longevity and invulnerability. *Sapphire* holds within it worldly truth, heavenly virtues, celestial contemplation and the feminine side of chastity. *Sardonyx* represents codes of honour, renown, brightness, vivacity, and aspects of self-control. *Topaz* holds the beauty of the Divine; goodness, faithfulness, friendship, love, sagacity. A topaz also symbolises the sun. *Tourmaline* inspiration and imagination are represented by the tourmaline. Friendship also comes under the same influence. *Turquoise* symbolises courage – physical and spiritual – fulfillment, and also success. *Zircon* Much worldly wisdom is held within zircon, as well as the virtues of honour, and the glories (or otherwise) of riches.

③ From a spiritual point of view, jewels and their understanding can enhance personal development. In most dreams it is the better known stones which appear, but when the lesser known ones are seen, there is much benefit to be gained by learning more on a conscious level. Many stones have healing properties, and this is a whole area in itself. There are many good books and internet sites available which will help you in your research.

Job
– see Career and Work

Journey

① The idea of a journey representing the story of our lives is perhaps one of the most powerful there is. The image of a journey becomes more recognizable as time goes on and we reach maturity. If we accept that any journey consists of moving between two points, there is much to be learnt. Indeed, if we translate our dreams in terms of a journey we can often uncover fresh insights into our motivation and hidden agendas. As age mellows us and we accept the knowledge of experience, we tend to become more aware of reaching our final destination.

② Often the symbolism of a journey is highly graphic, giving us the opportunity to work out what is holding us back in life. Frequently, as we become more proficient at interpretation, it highlights what is around to help us to move forward. The dreaming mind will call on our experiences to date to highlight particular patterns of behaviour, courses of action or recognisable events and environments. These can help us to manage our waking lives. Below are some of the more common elements of journeys which appear in dreams:

Arriving at a destination shows that we have had some success in what we are attempting to do. *If we feel that we have arrived but have forgotten something along the way*, we are perhaps not recognising the effort we have put in, or the external help we have had. *If we do not know where we are,* then it is perhaps important that we make an effort to orientate ourselves within a new or unfamiliar environment. *A sense of anticipation* may show we are now capable of moving on confidently, whereas a feeling of dread suggests that we should try to manage our fears better. *If we sense that a difficult journey is behind us,* then we have come through the problems and pitfalls of the past. *Turning a corner* in dreams suggests that we have accepted the need for a change of direction in waking life; we may have made a major decision.

Departing/Leaving Any dream which deals with departures of any sort usually suggests new beginnings. Formerly all departures were interpreted as death, but today are mostly to do with some form of transition which leaves behind the old and allows room for the new. To dream of *wanting to leave but not being able to* suggests that there is still some unfinished business we need to complete before we can move on. To be conscious of *the time of departure* might suggest that we are aware of a time limit or constraint in our everyday lives.

Destinations When our destination is *known or becomes apparent,* it gives some indication of our aims and objectives in life. Because these can alter according to our ability to accommodate change, we may discover – through dreams –that we actually need to adjust our behaviour in order to focus on a new goal. A workable plan for a particular section of our journey may surface in dreams. We often don't know our exact destination in a dream, until after we have confronted the obstacles and challenges along the way, reflecting real life. Such a dream suggests that our inner motivation may be totally different from our outer behaviour.

Driving The whole of the symbolism of driving in dreams is particularly obvious; it represents our basic urges, wants, needs and ambitions. If *we are driving* in a dream we are usually in control of circumstances around us. We may, however, be aware of our own inadequacies, particularly if we do not drive in everyday life. If we are *uncomfortable when someone else is driving* we may not trust or have confidence in that person, and may not wish to be dependent on them or what they represent. When *someone else takes over the driving*, there is a situation in which we are becoming passive in our lives. If we are *overtaking the vehicle in front* we are achieving success, but perhaps somewhat aggressively. When *we are overtaken*, we may feel someone else has got the better of us. Once again, the way we are in everyday life is reflected in our dreams. Our drives, aggressions, fears and doubts are all reflected in the way we drive.

Obstacles Obstacles ahead in dreams may indicate that we are, or need to be, conscious of the difficulties which may occur. We do need to be aware in waking life that we ourselves can cause our own problems and that our attitude to life is perhaps responsible. Any obstacle will reflect difficulties on our chosen path in life. Exactly *what the obstacle is* will also need interpreting. To be *stopping and starting* suggests that there is conflict between inertia and drive. When we are *at a standstill* we are being prevented, or are preventing ourselves, from moving forward. This interpretation needs handling with care, since to stop may also be appropriate.

Passenger In dreams, if we find that *we are a passenger* in a vehicle, we are probably being carried along by external circumstances in everyday life and have not planned for all eventualities. *Travelling along with one other passenger* is said to indicate that there may be a one-to-one relationship on the horizon, while if as drivers *we are carrying passengers* it suggests we may have made ourselves responsible for other people –knowingly or inadvertently. Other people may not be pulling their weight.

Road/Path A road or path in dreams reflects our course of action in everyday life. For instance, a *road which meanders* all over the place may indicate that we have no real sense of direction. Any *visible turns* in the road, particularly a blind corner, will suggest some change in direction. *Crossroads (also see individual entry)* indicate there are several choices we can make, whereas while a cul-de-sac would signify a dead end or wasted effort. When a *particular stretch of road* and it environs are accentuated in dreams it may be that a period of time, is highlighted or an extra effort is needed. Finding ourselves *going uphill* will suggest additional exertion, while going *downhill* will suggest lack of control and perhaps the need to our inner motivation.

Traffic accidents, jams and offences These may all be to do with self-image or sexuality. Such incidents may bring into prominence the way we handle aggression or carelessness, both in ourselves and others. A *collision* might suggest, therefore, a conflict with someone whereas *avoiding an accident* typifies being able to control our impulses and emotions. *Road rage* in dreams signifies not being in control of our emotions. A *traffic jam* appearing in a dream would suggest that there are a number of factors preventing progress. It may be that it takes a professional who is capable of prioritising the way matters should 'flow' to disentangle the problem.

Voyages Making a long sea voyage suggests leaving friends and family or the known for the unknown, as would *running away to sea* – a more deliberate act of escape. *Disembarking* from such a voyage shows the end of a pet project or period of time, whether successful or otherwise. *Running aground, pulling into harbour, arriving at a jetty or pier* has the same significance as arriving at a destination on land.

③ Not only does a journey of any sort in a dream describe our path to an understanding of ourselves in the spiritual sense, but it also reflects our everyday lives in a purely practical sense. Using the symbolism of a journey, dreams often show us how we are progressing in life and reveal obstacles as difficulties on that journey. The pilgrim's journey, or rather the idea of a search for a spiritual place, has resonance in the Hero's Journey towards psychological integration.

Jubilee

① The time of a jubilee represents a fresh start. This has significance in that it is the 49th part of the life cycle. After 7 x 7 years, the fiftieth year becomes sacred and gives a new beginning. To be dreaming of a jubilee or jubilee celebrations would indicate a rite of passage – a passing from the old into the new.

② Dreaming of a jubilee or jubilant occasion can represent the natural spontaneity with which we greet changes.

③ A sacred start to Spiritual celebration, marking the passage of time and the reaching of Spiritual maturity.

Judge
– see Magistrate and also Authority Figures and Judge/Magistrate in People

Judgement
– also see Acquit/Acquittal, Jury and Justice

① A judgement in practical terms is a considered opinion passed after all evidence has been heard. Such a situation will surface in dreams when we are dissatisfied with our own performance or with that of others around us.

② To have someone pass judgement on us in dreams, whether that is an authority figure or a friend, suggests that the critical part of our personality has become alerted to a misdemeanour against our own personal code of behaviour.

③ Most systems of belief develop a set of rules and strictures which must be adhered to. Having a judgement passed against us will highlight how we appear to have transgressed.

Jungle

① The jungle in dreams is an image belonging to mysticism and fairy tales. It can often represent chaos. This chaos can be either positive or negative depending on the circumstances of the dream. It is the eruptions and urges of feelings from the unconscious, perhaps from those areas which could be considered to be uncivilised. In myths the jungle symbolises an obstacle or barrier that has to be passed through in order to reach a new state of being. With this meaning it has the same significance as the enchanted forest *(see Forest)*.

② To be **trapped in a jungle** indicates that we are trapped by negative and frightening feelings from the unconscious with which we have not yet come to terms. To be conscious of **having come through a jungle** would indicate that we have passed through, and overcome, those aspects of our lives which we have never dared approach before. Psychologically, without the ordering of information that we receive, our minds can simply become a jungle of information. We need to use logic to apply order so that we can make sense of ourselves and our environment.

③ The jungle can symbolise spiritual chaos due to its unpredictability. Spiritually for us it may be 'a jungle out there'.

Jumping/Bouncing

① The act of jumping can be somewhat ambiguous in a dream. It can indicate either **jumping up** – attempting to attain something better for ourselves – or **jumping down**, which can mean going down into the unconscious and those parts of ourselves where we may feel we are in danger. Both **jumping on the spot** and **bouncing up and down** can indicate joy and exuberance and have the same significance as dance *(See Dance/Dancing)*. **Leaping** suggests bridging a gap.

② Repetitive movement of any sort in a dream usually indicates the need to reconsider our actions, to look at what we are doing and perhaps to express ourselves in a different way. On a psychological level, jumping up and down in a dream may indicate being caught up in a situation without having the power to move either forwards or backwards.

③ In certain religions, spiritual ecstasy is induced by jumping. This is a way of employing the physical in order to reach the spiritual. There were once agrarian rituals which encouraged plants to grow by jumping up and down near them.

Jury
– also see Judgement

① When a jury appears in a dream we are usually struggling with an issue of peer pressure. We may fear that others will not understand our actions, they could judge us and find us wanting.

② If **we are a member of the jury**, it depends on the circumstances of the dream whether we agree with the group or not. We may not feel we can go along with the group decision. We might have to decide to 'go it alone' and make a unilateral decision. Such a dream would probably reflect a situation in our everyday lives.

③ Often in the process of personal development we may have to make judgements which are not popular. Provided we adhere to our own inner truth, we cannot be judged.

Justice
– also see Judgement, Jury and Authority Figures in People

① Very often in a dream we do not seem to be capable of expressing our right to be heard, to articulate those things we believe are correct. Therefore, to dream of either **justice or injustice** can indicate that the unconscious mind is trying to sort out right from wrong. This is usually on a personal level, although it can have a wider implication as to what is morally right and the norm within society.

② Often when we are attempting to balance two different states or ways of being, the figure of justice can appear within a dream. This is to alert us to the fact that we may need to use both sides of ourselves successfully. To be **brought to justice** can signify that we must pay attention to our actions or to our attitude to authority.

③ In spiritual progression there needs to be a balance between our more spiritual selves – what might be called ideal behaviour – and the physical. This balance can be difficult to both attain and maintain. The figure of Justice in dreams is a representation of fairness and honesty. Such a figure may also represent the astrological sign of Libra.

Kaleidoscope

① A kaleidoscope connects us with our childlike selves, and the patterns that such a toy creates reminds us of the mandala *(see Mandala)*. We are able in dreams to appreciate the beauty of basic patterns. Just as a child is fascinated by the pattern that a kaleidoscope creates, so the dream image can introduce us to the creativity which can often become trapped.

② The magnification of the pattern created by small objects harks back to the sense of wonder that is felt in being human. We become aware of our own 'smallness' within the larger scheme of things.

③ A kaleidoscope can symbolise the patterns that we form for ourselves in times of spiritual self-improvement.

Kangaroo
– see Animals

Keepsake

① A keepsake in olden times was something which was often exchanged by lovers. To be conscious of having such an object in a dream signifies our ability to love and be loved. Any object which links with the past reminds us of what we have been capable of doing or being.

② Romantic memories figure largely in dream imagery. To dream of something which is very precious to us, and has been given by someone else, allows us to recognise the beauty held within.

③ A keepsake in the spiritual sense is an object which, because of the high regard the owner has for it, is sacred. It will probably have been blessed in some way.

Kennel
– also see Dog and Niche

① The word kennel actually means 'a place for a dog', and through association of ideas can, in dreams, represent a safe space for the potentially more difficult side of our personality, away from harm.

② Being 'in the doghouse' for some supposed wrongdoing in waking life can be developed in a dream scenario into being put into a kennel. This idea is demonstrated very ably in the original story of *Peter Pan* by J.M. Barrie.

③ In mythology the dog-headed god Anubis judges our suitability to enter the underworld. As we become more spiritually aware we become our own judges and the kennel can signify a type of halfway house where we can sort out our loyalties. It is a sacred space which is ours alone, and has the same significance as a niche.

Kettle
– also see Cauldron

① Because a kettle is such a mundane everyday object, to dream of one indicates our more practical, pragmatic side. If the kettle is unusual – such as an **old fashioned copper kettle** – it denotes outworn, but still appreciated, beliefs.

② A kettle is very often taken to symbolise transformation and change. To dream of one in this context suggests that we need to accelerate a process of learning and growth.

③ A kettle by way of its association with a cauldron (but also by its own strength) can symbolise magic and magical forces working for the Greater Good. It also represents the Feminine Principle.

Key
– also see Lock and Prison

① Keys often appear in dreams. They represent fresh attitudes, thoughts and feelings which are capable of unlocking memories, experiences and knowledge which we have previously hidden. To dream of a **bunch of keys** suggests the need to open up the whole of our personalities to new experiences.

② When we experience ourselves as trapped, the key to freedom can often appear as if by magic. We hold within us many of the answers to our difficulties, but often need a down-to-earth mundane symbol to trigger off our ability to work out solutions.

③ A key can represent our need for liberation from a stressful situation and then initiation of a positive move. **Silver and gold keys** represent – respectively – temporal and spiritual power.

Keyboard
– also see Musical Instruments

① A keyboard appearing in dreams will mean different things to different people. A **musical keyboard** will generally have the same as a musical instrument, whereas a **computer keyboard** would signify a means of communication or a creative tool to someone else.

② As we all become more technologically competent, the keyboard represents an interface between us and the rest of the world. Dreaming of a **disconnected keyboard** would signify loss of contact, whereas one which was **not working** might suggest a feared loss of competence. Recognising that any type of keyboard has a place in our ways of communicating indicates our awareness of our relationship with others.

③ In terms of spiritual resonance, the keyboard will represent our ability to create our own 'note' and way of being.

Keyhole

① When we dream that we are **peering through a keyhole**, we are conscious of the fact that our ability to see and understand is somehow impaired. Conventionally, the keyhole has been taken to represent the feminine, so that impairment could result from our attitude to the feminine.

② Since a key usually requires a keyhole, to dream of one without the other indicates some kind of confusion between the inner and outer self.

③ A keyhole symbolises our tentative entry into the Sublime.

Kick

① Aggressiveness can be represented in many ways, and to dream of **kicking someone** often allows the expression of aggression in an acceptable way. We would not necessarily do this in waking life. To dream of **being kicked** highlights our ability to be a victim.

② **Kicking a ball** around in a dream signifies our need for self-control, but also our control of external circumstances.

③ A kick can be taken symbolically as a need for spiritual motivation; it may be the kick that we need in order to continue (or maybe even begin) the spiritual journey.

Kidnap

① If we find ourselves **being kidnapped** within a dream, we are conscious of the fact that our own fears and doubts can make us victims. We are being overcome by our own 'demons', which have ganged up on us and caused us to become insecure.

② In dreams we may find ourselves **trying to kidnap someone else** and this would indicate, at its simplest level, that we are trying to influence someone else. It may also suggest that we are trying to absorb some quality from the other person which is not freely available.

③ Some sort of psychic theft may be symbolised here or, on a darker level, a thread of spiritual vampirism may be running through our subconscious. It is up to us thoroughly to define this image.

Kidneys
– see Body

Kill
– also see Murder/Murderer

① To dream of **being killed** indicates that we are coming under an influence – usually external – which is making him, or an aspect of his personality, ineffective in everyday life. To be **killing someone** in a dream is attempting to be rid of the influence they have over us.

② Killing is an extreme answer to a problem. It is such a final act that in dreams it can often represent our perception of the need for violence, particularly against ourselves. Perhaps the only way a solution to a problem can be reached is by 'killing off' part of us. There is no denying in this case the potential for violence, although ultimately the impulse may not be correct.

③ A spiritual slaying and therefore sacrifice is represented here. We need to be aware that what we consider worthy may need further nurturing, lest it be relinquished.

King
– see People

Kingfisher
– see Birds

Kiss

① When we dream about kissing someone, it can suggest an acceptance of a new relationship with that person. Such an act can also signify that, on a subconscious level, we are seeking to develop a quality in ourselves belonging to that other person. A kiss formerly indicated a mark of respect and in dreams can still have that meaning.

② We are sealing a pact – perhaps coming to some sort of agreement. This agreement may be sexual, but it could also be one of friendship. We may also be moving towards unity. **Being kissed** indicates that we are appreciated and loved for ourselves.

③ A single kiss (particularly on the forehead) has often had spiritual and religious undertones, and here the image symbolises a blessing of a spiritual kind.

Kitchen
– also see House

① For most people, the kitchen represents the 'heart' of the house. It is the place from which we go out into the world and to which we return. In dreams, the kitchen can often represent the mother, or rather, the mothering function. It is the place which is usually busiest and therefore the place where many relationships are cemented, and where many exchanges take place.

② The kitchen is a place of creation, and usually of warmth and comfort. It has therefore come to represent the nurturing aspect of Woman.

③ There are folk tales in most cultures to do with the kitchen, and spiritually it represents transformation and transmutation. This is much more to do with desired transformation, rather than one which is enforced. The rituals associated with the hearth and with fire were, and still are, a significant part of spiritual development. Even in today's climate of convenience foods there is the sense of work in the kitchen being an offering.

Kite

① In Chinese lore, the kite symbolised the wind – and even today it represents freedom. So, to dream of flying a kite can remind us of the carefree days of childhood when we were without responsibility. Often the colour is important (*see Colour*), as may be the material from which it is made.

② While flying a kite, we are at the mercy of the wind unless we have a fair degree of expertise. In dreams it is recognisable that we have some expertise in our everyday lives.

③ A kite represents the our need for, or recognition of, forthcoming spiritual freedom. To be free of constraints and to be 'pulling our own strings', as it were.

Knapsack/Rucksack
– also see Luggage

① When we discover that we, or someone else, is wearing a knapsack in a dream, we are dreaming either about the difficulties we are carrying – for instance, anger or jealousy – or about the resources we have accumulated.

② In Tarot imagery, the Fool carries in his knapsack the lessons he has to learn in life. If we believe in reincarnation, the knapsack is also reputed to carry those things we have brought forward from a previous life. These can also be the resources which we have in order to deal with problems.

③ Spiritually the knapsack suggests those qualities which are external to ourselves, and which we must learn to handle. These may be negative or positive – it depends on how we handle them.

Knead/Kneading

① In everyday life kneading is the mixing of more than one ingredient into an amorphous mass, usually to create another article altogether. In dreams therefore such an action would suggests that we need to consider our own creativity and how we can best combine the talents we have.

② To be **kneading bread** suggests a 'need' to sustain ourselves or others by our actions. If the substance we are working is **clay** then this would identify the possibility of using the raw material of life to create a different perception. **Kneading muscles** as in massage indicates that there is some long-held tension in us that needs to be released.

③ In spiritual development there is a stage where we begin to appreciate that the various qualities we possess can be combined in a different way. This might be likened to kneading.

Knee/Kneeling
– see Body

Knife
– also see Dagger and Weapons

① A cutting instrument in a dream usually signifies some kind of division. If we are **using a knife** we may either be freeing ourselves or trying to sever a relationship. If we are **being attacked with a knife,** it indicates either violent words or actions may be used against us. **In a woman's dream** this is probably more to do with her own fear of penetration and violation, whereas in a **man's dream** it is highlighting his own aggression.

② It can be important in a dream about a knife to notice what type is being used. For instance, a **table knife** would be interpreted very differently to a **Swiss Army knife**. Both are functional, but the former would only be appropriate under certain circumstances, whereas the latter might have a more universal application.

③ A symbol of division, of cutting through. Although we are on our way to achieving what we want at this time, it is not making us particularly happy, so there is confusion as to which road we should have taken.

Knight

① A knight appearing in a dream, particularly a woman's, can have the obvious connotation of a romantic liaison – the knight in shining armour. This actually is a manifestation of her own Animus *(see Anima/Animus)* – her own inner masculine – and is to do with her search for perfection. In a man's dream it indicates that he may be searching for the Hero *(see Archetypes and People)* in himself.

② Psychologically, the knight in a dream signifies the guiding principle. He is that part of ourselves which is sometimes known as the Higher Self, the spirit guiding the physical. The **black knight** is the embodiment of evil. It is interesting that often the **white knight** appears with his visor up, whereas the black knight appears with his visor down.

③ Initiation, in order to develop our finer qualities. Interestingly, though historically some of the knights in the Crusades were initially pressed into service, this would have brought out the intrinsic worth of commitment and loyalty to a cause, still needed by us today.

Knitting

① The first symbolism connected with knitting is that of creating something new out of available material. A project or idea which is being worked on is beginning to come together. To be **unravelling knitting** suggests that a project that is being worked on needs reconsideration.

② Often it is worthwhile taking note of the colour of what is being knitted *(see Colour)* in order to make sense of why the image of knitting should appear in a dream. It may well be that we are working at creating a relationship, or working on emotions.

③ Knitting can symbolise a form of creativity, which we may not have fully realised we have available to us. Formerly it was a recognisable symbol of feminine expertise.

Knob

① To be dreaming of a knob such as a **doorknob** can indicate some kind of turning point in our life. A noticeable contrast between the door and the knob can present us with certain insights. For instance, **a very plain knob on an ornate door** may indicate that the process of moving forward from a situation is very easy. To dream of any other sort of knob is often to do with one's hold on a situation.

② Since many people still have difficulty in calling 'private parts' by their correct name, a knob appearing in a dream can represent the penis or, if the dreamer is a man, his masculinity.

③ Spiritually, a knob can suggest changes occurring in the way we access our subconscious self.

Knock

① To **hear knocking** in a dream generally alerts us to the fact that our attention needs to be re-focused. We may be paying too much attention to one part of our personality. For instance, we may be too introverted when in fact we need to be paying more attention to external matters.

② If **we ourselves are knocking** on a door, we may be wanting to become part of someone's life. We are waiting for permission to be given before moving forward.

③ We are being given permission from our spiritual self to progress on our current spiritual journey.

Knot

① A knot is one of the most interesting symbols to appear in dreams, since it can have so many meanings. Negatively, if it seen as a **tangle**, it can represent an unsolvable problem or difficulty. The answer can only be 'teased out' gradually. Positively, a knot can represent the ties that one has to family, friends or work.

② A **simple knot** seen in a dream could represent the need to take a different direction in a project. A **more complex knot** could indicate that we are bound to a situation by a sense of duty or guilt. It may well be that, ultimately, the only way to escape from such restraint is by loosening the ties in our relationship with someone else, or with a work situation.

③ Spiritual continuity or connection, timelessness. A three-cornered knot can represent the Holy Trinity or the three stages of femininity: Maid, Mother and Crone.

Label

① Often, dreaming of labels links with the human being's need to name things. Our sense of identity comes from the name we are given, and our label is much to do with the way that others see us and understand us.

② To dream of having **the wrong label** suggests that we are aware that we are not perceiving something in the correct way. To be **re-labelling something** suggests that we have rectified a misperception.

③ In the spiritual sense a label can give us a sense of Identity *(see Name)*.

Laboratory

① Dreaming of **working in a laboratory** indicates that we need to be more scientific in our approach to life. We may have certain talents which need to be developed in an objective fashion, or we may need to develop our thinking faculty further.

② A laboratory can suggest a very ordered existence, and how we interpret the dream will depend on whether we are working in, or are specimens in, a laboratory.

③ Dreaming of a laboratory indicates we need to make an objective assessment of what is going on in our lives.

Labour

① **To be labouring** at something, in the sense of working hard, suggests that we have a goal we wish to achieve. To dream of '**hard labour**' will alert us to an aspect of self-flagellation or self-punishment in what we are doing.

② If a woman dreams of **being in labour** she should look at her wish and desire to be pregnant.

③ **The twelve labours of Hercules** are reputed to represent the passage of the sun through the twelve signs of the Zodiac. They are also the hardships and effort man uses to attain self-realisation.

Labyrinth

– also see Maze

① On a purely practical level, the labyrinth appearing in dreams signifies the need to explore the hidden side of our own personality. With its many twists, turns and potential blind alleys it is a very potent representation of the human being. Within the labyrinth one meets and overcomes the difficulties in life which could impede progress.

② Psychologically, in undertaking our own Heroic Journey, we must at some point go through some kind of labyrinth experience. It is undertaken at a point when we must travel into the differing areas of our subconscious and come to terms with our fears and doubts, before confronting our own Shadow *(See Shadow)*. In dreams the labyrinth can be suggested by any dream which has us exploring a series of underground passages. It is held by some to be an exploration of the hidden feminine.

③ Spiritually the labyrinth experience marks a watershed. It is a symbol for the transition stage between the physical and practical world and a deeper understanding of all mankind. The route in one type of labyrinth is 'unicursal' – that is, it goes by a straightforward route which covers maximum ground straight to the centre and out again. The second type is designed with the intention to confuse, and has many blind alleys and unexpected twists. This represents spiritual progress, through having to work out the key or code. Many trials and tribulations are met and overcome or negotiated on the path to attainment. Each individual will undertake his or her own route to the centre of his existence.

Ladder

① The ladder in dreams suggests how secure we feel in moving from one situation to another. We may need to make a considerable effort to reach a goal or take an opportunity. Often this dream occurs during career changes, and so has obvious connotations. If the **rungs are broken** we can expect difficulty. If **someone else is carrying the ladder** it could suggest that another person, perhaps a manager or colleague, has a part to play in our progression.

② The ladder denotes our ability to break through to a new level of awareness, moving from the physical to the spiritual, but also being able to move downwards again. It also suggests communication between the physical and spiritual realms as a stage of transition. Occasionally it may also represent death, though this may be the death of the old self, rather than a physical death.

③ In a dream, the rungs of the ladder are often either seven or twelve in number, these being the stages of growth towards spirituality.

Lagoon/Lake
– also see Water

① A lagoon or lake represents our inner world of feeling and fantasy. It is the unconscious side which is a rich source of power when it can be accessed and understood. If **the lake is contaminated** we have taken in ideas and concepts which are not necessarily good for us. **A clear stretch of water** would indicate that we have clarified our fears and feelings about ourselves.

② Often thought to be the home of the magical feminine and of monsters, the lagoon stands for the darker side of femininity. This is seen clearly in the legends of King Arthur and this type of image will appear in dreams as we lose our fear of that particular part of ourselves.

③ The unconscious and the primordial substance are often pictured as a lagoon. The Chinese concept of a kind of soup from which came all existence, links with the lagoon.

Lamb
– see Animals

Lame
– also see Immobility

① Dreaming of being lame suggests a loss of confidence and strength. If **we ourselves are lame** there can be a fear of moving forward or a fear of the future.

② To be aware that **someone else is lame** has two meanings. **If the person is known** to us, we need to be aware of their vulnerability and uncertainty. **If they are not known**, it is more likely to be a hidden side of ourselves which is insecure.

③ Lameness in the spiritual sense suggests the imperfection of creation, when an imperfect world is formed.

Lamp/Lantern
– also see Light

① In dreams a lamp or a light can represent life. To be **moving towards a lamp** suggests a clarity of perception, which may be slightly old-fashioned. The lamp in its most practical aspect in dreams signifies the intellect and clarity.

② The lamp in dreams often signifies guidance and wisdom. It can also represent previously held beliefs which may need to be updated. **An infra-red or heat lamp** has the significance of more modern thinking, whereas **a lantern** being more old-fashioned, is likely to represent the past.

③ Spiritually the lamp can suggest the idea of a personal light in darkness. The

Hermit in the Tarot demonstrates this in his need to be able to move forward despite the darkness around him. The lamp can also signify the light of the Divine and immortality.

Lance

① A lance – **as in a Knight's lance** – in a dream suggests an aspect of masculine power, penetration and therefore sometimes the sexual act.

② A lance as **a surgical instrument** is also penetrative, but has a more healing connotation, as it is designed to release the negative. We may need to take short, sharp action in order to improve a situation.

③ A phallic image of solar power, light within darkness.

Landscapes
– also see Places/Environments

① The landscape in a dream can be an integral part of the interpretation. It usually mirrors feelings and concepts that we have and therefore reflects our personality. A **rocky landscape** would suggest problems, whereas a **gloomy landscape** might suggest pessimism and self-doubt. **A recurring scene** may be one where in childhood we felt safe, or may reflect a feeling or difficulty with which we have not been able to come to terms. Landscapes do tend to reflect habitual feelings rather than momentary moods.

② Dream landscapes can have a bizarre quality about them in order to highlight a particular message. For instance, there may be **trees made of ice, or rocks made of sugar**. The plot and other aspects of the dream may be important in arriving at the correct interpretation of these symbols. The landscape in a dream can also indicate how we relate to other people. To be **in a desert** might represent loneliness, whereas to be **in a jungle** might represent a very fertile imagination.

③ Spiritually, the landscape in a dream can suggest improvements which we can make in handling our own moods and attitudes. **If the landscape changes** between the beginning and end of the dream, we perhaps need to make corresponding changes in everyday life.

Language

① Hearing **foreign or strange language** in dreams illustrates some kind of communication, either from within or from the Collective Unconscious. It has not yet become clear enough for us to understand it.

② As we become more open to possibilities, the various facets of our personality can achieve their own method of communication with us. This is often experienced in dreams as strange language, and often comes across as sleep-talking.

③ In Spiritualism, hearing language is communication by discarnate beings.

Larder
– also see Refrigerator

① A larder, being a repository for food, usually indicates sustenance or nurturing in a dream. It will depend to a certain extent what is in the larder as to the interpretation of the dream. In previous times it would have referred to having harvested *(see Harvest)* food, but it may be significant here if we register that a particular food is missing.

② As life moves on, many people no longer have larders, this image being replaced by the refrigerator or fridge freezer. All these images indicate that conservation is necessary. This may be conservation of energy, resources or power.

③ A larder in spiritual terms suggests conserving gifts or talents.

Large
– see Size

Lark
– see Birds

Laser

① The laser is a very focussed beam of light which has an ambivalence about it, in that it can be both healing and yet destructive. In dreams we must decide which function is paramount. In fact, the light emitted is of a particular quality, so a further interpretation of the image is of energy being used effectively.

② Lasers in waking life are used to pinpoint certain areas worthy of note, so in dreams will appear as a means of highlighting certain ideas or principles.

③ Spiritual energy used effectively in healing – or such powers as clairvoyance – is similar to the high frequency use of phased light in lasers and may manifest initially as such as image.

Late
– see Time

Laugh/Laughter

① **Being laughed at** in dreams suggests we may have a fear of being ridiculed, or may have done something which we feel is not appropriate. We may find ourselves embarrassing. It can also be seen as a sign of rejection.

② If **we ourselves are laughing** we may be experiencing a release of tension. Often the object of our amusement will give a clue to the relevance in everyday life. **To hear a crowd laughing** suggests a shared enjoyment.

③ Laughter in the spiritual sense signifies pure joy.

Laurel/Bay leaves

① The laurel or bay tree is less likely to appear in dreams nowadays, unless we are either a gardener or has particular knowledge of symbolism. In former times, it would have represented a particular type of success. Traditionally the laurel or bay is difficult to grow, so it would have symbolised triumph over difficulty.

② **The laurel wreath** is often used to indicate triumph and victory, and therefore is an acknowledgement of success. It also suggests immortality.

③ The laurel or bay tree signifies chastity and eternity and overcoming tribulation.

Lava
– see Volcano

Lavatory
– see Toilet

Law/Legal
– also see Acquit/Acquittal, Judge, Judgement and Jury

① If an action is legal it has been approved of by higher authority and therefore is within the law as set by that authority. In dreams, to be dealing with legal papers suggests some kind of binding contract or promise. Law generally is a decree which benefits the most people within a community and will have that meaning in dreams.

② While laws are apparently developed to differentiate between right and wrong, their real purpose is to create a system of rules and edicts which creates a stable way of life for all. In dreams this may come across as restrictive. Legal matters such as courts, judges and juries may highlight such problems.

③ Spiritual law might be taken as a divinely appointed order, a perfection of rightness. Interestingly, it is left to each individual to interpret this in his or her own way and dreams have a way of revealing what is right for us.

Lead (Metal)

① The conventional explanation of lead appearing in a dream is that we have a situation around us which is a burden to us. We are not coping with life as perhaps we should be, and as a result it is leaving us heavy-hearted. Lead, as in the **lead of a pencil**, has obvious connections with the life force and masculinity.

② Lead as a substance is less used nowadays than it used to be, but still has the connotations of a base metal. In dreams it can indicate that the time is ripe for transformation and transmutation. We need to instigate changes to give a better quality to our lives.

③ Lead in spiritual symbolism stands for bodily consciousness. It is the metal of Saturn and we should look at how that planet may help us progress.

Lead/Leader/Leading

① Dreaming of a **dog lead** (also see Harness and Halter) would symbolise the connection between ourselves and our lesser nature. To have **lost the dog lead** would indicate a loss of control. **Leading someone** in a dream pre-supposes that we know what we are doing and where we are going. **Being led** suggests that we have allowed someone else to take control of a situation around us.

② Leadership qualities are not necessarily ones that everybody will use. Often we can surprise ourselves in dreams by doing things that we would not normally do, and taking the lead is one of them.

③ We are able to take authority by virtue of our spiritual knowledge. This can be done with humility and without ego.

Leaf/Leaves

① A leaf very often represents a period of growth and can also indicate time. **Green leaves** can suggest hope and new opportunities, or the Springtime. **Dead leaves** signify a period of sadness, barrenness or Autumn (see Autumn).

② When looking at our lives as a whole, leaves can give some indication of a particular period of our lives – perhaps a period that has been meaningful and creative. Following a dream about leaves we may need to assess how to go forward in order to avail ourselves of the opportunities offered.

③ Leaves signify fertility and growth. Since each leaf is completely unique, we may be being alerted to the beauty of creation.

Leak
– also see Water

① Dreaming of a leak suggests we are wasting or losing energy in some way. If it is a **slow leak** we are perhaps not aware of the drain on our energies. If it is **gushing** we need to look at 'repairing' the leak, perhaps by being more responsible in our actions.

② A leak can indicate carelessness. We may not be paying attention to necessary repairs either on a physical, emotional or mental level.

③ A leak of any sort suggests wastefulness and misuse of resources.

Leather

① At its basic meaning, and depending upon the circumstances in our life, leather can be associated with self image. Often it is connected with protection, and subsequently with uniform. For instance a **motorcycle rider's leather suit** will make him easily identifiable, but will also protect him in all weathers. Dreams will often bring forward an image that has to be considered very carefully.

② Leather can also be connected with sadistic methods of torture, and thus can become connected with the wider issues of sexual behaviour, either ours or others which we may, or may not find appropriate.

③ Self-flagellation as with a whip *(see Whip/Lash)*, or the power of protection.

Left/Leaving
– see Journey and Position

Leg
– see Limbs in Body

Legal
– see Law/Legal

Lens
– also see Glasses/Spectacles and Goggles

① Just as in everyday life a lens helps to focus the attention, so in dreams it can signify our need to perceive something very clearly.

② When a lens appears in a dream we need to be clear as to whether it is enlarging the object being looked at, or is intensifying it. A proper interpretation can only be made in the light of other circumstances in the dream.

③ Visionary clarity and the ability to focus on detail in spiritual matters. This image may appear as we develop the clairvoyant faculty.

Lemon
– see Fruit and Food

Lend/Lending
– also see Loan

① If in a dream we are **lending an object** to someone, we are aware that the quality that object represents cannot be given away, that it is ours to have, but that we can share it. If **someone is lending us an article** then we are perhaps not responsible enough to possess what it represents on a full-time basis. Conversely, we may only need it for a short time.

② If we are **lending money**, we are creating a bond of obligation within our lives. If we are being **lent money** we need to look at the way we are managing our resources, but more importantly what help we need to do this.

③ In spiritual terms, the concept of lending is connected with healing and support, allowing our energy to be used.

Leopard
– see Animals

Leper

① To dream of a leper suggests that we are aware of some aspect of ourselves that we feel to be unclean. We feel that we have been rejected by society without quite knowing why. We may also feel that we have been contaminated in some way.

② If we are **caring for a leper** we need to attend to those parts of ourselves we consider unclean, rather than trying to dispose of them. If **the leper is offering us something**, it may be that we have a lesson to learn about humility.

③ Spiritually, a leper in a dream can suggest that we are having to deal with a moral dilemma which takes us away from compassion and caring.

Lesson
– see Education, School and Teacher

Letter/Email
– also see Writing

① Whereas letter writing was previously a valid way of communicating, as more people become proficient at using modern technology, the email has taken on the same significance as the letter. Shorter and more concise by nature it can symbolise more efficient communication is necessary. If we **receive a letter or email** in a dream we may be aware of some problem with the person it is from. It is possible that the sender has moved away from us or has died, in which case we have unresolved issues with them. If we are **sending a letter or email** we have information which may be useful to others.

② Often we can dream about a letter without knowing what the contents are. This suggests some information which is being witheld. If a particular **letter of the alphabet** is highlighted, it may be because it has some personal relevance. As **texting** becomes another way of communicating, an initially meaningless jumble of letters may become understandable in dreams and brought into conscious knowledge.

③ The Hebrew system of letters still retains much rich symbolism and, as we explore the spiritual more fully, can appear in dreams, at first unrecognisable but later comprehensible. Hidden information can often become acceptable if we have made the effort to understand.

Level

① Usually a level surface suggests ease and comfort. Dreaming of **a road being level** would indicate our way ahead is fairly straightforward. **A level crossing** suggests that we are approaching a barrier which requires our attention. We may not yet have enough information to take avoiding action.

② There are many levels of understanding which are available to us in the dream state. These levels may be pictured as, for instance, a plateau of some sort (*see Plateau*).

③ In dreams, differing states of awareness may be symbolised by different levels of any sort. A level in sacred architecture represents knowledge outside the norm.

Library
– also see House

① A library in a dream can often represent the storehouse of our life's experience. It can also represent our intellect and the way we handle knowledge. A **well-ordered library** suggests the ability to create order successfully. A more **chaotic, untidy one** would suggest that we have difficulty in dealing with information.

② At a certain stage in psychic and spiritual development, the library is an important symbol. It suggests both the wisdom and skills that we have accumulated, but also the collected wisdom available to all humanity. As we are able to look more objectively at our lives we have more access to universal knowledge.

③ A library represents the Collective Unconscious – all that is, was, and ever shall be. It is often taken as the Akashic records – that is, the spiritual records of existence.

Lice
– see Insects

Lifeboat
– also see Sea in Water

① Dreaming of a lifeboat could indicate that our need to be rescued, possibly from our own stupidity or from circumstances beyond our control. If we are at **the helm of a lifeboat** we are still in control of our own lives, but are perhaps aware that we need to offer assistance to someone else. Because the sea often represents deep emotion, in dreams a lifeboat may be of help in handling our own emotions.

② Since a lifeboat requires a degree of dedication from the members of the crew, we may be alerted to the need for such selfless dedication in our lives. We may also be being made aware of the degree of skill we require to navigate life's difficulties.

③ Spiritually we can only be 'rescued' by a greater knowledge, wisdom and experience. There is always an element of risk in undertaking a difficult task.

Light
– also see Lamp/Lantern

① Light in a dream usually means illumination. For instance, 'light at the end of the tunnel' suggests coming to the end of a difficult project. 'He saw the light' means the recognition of the results of actions. It is much to do with confidence. To **feel lighter** signifies feeling better about ourselves. When an **article is light**, it has the qualities of joy or airiness about it.

② When light appears in dreams we are usually in process of trying to improve who we are. A **very bright light** often symbolises the development of intuition or insight. There are various techniques using candle flames and other sources of light which can be used in the waking state to enhance this faculty.

③ Spiritually in dreams a bright light symbolises the manifestation of divinity, truth or direct knowledge. Often this knowledge is beyond form and therefore appears as energy which the dreaming mind translates as light.

Lighthouse

① A lighthouse is a warning system, and in dreams it tends to warn us of emotional difficulties. It will depend on whether we are aware in the dream of being on land or at sea. If we are **on land** we are being warned of difficulties to come, probably from our own emotions. If we are **at sea** we need to be careful not to create misunderstandings for ourselves by ignoring problems.

② A lighthouse can act as a beacon and can lead us into calmer waters. It can often have this significance in dreams whether emotionally or spiritually. A lighthouse can also take on the symbolism of the tower *(see Tower)*.

③ Spiritually a lighthouse highlights the correct course of action to help us achieve our spiritual goals.

Lightning

① Lightning in a dream denotes unexpected changes which are taking place or are about to take place. These may come about through some type of realisation or revelation. Often such a revelation has the effect of knocking down the structures we have built in as safeguards in our lives. Alternatively, we may have to make changes in the way we think while leaving our everyday structure and relationships in place. Lightning can also indicate strong passion – such as love – which may strike suddenly but be devastating in its effect.

② When we dream of lightning we are marking a discharge of tension in some way. There may be a situation in our everyday lives which actually has to be blasted in order for something to happen which will change the circumstances. This may seem like a destructive act on our part, but is nevertheless necessary. If we take all the known facts into account, our intuition will make us aware of the correct action.

③ Spiritually, lightning denotes some form of spiritual enlightenment. This may be the sudden realisation of a personal truth, or of a more universal awareness. Literally something which had not 'struck us' before. In dreams **a lightning flash** can also represent the Holy Spirit.

Lily

① Because of their connection with funerals, for some people lilies can symbolise death. They can, however, also symbolise nobility and grace, and the interpretation needs to be carefully thought out. If we are **planting lilies** we are hoping for a peaceful transition in some area within our lives. If we are **gathering lilies**, particularly in **a woman's dream** we are developing a peaceful existence.

② One symbol of lilies is that of purity and, particularly in a teenager's dream, lilies can suggest virginity. Lilies in dreams, other than the white funerary arum lily, can suggest aspects of femininity.

③ Spiritually lilies are a symbol of resurrection and of everlasting life. They are often used in religious ceremony to denote this.

Limb
– see Body

Line

① A line in a dream often marks a boundary or denotes a measurement. In dreams, it can also signify a link between two objects to show a connection which is not immediately obvious. **A line of people or queue** would suggest an imposed order for a particular purpose. If we are **waiting in line**, it may be that we need to have patience in waking life.

② Psychologically, we tend to need boundaries or demarcation lines, and those lines can be demonstrated in dream symbolism in ways which might not be feasible in everyday life. For instance, **jumping over a line** would suggest being brave enough to take risks. A **line of objects** might signify the choices we are offered.

③ Symbolically in dreams a line can have great significance. The **straight line** can represent time and the ability to go both forward and back. When **horizontal**, the line is the earthly world and the passive point of view; when **vertical**, it is the spiritual world, the active aspect and the osmic axis.

Linen

① Linen in dreams on a purely practical level can suggest an appreciation of fine things. **Linen tablecloths**, for instance, may suggest some kind of a celebration in the sense of only using the best. **Linen bed sheets** might signify sensuality.

② In today's world, where everything is done as quickly and as easily as possible, linen appearing in a dream would suggest a slowness of pace and caring which enables us to appreciate our lives better.

③ Spiritually, fine linen signifies purity and righteousness. It was the cloth used to wrap Christ with in the tomb, and therefore suggests reverence and love.

Link
– see Chain

Lion
– also see Animals

① The lion in dreams signifies both cruelty and strength. In terms of how we react to people, the lion can suggest leadership or leadership qualities.

② In psychological terms, the lion represents all those qualities it shows – majesty, strength, pride, courage and so on. It is easier to recognise the necessity for such qualities in ourselves when symbolised in something else.

③ Spiritually the lion symbolises all those attributes that belong to the fiery principle. It is an ambivalent symbol, since it represents both good and evil. It plays a part in the recognition of the four elements – Fire, Earth, Air and Water – and represents fire.

Liquid

① Liquid in dreams can have more than one meaning. Because it is always connected with 'flow' it can represent the idea of allowing feelings to flow properly. The colour of the liquid in the dream *(see Colour)* can be important since it can give an indication of exactly which feelings and emotions are being dealt with. **Red** might represent anger, whereas **violet** might signify spiritual aspiration.

② When **something is unexpectedly liquid** in a dream, we need to be aware that in everyday life we are in a situation which may not remain stable. At that point we need to be ready to 'go with the flow' in order to maximise the potential within that situation. One of the symbols of liquid is to do with liquidity – that is, having assets or possessions which can be realised. This can be on either a physical or emotional level.

③ A strong symbol in spiritual development is golden liquid which can represent both power and energy.

List

① To be dealing with a list in dreams suggests that we need to create order in our lives. The type of list will be important: a random list such as a shopping list will perhaps signify the imposing of order on a more chaotic task. An alphabetical list will require one type of logic, whereas a numerical list suggests sequential action.

② When on waking we find our dream images totally chaotic it is useful to attempt to list them in various ways. This allows us to discover whether there is some inherent order in them. We can then discover the theme of the dream and allow ourselves additional interpretation.

③ Developing spiritually is not a linear process. However, it frequently helps to look back and make a list of the steps we have taken so far.

Listening/Hearing
– see Hearing/Listening

Litter
– see Garbage/Rubbish/Litter

Liver
– also see Body

① We do not often dream about our internal organs, but since the liver is probably – after the heart – our most vital organ we may be being alerted to problems in our physical body by dreams of this organ.

② As we begin to understand the workings of our physical body we also understand how interconnected our emotions are with our physical body. Irritability in dreams can be a sign that our essential life force is being compromised, perhaps by our lifestyle.

③ The liver has been described as the body's most forgiving organ. In traditional Chinese medicine it governs the smooth flow of the life energy and so dreams can be an early warning system of a difficulty.

Lizard
– see Reptiles in Animals

Loan

– also see Bank/Banker, Debt, Finance, Lend/Lending and Money

① In today's financial climate it would not be unusual to dream of **applying for a loan**. If we are able to decide whether the loan in the dream is retrospective, to buy material goods or to manage our resources better we should be able to identify its relevance in everyday life.

② To dream of **paying off a loan** suggests we feel we have repaid a debt, whether that is emotional or material. **Not being able to repay a loan** indicates a continued lack of resources. **Lending money** in a dream implies our continuing care about our input into a situation.

③ Being conscious of a loan or lending suggests that we are able to draw on our spiritual reserves in order to facilitate a successful conclusion. We can literally lend our energy.

Loaf/Loaves

– also see Baker, Bread and Food

① In less sophisticated times bread, because it was made from grain, was also a fit offering for the gods. It was formed into loaves which then became symbols of fertility, nourishment and life. This symbolism remains visible today at Harvest and Jewish festivals. In dreams, loaves can represent our need for nourishment.

② The Biblical parable of five loaves and two fishes signifies the principle of being fed through caring. In most cultures, the sharing of a loaf denotes friendship. It can have the same significance in dreams.

③ Spiritually the loaf represents the Bread of Life, the love of God and charity in the sense of caring.

Lock/Locked

– also see Key and Prison

① It is very easy to lock away the emotions, supposedly to keep them safe. A lock appearing in a dream may alert us to the fact that we need to free up whatever we have shut away. **To force a lock** would indicate that we need to work against our own inclinations to lock things away in order to be free of inhibitions. **To be mending a lock** suggests that we feel our personal space been trespassed upon and we need to repair the damage.

② To recognise in a dream that a **part of our body has become locked** suggests that we are carrying extreme tension. We need to release that tension in a physical way in order to be healthy. To realise **a door is locked** suggests that somewhere we thought of as sanctuary is no longer available to us. It may also be that a course of action is not right.

③ Spiritually, a lock can represent that either a new freedom is being offered to us or that the way forward is barred. Our actions are not appropriate.

Locust

① The image of a plague of locusts is so strong in Western thought that even in dreams it has come to represent retribution for some misdemeanour.

② As a flying insect the locust can signify scattered thought and concepts which have not been properly thought out and marshalled. Put together they may be a very powerful tool, but should be used wisely.

③ Spiritually locusts signify divine retribution, but also a misuse of resources. We may also be linking with the idea of a group mind.

Loom
– also see Weaving

① A loom in dreams will obviously have a different significance if it is a work tool, or if one is a creative artist. By and large a loom suggests creativity, whether more mechanical or craft oriented. We all have the ability within ourselves to create beautiful objects and the loom is one of these symbols.

② A loom picks up on the symbol of weaving and the idea of creating our own lives. We have certain basic materials which can lay down an elementary pattern, but we must add our own touches which give the individuality to the overall woven object. The loom is the tool we need to achieve the right pattern.

③ The loom in spiritual terms suggest fate, time, and the weaving of destiny.

Lorry
– see Transport

Lose/Lost
– also see Searching

① To have **lost something** in a dream may mean that we have forgotten matters which could be important. This may be an opportunity, a friend or a way of thought which has previously sustained us. To suffer loss suggests that part of ourselves or our lives is now dead and we must learn to cope without it. **To lose a much-loved article** suggests perhaps some kind of carelessness on our part.

② To experience ourselves as **being lost** denotes confusion on whatever level is depicted in the dream. It may be emotionally or mentally as much as physically. It shows we have lost the ability or the motivation to make clear decisions.

③ The search for the **lost object or the lost chord** epitomises the search for enlightenment. In spiritual terms we do not know what we are looking for until we have found it.

Lottery

① A lottery – particularly in today's climate – suggests the idea of gaining through taking a risk. To dream of **winning a lottery** would suggest that one has either been lucky or clever in waking life. To dream of **losing** might suggest that someone else was in control of our destiny.

② A lottery can highlight all sorts of belief systems, some valid and some not. The idea of random selection – particularly mechanically – links with belief in a mechanistic universe. The lottery also denotes one's attitude to greed and poverty and to the principle of winning through luck rather than effort.

③ Spiritually the lottery represents the ability to take chances, to rely on fate rather than good judgement.

Low
– see Position

Luggage
– also see Knapsack/Rucksack

① Luggage in a dream can be slightly different to baggage in that luggage will symbolise what we feel is necessary to have us go forward. It can be those habits and emotions which have helped us in the past, but which can now be reappraised before being 'repackaged'.

② When luggage appears as a symbol in our dreams we should perhaps look at whether it is **ours or someone else's**. If ours, it signifies those views, attitudes and behaviours which we have brought through from the past. If it is someone else's, then we may be looking at family or global concepts which no longer are useful to us.

③ Spiritually if we are to travel 'light' we must often find a way of unburdening ourselves. Luggage in a dream can help us to envisage this.

Lungs
– see Body

Lynx
– see Animals

Machine/Machinery

① When a machine of any sort appears in a dream, it is often highlighting the body's automatic functions such as breathing, heart beating, elimination – those mechanical drives towards life that help us to survive. It is usually to do with some kind of mechanical, habitual form – that is, the ordinary everyday things that take place. The 'mechanics' of the body are an important part of our well-being and often when we perceive a **machine breaking down** in dreams, it warns us that we need to take care, that perhaps we are over-stressing a particular part of our being.

② A machine of any sort appearing in a dream is very often to do with the brain and thought processes, so psychologically it is the process of thinking that is important. If a machine seems **large and overpowering** we perhaps need to reassess what we are doing to ourselves. The type of machine is important and may give insight into our motivations. A **static piece of machinery** might suggest security, whereas a moveable one such as a **lawnmower or fork-lift truck** would signify hard work.

③ A machine may well represent the machinations of everyday life, which would be interpreted spiritually as The Life Process.

Mad

① When we are confronted by madness in a dream, we are often meeting those parts of ourselves that have not been integrated within our present situation. We are facing a part of ourselves that is out of control and which, under certain circumstances, can be frightening. Without imposing an inner control, not only we, but also others, may find this to be so.

② Being mad in a dream represents the uncontrollable aspects of extreme emotion. If we are conscious of being at odds with other people, and therefore considered to be mad, we are not integrating fully within society or the group to which we belong.

③ Madness can also be translated into feelings of Spiritual ecstasy. This gives rise to the concept of the Holy Fool, who follows only his own intuition and sense of rightness.

Maggots

(1) Maggots appearing in dreams in their correct context can represent the feelings we have about death. If a **fisherman was using maggots** we would be referring to power and energy, but if someone else was using maggots their use of nastiness might be in question.

(2) Maggots can represent impurities in the body and the sense of being eaten up by something, of having something within our body – such as an idea or feeling – that is alien to us and can therefore overtake and overcome us.

(3) Maggots in dreams may reflect our own fears about death and illness.

Magic
– also see Wand

(1) Magic previously was all about controlling external forces and may still have that significance in dreams. When we are using magic in a dream, we are using our energy to accomplish something without effort or difficulty. We are capable of controlling the situation that we are in, to have things happen for us and to create from our own needs and wants.

(2) Psychologically, when there is magic in a dream it is to do with our ability to link with our deepest powers. They can be the powers of sexuality or the powers of control, or of power over our surroundings. As mankind grows and matures psychologically, we return to an earlier form of magic and learn to live in harmony with our surroundings. This may give rise to magical images in dreams such as tree spirits and other forces of nature.

(3) Magic has always had an appeal. This may well be due to the mystery that surrounds it, and also the idea of something which is beyond our own understanding. Spiritually, ancient systems of understanding the Cosmos and the Divine give rise to many archetypal dream images which seem magical to the uninitiated.

Magistrate
– also see Judge/Magistrate in Occupations and Authority Figures in People

(1) Whenever an authority figure appears in a dream, it is very often harking back to our relationship with our father, with the need to be told what to do, or perhaps to have somebody who is more powerful than we are take control within our lives. Since a magistrate imposes the laws of society, it is also to do with our willingness to submit to authority on behalf of the Greater Good. Throughout life, we learn to belong to groups and to act in a way that is more in keeping with the needs of those groups.

(2) Authority figures are part of our make-up. It may well be that part of our being

knows best what we should be doing, and our conscious, everyday working self is not operating in keeping with that inner authority.

③ Spiritual authority coupled with spiritual knowledge is often represented by a dream of a magistrate. It signifies that we can be open to both.

Magnet

① We all have within us the ability to attract or repel others, and often a magnet appearing in a dream will highlight that ability. Since of itself the magnet is inert, it is the power it has that is important. We often need to realise the influence that we have over other people comes not only from ourselves, but also from our interaction with them.

② The magnet has the ability to create a 'field' round itself, a field of magnetic energy. Often the magnet appearing in a dream alerts us to the intrinsic power that we have, which is inert until such times as it is activated by situations around us in everyday life.

③ A magnet will suggest a degree of charisma within us which can be used in various ways, depending upon our inclinations.

Magnifying glass

① When anything is magnified in a dream it is being brought to our attention. **To be using a magnifying glass** indicates that we should be making what we are looking at conscious. It needs to be made part of our everyday working life and we do have the power to create something out of the material that we have.

② Where it strikes us that it is the magnifying glass itself, and not what we are looking at, that is important we are recognising our own abilities, our own power within a situation.

③ Making Spirituality manifest would initially mean being more aware of our own actions. We need to examine ourselves minutely, perhaps using spiritual techniques.

Magpie
– see Birds

Make-up
– also see Cosmetics

① Make-up normally indicates our ability to change the impression we make on others. If we are **making ourselves up** it can very often indicate a happy occasion or celebration. We need to put on a facade for people – we may even need to put on a facade for ourselves – so that we feel better about our own self image. If we are **making someone else up**, then often we are helping them to create a false – or perhaps better – impression. Recognising that we have the use of **a box of make-up** suggests that we are able to change our personality to suit our surroundings

② To be dealing with make-up means that we have a choice as to the sort of person we want to be. We can choose our outward appearance and can create an impression that perhaps is different from the one we naturally make use of. **'Making up' with someone** in the sense of having a reconciliation suggests being able to make adjustments in our perception of one another. We are prepared to be tolerant.

③ Spiritually we must be aware of the way we are 'made-up' (constructed) and must be conscious of the facade we present to other people and whether it differs greatly from the person we feel ourselves to be.

Mandala
– also see Mosaic

① The mandala is a sacred shape which is so powerful that it is found in one form or another in most religions. Typically, it is a circle enclosing a square with a symbol in the centre representing the whole of life. It is mostly used as an aid to meditation. The principle is that one travels from the outer circle (which stands for the whole of existence) through the creation of matter – the square – to the centre of existence – the central figure. Finally, one moves back out to take one's place in material existence again. It is often consciously depicted as an eight-pointed star, and represents both man's aspirations and his burdens. It often appears in dreams in this form, and can then become a personal symbol of the journey from chaos to order. It has also been found that, in a healing process, this symbol will occur over and over again. It is seen more frequently in Eastern religions, often as very ornate pictures or patterns.

② Jung judged this figure to be an important part of psychological wholeness. The word means 'circle', and he saw the mandala as being an archetypal expression of the soul. In dreams this symbol often appears without us knowing what it represents. It is only when it is drawn afterwards that it is recognised as a mandala. This would suggest that it is a true expression of our individuality and of his connection with Unity, whatever we see this to be.

③ When ego and individuality are understood, the soul searches for representation. The expression of wholeness and yet separateness in this figure moves us into a space which enables us to create a whole new concept of the principles of existence. Often, by creating and recreating this figure, we move towards and experience a wholeness and tranquillity which would not otherwise be available. The particular shape, number of sides, and colours in the mandala will be significant *(see Shapes/Patterns, Numbers and Colour)*. The mandala seen in dreams can become a gauge for spiritual progression.

Mallet

① The mallet is a symbol of authority and masculine force. For something like a hammer *(See Hammer)* or a mallet to appear in a dream indicates that we may be using undue force or power to achieve a certain outcome.

② The mallet is also the directing will, and to have such an item in a dream indicates that we may be attempting to make things happen in a way that is not necessarily appropriate for that particular situation.

③ A mallet suggests a form of spiritual power and energy. However, we do need to be aware of how the power and energy is being channelled.

Mandrake

① In olden times the mandrake root was taken to symbolise Man. It was often used in magical ceremonies, and thus became significant in the same way that a voodoo doll can be significant. When the mandrake root or a manikin is recognised in a dream, we are linking in with our own wish to harm other people and with our conflict with someone else. Interestingly enough, the mandrake root is also a symbol of the Great Mother *(see Great Mother/Mother Earth)*, and therefore represents feminine aspects. So, in witchcraft, the witch was in fact linking with the destructive powers of her own Self.

② The significance of mandrake within a dream is that perhaps of word association. We are not necessarily dreaming of the root itself, but are trying to make sense of some aspect of the personality around us that appears not to be fully formed in some way.

③ In less sophisticated forms of magic it is believed that we have power over the physical being. In former times mandrake represented the physical realms. Though we are less likely to have malign thoughts as we advance spiritually, old significances can still surface in dreams.

Manna

① Manna represents food and therefore has the same significance as bread. It is food for the soul and food which is in some way miraculous. For this to appear in a dream usually represents the ability we have to transmute something from the ordinary to the sacred.

② When we are seeking something, perhaps to change our lives in some way, we often need external help when everything around us is going wrong and we are beset by problems. The symbolism of manna – of the miraculous bread appearing – is something which makes us realise that we can in fact carry on. This symbol of the miraculous appears in many religions and therefore represents the aspect of ourselves that links with the Divine.

③ The Grace of God and his goodness is implicit in manna. We are in the right place at the right time for the right reasons.

Mansion
– see House

Mantis

① As with most insects, the mantis often represents something devious within our lives, that Trickster part of us *(see Trickster)* that can create problems when things are effectively working out for us. It is that aspect of our personality which perhaps preys on the other parts and will not take its place within our overall integration.

② In dreams, we often translate a quality or a situation we are struggling with into an object. To be aware of the mantis may indicate that on some level we are aware of trickery around us.

③ We should look carefully at the appearance of a mantis as it represents deviousness, particularly of an emotional kind.

Mantra

① The Mantra is the creation of a sound, corresponding to a name or an aspect of god, and is a creative vibration. Often it is three syllables long, and is an aid to becoming closer to the centre of both oneself and the universe. In dreams it is frequently first heard as the sound of one's own name *(see Name)*, and can be developed from there. It is (or rather becomes) the personal 'key' to universal knowledge.

② The intense concentration and repetition needed to fill the mind with one concept of whichever God one believes in – coupled with a sense of spiritual union – is a conscious activity designed to achieve a state of restful alertness. If dreams are considered to be alert restfulness, the use of Mantra can have a profound effect on the dream state in allowing us to be more focused in our dreaming. We are thus able to accept the spontaneity of the images evoked by Mantra when they also appear in dreams.

③ Spiritually, sound repeated over and over induces a change of consciousness and awareness. Mantra permits this to be positive and opens up possibilities for enhanced wisdom and knowledge.

Manure

① Some of the experiences which we have to go through can be painful or downright unwholesome. If we do not manage to understand what has happened to us and make use of it as part of our growth process, we can often find that those experiences remain within our subconscious and cause difficulty later on. These bad experiences may appear as manure within a dream and alert us to the fact that we should be breaking down our problems and making positive use of them.

② Manure can represent something which is disintegrating in our lives. To be aware for instance, of a pile of **manure in an inappropriate position** would indicate that we have something in our lives which will have to disintegrate, to change form before it can be used properly by us.

③ Manure can be seen also as the prelude to spiritual breakdown. This does not have to be a negative thing, as a rebuilding process is often what is required to enable us to find solutions to current problems.

Map

① For a map to appear in a dream often indicates the clarification of the direction we should be taking in life. We may feel that we are lost and need something to indicate the way forward, particularly so far as ambition or motivation is concerned. **A map that has already been used** by other people would therefore indicate that we are capable of taking a direction and learning from those people.

② When we first set out on the journey of discovery which makes us grow into capable human beings, we often need clarification of the way that we must undertake the journey. In dreams this often appears as a map. The **direction we are being shown to take** *(See Position)* is important; i.e. forwards, backwards, left or right and we are often helped by the idea of having a course to follow.

③ A map can obviously help us in our quest to find the spiritual way forward. It is worth remembering that we would need to read the map ourselves, and therefore we are our own guides.

Marble
– also see Obelisk

① Because it is a fine substance, marble appearing in a dream often indicates age or perhaps permanence. We all need some quality of permanence within our lives and marble can symbolise this.

② When we are in trouble, it can often seem that we are 'between a rock and a hard place'. Marble in a dream – because it is a beautiful substance – can reconcile us to the fact that we must move forward in an appropriate way.

③ Marble can represent spiritual firmness and the permanence of belief.

Mare
– see Horse in Animals

Marigold
– see Flowers

Market/Marketplace
– also see Shop

(1) Dreaming that we are **in a market** indicates our ability to cope with everyday life, of being able to relate to people, but particularly to relate to crowds. It is also the place of buying and selling and therefore often gives us some sort of indication as to how we value our various attributes, whether we have something to sell or whether we are buying.

(2) A market is a bustling, happy place and to dream of one may indicate that we need to look after ourselves more and to spend time with more people. It could also suggest that we need to become more commercial in the work that we are doing, or perhaps to be more creatively influenced, rather than doing something purely and simply because it is commercial – thus it has quite an ambivalent meaning.

(3) A marketplace can be viewed as a place of spiritual exchange in dreams. We can establish a balance between our everyday reality and our spiritual or inner world.

Marriage
– also see Wedding and Wedding Ring

(1) A marriage in a dream often indicates the uniting of two particular aspects of our personality which need to come together in order to create a better whole. For instance, the intellect and feelings – or perhaps the practical and intuitive sides – may need to be united. Often a marriage in dreams can be precognitive in that one may subconsciously be aware of a relationship between two people, but it has not yet registered on the conscious level. In today's secular society, to realise in dreams that two people are in fact married is to recognise the commitment involved.

(2) Because the human being is generally looking for someone to complement him or herself, to dream of being married can give some indication of the type of person we are looking for as a partner. We may, for instance, dream that we are marrying a childhood friend – in which case we are looking for somebody who has the same qualities as that person. We may dream we are marrying a famous figure and again the qualities of that particular person will be important. To be married to someone of a different age to ourselves may signify that we need to adjust our perception of ourselves. Perhaps we need a younger, more light-hearted outlook or a more mature, considered one.

(3) Spiritually, there is a process of integration which needs to come about. Firstly the masculine and feminine sides of our personality need to unite, making both drive and intuition available to us. Then the physical and spiritual sides need to harmonise. This is usually known as a Mystic Union or sacred marriage.

Marsh

– also see Swamp

① When we dream of a marsh or a swamp, it can indicate that we are feeling 'bogged down'. We feel that we are being held back in something we want to do, and perhaps we lack either the self-confidence or emotional support that we need to move forward. A marsh or a swamp can also indicate that we are being swamped by circumstances, being trapped in some way by the circumstances round us.

② Dreaming of marshy ground very often represents difficulty on an emotional level. Perhaps we are creating emotional difficulties for ourselves – or even having them created for us – which make it difficult for us to feel secure.

③ Spiritual and emotional conflict. We may be spiritually on 'dodgy ground' and should consider whether we are acting appropriately.

Martyr

① Actually experiencing ourselves in dreams as **playing the martyr** highlights our tendency to do things without being sufficiently assertive to say no, and to act from a sense of duty. When we are aware of **someone else being a martyr** our expectations of that person may be too high.

② Dreaming of a **religious martyr** often means we need to question our own religious beliefs and upbringing. We are perhaps allowing excessive enthusiasm to guide us.

③ We may feel the need, spiritually, to become a sacrificial victim and hence give our life some meaning. However, this should be looked at closely, as it may not be necessary.

Mask

① Most people have a facade they put on for others, particularly at a first meeting. To dream of a mask often alerts us to either our own or other people's facade. When we are not being true to ourselves we can often experience this in dreams as a 'negative' or frightening mask.

② When we are trying to protect ourselves and prevent other people knowing what we are thinking or feeling, we 'mask' ourselves. A mask appearing in a dream can therefore represent concealment. Additionally, in primitive cultures, **to wear a mask** such as that of an animal gave the wearer the powers of that animal. In Shamanism that is still accepted today.

③ The Death Mask, either our own or another's, can appear in dreams as a signal that it is time to put an end to a spiritual game we are playing. It is a memento of past behaviour.

Masturbation
– see Sex

Mattress
– also see Bed in Furniture/Furnishings

① Similar to a bed, to dream of a mattress indicates the feeling we have about a situation we have created in our lives, whether it is comfortable for us or not. We are aware of our own basic needs and are able to create relaxed feelings that allow us to express ourselves fully.

② Sexual comfort is important to most people. To dream of a mattress can very often indicate the way that we handle our own sexuality – whether we are comfortable with it, or whether we find it an uncomfortable thing to deal with.

③ The mattress can signify the spiritual support we receive. It is also a sign of a comforting environment.

Maypole

① A maypole in a dream can very often represent the masculine and may indicate the 'dance' which we go through when coming to terms with our own universe. It is the central pole of the world that we create for ourselves; thus to dream of a maypole may indicate the way in which we handle our own lives. It may also have sexual connotations.

② Psychologically, festivals, celebrations and occasions for ceremony are necessary for the human being to be at ease with himself. Often, the maypole may be one such symbol – of celebration, of new life. It may also represent time in a dream, and the way in which a dream indicates the type of timing that is necessary within certain situations.

③ The maypole in a spiritual sense is a representation of the phallic, of masculine spirituality and of life-giving energy. It is also a representation of the World Tree.

Maze
– also see Labyrinth

① A maze often represents a confusion of ideas and feelings. There are conflicting urges and opinions and we often discover that in attempting to find our way through the maze we have learnt something about our own courage, our own ability to meet problems. Often there is the apparently irrational fear and doubt that arises from not being able to find our way in and out of the maze. This can allow us to release feelings of self doubt and fear.

② Psychologically, the maze may represent the variety of opinions and authoritative beliefs that we come up against in our ordinary, everyday world. We may be trying to find our own way through this mass of detail and we picture it in a dream as actually trying to find our way through a maze.

③ The path to the Divine. The feminine intuitive path.

Meander

① In a dream, to have a path or the road in front of you meandering – that is, not going in any specific direction – suggests that we very often have to 'go with the flow', to simply follow what happens without actually thinking of the particular direction in which we are going. Sometimes the meandering has a kind of purpose, in that by moving about in an apparently aimless fashion we are actually finding out more about ourselves or the circumstances we are in.

② Water moves in its own way, and often to be conscious of a **river or a road meandering** around us indicates that we should be more aware of our own emotions, that we are capable of dealing with these emotions in a much gentler way than by being very direct. This may also refer to our relationship with other people. It could be that we need to recognise that other people cannot be as straightforward as we are.

③ The Spiritual Spiral. We should look at whether it is a downward spiral, an aimless wandering or a purposeful – if indirect – exploration.

Medal

① A medal is often a reward for good work or for bravery, so when one appears in a dream, it is a recognition of our own abilities. If we are **giving someone else a medal** then we are honouring that part of ourselves represented by the other person.

② Human beings both like and need to feel good about themselves. A medal in a dream acknowledges our talents and/or successes – not just in the immediate moment – but gives a permanent reminder of what we have done.

③ A badge of honour reflecting our attunement with the Spiritual code can be symbolised in dreams by a medal.

Media
– also see Celebrity and Fame

① In its original meaning media meant 'the means of communication' and will often appear in dreams as simply that – a way of getting information across. To dream of **being interviewed**, for instance, might signify needing to reach a wider audience or overcoming our own reticence.

② Nowadays, the media in the form of newspapers and television can often be considered intrusive and not necessarily to be trusted. When we ourselves are learning to be more communicative through such media as social networking sites we perhaps feel more in control of what others know about us. Dreaming of using such tools may signify such control.

③ Speaking wisely and well is an aspect of spiritual development which needs to be developed in order to put our own personal message across. This may be perceived in dreams as using the media in some way.

Medicine
– also see Chemist/Pharmacist

① **To be taking medicine** in a dream suggests that on some level we are aware of part of ourselves which needs healing. Often we are aware of what the medicine is for and are thus alerted either to a health problem, or to a situation which can be changed from the negative to the positive.

② Sometimes an experience which we have in waking life can be unpleasant in the immediate moment, but ultimately is good for us. In dreams, medicine can stand as such a symbol.

③ The spiritual need for a healing influence in our lives is indicated by medicine appearing. It does not necessarily mean we are, or will be, unwell – merely that changes are necessary.

Meditation

① Interpreting the act of meditation will depend on whether we meditate in waking life. In someone who does, it will suggest a discipline that is helpful to us when putting ourselves in touch with intuition and spiritual matters. In someone who does not, it may indicate the need to be more introverted in order to understand the necessity to be responsible for oneself.

② Often on an unconscious level we are aware of the need to change consciousness or attitude, and to dream of meditating can highlight this for us. We can access the more creative, spiritual side.

③ We need to have a degree of discipline if we are to succeed in our spiritual goals.

Medium

① Dreaming of **visiting a medium** very often means that we are looking for some kind of contact with our own unconscious, or with the dead. We may also be attempting to alert our own intuition and use it differently to a way we have done previously.

② To dream of **being mediumistic** would indicate that we are aware of greater powers than we believe we have in ordinary everyday life.

③ Mediumistic aspects in a dream can represent our wish to be in contact with the dead. This does not necessarily have to be dead in literal terms, it can merely be what we consider to be 'dead' in our life, that which we may wish to resurrect.

Melt
– also see Thaw

① To see **something melting** in a dream is an indication that our emotions may be softening. We are perhaps losing the rigidity we have needed to face the world with previously. We are undergoing a change and are becoming softer.

② When we **feel ourselves to be melting** we may be becoming more romantically inclined and less likely to drive ourselves forward. We may need to sit and simply let a situation develop around us to the point where it is safe for us to give up control.

③ On a spiritual level 'melting away' has sometimes had connections with evil, or badness. When challenged, evil disappears.

Memorial
– also see Obelisk

① To see a memorial such as **a war memorial** in a dream takes us back to a previous time, to a memory which may be 'cast in stone'. We need to be able to come to terms with, and accept, this memory in order to be able to move on.

② A memorial appearing in a dream may simply be a recognition of a happier time which needs to be remembered. Perhaps we can apply those happy feelings to something in our lives today.

③ A memorial is a tangible representation of homage and esteem.

Menstruation
– also see Blood

① To dream of menstruation may be linking with the creative side of ourselves which can conceive new ideas and can create new and more wonderful 'children' out of simple material. We are linking with the mystery of life and with the procreative drive.

② Since menstruation is such an integral part of the feminine life, it can indicate in **a woman's dream** her acceptance of her own emerging sexuality. In a **man's dream** however, it can alert him to his fear surrounding relationships and union with the feminine. It can also indicate his own feminine side and his need to understand his own sensitivity.

③ The Cycle of Life and all that is mysterious in women can be symbolised by menstruation. It is only in a patriarchal society that it is seen as unclean.

Merge/Merger

① In mundane terms a merger is a business device to allow two different companies – often with very disparate cultures – to combine. Where there is a great deal of stress involved in our lives the concerns of the day will often overshadow dreams and we will dream of trying to combine two very different ideas, objects or concepts.

② When two things merge, they both lose their singular identity and create a third entity, often completely different from the originals. Dreaming, for instance, of **two roads merging** may mean combining two ideas which will take us in a totally different direction to our present one. If **two objects merge** to become one in a dream, it indicates we must take into consideration the qualities of both.

③ In the course of spiritual development there is a point at which, rather than treating the spiritual realms and the mundane world as being two different modes of awareness, we must merge the two in order to live our lives successfully. This is known as living life mindfully.

Mermaid/Merman

① Traditionally, the mermaid or merman belongs to the sea as well as being able to exist on land. This symbolically represents an ability to be deeply emotional and also entirely practical. Until these two separate parts are properly integrated, the human being cannot fully exist in either realm.

② Mermaids and mermen are feminine and masculine representations of the link between the darker forces – which we do not necessarily understand – and the conscious self. Many stories exist of the human's attempt to mate or link with these creatures of the sea. Most end in hurt and distress for one party or the other. This is an example of how difficult it is to integrate the two sides of our nature.

③ We must each bring about integration between the Spiritual Self and the emotional self before there can be wholeness. This can be represented in dreams by mermaids or mermen.

Metal

① Any metal which appears in dreams represents the restrictions and limitations of the real world. It can represent our basic abilities and attributes, but can also indicate a hardness of feeling or emotional rigidity.

② Most metals have symbolic meanings. They can also be connected with various planets: Sun is represented by gold, the Moon by silver, Mercury by quicksilver, Venus by copper, Mars by iron, Jupiter by tin, Saturn by lead.

③ Spiritual elements and how they can enhance our progression.

Microscope

① A microscope in a dream very often indicates that we need to pay attention to detail. Also we may need to be somewhat introspective in order to achieve a personal goal.

② We have the ability to look at things in dreams in much finer detail than we would necessarily do in the waking state. While the mind can be creative it sometimes also needs to apply scientific and perhaps logical thought to a problem, and the symbol of a microscope can draw attention to this.

③ A degree of detailed introspection is called for, either spiritual or physical.

Milk
– see Food

Mill/Millstone/Millwheel

① A mill extracts what is useful from the crude material it is fed. It is this quality that is symbolised in dreams. We are able to extract from our experiences in life what is useful to us and can convert it into nourishment. A **millwheel** has the symbolism of picking up and utilising necessary energy.

② There is a transformation which occurs when a material of any sort is ground, and any dream containing a mill will signify that transformation. The two stones are believed by some to signify will and intellect, the tools we use in transformation. Because of its connection with water, a millwheel symbolises the efficient use of emotion.

③ Both the millstone and the millwheel represent transformative Spiritual energy, turning crude information into usable knowledge.

Mines
– also see Digging/Excavation

① Dreaming of mines signifies bringing the resources of the unconscious into the light of day. We are able to use the potential we have available. Interestingly, in dreams, mines can also represent the workplace. **Landmines** and other such devices suggest short, sharp, sudden trauma.

② This is one of those symbols which can actually be a word play. The things in the dream are 'mine'. It could also be that there is a potentially explosive situation which needs handling carefully.

③ Mines spiritually suggest the ability to 'mine', or learn from the emerging unconscious. We can go into the depths of our being to discover the valuable material that can be brought to the surface and utilised.

Minotaur
– See Fabulous Beasts

Mirror
– also see Reflection

(1) Dreaming of a mirror suggests concern over our self-image. We are worried as to what others think of us, and need self-examination in order to function correctly. There may be some anxiety over ageing or health.

(2) To be **looking in a mirror** can signify trying to look behind us without letting others know what we are doing. We may have a concern over past behaviour. We may also need to 'reflect' on something we have done or said. When the **image in the mirror is distorted** we are having a problem in understanding ourselves. When the **mirror image speaks to us** we should be listening more closely to our inner selves.

(3) Self-realisation which reflects wisdom. As a means of understanding ourselves on a deeper level, we can set up a dialogue in real life between one's mirror image and oneself. Many of the insights gained can be quite startling.

Miscarriage

(1) Dreaming of a miscarriage **whether our own or someone else's** suggests that we are conscious of the fact that something is not right. **In a woman's dream** it will depend on whether she has suffered a miscarriage, since nowadays she may well not have given herself time to grieve properly.

(2) Dreaming of a miscarriage can also suggest the loss of work, a project or even a part of ourselves, and we need time to acclimatise.

(3) A miscarriage can represent aspects of early death and the fear it can engender.

Mist

(1) Mist is a symbol of loss and confusion – particularly emotionally – so when this image appears we may need to sit down and reconsider our actions.

(2) Mist in a dream can indicate a transition state, a way from one state of awareness to another and will often manifest to signify this.

(3) Mist can symbolise Spiritual initiation and learning, the state of limbo.

Mistletoe
– also see Flowers

(1) Conventionally, mistletoe represents a time of celebration, love and partnership.

Because of these well-known associations it is most often dreamt of around Christmas.

② As a parasite, mistletoe has the ability to draw strength from its host, but also to be useful in its own right. It can therefore symbolise relationships where there is a dependency on one partner.

③ Mistletoe represents the Essence of Life. It is a divine healing substance.

Moat

① A moat is a representation of our defences against intimacy. In dreams we can see for ourselves how we build or dig those enclosures. We can also decide what steps we need to take to remove them.

② When we need to contain our own emotions we will often create a way of monitoring to whom we need to relate. A moat can be a symbol for this ability. A moat can be also represent an emotional barrier or defence.

③ A moat can represent our spiritual defences. Because a moat is man-made it may suggest that we are using our emotions from a logical perspective rather than allowing them to flow freely.

Mob
– see Crowd/Mob

Mobile
– see Immobility and Telephone

Mole
– also see Animals

① A mole lends itself to many dream interpretations. In dreams awareness of a **skin blemish** or disturbance may alert us to a problem which has not yet become fully apparent in our everyday lives. This need not be a health problem, but is most probably a difficulty which if not handled efficiently may give us problems later on. The **animal mole** appearing in a dream signifies someone, or something, that will not go away.

② Another interpretation of mole is as a bulwark against an excess of emotion. Properly constructed, in waking life we can create a safe space for ourselves free from emotional storms (*See Pier/Harbour*).

③ Following the idea of a burrowing animal, in spiritual terms a mole may represent infiltration by a negative or external influence, particularly one which remains unnoticed for a period of time. It can also represent subversive behaviour, usually through lack of perception or – as with a spy – due to a conflict of beliefs.

Money

– also see Debt, Finance, Income, Poverty and Wealth

① Money in dreams does not necessarily represent hard currency, but more the way in which we value ourselves. This symbol appearing in dreams would suggest that we need to assess that value more carefully, and equally to be aware of what we 'pay' for our actions and desires. Being aware of money in dreams can also alert us to our need for security or status.

② Money can also represent our own personal resources – whether material or spiritual – and our potential for success. In some circumstances a dream of money can be linked with our view of our own power and our sexuality. Being conscious of 'small change' is obvious in its symbolism, whereas larger quantities of money might represent reward or available energy.

③ Money is a unit of exchange and is a representation of the effort that is put into making life work for us. In dreams – similar to using techniques such as meditation to enhance our spirituality – it can be a symbol of self worth or of the esteem that others have for us.

Monitor

① In its original meaning a monitor was a student given the task of keeping others up to scratch. If we dream of someone in that position we are accessing that part of ourselves which judges our own behaviour. A computer screen on the other hand would have different meanings. If it is active it is a receiver of information. If not switched on it would suggest that we are not in tune with those around us.

② To be monitoring something suggests that we are following its progress. Being monitored on the other hand can indicate that we are undergoing a lack of confidence or feel that someone is spying on us.

③ Witnessing in the spiritual sense is being able to observe dispassionately without making any judgement whatsoever. Experiencing monitoring or being monitored in a dream indicates that we are aware of that part of us which is capable of being dispassionate.

Monk

– see Monks in Occupations

Monkey

– see Animals

Monster

① Any monster appearing in a dream represents something that we have made larger than life. We have personalised it so that whatever is worrying us appears as a creature. It usually stands for our negative relationship with ourselves and fear of our own emotions and drives.

② When, in everyday life, events get out of proportion we often have to suppress our reactions. In dreams we cannot do this and so our minds create some way of dealing with the problem. Often the colour of the monster (*see Colour*) will give us some indication of what the problem is, thus a **red** monster would indicate anger (possibly uncontrolled), whereas a **yellow** one might suggest resentment.

③ Fear of death or sudden change and all that goes with it. A monster can highlight a more childlike fear, and can be looked at thus.

Moon
– also see Planets

① The moon has always represented the emotional and feminine self. It is the intuition, the psychic, love and romance. To dream of the moon, therefore, is to show we are in touch with that side of ourselves which is dark and mysterious. Often in dreams the moon can also represent our mother or the relationship with her.

② It has always been known that the moon has a psychological effect on the human being. In Pagan times, it was suggested that she ruled men's emotions and guarded women's intuition. Even today, that symbolism still stands. **In a man's dream** when the moon appears, he either has to come to terms with his own intuitive side or with his fear of women. **In a woman's dream** the moon usually indicates her inter-relations with other women through their collective intuition.

③ The Great Mother (*see Great Mother/Mother Earth*), or the darker, unknown side of Self, is symbolised by the moon. It is also symbolic of the unapproachable.

Morning
– see Time

Mortgage
– also see Debt, Finance and Money

① Dreaming of a mortgage or problems with the ability to pay it is not surprising in times when our security is threatened. This may be due to necessary or enforced changes regarding the best use of our material resources. In that a mortgage is a personal responsibility, such dreams reveal what is truly important to us and often what risks we are prepared to take to maintain stability.

② From an emotional perspective, a mortgage can variously represent a necessary expenditure to enable us to feel that we have a secure home or a commitment to future security. As financial authorities in waking life prove less amenable to lending, a mortgage in dreams may also symbolise an unattainable goal.

③ Interestingly, the true meaning of mortgage – a pledge against death – gives us the spiritual interpretation of this in dreams. We have given a promise which dictates our spiritual conduct for the rest of our lives.

Mortuary

① In everyday life, a mortuary is a frightening place, connected as it tends to be with the trauma of death. When a mortuary appears in a dream, we are usually having to consider our fears and feelings about death.

② If we are **viewing a dead body** we may be having to consider a part of ourselves that has died, or perhaps a now defunct relationship. If **we are the body in the mortuary**, we may have induced a state of inertia which does not allow us to enjoy life properly.

③ Death and dying, again not necessarily the final calling, but possibly new spiritual awareness.

Mosaic
– also see Mandala

① Any intricate pattern appearing in dreams usually signifies the pattern of our lives. We probably need to consider life as a whole, but also to understand and respect the many separate parts of it.

② Within a mosaic, made up of many small parts, there is a deliberate act of creation. When such a symbol appears in dreams we are being alerted to our abilities as creator. The colours and shapes used will be important *(see Colours and Shapes)*.

③ The Kaleidoscope of Life with its many facets is a potent spiritual symbol represented in dreams by the mosiac.

Moses
– see Religious Iconology

Moth

① The moth is largely associated with night-time and therefore connects with the hidden side of our nature. Also, because the moth can be self-destructive when there is light around, it tends to symbolise our dream self and the more transient side of our personality.

② As the butterfly is taken as the symbol for the soul, so the moth symbolises the darker side of us which uses fantasy. The **moth emerging from darkness** signifies the recognition of self we must all achieve to survive.

③ The moth symbolises the Self (*see Self*), but perhaps in its darker, less well understood, sense.

Mother
– see Family and Archetypes

Motorbike
– see Transport

Mould/Mouldy
– also see Putrefaction

① When mould is present in a dream it will represent one of two things. Firstly there is some kind of contamination or unpleasantness present in our waking lives and secondly there is not enough energy in a project or idea to stop it from deteriorating badly.

② When organic matter goes mouldy it has been invaded by another organism. It is this symbolism which becomes apparent in dreams. We are perhaps experiencing unwanted interference in our waking lives. Interestingly, not all invasive material is negative, but may sometimes be beneficial in outcome, once we have understood its purpose.

③ Mould or mouldiness usually signifies the presence of negativity, often parasitic in nature. This would suggest that given the opportunity, the negativity will grow, depleting the energy of positive thought, unless we take steps to deal with it.

Mound
– also see Hill

① Traditionally, any mound appearing in a dream is supposed to link back to our very early childhood needs and the comfort that mother's breast brought.

② Emotionally, Man's need for comfort and sustenance continues throughout his life. At the same time, he needs to come to terms with his dependence on the feminine. Often to dream of mounds helps him to understand this.

③ The mound symbolises the Earth Mother (*see Great Mother/Mother Earth*) or the entrance to the Underworld.

Mountain
– also see Climb

① In dream sequences the mountain usually appears in order to symbolise an obstacle which needs to be overcome. By daring to **climb the mountain** we challenge our own inadequacies and free ourselves from fear. To **reach the top** is to achieve one's goal. To **fall down the mountain** is to indicate carelessness.

② .We all have difficulties to face in life. Often it is how we face those difficulties that is important. The symbol of the mountain offers many alternatives and choices. This means we can work out, through dreams, our best course of action in everyday life.

③ Representing the centre of our existence in earthly terms, the mountain is an image that can be worked on from many different perspectives.

Mourning

– also see Funeral and Weeping

① The process of mourning is an important one in all sorts of ways. We not only mourn death but also the end of a relationship or a particular part of our lives. Since sometimes mourning or grieving is seen as inappropriate in waking life, it will often appear in dreams as a form of relief or release.

② In many cultures less emotionally repressed than our own, the period of mourning is seen as a way of assisting the departing soul on its way. In dreams we may find that we are helping ourselves to create a new beginning through our mourning for the old. Psychologically, we need a period of adjustment when we have lost something. Our grief may be as much for ourselves as for what we have lost, or had taken away.

③ Grief. We may need to look at how we deal with grief on both a spiritual and physical level.

Mouse

– see Animals

Mouth

– see Body

Movement

① Movement in dreams is usually highlighted to make us aware of progress. **Moving forward** suggests an acceptance of our abilities, while **moving backwards** signifies withdrawal from a situation. **Moving sideways** would suggest a deliberate act of avoidance.

② The way we move in dreams can indicate a great deal about our acceptance of ourselves. For instance, to be **moving briskly** would suggest an easy acceptance of the necessity for change, whereas **being moved** – such as on some kind of moving walkway – would signify being moved by outside circumstances or at the wish of other people.

③ A movement towards Spiritual Acceptance can be undertaken when the time is considered to be right.

Mud

① Mud in a dream suggests that we are feeling bogged down, perhaps by not having sorted out practicality and emotion (earth and water). Mud can also represent past experiences or our perception of them which has the ability to hold us back.

② Mud represents the fundamental substance of life which, handled properly, has a tremendous potential for growth but handled badly can be dangerous. Other circumstances in the dream will indicate what we should be doing.

③ Spiritually mud represents the very basic material from which we are all formed, and the need to go 'back to basics'.

Mummy (Egyptian)

① The obvious connection between Mummy and mother is a play on words. In many ways our mother must 'die', or rather, we must change our relationship with her, in order to survive and grow. The Egyptian mummy in dreams can also symbolise our feelings about someone who has died.

② The Egyptian mummy symbolises death, but also preservation after death and therefore the afterlife. We may be trying to understand such a concept in real life, or we may realise that life has got to continue on a more mundane level.

③ The Self, the unbending Mother and self preservation are all symbolised in the mummy.

Murder/Murderer
– also see Kill

① We may be denying, or trying to control, a part of our own nature that we do not trust. We may also have feelings about other people which can only be safely expressed in dreams. If we ourselves are **being murdered** a part of our lives is completely out of balance and we are being destroyed by external circumstances.

② **To be angry enough to kill** suggests that we are retaining some kind of childhood anger, since it is quite natural for a child to wish somebody dead. If we are **trying to murder somebody else** in a dream, we first need to understand what that person represents to us before recognising the violence of our own feelings.

③ Wilful destruction is the relevant symbol here. Spiritually we need to take a look at what is in our path and also what we need to change in order to progress.

Museum
– also see Fossil

① A museum in a dream denotes old-fashioned thoughts, concepts and ideas. We may need to consider such things but perhaps more objectively than subjectively.

② A museum can represent a place where we store our memories and therefore can represent the subconscious – it is that part of ourselves which we will usually only approach in an effort to understand who we are and where we came from.

③ The past as an interesting relic that can be observed at some length, and then moved away from in order to progress.

Music/Rhythm
– also see Musical Instruments and Orchestra

① Music and rhythm are both an expression of our inner selves and of our connection with life. To **hear music** suggests that we have the potential to make that basic association. Music can also represent a sensuous and sensual experience.

② **Sacred music** such as chanting, drumming and **pipe playing** is used to induce an altered state of consciousness, and this can be represented in dreams by the hearing of music.

③ Sacred sound has always been used in acts of worship, as has dancing (*see Dance/Dancing*).

Musical Instruments
– also see Drum, Flute, Organ and Piano

① Musical instruments in a dream often stand for our skills and abilities in communication. **Wind instruments** tend to suggest the intellect. **Percussion instruments** suggest the basic rhythm of life.

② Sometimes in dreams, musical instruments can suggest the sexual organs and therefore one's attitude to one's own sexuality.

③ Ways of self-expression (for example, playing a musical instrument) are offerings of our own creativity and are spiritual acts.

Mystic knot

① Traditionally, the mystic knot had no beginning and no end. Its basic meaning suggests an unsolvable problem. We probably need to leave such a problem until it is solved by time.

② The mystic knot usually appears as we are attempting to understand ourselves and our relationship with the spiritual.

③ The mystic knot suggests Infinity or the unsolvable mystery of Life itself.

Nail

① Dreaming of nails, as in **woodworking**, suggests our ability to bond things together. The holding power of the nail may also be significant. **Finger and toe nails** usually suggest claws or the capability of holding on.

② The penetrative power of the nail may be significant if we are experiencing issues to do with gender. In **a woman's dream** the nail may represent drive and assertion, whilst in **a man's dream** the issue may well be one of sustainability.

③ Spiritually the nail represents necessity and fate. In the Christian faith, nails also signify ultimate sacrifice and pain.

Nakedness
– see Nude

Name

① Our name is the first thing we are conscious of possessing. It is our sense of self and of belonging. If we **hear our name called** in a dream, our attention is being drawn specifically to the person we are. There is a suggestion that parents name their child so that the meaning of the name carries the biggest lesson that the child has to learn in life. For instance, Charles means 'man', and Bridget means 'strength'.

② When we are aware of **other people's names,** we are probably also aware of the qualities that person has and it is those qualities we need to look at. When the **name of a place** comes up in a dream, we are considering the way we feel about that place, or something we know about it. There may also be some word-play on the names.

③ Spiritually, when something is named it then has form and therefore meaning. The name allows us to link with the Essential Self.

Narrow

① When we dream of anything which is narrow, we are aware of restrictions and limitations. Sometimes we have created them ourselves, sometimes other people will have created them for us. A **narrow road** would perhaps suggest some kind of restriction, and a warning that we must not deviate from our path.

② We should take care not to be narrow-minded and judgemental. We may be being intolerant and parochial in our opinions. A **narrow bridge** might suggest a difficulty in communication, perhaps in putting our ideas across.

③ One-pointedness and bigotry are not qualities which are particularly spiritual, but self-discipline may require us to keep to the 'straight and narrow'.

Native American
– see Guardian Spirits

Nausea

① Nausea in a dream usually indicates the need to get rid of something which is making us feel uncomfortable. It may be a reflection of our physical state, but since the stomach is the seat of the emotions, it may be a representation of an emotion that is distressing us.

② The body often has its own way of alerting us to difficulties, and it may be that nausea in a dream indicates a problem before it manifests in the physical.

③ Nausea can also suggest an awareness of something spiritually rotten or putrid.

Navel

① To be conscious of the navel, whether **our own or another's**, is to be aware of the way in which we connect our inner-self with the rest of the outside world. It is the way in which the baby in the womb first becomes aware of its physicality. In dreams we often need to be aware of our bodily image, which will help indicate the way we see ourselves, which in turn enables us to work out the way we fit in to the everyday world.

② The navel in a dream can signify our dependency on others, particularly our mother. The navel is our emotional centre, and also, as adults, initially the seat of our power. Often in nightmares we become conscious of something, perhaps a Devil sitting on our navel, and this can be a personification of our own fears.

③ The navel or solar plexus is spiritually the point of connection between the spiritual and the physical. It is the lower *Dan Tien (hara)* in Eastern martial arts.

Navigate/Navigation

① In the sense of finding one's way, navigation is a very strong image. When new experiences happen in waking life, navigation highlights the idea of moving into the unknown, often without enough information. We must act with circumspection.

② In times of stress dreams about navigating a steady course or successfully avoiding obstacles can confirm our sense of rightness. Originally used in the sense of steering a craft, navigation now encompasses not only vehicles but also moving from point to point to accomplish a task such as research. Each point gives more usable information.

③ In mythology it was thought that the gods navigated the sun and moon in boats or barques across the sky, and navigation has thus taken on the meaning of moving in the right direction through the Journey of Life.

Near

① When we are conscious of being near someone or something in a dream we are on the point of recognising them in waking life. We may be becoming emotionally closer or more able to handle whatever is happening.

② When an object or image in a dream is near us – that is, when we are passive within the dream situation – we are often alerted to the fact that something will happen quickly. Spatial awareness in dreams can give us a concept of time and vice versa.

③ Conscious Awareness of those aspects of life which are spiritual often manifest as a nearness.

Necklace
– also see Jewels/Gems

① A necklace suggests a special object, and thus translates into special qualities or attributes. There is a richness to be acknowledged. This may be of feeling or of emotion. An old interpretation of a man giving a woman a necklace was that he would soon ask for her hand in marriage.

② Necklaces arose from the wearing of a chain of office and in dreams suggests a dignity or honour which has been conferred on the wearer.

③ The necklace is an acknowledgement of honour and power. The rosary is a special kind of necklace which aids one in prayer.

Needle

① In dreams needles suggest irritations, but can also signify the power to heal through penetration. A concept or knowledge has to be introduced from the outside, which may hurt, but will ultimately make us better from the inside.

② The ability to have some penetrating insights about our own state can help us to cope with everyday life. It will depend if the needles are being used by us, as in sewing, or on us – for instance medically.

③ The needle can suggest masculine sexuality, but also the type of penetrating insight which changes our view of life.

Nephew
– see Extended Family in Family

Nest

① The nest symbolises safety and perhaps home life. We may be emotionally dependent on the people around us and afraid of 'leaving the nest'.

② It is perhaps interesting to note that just before giving birth many women have a nesting instinct. This will sometimes emerge in dreams before it is recognised in waking life.

③ Security within our known environment and the safety of a sacred space.

Net/Network
– also see Computer and Internet

① A net in dreams usually indicates that we are feeling trapped and entangled in a scheme or situation. **In a woman's dream** she will be aware of her own seductive power, whereas **in a man's dream** he will be conscious of his fear of women.

② Women are often able to create a network of 'sisters' through the use of intuition, and often will symbolise this in dreams as a tangible bonding. In business terms, partly because of the spread of technology, a network of associates is an integral part of daily life. Dreams will often demonstrate in graphic form how to make the best use of such networks.

③ Nets and networks represent the many levels of interrelationship that are possible, particularly in spiritual terms. Some are more subtle than others.

Nettle

① A nettle in a dream suggests that there is a difficult situation which will have to be avoided. There may be irritation, particularly if we are not interacting with others or with the environment we are in. **A patch of nettles** could also suggest difficulty in communication if we are in the middle of it. Others round us may be using words or circumstances to hurt us. Nettles in a dream can also signify a worthless transaction: 'I got stung'.

② Nettles are wild plants with the quality of irritating the skin. This symbolism can come across in dreams as having allowed ourselves to be over-stimulated by a display of wild behaviour. This may be sexually, but could be in other ways as well, such as through dance. There is a point at which there is loss of control. Nettles can also suggest a kind of healing, both through the vitamins and minerals they contain when eaten, and also because they can be used to stimulate the system through external application. Folk medicine often suggested applying poultices of nettles to stimulate the blood supply.

③ In spiritual terms, nettle is supposed to be a specific against danger. It is also used in purification rituals. Fresh nettles are reputed to aid a sick person's recovery.

New

① Dreaming of something which is new suggests a new beginning, a new way of looking at or dealing with situations, or perhaps a new relationship. Thus, **new shoes** might suggest either a different way forward or a way of connecting with the earth. A **new hat** might suggest a novel intellectual approach, whereas **new spectacles** indicate a fresh way of seeing things.

② To be **doing something new** in a dream highlights the potential in a fresh learning situation. We are stimulated and excited initially. When we move into a new situation in real life our dreams can highlight our fears and difficulties. We may often dream of possible scenarios where we are not functioning as well as we should, or of actions we might take to enhance our performance.

③ The new, within the spiritual, is information which comes to us at the right time to enable us to progress. What is new to us may not actually be new but has impact because we have not previously known it.

New Year

① To dream of the New Year is to recognise the need for a fresh start. It may also signify the measurement of time in a way that is acceptable, or a time when something can happen.

② Psychologically, when there is a need for renewal or a new growth in understanding we need to acknowledge the effort we must make. This is often symbolised as a New Year, a new beginning.

③ Spiritually, in any culture, the New Year with its attendant celebrations can signify enlightenment or new knowledge becoming available. We are no longer in the depths of darkness.

Newspaper

① Although less popular today than they once were, newspapers will suggest knowledge which is publicly available. It may be information that we require in order to make sense of the world around us, or it may be something which is specific to us. A **tabloid newspaper** may suggest sensational material, whereas **a quality one** would suggest better researched data. **A Sunday newspaper** may suggest that we have the ability to assimilate the knowledge we need in periods of rest and relaxation. **A local newspaper** signifies that the facts we require are close to hand.

② Newspapers in dreams signify new information available to us which is now conscious, rather than being held subconsciously. It is information which we need. A **blank page** can have two meanings. Firstly, the information may not be available to us for various reasons. Secondly, it may be for us to provide the information for other people to make use of.

③ Spiritually, we should be aware that what we do needs to be for the Greater Good. We need to be more publicly visible.

Niche

① Everyone has a basic need to belong and often we are conscious in dreams of finding our particular place. It manifests itself in dreams as a place where we are protected on all sides except from the front. It has been suggested that this is a return to the childhood state prior to the age of four when the child begins to realise that he is vulnerable from the rear. A niche is therefore our 'spot' – the place where we are safe.

② In new situations we have a need to understand the world we are entering. Often our dream scenarios can open up possibilities by showing us where we belong – what niche we need to find for ourselves. Not only must we find the space where we belong but we must know which external factors are going to help us and which will hinder. Dream images connected with the niche will give us such information.

③ In religious iconology, the niche is consecrated so that it is a fit place to contain the Divine. It then symbolises the holiness and special powers relevant to the particular deity. If an icon *(see Icon)* is placed within the niche, then the energy of the god or goddess is present and available to us.

Niece
– see Extended Family in Family

Night
– also see Time

① Night signifies a period of rest and relaxation. It can, however, also suggest a time of chaos and difficulty. It is a time for 'ghosties, ghoulies and things that go bump in the night'. More positively, it is a period which allows us to create a new beginning with the dawning of the new day. Used constructively, night is therefore the fallow period before fresh growth.

② Physiologically night is a time when the body is supposed to be renewing itself. In Chinese medicine, certain hours of the night correspond with the renewal of certain organs in the body. Insanity may eventually ensue if the body were not able to repair itself properly over a period of time.

③ Night symbolises the darkness that occurs before rebirth or initiation. There is a disintegration which has to occur before there can be enlightenment. Night can also signify death or drastic change.

Nimbus
– also see Aura

① The force field – or electro-magnetic energy – that emanates from each of us has a particular quality in those who have undertaken to develop themselves spiritually. To the clairvoyant eye it can appear as a type of mother-of-pearl radiance.

② The charisma which many world and spiritual leaders have is felt by many. The nimbus is usually slightly more subtle, and therefore more far reaching, than the normal person's aura.

③ The nimbus is often portrayed in religious pictures as the halo or divine radiance around saintly people.

No

① To be aware of saying no in a dream may be an important part of our growth process. We are capable of making decisions which go against the wishes of other people, without feeling that we are going to be punished. We are coming to terms with rejection and are no longer fearful. We are capable of standing on our own two feet.

② The right to refuse is an important aspect of making choices. We may have no coherent reason for refusal, except the right to say no. In terms of relationships, saying no suggests that we know what is right for us.

③ Saying no in spiritual terms entails rejecting that which is not compatible with our progress.

Noose
– also see Hanging and Rope

① A noose in a dream suggests that we have a fear of being trapped, perhaps by others' actions. We are aware that we can create a trap for ourselves, thereby 'putting a noose round our own necks'. Traditionally, a drawing of a **hangman's noose** was a threat of death and it can still have that significance in dreams. As always, this death may be of part of our personality.

② A noose, like the halter, harness and other symbols of restraint suggests the taming of something wild. So, for a **young man about to be married** to dream of a noose might indicate a fear of being restrained unduly. For a **young woman wishing to leave home,** a noose might represent a fear of becoming trapped in the parental home. A noose can also imply the prevention of self-expression.

③ At its simplest, the noose represents a traumatic death. In a more complex sense it can represent the binding of spiritual intent, the harnessing of spiritual energy.

North
– see Position

Notice

① There are so many interpretations of notice in dreams that it is worthwhile considering other aspects of the dream scenario for accuracy. Notice being taken of **an object** in dreams suggests consideration needs to be given to what that object represents. A notice in the form of a **leaflet or poster** will convey information or instruction. When we are being noticed in dreams we usually have issues with approval or disapproval which need to be resolved.

② If we are being **given notice** in dreams, for instance of **termination of a contract,** we need to be aware that new ideas and thoughts need to be introduced and we perhaps should be proactive rather than reactive. A past method of working or of behaviour is no longer appropriate. **Giving notice to someone else** suggests that a useful association is coming to an end. From a psychological perspective we may no longer require the behaviour being shown by our dream character.

③ Spiritually noticing a particular facet in dreams is a way of alerting us to changes which may be necessary. Changes in behaviour in line with greater understanding often need due consideration before we can incorporate them in our way of operating.

Nourishment/Nurturing
– also see Eating and Food

① In dreams, all symbols of nourishment are associated with basic needs. Firstly, we require warmth and comfort; secondly, shelter and sustenance. Initially we experience this as coming from mother. Any dream in which we become aware of our needs then links with our relationship with mother. If our need for nourishment and nurturing is not met we experience rejection and hurt. In dreams the two become interchangeable.

② All symbols of containment (the vessel, cup, cauldron, bowl etc.) are symbols of nurturing and femininity. Food-producing animals are also associated with the nourishing aspects of the mother and therefore of Mother Earth.

③ The suggestions of nourishing the soul and conferring immortality all belong to the nurturing of the Mother Goddess.

Novel
– also see Book and Reading

① Strictly, a novel represents a different way of looking at things. If we are aware in dreams of reading such a book, we need to ascertain what kind of a novel it is. The storyline may have relevance in our lives at that particular moment. For instance, a **historical novel** might suggest we need to explore the past, whereas a **romantic novel** would suggest the need to look at relationships.

② Novel also means new, and psychologically we are often searching for stimulation. In dreams, therefore, there can be a play on words to indicate that we should be looking for some new way of dealing with our lives.

③ New spiritual learning can often be explained in terms of a story or a myth.

Nuclear Explosion
– also see Atom Bomb

① A nuclear explosion can be accidental (as, for instance, was Chernobyl). Such an accident can unintentionally have very far-reaching effects. To dream of a nuclear explosion can highlight our anxiety about great change in our lives. We do not yet know what effect that change may have. We do, however, know we must undertake radical change, but would prefer it to be a more gradual process.

② When we have suppressed certain parts of our personality rather than handling them, there may be some type of synergy (combined energy) which can become destructive. We would be alerted to this by dreaming of causing a nuclear explosion.

③ Spiritually, a nuclear explosion would suggest a discharge of power which, if not handled properly, could be destructive.

Nude
– also see Bare

① Freud assumed that dreaming of being nude was linked with sexuality. It is, however, more to do with self-image. We have a desire to be seen for what we are, to reveal our essential personality without having to create a facade. To interpret a dream of **walking down a street naked** will depend on whether we are **seen by other people** or not. If we are seen by others there may be something about ourselves which we wish to reveal. If we are **alone** we may simply have a wish for freedom of expression.

② Nudity signifies innocence. It may be that there is a situation in our lives which requires honesty and truth. If we are sufficiently secure within our own self-image, we will not be afraid of being 'stripped' in public. Dreaming of appearing nude, for instance in a **strip show**, could suggest we have anxiety about being misunderstood. We are conscious of the fact that we are prepared to be open and honest, but others may not understand.

③ Nudity can suggest a new beginning, a rebirth. It is the paradise state and the state of natural innocence we all, at one time, had. It can also represent renunciation of the material world.

Nugget

① More often than not a nugget is made of gold and therefore signifies the best part of a situation. In dreams we may find that there is a piece of information or knowledge that is represented by a nugget.

② Precious metals are usually found in nuggets in a raw state. Often **gold** will represent the masculine, and **silver** the feminine. So to find either in a dream signifies finding a part of ourselves that we did not know existed. It may be in a rough state, but with some work can be made into something beautiful.

③ Spiritually a nugget will represent knowledge, power and psychic ability. It is the kernel of an idea or concept.

Numbers

① When numbers are drawn to our attention in dreams they can have either a personal or a symbolic significance. Often a number will appear which has personal meaning, such as a particular date, or the number of a house we have lived in. Our minds will often retain the significance of the number even though we do not necessarily consciously remember it ourselves.

② Symbolically numbers have some kind of significance in all systems of belief and religions. Also used often in divinatory practice, there are numerous levels of interpretation. Below are the most often found meaningful interpretations, which have been divided into three subsections.

a) Supposed divinatory meanings: *One* You will accomplish outstanding skill in the work you do. *Two* Business or personal relationships need handling carefully. *Three* Your ideas for stability and success will materialise. *Four* A secure and sheltered home is yours for the asking. *Five* You are about to make an important discovery which will bring about changes. *Six* A loving relationship is available to you. *Seven* With personal effort you can solve your problems. *Eight* Your life holds the potential for a wonderful offer. *Nine* Take care not to overreach yourself. *Zero* The cipher holds within it all potential.

b) Characteristics attributed to numbers: *One* Independence, self-respect, resolve, singleness of purpose. Intolerance, conceit, narrow-mindedness, degradation, stubbornness. *Two* Placidity, integrity, unselfishness, gregariousness, harmony. Indecision, indifference, lack of responsibility, bloody-mindedness. *Three*

Freedom, bravery, fun, enthusiasm, brilliance. Listlessness, over-confidence, impatience, lackadaisical behaviour. *Four* Loyalty, stolidity, practicality, honesty. Clumsiness, dullness, conservatism, unadaptibility. *Five* Adventurousness, vivaciousness, courage, health, susceptibility, sympathy. Rashness, irresponsibility, inconstancy, unreliability, thoughtlessness. *Six* Idealism, selflessness, honesty, charitableness, faithfulness, responsibility, superiority, softness, impracticality, submission. *Seven* Wisdom, discernment, philosophy, fortitude, depth, contemplation. Morbidness, hypercriticism, lack of action, unsociability. *Eight* Practicality, power, business ability, decision, control, constancy. Unimaginativeness, bluntness, self-sufficiency, domination. *Nine* Intelligence, discretion, artistry, understanding, brilliance, lofty moral sense, genius. Dreaminess, lethargy, lack of concentration, aimlessness.

c) The more esoteric interpretations are: *One* Oneself, the beginning, the first, unity. *Two* Duality, indecision, balance, male vs female, two sides to an argument, opposites. *Three* The triangle, the triad, freedom. *Four* The square, strength, stability practicality, the earth, reality, the four sides of human nature – sensation, feeling, thought, intuition; earth, air, fire and water. *Five* The human body, human consciousness in the body, the five senses. *Six* Harmony or balance. *Seven* Cycles of life, magical, spiritual meaning; human wholeness. *Eight* Death and resurrection, infinity. *Nine* Pregnancy, the end of the cycle and the start of something new, spiritual awareness. *Ten* A new beginning, the male and female together. *Eleven* Eleventh hour, the master number *Twelve* Time, a full cycle or wholeness. *Zero* The Feminine, Great Mother *(see Great Mother/Mother Earth)*, the unconscious, the absolute or hidden completeness.

③ Spiritually, as we progress we put ourselves in a position to make the best use of the vibratory effect of numbers. It has long been accepted that by combining numbers in certain ways, influence can be brought to bear on our environment. The Hebrew Kabbalists worked out a whole system on which they based their esoteric knowledge.

Nun
– see Carers in Occupations

Nurse/Nursing
– see Carers in Occupations

Nut

① To dream of a metal nut, as in **nuts and bolts**, is highlighting our ability to construct our lives in such a way that it will hold together. In the old-fashioned sense a nut was considered to be feminine, and the screw masculine.

② **Edible nuts**, because of their shape, have significance as inner nourishment. It was thought that they fed the brain, thus giving wisdom. They can still have this significance in dreams. Again, because of their shape, there is a connection with masculine sexuality and fertility. To dream of nuts may suggest that we are trying to de-personalise issues to do with sexuality.

③ Nuts were reputed to be the food of the Gods, and so spiritually enhance the psychic powers.

Nymph

① Nymphs are personifications of feminine universal productivity. They have an innocent and care-free energy which is naive and clear. They tend to be guardians of sacred spaces such as woods, mountains and lakes. In dreams, therefore, they are connected with a woman's sense of beauty and her own femininity.

② Psychologically the nymph most clearly has associations with the princess (see Princess in Archetypes and People). She is the carefree, fun-loving aspect of energy which glories in movement and light. As pure energy, when we work with dreams, the nymph allows us the opportunity to connect to the qualities of purity and grace.

③ Nymphs are Earth spirits that deal with pure energy. Their charm is their youthfulness, beauty and vitality. Each group of nymphs has their particular own role and guardianship of specific areas, such as forests and lakes, woods and valleys, mountains and grottoes. Dryads, for instance, do not mingle with others nymphs. Their significance spiritually is that they epitomise most of the feminine qualities in their purest states.

Oak
– see Tree

Oar

① The oar is a tool that enables a boat to move forward successfully, but its use requires some skill. Thus it stands for our own set of personal skills. We have certain skills which help us to 'navigate' our lives.

② **To put one's oar in** indicates our ability to interfere with other people's lives. **To lose an oar** indicates losing an ability we have formerly valued.

③ The oar symbolises a guiding principle in life. Two oars signify balance particularly between two polarities – masculine and feminine, physical and spiritual for instance – particularly in relation to the emotions (water).

Oasis
– also see Desert

① Most people see an oasis as a place of refuge in a desert. Because of its association with water, in dreams it becomes a place where we can receive whatever emotional refreshment we require.

② When people are in difficulty, they need a place where they can express themselves – or perhaps renew their own strengths and ability to cope. In dreams an oasis, particularly when we are lost *(See Lose/Lost)*, represents such a place. It highlights a particular type of sanctuary.

③ An oasis in spiritual terms represents refreshment, and the idea of being able to slide away from old oppressions.

Oats

① Oats in the form of **porridge** signify an almost 'magical' food. Because they have been used since time immemorial as a staple food, they represent warmth and comfort. Incidentally, since oats are known to support the function of the heart, they also represent a loving nature.

② **Wild oats** obviously have a connection in people's minds with sexual satisfaction and freedom. To dream of **sowing grain** suggests that we are expecting to reap a benefit from a situation at a later date.

③ Symbolically oats are indicative of fruitfulness, and as with all grains suggest a good harvest and spiritual sustenance. There may also be a need for simplicity in our lives.

Obedience

① When in dreams we **expect obedience from someone**, we are acknowledging our own power and authority over others. To dream of having to be **obedient to others** indicates we are aware of their greater authority and knowledge, and also of the disempowerment that has occurred.

② If we find ourselves in the position of **being obedient to someone we know** in an unexpected situation, we can often expect to have an easier relationship with them in the future, perhaps because we are able to acknowledge them in a different way.

③ To be obedient, in the spiritual sense, suggests a submission to the Greater Good, and after much struggle, to the spiritual side of oneself.

Obelisk
– also see Marble and Stone

① Any carved stone appearing in a dream suggests we are considering how we have shaped our own basic nature. The simpler it is, the more room we have for improvement; the more ornate it is, the more successful we are at using our creative energy.

② An obelisk often represents a marker outlining a particular area – such as a sacred space. It can also represent old instinctive knowledge.

③ An obelisk is often representative of a Sacred Stone. We also need to be clear regarding our spiritual beliefs and that we are progressing on our journey without too much hindrance.

Obese
– see Fat

Obligation

① When we find ourselves **under an obligation** to one of our dream characters we are being reminded of our innate sense of duty. We may feel that we have done, or need to do, something for them which, in our heart of hearts, we do not feel is appropriate for us.

② If we are conscious of **others' obligation to us** we need to be certain we are not forcing our will within a situation. When we feel **no obligation**, we are free from duty and commitment.

③ To feel obliged in a dream may lead us to the performance of a spiritual task or duty that we may, subconsciously, have been putting off.

Obscenity

① Often dreams will link with the lower aspects of ourselves, those parts we will not normally face in waking life. To have obscenity appear in a dream allows us to deal with these impulses safely, in a non-judgemental way.

② Often obscenity is connected with our perception of ourselves. If we are **performing obscene acts**, we need to be aware of suppressed impulses. If such acts are **performed against us**, we need to decide how we are being victimised in our daily lives.

③ In previous times, obscene and lewd acts were deemed to be the work of the Devil. While attitudes have largely changed, in dreams the symbolism may still be associated with wrongdoing and evil.

Obsession

① Obsession is an unnatural focusing on a feeling, belief or object, and may simply indicate that we need to take time to work a difficulty through. There is often anxiety about some past occasion or deed, with which we have not been able, or allowed, to deal.

② Obsessive or repetitive behaviour in dreams is often occurs in order to ensure that we have fully understood the message being conveyed by the unconscious.

③ There is a point in spiritual development where belief can take on the qualities of obsession – a focusing on one aspect to the exclusion of everything else. In dreams we may find ourselves mirroring this obsession before it becomes conscious action. We can become obsessive over putting our ideas across or fanatical when others do not agree.

Obstacle

① Obstacles in dreams can take many forms – a wall, a hill, a dark forest, etc. Largely, we are aware that these obstacles need to be overcome. How we do this in a dream can often suggest how to tackle a problem in everyday life.

② Indecision and self-doubt can often translate themselves in dreams into actual physical objects. At times, our own inhibitions and anxieties cannot be faced unless we give them tangible forms.

③ Difficulty, indecision and doubt are the three main blocks one will come up against in this particular spiritual 'obstacle course'. We will have to overcome each one if we are to finally achieve our spiritual goal.

Obstruction

① Any obstruction in a dream is simply an obstacle to progress. Through dreams, once given the opportunity to consider the nature of the obstruction we can identify the problem in waking life. We must decide whether the difficulty has simply arisen, whether it has been deliberately placed there either by us or other people, or whether it is an integral part of the situation.

② Dreams may give us information as to how we need to deal with obstruction. If it is insurmountable then we must consciously find our way round it, if too difficult to 'get over' then we may need to use alternative ways of dealing with what it represents. An obstruction may also suggest that we are going the wrong way about achieving a goal and need to reconsider our options.

③ Obstruction in dreams in the spiritual sense is often a warning that we are not acting in a way that will allow us to achieve a successful outcome. We may have to reconsider how we have got into that position in the first place, or whether the goal itself is an appropriate one.

Occult
– also see Magic

① The word occult actually means 'hidden', so for someone to dream of the Occult when they have no knowledge of the subject usually suggests the need to come to terms with all their hidden fears. Most people tend to think of the Occult in its most negative sense, as in black magic or Satanism, and thus may link with the egotistical side of their natures.

② If we have Occult knowledge it may be important to apply that awareness in an everyday situation. The rule is always then 'harm no-one'.

③ In dreams, the Occult, due to its many strange facets, may well be alerting us to an as yet untapped arcane wisdom.

Occupations

① From the time that we are very small we accept certain stereotypes as having relevance in our lives. Children's story characters such as Bob the Builder or Postman Pat give a sense of the values and requirements of such occupations. As we mature, we give each occupation we encounter certain attributes which will often appear in our dreams.

② As we progress through life, we come to realize that there is a huge store of knowledge which can be worked with to enhance our lives. People appearing in dreams are likely to have a particular significance for us depending on our upbringing and also our own way of working. It would not be unusual, for instance, for nurses and doctors to appear in a therapist's dreams. Below are some occupations and their better-known significances.

Actor/Performer Dreaming of an actor suggests that we need to take responsibility for our actions and for who we are. Performers of one kind or another may also serve in dreams as a projection of the type of person we would like to be. We may, for instance, in real life be shy and withdrawn, but need to be admired and loved.

Analyst/Therapist We may well be in contact with our own inner analyst. Our instinctive knowledge of what is right for us – our Higher Self – will make itself known in dreams when, on a conscious level, we have diverted from the correct path.

Artist Though we ourselves may have no apparent artistic ability, as a stereotype such a figure often represents our creative force and energy. Nowadays encompassing much more than did the painters of previous times, we have available a wider concept of creativity.

Bailiff This oppressive figure usually represents a particular kind of authority figure. In waking life the bailiff acts on behalf of someone else and is often dreaded because of what they represent. In dreams therefore he comes to signify a figure of retribution.

Baker/Chef The old-fashioned figure of the *baker* symbolises nurture and caring, and our ability to change and improve our circumstances by our own abilities. Particularly as television reaches wider audiences our domestic talents become more discernable and attainable, though sometimes only by proxy. The *chef* symbolises ultimate skill in a particular art.

Banker (also see entry for Bank/Banker) A banker in dreams originally suggested that part of our personality that we entrust with our resources, both emotional and material, ideally in an effort to conserve them or use them well. Initially an authority figure, he may now sometimes be perceived in dreams as the wastrel or the archetypal Villain. A great deal will depend on our individual relationship with our own bank in waking life.

Beggar/Tramp The *tramp* tends to personify the 'drop-out', the archetypal wanderer or freedom-lover in us. If in dreams this figure appears a *beggar* or someone down on their luck it can suggest that our emotional drives and thoughts in waking life have become starved and we need to ensure their wellbeing.

Butcher Traditionally seen as the Grim Reaper or a sign of death, this figure now more properly suggests a skilled operator – someone who uses the available resources to the best of their ability and for the Greater Good. He is of service within the community.

Carers appearing in dreams suggest the more compassionate, nurturing side of ourselves. Often it is that part of the personality which has been 'called' or has a vocation in which case the dream figure may be that of a *nun*. Nurses or carers in the community may suggest some kind of healing or specific act of palliative care. In men's dreams such figures may indicate the idea of a non-sexual relationship.

Chemist/Pharmacist Psychologically, the *chemist or pharmacist* represents the part of ourselves which is capable of making changes and is concerned about bodily health. By making calculated adjustments, a situation may be made more positive. Traditionally, when an *alchemist* appears in dreams the 'crude' or basic may be turned into something worthwhile. Such a figure may also represent ancient or arcane knowledge.

Dancer/Ballerina As we become more aware of the rhythm of life, motifs associated with dance become more prevalent in dreams. This figure of a ballerina often symbolises our search for balance and poise, and can also suggest the joy of movement.

Doctor/Physician/Surgeon A doctor in our dreams may suggest a known authority figure, or someone who has our best interests at heart. Such a figure may represent a healer, in which case a surgeon would suggest the cutting out of something negative in our lives.

Estate/Real Estate agent Dreaming of such a figure, or indeed anyone who is selling security in some way, epitomises that part of us which needs a safe base from which to operate successfully in the world. Interestingly, we may not fully trust that aspect of our personality and there may be issues of commitment to something in our waking lives.

Fisherman Often a fisherman will represent a provider, or perhaps bravery, as represented by deep-sea fisherman. A fresh-water fisherman may indicate the need for rest and recuperation. Whenever one of our dream figures is carrying out a specific action we need to look at what is represented by that particular action. Because of the Christian connection a fisherman may also suggest a priest or other religious figure in dreams.

Gardener The gardener can represent the insights which we have gathered through our experiences in life. They can also represent a specific kind of practical, down-to-earth wisdom on which we can rely. A gardener can also signify that part of us which is in touch with the forces of nature.

Hairdresser/Barber In dreams the hairdresser or barber appears as the part of us that deals with self-image, the way we feel about this and the way we project ourselves to the world at large. The connection between self-image and beauty is obvious, and we cannot make progress in our lives unless we feel good about ourselves. The hairdresser can also be taken to represent a person whom we trust greatly.

Hermit The hermit signifies the Wise Old Man *(see Wise Old Man)*. He is often a lone figure with principles, who has come to terms with his chosen way of life. In dreams he suggests that side of us which finds itself wary of relationships, lest they divert us from our chosen path.

Hunter/Huntsman In traditional dream interpretation the hunter or huntsman represented Death. More properly nowadays it is the inevitability of an enforced ending of a situation or some kind of threat specifically targeting us. We may be conscious of some kind of vendetta being waged against us in waking life. The hunter may also suggest the provider, though in this time of political correctness he may also represent an outmoded way of behaving.

Inventor Dreaming of an inventor connects us with the more creative side of ourselves – someone who is capable of taking an idea and making it tangible. We are also linking with the wiser, if more introverted, side of our personality.

Jailer An aspect of legitimate authority, in dreams such a figure represents some kind of restriction in our waking life. This figure, while representing that which is causing our incarceration, may also hold the secret to our freedom.

Judge/Magistrate An authority figure, the judge or magistrate suggests power vested in him by society. He is therefore that part of us which monitors our behaviour and may sometimes represent the Higher Self.

Leper To dream of a leper suggests that we feel contaminated or 'infected' in some way by negative perceptions. It is that part of us which feels cut off and alienated from everyday society.

Monks/Priests/Ministers of all Religions Ministers of all religions are vested with a certain type of authority that many people find daunting. When such figures appear in dreams there seems to be an aura about them which highlights moral and correct behaviour. The monk links with the more reclusive religious side of our lives.

Musician/Organist It is now widely accepted that music itself has a particularly beneficial healing effect. Any musician therefore may suggest a healer, or therapist. The co-ordinator of our life force, personal vibration or ch'i as it is known in the Eastern martial arts is often seen as an organist in dreams.

Official An official of any sort in a dream often links back to someone who has been given authority or status by others. Someone in uniform, particularly of the armed forces, may suggest an element of service to the community into the dream.

Occupations

Optician An optician, as someone who cares for the eyes of others, most often represents the need for clarity and wisdom, or rather knowledge specifically applied in our waking lives. It suggests the need to understand a situation which may be confusing us.

Osteopath An osteopath in dreams may suggest that part of us which is capable of manipulating the structure of our lives in order to achieve success. He may also represent the release of trapped energy on any, or all, levels to enable us to reach our full potential.

Pilot A pilot or *airman* signifies that part of us which is in control of our means of 'getting there'. It is a romanticised picture of the either the Self *(see Self)* or the Animus *(see Anima/Animus)*. A *train driver* would have a similar significance, if a little more down to earth.

Pirate/Outlaw Both the pirate and the outlaw suggest the anarchic, rebellious side of our personality. Dreaming of a pirate suggests there is a part of us that is capable of stealing away some basic attribute. This would have the potential to destroy our emotional connection with all that is good in us. Both figures may represent the archetypal Villain *(see Archetypes)*.

Police Often the police will appear in dreams as our conscience. This may reflect the judgemental side of our personality, that which is formed by the norms and attitudes of society. Occasionally the police will be seen as a force to be opposed – not fitting in with our own sense of right or wrong.

Politician Dreaming of a politician may depend on our attitude towards them and what might be defined as good for society. As one able to convince people of a particular course of behaviour a politician may represent that part of us which cares for the community. As someone who represents our needs and wishes they may signify the self-absorbed, more selfish side of our personality.

Pope/Religious Leader The Pope or other religious leader often appears in dreams as a substitute for the father, or as a personification of God. To meet such a figure in a dream is to meet the side of ourselves which has developed a code of behaviour based firmly on our own system of belief. This leader may be benign or judgmental.

Prostitute As what is known as 'the oldest profession', the original definition of the prostitute or siren was she who led man back to God. This indicates some kind of need, whether it is to understand an extrovert side of the personality, or to understand the Siren *(see Archetypes)*.

Tailor Any professional person develops certain talents, such as, in this case, the ability to do precise work and to 'fashion' something new. The tailor particularly is a craftsman in his own right and signifies the trained creative energy. It is these qualities which are highlighted in dreams.

Waiter/Waitress The interpretation of this dream depends on whether we ourselves are *waiting at table*, or whether we are *being waited upon*. If we are in the role of waiter or waitress, we are aware of our ability to care for, and nurture, other people. If we are being waited on, we perhaps need to be nurtured and made to feel special.

③ Just as fairy tales and myths give us concepts of times past, modern-day occupations root us firmly in the present and allow us points of contact with creativity and spirituality – the search for Self.

Ocean
– see Sea/Ocean in Water

Octopus

① Because the octopus has eight legs, it picks up on the symbolism of the mandala *(see Mandala)*. Often the tentacles can have particular significance, indicating that we can be drawn into something that we find frightening and from which we cannot escape.

② Creatures that are unusual and are not familiar to us appear in dreams to alert us to certain qualities within ourselves. The octopus is capable of moving in any direction and it is this symbolism of which we need to be aware.

③ An octopus can represent the unrestricted movement of the Spirit.

Offence

① **To take offence** in a dream is to allow a display of emotion and feeling about our own sensitivity which may not be appropriate in waking life. **To give offence** to someone in a dream is to recognise that we are not as aware of other people's feelings as we should be.

② **To be committing an offence** suggests that we are not, either consciously or unconsciously, following our own code of moral behaviour. We have put ourselves outside the norms of society.

③ A suggestion of spiritual wrongdoing may be relevant. It is, however, for us to assess the seriousness of the offence and then to act accordingly.

Office

① Often our work or office situation gives an environment in dreams with which we feel comfortable. It is slightly more formal than our home, and often deals with our feelings about, or our relationship with, work and authority. As a place where we spend a great deal of time it can also highlight issues of relationship, control and management of emotions.

② **To be in an office**, particularly if it is not known to us, would suggest some kind of order or bureaucracy is necessary in our lives. **To be in office**, in the sense of holding a post, signifies taking responsibility for what we do. Because of the need for a degree of formality, a dream about an office may symbolise our attitude to colleagues and the day-to-day interactions which take place.

③ An office in spiritual terms suggests having taken responsibility for who we are.

Officer/Official
– also see Official in Occupations and Authority Figures in People

① To be dreaming of an officer, unless we have a relationship with that person in real life, is to be looking at that part of ourselves which co-ordinates and directs our lives. Any official figure, and particularly one in uniform *(see Uniform)*, alerts us to that part of our being which needs to belong to an organised group. On a conscious level we may rebel, but there is a part of ourselves which recognises that we must fit in some way.

② Often, if our father has been particularly strict or overbearing, we will picture him in dreams as an officer. We learnt in childhood to conform to authority. Interestingly, different armed forces will represent different aspect of our personality. The **Army** will signify the more down-to-earth practical side, the **Air Force** the intellectual, and the **Navy** the freedom-loving, more emotional side.

③ The need for Spiritual Authority may well be represented here. We are seeking a higher guidance, and needs to be 'told' what to do.

Ogre
– see Archetypes

Oil
– also see Fuel and Petrol

① It will depend on which type of oil is being used in the dream. **Cooking oil** will often signify the removal of friction, or a way of combining different components. **Massage oil** suggests caring and pampering, whereas **engine oil** will highlight our ability to keep things moving. As petroleum oil supplies increasingly become a bone of contention we may dream of the various arguments and processes which are an integral part of using those resources. These might be financial, ecological or aesthetic.

② Psychologically, we may recognise that a situation can only be dealt with by removing the stress, e.g. 'Pour oil on troubled water.' While we give little thought to the properties of any oil *per se*, in the present day concerns about the huge costs – both financial and in environmental damage – triggered off by the production of any oil, be it natural, olive or palm, may surface in dreams. In this case images such as barrels, oilwells and so on are likely to appear.

③ From ancient times oil – whether burned or perfumed – has been considered as a special commodity, worthy of offering to the Gods. It still retains this symbolism in dreams today, particularly as we learn more about ancient customs. It also signifies consecration and dedication.

Ointment

① Dreaming of ointment means we need to be aware of the part of ourselves that either needs, or is capable of, healing. The kind of ointment will often give information as to what we need. For instance, to be dreaming of a **well-known brand** can suggest a non-specific type of healing, whereas an ointment that has been **prepared specifically for us** suggests a more focused approach.

② Since ancient times, ointments have been used to preserve and to prevent decay. Often the use of ointments was a mark of respect.

③ Ointment in dreams can point to our Spiritual need to care and heal, or alternatively, our need to be cared for. Anointing signifies the acknowledgement, and creation, of Holiness.

Old/Ancient/Antique
– also see Historic

① When we dream of old things, we are touching into the past and perhaps need to bring some kind of knowledge forward, so that we can make use of it in the present day. Dreaming of **historical figures** usually means we are aware of the qualities that those people possessed. Perhaps we need to develop those qualities within ourselves.

② **Old people** in dreams tend to suggest traditional thought or wisdom arising from experience *(see People)*. We may also need to consider our attitude to death. **Old buildings** can signify a past way of life which we thought we had left behind. **Antiques** will often represent elements of our past experience which might be worth keeping.

③ The Wise Old Man *(see Wise Old Man)* is a part of ourselves which is not always consciously available to us. An old man appearing in our dreams puts us in touch with this part of ourselves. He can also represent our feelings about time and death.

Onion
– also see Food

① Oddly enough, the onion can appear in dreams and meditation as a symbol of wholeness, but a wholeness which is many-layered. **Peeling an onion** can suggest trying to find the best part of ourselves, or of somebody else. It may also indicate attempting to understand the various facets of our personality.

② **Chopping onions** can signify an attempt to increase the energy available to us in some way.

③ The Cosmos, revelation and a many layered existence.

Opal
– see Jewels

Opera

① **To be attending** an opera in a dream suggests observing the 'drama' of a situation around us; it may be more appropriate to observe rather than take part. To **be taking part** in an opera highlights our need for some kind of dramatic input into our lives.

② When we find ourselves **singing in an opera**, we should be able to express ourselves in a more dramatic and tutored way within everyday situations.

③ The Drama of Life and supreme emotion played out in full.

Operation
– also see Hospital and Surgery

① An operation in hospital is frightening and invasive. In dreams it can signify not only our awareness of our own fears of illness and pain, but also a recognition of our need to be healed.

② **If we are performing an operation** we are recognising our own level of skill within a situation in waking life. **If the operation is being performed on us** we are attempting to access some inner knowledge but are possibly fearful of the outcome.

③ Incisive Healing and the cutting out of the negative, creating a deep healing of the Spirit.

Optician
– also see Occupations

① To be **visiting an optician** in a dream probably indicates that we do not feel we can see a situation clearly – we need assistance. It may also indicate that we need to develop a new way of looking at things.

② The optician in a dream may suggest that we need to understand the skill and value of seeing things properly. This may also signify clairvoyance.

③ This dream indicates our ability to enhance our perceptions and understanding.

Oracle

① Most of us like to know what is going to happen to us and also like to be told what to do, so dreaming of an oracle links us with that part of ourselves which knows what our next moves are. Often an oracle can appear as a person – for instance as a goddess (*see Goddess/Goddesses*) or wise old man (*see Wise Old Man*) – or we can dream that we are using one of the many systems of prediction which are available in everyday life.

② The need to know is very strong and the assumption is that an oracle has more information than we do. Often that information has to be unscrambled, since it is presented in odd ways and sometimes it cannot be made sense of until such time as we have considered it in waking life.

③ Foretelling of the future and Hidden Knowledge – depth of perception.

Orange
– see Colour and Fruit

Orchard

① In dreams an orchard may represent our attempts to look after ourselves. It will depend on whether the trees are showing flowers or fruit. If they are showing **flowers** then this will represent the potential we have for success; if they are showing **fruit** we are being reassured as to the harvest we may gather.

② Any collection of trees can represent our own fertility. As an orchard tends to be more ordered than, for instance, a forest, dreaming of one indicates we are appreciating the more structured side of our personalities.

③ Fertility and an ordered approach to life. The cultivated fruits of labour.

Orchestra
– also see Music, Musical Instruments and Organist

① We all have certain aspects of our personality which must work in harmony with one another for us to function properly. Dreaming of an orchestra represents ways in which we can bring all those aspects together and make a coherent whole.

② When we wish to orchestrate something, we want to make it happen. This occasionally means that we must take action which enables us to be heard and to have people understand us. When we find we are **conducting an orchestra** we can accept we are in control. When we are a **member of an orchestra** we are simply part of a greater task.

③ We are capable of operating in spiritual harmony.

Ore

① Ore is a crude material which needs refining in order to make it usable. In dreams this can represent the resources we have available, although these may be initially rather crude. It can also represent new ideas, thoughts and concepts which have not yet been totally understood.

② Whenever any basic material – such as ore – appears in a dream, the unconscious is asking us to 'dig for information'. It may not present itself as usable material to begin with but will need working on to enable us to make use of the information we have.

③ There is both basic and core spiritual knowledge available which can be revealed to us.

Organ

① The various organs of the body can represent the different aspects of the self. In dreams they can signify diverse weaknesses and strengths. A **musical organ** will tend to highlight our views and feelings about religion. In slang terms, the organ suggests the penis.

② In Chinese medicine, the different organs of the body represent different qualities. For instance, the gall bladder deals with the ability to make decisions, while the liver is the seat of irritability. In dreams, therefore, being conscious of a bodily organ would require us to be aware of what is bothering us and dealing with it in an appropriate manner.

③ Spiritually, perfect health of mind and body would be possible provided we understood the workings of the physical body. If we know what perfect is, then self-healing would ensure proper working of the organs.

Organist
– also see Orchestra

① The organist as an image is the part of us which knows how to make use of the various vibrations of which we are formed. When we dream of such a figure we are appreciative of the fact that, as with an orchestra, the various notes that we play can be brought into harmony. This, however, requires some skill in making the sounds available.

② Expressing ourselves successfully is a learnt skill. The organist represents that part of us which is prepared to be disciplined and determined in order to enable us to be listened to and heard properly.

③ The Higher Self. The player of our various talents which enables us to make use of our abilities for the Greater Good.

Orgy
– also see Sex

(1) An orgy relates to a tremendous release of energy which can take place when we give ourselves permission to access our own sexuality. This permission will often be given subconsciously first, and can be expressed in dreams more fully than we would allow ourselves to do in everyday life. To dream of an orgy can also highlight the way we relate to other people.

(2) Often our dreams will express a difficulty or blockage we may have in any one area of our lives. Since most people's self-image is very much connected with their sexuality, dreaming of an orgy can indicate the way in which we can release blocked energy. Behaviour which would not necessarily be appropriate in ordinary everyday life can be used in dreams to balance the difficulty.

(3) Spiritual excess. The need for other people to love and understand us is quite strong and, when seen as an orgy, can perhaps indicate that we are afraid of loss of control.

Orient

(1) For many people the Oriental or Eastern way of life is seen as being very exotic. Dreaming of this may give us access to that part of us which becomes suppressed by the demands of everyday life. Of late, as our viewpoint becomes more globally orientated, we perceive a dichotomy between ancient and modern ideas and in dreams it is this polarity which may be highlighted.

(2) From the wider perspective engendered by travel, we become more conscious of emerging trends coming from oriental sources. From a cultural viewpoint, differences and similarities are sometimes difficult to understand and it is only through dreams that we are able to decide if they are appropriate for us on an individual basis.

(3) The Oriental way of life appears to be more gentle and perhaps more intuitive than the Western. In dreams we tend to link with that side of ourselves which has access to wisdom and clarity. This tends to be quite a feminine way of working, so the figure often appears as an oriental woman *(also see Woman in People)*.

Ornament

(1) It will depend on whether the ornament seen in a dream belongs to us as to what the interpretation is. Dreaming of **personal ornamentation** *(see Necklace and Jewels/Gems)* suggests an attempt to enhance something that we have and value, but that we want to make more valuable. In dream terms this can represent either our feelings, emotions or ideas.

(2) To be conscious of ornaments in a dream tends to indicate that our personal

space can be used more fully and therefore bring us greater success. We are not simply going back to basics but are actively taking step to improve our situation.

③ Tangible and recognisable spirituality.

Orphan

① To dream of an orphan indicates that we may be feeling vulnerable and possibly abandoned and unloved. If we are **looking after an orphan** we are attempting to heal that part of us that feels unloved. If we experience ourselves as **having been orphaned** it may indicate that we need to be more independent and self sufficient.

② We have to come to terms with our ability to grow up and to move away from our parents. When our lives force us into losing them, either by death or other circumstances such as moving away, we may experience ourselves as being orphaned.

③ Spiritual desertion. We feel unloved by our God or Gods.

Osteopath
– also see Occupations

① In dreams an osteopath would signify our need to manipulate the circumstances of our lives to a point where we are comfortable. Because an osteopath heals, for one to appear in a dream would suggest concern over health matters and the way the body works.

② Oddly enough, because an osteopath manipulates the physical body, such a person appearing in a dream could alert us to manipulation that is going on in everyday life. Psychologically, any healing treatment is going to have an effect on the energy within the body and we often need to be conscious of the subtle changes necessary in our lives.

③ On a spiritual level an osteopath may represent a kind of spiritual manipulation or change in awareness.

Ostrich
– see Birds

Otter
– see Animals

Outlaw

① Inherent in the figure of the outlaw is someone who has gone against the laws of society. In dreams therefore, that part of ourselves which feels that it is beyond the law will appear as the outlaw. To be **shooting the outlaw** is attempting to control our wilder urges.

② Psychologically, we all have a part in us that is anarchical or wishes to rebel. Occasionally this can appear as a **person of the opposite sex**, in which case we are dealing with the Anima/Animus *(see Animus/Anima)*. If however, the outlaw is of the **same sex**, then we are dealing with the Shadow *(see Shadow)*.

③ To put ourselves beyond the reach of spiritual law, and correct behaviour is to play a dangerous game which may have to be paid for in various ways in the future.

Oval
– see Shapes/Patterns

Oven
– also see Baker

① An oven is representative of the human ability to transfer raw ingredients into something palatable. In dreams, therefore, this can suggest the ability to transform character traits and behaviour from something coarse to the more refined.

② As a hollow object, in dreams an oven can also represent the womb. With its ability to change ingredients into something else, the oven can also represent the process of gestation and birth.

③ The oven represents the transmutation of base qualities, and thus suggests spiritual transformation, perhaps through challenge.

Owl
– see Birds

Ox
– see Animals

Oyster

① The oyster is reputed to be an aphrodisiac food. In dreams it can therefore represent an increase in energy. It may also in today's society represent prosperity and good living.

② The oyster is almost unique because of its ability to transform a grain of sand into a pearl. It is this quality which tends to be brought to notice in dreams to demonstrate how we can change something which seems to be an irritant into something beautiful.

③ The oyster represents spiritual transformation. We can build on negative qualities in our lives without trying to eradicate them completely.

Packing
– also see Wadding

① When we dream of **packing suitcases**, as though going on a journey, we are highlighting the need to prepare carefully for the next stage of our lives. There is a need, or want, to get away from past ideas and difficulties. To be **packing a precious object** very carefully, indicates we are aware of the intrinsic value to ourselves, or others, of what is represented by that object.

② We need to establish some kind of order in our lives. To dream of packing suggests an internal selection process must be undertaken in order to decide what is important to us.

③ We need to make a choice about relevant spiritual information and decide what needs to be retained.

Padlock
– also see Key and Lock

① Dreaming of **locking a padlock** suggests that we are attempting to shut something (perhaps a feeling or emotion) away. This may either be through fear or possessiveness. Conversely, if we are **opening a padlock** we may be trying to open up to new experiences.

② Often when we feel our security is being threatened, a symbol which reinforces our need for defence mechanisms appears; the padlock comes into this category.

③ Just as a padlock keeps objects secure, so in dreams it 'locks away' our spiritual integrity, our ability to keep our spiritual self free from contamination.

Pagoda
– see Temple in Buildings

Painting

① To be using paint in dreams suggests we may be trying to change an image in some way. The colour may also be important *(see Colour)*. Often in waking life we will not recognise our own creative ability, and **to be painting** in a dream may alert us to other talents we have not realised we possess. We may not actually have the ability to paint successfully in everyday life. **To be looking at paintings** in dreams indicates that we are questioning or paying attention to ideas and concepts of which we have not been consciously aware. **Painting as in decorating** suggests we are making recognisable changes in the way we think and feel.

② Because painting has such a lot to do with self-expression, the way that we are painting in a dream may be important. If, for instance, we are **painting miniatures** we may need to concentrate on detail. If we are painting **large pictures** we may need to adopt a more global perspective.

③ We are developing a spiritual scenario and creating a way of life.

Pairs

① Particularly when we are aware of conflict within ourselves, we may dream in pairs (e.g. old/young, masculine/feminine, clever/stupid). It is almost as though there is some kind of internal pendulum, which eventually sorts out the opposites into a unified whole.

② A dream clarifying the masculine side of ourselves may be followed by a dream clarifying the feminine. The juggling that goes on in this way can take place over a period of time. Pairs may also highlight a polarity.

③ The unconscious mind appears to sort information by comparing and contrasting. The appearance of pairs in dreams shows we are trying to achieve a Spiritual balance.

Palace
– see Castle in Buildings

Palm
– also see Oil

① To see a **palm tree** in a dream is most often to do with rest and relaxation. Previously the palm was associated with honour and victory, but as foreign holidays have become more available it has largely lost that significance.

② The **palm of the hand** is significant as a recognised symbol of generosity and openness, and gives an indication of how we deal with money and finance.

③ The palm in spiritual terms suggests blessings and goodness.

Pan/Pot

① In dreams a pan or a pot signifies nurturing and caring. It can also suggest a receptive frame of mind.

② Just as a cauldron can be taken to indicate the transformative process, so a pan can suggest the ability to combine several 'ingredients' to make something completely different.

③ As always, any receptacle suggests the containing Feminine Principle, usually the nurturing side.

Panel

① Panels predispose surfaces which can, or have been, worked on or decorated and will have this significance in dreams. It will depend on whether they are blank or not as to the interpretation. A plain panel suggests that there is work to be done within a particular project, while one which has been worked on perhaps signifies the need for admiration. An intricately worked or decorated panel indicates a complexity of ideas.

② A panel of colleagues or judges indicates that we feel that someone is being judgemental. There is a consensus of opinion over our actions or feelings. Being interviewed by such a panel may mean that we feel we must justify who we are or conform to a certain standard. It is worth remembering that such a panel may be representative of various aspects of the Self (see Self) which can only achieve expression in dreams.

③ From time immemorial there has been the idea that those of greater experience can pass judgement on others. Most religions allowed elders or those with special powers to pass judgement on misdemeanours. This concept is so ingrained in the psyche that we dream of such panels of judgement. It could be that this is why celebrity panel games and reality shows are so successful. We allow ourselves to be judged.

Panther
– see Wild Animals in Animals

Pantomime

① For many people the pantomime is a happy childhood memory, and often appears in dreams as a reminder of happier times. It can also suggest the more spontaneous, humorous side of our nature.

② Because the images associated with pantomime are often exaggerated and larger than life, the pantomime can be used in dreams as a setting to draw our attention to something of which we need to be aware.

③ Most images connected with the theatre suggest the idea of life being a play. In the case of pantomime it is a very surreal image – everything tends to be grossly exaggerated and therefore warrants our particular and detailed attention to recognise its import.

Paper

① Paper is one of those images which, in dreams, is dependent on the circumstances in our life. For instance, in a **student's** life, paper would suggest the need to pay attention to the studies. In a **postman's** life there may be job anxieties, whereas **festive wrapping paper** could indicate the need for, or the possibility of, celebration.

② **Blank writing paper** points to a lack of communication, or need to communicate with someone, but can also suggest a new beginning. **Brown paper** can highlight the utilitarian side of our nature.

③ There is potential for Spiritual growth through both learning and our own creativity.

Parachute

① Dreaming of a parachute suggests that, whatever is happening to us in waking life, we have protection that will see us through. It may also indicate that we are able to face our anxieties and still succeed.

② Parachuting as a sport has become very popular, and the sense of freedom and adventure it gives can easily become apparent in dreams.

③ There is intellectual freedom in the image of parachuting. We have the ability to rise above the mundane, but equally to be 'down to earth'.

Paradise

① To dream of Paradise links with our innate ability to be perfect. We can experience total harmony within ourselves, and then are totally innocent.

② Psychologically, Paradise is that part of ourselves which is enclosed within and does not need to be available to anyone else. It is separate and the part from which we can develop perfect union with the universe.

③ To dream of Paradise is to be aware of the perfect Soul. In this state there is no right and no wrong, only completion.

Paralysis
– also see Immobility

① When paralysis is felt in a dream we are probably experiencing great fear or suppression. Feelings that are emotionally based are experienced as paralysis in order to highlight the physical effect those feelings can have.

② Imagination can often play tricks on us, and we experience as real some kind of reaction we would not normally allow ourselves. Paralysis is one such reaction.

③ Paralysis can signify spiritual inadequacy, inability to create movement, and inertia. There is a condition which sometimes occurs during development when we are forced into facing our own fears, and this can be experienced as paralysis.

Parasites

① Parasites such as **lice, fleas or bugs** in a dream suggest that we may be aware that someone is attempting to live off our energy in some way. Our lifestyle may, to them, appear to be exciting and more interesting than their own or provide them with amusement.

② We may feel unclean in some aspect of our lives which makes us ashamed or uncomfortable. We are aware that we cannot exist without support.

③ We realise that we are not satisfied with our own lives and why we may be living vicariously.

Parcel/Package

① When we **receive a parcel** in a dream, we are being made aware of something we have experienced but not explored. At this stage, we do not quite know what the potential of the gift is, but by exploration can find this out. When we are **sending a parcel or package** we are sending our energy out into the world.

② Parcels and packages in dreams can also represent the gifts that one receives from others. It can often be important to note who is actually giving us the gift, whether it is being directly received from the person concerned or whether we are simply aware who the donor is and that it is something that we can receive with joy.

③ Parcels and packages can suggest latent potential and gifts or skills.

Parents
– see Family and Archetypes

Parliament

① Dreaming of parliament or government often alerts us to that part of ourselves that is involved in decision making. The higher aspects of Self *(see Self)* have a degree of authority over us and are the part of ourselves that deals with the Greater Good. Parliament thus represents those aspects that connect us with the rest of the world.

② Any gathering of people is important in a dream, since it shows us how we relate to that group. To dream that we are in the **Houses of Parliament** represents that we are in a decision-making place; we may not be capable of making decisions which affect other people, but we do have access to that space. We may need to rake more responsibility for ourselves.

③ Parliament should stand for Spiritual Clarity and those who have our welfare at heart. Expressing opposing views brings about Right Action.

Parrot
– see Birds

Parsley

① In Pagan times parsley was considered to have mystic powers. Like all herbs, it was used very specifically in teas and flavourings to achieve certain results. We still, at some level of awareness, hold this knowledge, so when parsley appears in a dream we are linking with this information.

② One of the qualities of parsley is as a cleanser, or purifier, and it is as this that it may appear in dreams. We are aware that we need to get rid of something which is contaminating us.

③ Parsley is a symbol for the Feminine Principle and occult awareness.

Party

① When we find we are **attending a party** in a dream, we are often alerted to our social skills – or lack of such skills. In waking life we may be shy and dislike such gatherings, but in dreams if we are coping with the groups involved, we have a greater awareness of our own belonging. To belong to a **political party** would indicate that we are prepared to stand up for our beliefs, that we have made a commitment to a particular way of life.

② The human being often has need of celebration in his or her life. To be attending a party in a dream can indicate our need for celebration, for joining with other people to create a potentially happy atmosphere.

③ When a group celebrates a belief, which can be spiritual, it is an occasion for a party or festival.

Passage
– see Hall/Passages in Buildings

Passport

① The passport is normally taken to prove one's identity. In waking life, we may experience difficulty in maintaining a good self-image and in dreams may reassure ourselves by producing a passport.

② Often the passport can appear as a symbol of the permission we need to obtain from ourselves or others to move on to new things or situations. The passport is permission from a higher authority and in its symbolism of allowing us free passage signifies access to all parts of our personality.

③ The passport symbolises our growing ability to take responsibility for our actions and care for the wider world.

Path

① A path in a dream signifies the direction one has decided to take in life. The type of path, whether it is **smooth or rocky, winding or straight**, may be just as important as the path itself.

② Often a path can represent the way we feel a relationship or situation is developing. It can also suggest a way of following up a concept or line of enquiry. In waking life it is often the way a clairvoyant 'sees' the way in which the enquirer's life is changing.

③ A path in a dream can indicate a Spiritual direction, a way of progressing.

Pattern
– see Shapes/Patterns

Pawn-shop

① Dreaming of a pawn-shop can indicate that we are not being sufficiently careful with the resources, whether material or emotional, that we possess. We may be taking risks which we need to consider more carefully. Intrinsic in the image of the pawn-shop is that it is a place of exchange, where we can swap articles for which we have no use for something of value. In dreams it is more likely to be what we are exchanging that is important rather than the environment itself.

② We are aware that certain attributes and characteristics we have are being appropriated by other people, leaving us with nothing of value.

③ As recycling becomes more important, the pawn-shop in dreams can on the one hand represent the efficient use of resources. However, it may also represent the materiality which impedes our progress and an inappropriate use of the resources that we have. We may thus not be creating a correct exchange of energy in our lives.

Pay
– see Wages/Salary

Peacock
– see Birds

Pearl
– see Jewels/Gems

Pedestal

① When we become conscious in a dream that something, or someone, has been placed on a pedestal we have obviously attempted to make it special. We have elevated it or them to a position of power.

② Most human beings have a tendency to idolise or worship certain characteristics or ways of behaviour. Dreams will often show us the appropriateness – or otherwise – of such an action.

③ Putting someone or something on a pedestal suggests spiritual worship and idolatry, which can impede our spiritual journey if that worship is misplaced. It may also signify spiritual status.

Pelican
– see Birds

Pen/Pencil
– also see Toner/Ink

① If a pen or pencil appears in a dream we are expressing or recognising the need to communicate with other people. **If the pen will not work** we do not understand information we have been given. **If we cannot find one** we do not have enough information to proceed with an aspect of our lives.

② We all have an ability to learn but need to have some way of transmitting our learning to other people. A pen would suggest the learning would be more permanent than a pencil.

③ The powers to transcribe spiritual knowledge and to keep a record of that information are a necessary part of development. Dreaming of a pen or pencil may suggest that we could attempt automatic writing.

Pendant
– see Necklace

Penguin
– see Birds

Pension
– also see Finance and Savings

① Financial concerns in the modern day are of prime importance to most people. Whereas a pension was previously a reward for hard work and loyalty, it has now become our responsibility, to insure against problems and provide a means of financial survival in old age. Dreaming of **receiving a pension** may highlight other problems to do with being redundant (unwanted) or elderly.

② Providing for the future is a sensible act which, in today's commercialised world, has lost value. The idea of paying for a pension which could be drawn on in hard times is no longer valid since others have taken control of the wherewithal with which this could be done. Dreaming of problems with a pension highlights this lack of control and the minimising of adequate return for effort.

③ Pensions signify the reward for work well done. In dreams, a pension can symbolise deferred gratification – being rewarded later rather than immediately.

Pentacle/Pentangle/Pentagram
– see Star in Shapes/Patterns

People

① People appear in dreams in many guises. Sometimes they appear simply as themselves, because the dream scenario requires a particular set of circumstances. This may range, for instance, from shopping with our mother to climbing a mountain with an old friend.

A particular person's appearance in a dream may be significant because of the ordinariness of the occasion, or because their behaviour is bizarre. It may be that the dreaming self wishes to highlight a particular aspect of either our character or actions. They may be reminders of earlier, happier times, perhaps emphasise characteristics of their occupation or indeed may even offer explanations of past actions. Only you as the dreamer can be certain of the significance to you.

It is often necessary to decide of what or who each one makes us think in order to extract the information which each character brings to us. This is one area where free association comes into its own. That way we are able to reveal the deeper meanings and connections that we make. As an example, one particular old school friend of mine appearing in a dream invariably suggests some form of religious fervour, simply because of his teenage behaviour. As a matter of interest, any individual from the past could link us with a particular period in our lives, or with certain memories which may, or may not, be painful.

In waking life the people we meet have, through experience, developed their personalities and used the Jungian functions of thinking, sensing, feeling and intuition in their own specific ways. Dream characters will also exhibit certain characteristics which alert us to aspects we ourselves may need to consider more carefully in order to maximise our own potential.

Jung and his followers held that most people consciously used one of the above functions most frequently. Without the development of the least often used, however, there could be a lack of growth, both emotionally and spiritually; as a matter of interest, we will often indicate our predominant function frequently using such phrases as ' I think' or 'I feel'.

Our dream characters will often highlight the minor or neglected function. For instance, the 'princess' type who needs rescuing may need to develop, and dream of, the more competitive self-sufficient side of the Amazon *(see Archetypes)*. Equally, the carefree youth may need to develop his more dispassionate Hero in order to have the personal success he craves.

Sometimes, rather than trying to unravel the meaning of the dream it is enough to look at what bearing the dream character's actions have or could have on our everyday life. To interpret why our characters adopt a particular role in our 'dream play' it is necessary to consider our lifestyle. For instance, a member of someone else's family may, by association, suggest our own family members or possibly hitherto unresolved issues.

Sometimes we are more likely to dream about people when there is conflict between love and discord. Often in dreams there may be a noted difference between two of the characters, in order to clarify two sides of a dreamer's thoughts and feelings. Similarly, there may be a marked contrast in the way we handles a situation with two of our dream characters. It is as though two options are being practised.

As with composite animals, the composite character will emphasise more than one characteristic or quality in order to draw our attention to them. Not being able to decide if the dream character is one person or another may suggest a common characteristic between them. The fact that it is not just one person emphasises the many-faceted human being. Every character who appears in our dreams ultimately reflects a part of our own personality. Such characters can often be better understood if during interpretation we put ourselves in the position of that person.

② There is a particular group of behaviour patterns within each of us that makes us recognisable. In dreams these patterns and characteristics can be magnified so that they are easily identifiable – they can often appear as personalities. Much energy and power can become available once their significance is understood.

Dream characters and personalities themselves will often show a duality or overdevelopment which, with a little thought, can be interpreted to our advantage. When a dream image presents itself in a particular way we need to uncover not just the obvious – but also the hidden – message. In recurring dreams, which sometimes resist interpretation, taking notice of which function of the personality is predominant will clarify the message considerably. For instance, the overbearing prison warden female in dreams has elements of both Amazon/Competitor and Destructive Mother (carer) in her and highlights thinking and feeling. Dreaming of a stereotypical old-fashioned Alchemist brings to mind the Sorcerer, perhaps with aspects of the Tramp as freedom lover or Ogre as irascible old Man – an intuitive type tempered by sensing and/or feeling.

Deciding to work with the dream images, rather than simply looking for an interpretation, can heighten our appreciation of our own abilities and how we use the functions. We may decide to confront the negative aspects within our own make-up, enlist their co-operation or both. We can then consciously develop the lesser function.

Not everyone will be able to hold conversations with dream characters in the waking state. However, if we can suspend disbelief for a time, have patience with ourselves (and our dream characters) and learn to use visualisation as a tool, we can gain a great deal of information. This helps us to operate more successfully in everyday life and also enables us to understand other people and their motivation better.

When you have difficulty in understanding what part a character is playing in your dream it is worthwhile imagining yourself having a conversation with them, just as you would with a stranger. You would perhaps wish to find out more about them, and would ask pertinent questions.

With your dream characters you will sense the answers rather than hearing them. You might ask such questions as 'What are you doing in my dream?', 'What relevance does that have to my life?' and so on. It also is helpful for you to initiate the conversation and advantageous if you record the impressions you are getting for later consideration, as you gain greater understanding of the four functions. Below are some common figures which appear in dreams:

Adolescent Dreams of ourselves as an adolescent concentrate on the undeveloped, perhaps immature, side of the personality. Dreaming of *an adolescent of the opposite sex* often means having to deal with a suppressed part of our development. The emotions associated with adolescence are very raw and clear and to get back to such innocence is often possible only through dreams. There may be conflict over freedoms both given and taken by others.

Ancestors Our conformity, ways of behaving, ethics and our religious observances are all handed down from generation to generation. When we become conscious of our ancestors in a dream we are focusing on our roots, and perhaps questioning them. We may also come to an understanding of ourselves through our relationship with the past, either our own or others'.

Authority Figures Our impression of authority is usually first developed through our relationship with our father or father figure. Often, depending on how we were treated as children, our view of authority will be anything from a benign helper to an exploitative disciplinarian. Most authority figures in dreams will ultimately lead us back to what is right for us, although not necessarily what *we* might consider good. Authority figures in dreams initially appear to have power over us, though if worked with properly will generate the power to succeed, and may come to be viewed in terms of the Higher Self *(see Self)*. We may become aware that our wilder, more renegade side needs controlling.

Baby To dream about a baby, particularly *one that appears to be ours*, indicates that we need to recognise those vulnerable feelings over which we have no control. We may also be considering a new project or way of life which is literally 'our baby'. Dreaming of a baby can also indicate a need for innocence. *Dreaming of a foetus* rather than a live baby suggests that a project or idea has not yet been properly formed, sufficient for it to survive on its own. If the *baby is someone else's* in the dream we need to recognise a situation in waking life is not our responsibility or that we should not interfere.

Boy To have a dream about a boy shows the potential for development through new experiences. Emotionally, we may need to be in touch with ourselves at that particular age and with the unsophisticated naiveté and passion that a boy has. *If the boy is known to us* he reflects aspects of our personality which we are learning to understand. We are contacting our natural drives and ability to face difficulties.

Boyfriend We may need to consider the loving, nurturing side of masculinity. To dream of *a boyfriend, whether present or former,* allows us to associate with the feelings, attachments, sexuality and sensuality we have allowed ourselves within those relationships. We still search for the ideal lover – that perfect reflection of ourselves – in an effort to realise our own potential in waking life. To dream of *having as a boyfriend someone whom you would not anticipate,* e.g. someone you do not like, indicates our need to have a greater understanding of the way we relate to the masculine or to partnership in general. For a woman a boyfriend may represent her Animus *(see Anima/Animus).*

Child We all have parts of ourselves which are still child-like and inquisitive. Dreaming of a child gives us access to the less-developed sides of our personality – the inner child at a specific stage of development. When we are able to get in touch with that more innocent aspect, we give ourselves permission to clarify or rediscover a capacity for wholeness. *Dreaming of our own children* highlights the special dynamic inherent in family relationships.

Crowd (also see individual entry) Crowds in dreams can suggest how we relate to other people, particularly socially. A crowd may also signify the diverse archetypes inherent in us all. Additionally they may indicate how we can hide ourselves, or indeed how we hide parts of ourselves and do not single out any one attribute. Dreaming of a crowd suggests that we may also be attempting to avoid responsibility. *A huge crowd* suggests information or knowledge which we may not be able to assimilate, whereas a smaller crowd suggests a more efficient sharing of knowledge.

Dictators If we have had a domineering father, a known dictator may appear in dreams as representing that relationship. If we have difficulty with authority figures in general, a personification of dictatorship may appear in dreams. It will largely depend on our age and experience as to which figure is likely to appear.

Elderly People In dreams, the elderly very often represent either our forebears or grandparents, and hence wisdom accrued from experience. People older than us, who are not necessarily elderly, usually signify our parents or parental control. Interpretation of the exact meaning of elderly people appearing in dreams will depend on the gender of the dreamer. If the elderly person is male he will represent either the Self *(see Self)* or the Animus *(see Anima/Animus).* If female, then she will signify the Great Mother *(see Great Mother/Mother Earth)* or the Anima *(see Anima/Animus).* Groups of elderly people frequently appear in dreams and signify the traditions and wisdom of the past – those things which are sacred to the 'tribe' or family.

Girl When a girl of any age appears in our dreams we are usually attempting to make contact with the more sensitive, innocent, intuitive, feminine side of ourselves. If the girl is *known to us* we probably are aware of those qualities, but need to explore them more fully. If she is *unknown,* we can acknowledge that a fresh approach would be useful.

Girlfriend In dreams we frequently search for the lost or unidentified part of ourselves A girlfriend appearing in either a man or a woman's dream usually highlights matters to do with the dynamic between the various aspects of our personality. If a girlfriend appears in *a woman's dream,* there can either be a concern about her in the dreamer's mind, or she (the dreamer) needs to search for – and find – qualities belonging to the friend within herself. In *a man's dream* a girlfriend or ex-girlfriend highlights how he deals with a loving relationship and possibly with fears to do with his own sexuality. The dream figure is often a representation of his relationship with his own Anima *(see Anima/Animus).*

Hero/Heroic Figure When a hero or heroic figure of some sort appears in a dream, it often is as an antidote to some hated external figure within our everyday life. The heroic figure also demonstrates to us the 'journey' we must undertake in life. When the *hero is on a quest* in a dream we are struggling to find a part of ourselves which is at this time unrevealed. Our eventual integration needs the challenge of the negative, as is often seen in myths and fairytales. It is important that the darker forces within ourselves are conquered – but not annihilated, since they cannot be totally eradicated without harming the Wise Old Man *(see Wise Old Man).* In dreams, the *failure of the hero* may be brought about inadvertently. We all have a weak point through which we can be attacked, and in dreams we may be being warned of an element of self-neglect. We are not paying attention to the minutiae in our lives or to that part of ourselves we have developed. The *apparent death of the hero* can often suggest the need for resurrection, the development the more intuitive side of ourselves in order to be 'born again' to something new. A *conflict between the hero and any other dream character* suggests a basic disharmony between two facets of our own personality. In *a man's dream* the figure of the hero can represent all that is good in him, the Higher Self *(see Self).* In *a woman's dream* he will suggest the Animus *(see Anima/Animus).*

High Priest/Astrologer The Higher Self often presents itself in dreams as a character who appears to have knowledge of magical practices or similar esoteric wisdom. It is as though we need the personalisation of this deeper knowledge in order to gain access to it.

Intruder/Burglar To dream of any kind of intruder suggests that we feel threatened in some way. We may also need to defend ourselves against a violation of personal space, or we possibly feel threatened from a sexual perspective. The intruder can represent that part of us that has trouble dealing with doubt and fear. A change in attitude brings about a better and more meaningful relationship with our inner self. The intruder in *a woman's dream* is often an image of her own inner masculinity, i.e. the Animus *(see Anima/Animus).* In *a man's dream* it personifies the Shadow *(see Shadow).*

King A king emerging in a dream usually represents the father or father-figure and our need for approval. When the king is *old or on the point of dying* we will be able to discard old-fashioned family values which may be hindering us. *A new king* might suggest a new or different from of authority, such as a new boss, in our waking lives. An *emperor or foreign ruler* appearing on our dream may indicate that some of the father's attitudes and ways of being are alien to us.

Layabout/Inadequate Person It is a lot simpler to encounter our own shortcomings in the dream state, where we are safe. Often encountering a layabout or some kind of inadequacy in a dream is the first occasion we have to meet the Shadow, which will later become an ally. We must learn to deal with a sense of inferiority before we can progress. We shouldn't ignore this aspect of ourselves, nor can we afford to reject such an image when it does appear.

Man Any masculine figure which appears in a dream demonstrates an aspect or facet of our personality. Such a figure can identify the Shadow (the negative side of himself) for a man, and the Animus for a woman. Even when we are threatened by a negative character trait, we still have the ability to access room for improvement. *An older man,* particularly of he is white-haired or holy, can represent the innate wisdom we all have *(see Wise Old Man).* Such a person can also signify the father in dreams. *A man in woman's dream* highlights the more logical side of her nature. She has, or can develop, all the aspects of the masculine which enable her to function with success in the external world. If the man is *one she knows or loves* she may be trying to understand her relationship with him. *An unknown man* is generally that part of our personality which is not recognised. In a *woman's dream* it may be the masculine side of herself, and in *a man's dream* it is The Self *(see Self).* A *well-built man* appearing in our dreams indicates either our appreciation of the strengths, certainties and protection which our basic beliefs give us, or suggests that we may be feeling threatened or are made apprehensive by those very qualities. When we become aware of cultural characteristics in a male figure in dreams, we may be touching into our own understanding of stereotypes or the somewhat unconventional side of ourselves. As an example, depending on our personal experience, the figure of an Egyptian may represent either our magical knowledge, or perhaps the ability to make the best use of resources.

Prince/Princess These archetypal figures represent those parts of ourselves which exist by right. They are those aspects of our personality which we have deliberately made conscious and to which we have given authority. As the hero has taken responsibility for his own journey through life, so the prince and princess take responsibility for the lives they live. This translates into our waking lives as us being prepared to take responsibility for our own sense of duty to others.

Queen Such a figure most often represents our relationship with our mother, and thus with women in authority generally. Since the queen represents ultimate authority or approval, we may dream not only of any present queen, but also a *historical one* such as Victoria or even a *fantasy or mythical* one. These latter may suggest the need to move on from outdated concepts. Since fantasy and myth are such a rich source of imagery, it is worthwhile exploring the meaning of the fantasy or myth.

Stranger The stranger in a dream represents that part of ourselves which we do not yet know or appreciate. Such a figure can also represent the Shadow *(see Shadow)*. There may be a feeling either of reverence or conflict in our waking lives which must be dealt with before we can progress to full understanding.

Twins Twins in dreams (including the mirror-image of a figure in the dream) can suggest two sides of our personality. They may also signify our projections into the world of our own personalities. If the *twins are identical* we may be attempting to blend our unresolved feelings about ourselves into a coherent whole. If *not identical* they suggest the inner self and the outer reality.

Woman Any woman appearing in a dream represents all the qualities that we understand as feminine. Such a figure in dreams can suggest the softer, more intuitive aspects of the personality, whether the dreamer is male or female. *In a man's dream* such a figure describes his relationship with his own feelings and perhaps how he relates to his female partner. In *a woman's dream* a female family member or friend is often representative of an aspect of her own nature, but one she has not yet fully integrated. More spiritually a *goddess or holy woman* signifies the highest aspect of the feminine that can be attained. It usually suggests intuitive wisdom and the need to work for the Greater Good. *An Oriental women* appearing in a dream usually suggests the enigmatic mysterious side of the feminine. *In a woman's dream* they will reveal her own intuitive and instinctive ability for empathy. *In a man's dream,* taking into account the mystery of all women, such figures will often reveal his attitude to seduction of all types. An *older woman* most often represents our mother and her sense of inherited awareness and wisdom as epitomised by the Crone or Wise Woman. An *unknown woman* in dreams will represent either the Anima *(see Anima/Animus)* in a man's dream, or the Shadow *(see Shadow)* in a woman's. We can gain a great deal of information because the figure is unknown, and therefore needs to be carefully considered. It is the element of surprise and intrigue which permits us to explore the relevance of that previously hidden figure further.

③ The ultimate goal in understanding ourselves and living a successful life is what Jung called individuation. This is a growth towards maturity and an acceptance that all parts of our being can work together in harmony. Our interaction with people in ordinary life and with our dream people highlights that growth and allows us a great deal of freedom.

When we learn to use all of the four functions as successfully as we can, we consciously begin to integrate those parts of our personality and those archetypes *(see Archetypes)* which we may fear most. When we are no longer afraid of them, we do not project them on other people, nor do we permit other people to use us as 'punchbags' by pressing our particular triggers. One way of using our dream personalities to understand people in everyday life is to be able to classify them according to the broad categories shown above.

Not all dream personalities have a negative input. For total spiritual integrity, we must develop all sides of our personality, thus reaching for the True Self. As we do this we come to understand and be more tolerant of the idiosyncrasies in other people.

Pepper

① Pepper as a spice has the ability to 'spice something up' and it is this quality which is most symbolised in dreams. We need to liven up a situation we are in.

② To dream of pepper suggests we are changing our tastes. We may, in everyday life, be reacting to something in a relationship or particular situation that is not to our liking. It is this symbolism that often comes across when we need to make radical changes.

③ Pepper in dreams suggests spiritual warmth and love.

Perfume
– also see Smell

① When we dream of **smelling perfume**, we are often being reminded of particular memories. Smells can be extremely evocative and we may need to recapture a certain emotion associated with that specific perfume.

② Certain perfumes may remind us of people we have known. We may have a good – or bad – reaction to that smell. Just as people appearing in dreams remind us of our own qualities, so also can perfumes.

③ Intuitive information as well as spiritual learning can often be recognised because of a particular perfume or scent.

Pet
– also see Animals

① Whereas in the waking state we may not be aware of our need for love and affection, when a pet appears in a dream we are reacting to a natural drive in ourselves to give or receive love.

② On a subliminal level we may be aware that someone else has control over our lives. We can only do what is expected of us. Conversely, if we **own a pet in a dream** we perhaps need to question our ability to look after something or someone more vulnerable than ourselves.

③ Unconditional love which is without dependency often comes from our pets. They are often sensitive to our immediate emotional distress or pain.

Petrol
– also see Fuel and Oil

① Petrol is a form of energy and in dreams it is recognised as a requirement that we may have in order to keep us going. For instance, to be **putting petrol into a vehicle** would indicate that perhaps we need to be taking more care of our bodies.

Petrol is also explosive and dangerous, so to be **using petrol in a dangerous way** would indicate that we are creating problems for ourselves within a situation in ordinary everyday life.

② The energy we use in making decisions and in creating opportunities for ourselves can often be turned to drive. When we are handling petrol in a dream we are producing motivation. When we are at **a petrol station, being given or buying petrol**, we are taking energy from something external.

③ Spiritual power and energy can both be symbolised by petrol in dreams.

Pheasant
– see Birds

Phoenix
– see Birds

Photographs

① When we dream of **looking at photographs** we are often looking at an aspect of ourselves, perhaps our younger self or a part of ourselves that we no longer feel is particularly valid. To be **given a photograph of oneself** indicates that we need to be taking an objective view of situations round us or perhaps of ourselves within that situation. We need to stand back and look clearly at what is going on.

② Obviously photographs represent memories, past occasions, perhaps past difficulties. To be looking at photographs of **someone who belongs in the past** is to be looking at that person's qualities – perhaps bringing them forward into our own lives – and making use of those same qualities within.

③ Photographs in dreams can be used to represent a spiritual need to understand the past and how it may be relevant to the present.

Physician
– see Doctor

Piano
– also see Music/Rhythm

① Piano playing is something which satisfies all the aesthetic senses. The piano appearing in dreams is a symbol of our own creativity. Just as in everyday life we need to learn and practise playing the piano, so we also need to learn and practise using our creativity.

② One of the aspects of piano playing is that we are creative with someone else's composition. It may be that we need to look at our workaday situation in the light of making something happen in order to use our best potential.

③ Creative sound is a vital aspect in spiritual development, and our appreciation of music and rhythm in dreams can often give us an indication of our spiritual progression.

Picket

① In mundane everyday terms a picket is a group of workers surrounding a place of work to prevent entry, or to bring about a particular result. In dreams, therefore, to be **joining a picket line** is showing solidarity for a principle. To be **passing through a picket line** suggests that our own sense of self is more important than group feeling.

② In its original meaning a picket was a stake placed in the ground to defend a captured piece of land and it can still have shades of this meaning in dreams. We are defending our own emotional space.

③ A picket fence in dreams can symbolise our own spiritual boundaries – limits beyond which we cannot go.

Picture

① A picture in a dream is usually an illustration of something which is part of our lives. It will depend on whether it is **painted**, or a **print of another picture**, as to the interpretation. For instance, in a dream, a **picture that we have painted** might have more emotional impact than an **Old Master** (an Old Master can also suggest our attitude to the past).

② The condition of the picture may be important, as may also the colours in the picture *(see Colours)*. The subject matter may give us suggestions as to what we should be 'looking at' in our lives.

③ In the spiritual sense a picture is a captured image of our state of being at any one time. This may require some detailed study.

Pier/Harbour

① Dreaming of a pier would suggest happy times and memories to most people. We may have an association with a particular town or it may simply be that a seaside pier signifies rest and relaxation.

② A **pier** as a point of embarkation or arrival may suggest to us new opportunities or the end of a journey *(see Journey)*. A **harbour** has a similar meaning as pier, as a safe haven.

③ A pier signifies both a beginning and an ending and also moving to a new level of spiritual understanding. A harbour signifies a point of anchorage and spiritually suggests the safety of religious belief.

Pig
– see Animals

Pill
– also see Tablet

① For most people, taking a pill suggests doing something to make themselves feel better. In dreams, taking such a course of action will signify putting ourselves through an experience we need in order to improve our performance or potential. Dreaming of taking the **contraceptive pill** may in a woman's dream signify a fear of pregnancy or her fear of commitment.

② On a psychological level we may be aware of our ability to heal ourselves. **Taking a pill** in a dream may alert us to that capability. We may also be conscious of the necessity for taking care over what we put in our mouths, particularly if **someone else is giving us the pill**.

③ Spiritual or alternative methods of healing may be appropriate in a given situation. A bitter pill suggests there is something difficult to tolerate.

Pilgrim/Pilgrimage

① When we are **undertaking a pilgrimage** in a dream we are recognising the purposeful, directed side of our personality. We have a goal in life, which may require faith to achieve.

② A pilgrim can often represent the hermit or Wise Old Man *(see Wise Old Man)* within. That part of our personality which is secure and may not need much input from others has the ability to direct our lives provided we create the correct circumstances.

③ A seeker of Spirituality must always undertake a journey of some kind. This is often represented by a pilgrimage to a holy place.

Pillar

① One symbolism of a pillar is phallic, but another one is probably more accurate. We are able to create stability and to stand firm in the presence of difficulty. In dreams, to find that we are a **pillar of the community** suggests that we should be taking more responsibility for our actions.

② Pillars mostly indicate a sort of support, so to become aware of **supporting pillars** indicates that the structure that we have given our lives may need some attention. Esoterically, for there to be **two pillars** in a dream highlights the difference between the masculine and the feminine. The **left pillar** represents the feminine, and is often seen as being black. The **right** is masculine, and is seen in dreams as white.

③ The contrast between spiritual and material power is seen as two pillars in dreams. To be able to navigate through this duality is to attain Unity with the Divine.

Pillow

① In ordinary everyday life a pillow or cushion can offer support or comfort. So, in a dream, being conscious of a pillow may suggest such a need. Sometimes **what the pillow is made of** is important, and may have relevance in the interpretation of the dream. For instance, **a feather pillow** would suggest gentle support, whereas **a stone pillow** would represent a degree of rigidity.

② Sometimes, when we are going through a period of self-denial, we will deny ourselves any comfort symbolism and so our pillow may disappear. To dream of **a pillow fight** indicates a mock conflict.

③ Spiritual comfort and ease are represented by the pillow. We have reached a point in our journey where we can take a rest.

Pimple

① For most people the way they see themselves is important. To be overly conscious of something like a pimple in a dream is to suggest some worry as to how one comes across to others. A pimple can also represent some kind of blemish in our characters which at some time or another will have to be dealt with.

② Since a pimple usually suggests the body's inability to throw off toxins, such a symbol in dreams indicates our inability to throw off infection or negativity. It has only come partly to the surface of our consciousness.

③ A pimple can suggest a spiritual blemish – that is, something which causes difficulty or ugliness of some sort in our lives.

Pin

① It depends whether the pin is holding something together or is being used to pierce us, or an object, in our dreams. If it is **holding something together** it indicates the emotional connections or bonds that we use. If it is **piercing an object** a trauma is suggested, although it may be quite small.

② Occasionally in a dream we are reminded of a feeling we have in everyday life. To experience **a feeling of pins and needles** in our dream suggests that we are not ensuring an adequate flow of energy in a situation around us.

③ We may not be able to solve some sort of spiritual difficulty immediately. A temporary solution may be necessary and this can be symbolised in dreams by the use of a pin.

Pine cone

① If the pine cone does not have a personal connection for us – such as a childhood memory – it will denote fecundity and good fortune.

② The pine cone is an ancient fertility symbol, also representing eternal life. Interestingly, in waking life a forecaster of good and bad weather, in dreams it may be seen as a forewarning of difficult or changing times ahead.

③ In Masonic lore the pine cone has the same symbolism as the pomegranate, but in the sense of the connection between the physical and spiritual realms, the Third Eye or the pineal gland.

Pipe

① On a purely practical level a pipe can symbolise many things. A **water pipe** can give information as to how we might handle our emotions (the size and type in this case will be significant). A **tobacco pipe or chillum** might suggest a means of escape, whereas a **musical pipe** indicates our connection with the rhythm of life.

② When we are in difficulty in everyday life, a simple symbol such as a pipe will indicate how making connections between the various aspects of a situation will help resolve it.

③ A pipe suggests some kind of spiritual conduit, a way of clearing or increasing energy. We are ready to take in more knowledge.

Pirate
– see Occupations

Pistol
– see Gun and Weapons

Piston
– also see Car, Engine/Engineering and Machine/Machinery

① A piston in a dream can be taken to mean sexual drive or activity. In this context it is more of a mechanical action than a loving act, and may show our attitude to sex. **In a woman's dream** a piston may reveal her fear of being hurt sexually. She may also be aware that she is simply being used, and that there is no tenderness. **In a man's dream** such an image may be indicative of his sense of identity and masculinity. If the **piston is not rigid** a man may fear impotence, whereas a woman will feel perhaps that she cannot trust her partner.

② A piston may also represent a person's drive for success. We may need to assess the amount of effort that is necessary for us to be able to achieve our goals. They may need to recognise that concentrated effort – which is fairly mechanical – may, at this stage, achieve more than creative flair. The piston, being only part of an engine, requires the rest of the components to operate successfully. Often a great deal of help can be gained by considering the way in which the piston works. In other words, when at a particular stage of development our actions may have to be mechanical, we also need the fuel and the container with which to operate.

③ The spiritual drive – that is, the need to be complete, requires effort which can be enhanced by using our resources properly.

Pit
– also see Abyss

① Many people talk about the pit of despair and of feeling trapped within a situation. A pit in a dream makes us more conscious of this particular feeling. We may be in a situation which we cannot get out of, or may find that if we are not careful we will put ourselves in such a situation. If **we are digging the pit** in the dream, we have to be conscious of the fact that we may be creating the situation ourselves. If **others are digging the pit**, we may feel we have no control over our circumstances and that doom and disaster are inevitable.

② **Rescuing others from a pit**, particularly if they are members of our own family, suggests that we have information which may be of use to them to enable them to overcome their problems. **Pushing someone into a pit** indicates that we are trying to suppress a part of our personality. To be conscious that **the pit is bottomless** signifies that we do not have the resources to recover a previous situation.

③ The pit, like the abyss, represents the Void and most probably death – not necessarily a physical death, but more a death of the old self. We have no choice but to go forward, knowing that we may fail, but also that if we do succeed our lives will change for the better. To face the pit requires extreme courage.

Places/Environments

① Often the setting or environment in a dream can give an insight into our state of mind. This may be because our attention needs to be drawn to our ability to make choices in waking life. A particularly **dark and depressing atmosphere** can illustrate the feelings that we have about a situation at that particular moment, or might perhaps be a warning of conditions to come. However, a **bright airy space** may suggest happiness and potential, and may also be a representation of our own way of looking at life.

② The scenario in a dream, as we become more skilled in interpretation, can often provide as much information as the characters and actions. Some such scenarios are given below.

Landscapes (also see individual entry) Interpreting the attributes of certain places as they appear in dreams gives us a perception of our own 'inner landscape'. Thus, a landscape that becomes *fertile or lighter* in the course of the dream indicates that something we have not previously appreciated – or have found unpleasant – is now developing possibilities and potentials, maybe for spiritual development. *Dreary unfriendly* landscapes, or *tranquil favourable* places may well refer to our subjective view of the world.

The country where the dream takes place or the destination we are pursuing may have a certain resonance for us through our use of stereotypes. For example, America might signify a rather brash, commercially oriented culture; England tends to be seen as inhibited and dutiful; France will represent the volatile masculine and so on. Such a dream may also be highlighting cultural differences or wish fulfillment.

The countryside (also see individual entry) can suggest a particular mood or feeling, especially of freedom. An *urban environment* may well suggest stress or bustle and hurry, while quickly changing dream scenes may demonstrate the theme of the dream.

Places which are familiar to us will evoke certain moods and memories though the details may have changed. This perhaps depicts a change in our appreciation of that particular memory. For instance, in dreams the *place of our birth or a childhood home* suggests a secure space. However, if it now feels oppressive, it may no longer seem to be a sanctuary.

A *sheltered space* offers peace and tranquillity, whereas *wide-open spaces* offer us freedom of movement.

Unknown or unfamiliar places are aspects of ourselves of which we are not yet aware. A place that *seems familiar and yet is unknown* to us signifies a situation we are in in everyday life which contains a recurring theme without necessarily being able to fully comprehend it.

As our concerns move from the community in which we live to more global issues we become increasingly aware of the effect we have on our immediate surroundings, the environment in which we live. Each of us has a responsibility to make the best use of resources, so issues surrounding the use of those resources are likely to arise in dreams. We may find ourselves dreaming of recycling, reuse and renovation for instance, of making the environment better or perhaps when under stress recognising the effect our actions can have on the world.

In the same way as our ancestors dreamed of natural and agricultural matters, we may dream of technological and manufacturing environments. A factory *(see Factory)* with lots of machinery might signify a noisy atmosphere yet one where everyone knew their right position. A computerised environment might suggest a quieter atmosphere where speech is reduced to a minimum. Even in the home, our attention may be drawn to such technology. It is usually of benefit to pay attention to such small details in the dream environment.

There is a particular aspect of dreaming which is of interest to those who wish to use dreams in a more creative fashion. It would seem that the human mind operates more creatively when freed from the restraints of the conscious mind. To a large extent this happens naturally when asleep anyway, but can also happen within the framework of dreams. Dreams where the environment is one of space – whether outer space or merely a more open atmosphere – give us the freedom to do, and be, whatever we choose. It is as though we link in to a wider perspective than our normal everyday reality and can accept that anything is possible.

Man has always been fascinated by the idea of there being other worlds out there to explore, perhaps because he knows that within himself there is potential for the creation of many realities. The space environment in dreams gives him the opportunity to undertake such exploration in a safe way. Planets offer fixed points of reference, space travel gives a metaphor for exploration, and aliens offer scope for the idea of difficult concepts (*see Space, Aliens and Planets*).

③ From a spiritual perspective, as we become more aware and recognise dreams as a fertile basis for our instinctive creativity we can begin by manipulating our dream environments. On waking we can consciously work with a dreary landscape to turn it lighter, thus changing our mood. We need to remember that environments in dreams form a background to the 'play of life' as we live it. While it may seem that we have no control over this background, dreams teach us that we can alter circumstances to suit ourselves.

Plague

① In olden times, plague and pestilence was believed to come from an angry God. In fact, most plagues are caused by an imbalance in natural ecology. To dream of a plague will highlight some internal imbalance within ourselves. This may be physical, emotional, mental or spiritual. One quality of a plague, no matter what it is, is that there is too much. We can be overwhelmed by it, as happened with the plague of locusts chronicled in the Bible.

② One outstanding example of a plague in the Bible was that of Job who was plagued by boils. This suggests the old-fashioned idea that if one did not conform, retribution would occur. To dream of a plague, therefore, is to recognise that we will suffer in some way if we do not at least attempt to reach our highest potential in our waking lives.

③ In spiritual terms a plague signifies Divine Retribution. We should consider whether we are acting appropriately.

Plait

① In olden times, a **plait using three strands** indicated the interweaving of body, mind and spirit and with more natural belief systems still does. It also represented the influences which were assimilated by a growing girl and taken into her understanding of herself as a woman. In dreams it therefore represents womanhood. In the present day, as men become more sensitive, the more creative will often plait longer hair.

② **Plaited hair** was formerly a means of creating order and cleanliness. Often in dreams to see a plait reminds us of the talisman – or favour belonging to his lady – which a knight of old would carry into battle. Nowadays it is more of a lucky or magical charm. To be **plaiting string, rope, hair etc.** highlights our ability to weave the different influences of our, or someone else's, life into a coherent whole.

③ Very subtle influences come into play when we begin to develop spiritually. Hair **plaited into the shape of a crown – or wound round the head** – indicates spiritual attainment.

Planets

① Dreaming of planets is to be linking with very subtle energies which surround us and have an effect on our lives, even though we may not be consciously aware of them.

② The interpretations of the planetary significances are: *Jupiter* suggests growth and expansion, and also freedom from limitation. *Mars* indicates activity and war but also drive. *Mercury* signifies communication, intuition and mental powers. The *Moon* represents our emotions and our links with our mother. *Neptune* works with illusion – but also with inspiration. *Pluto* has charge of the unconscious and transformation. *Saturn* is a restraining influence and rules the past. The *Sun* usually symbolises the Self *(see Self)* and the energy that we have. *Uranus* governs sudden changes, whereas *Venus* highlights love and beauty.

③ Spiritually, once we become aware of how the subtle energies can help us live our lives successfully, we can learn to make use of planetary energy.

Plank
– also see Wood

① To dream of **walking the plank** suggests taking an emotional risk. A plank of wood appearing in a dream can indicate that something needs repairing, or that we feel safer carrying our own means of support. If the plank is to be **used in flooring** the symbol is one of security, but if to be used as a **door** or as **decoration** on a wall, it signifies defence or adornment of one's inner space.

② If the plank is to be **used for making something**, it suggests the material we have for undertaking a project. We may be aware in the dream of the type of wood we are using and this can have some significance or memory for us. If the plank is **used for making a box**, we should take care not to become trapped within a situation.

③ We have the raw material to enable us to become more aware of the process of life. We may need to look at what we consider to be our usefulness within the world.

Plants
– also see Gardener and Weeds

① Because of the process of growth and decay that plants go through naturally, they become a symbol for progressive change. If the **plants are cultivated**, then we should be aware of our ability to cultivate potential. If the **plants are dying** we may have reached a stage where there is no more advantage within a situation.

② If the **plants are growing wild**, there is a part of us that needs freedom. If they are **grown in regimented or formal rows** we are overly concerned about other people's views and opinions. Many plants have both healing and magical qualities which become apparent in dreams.

③ Plants in a spiritual sense signify the life force and cycle of life. Because they die only to grow again, they also suggest death and rebirth.

Plate

① A plate can be simple or ornate. In dreams the interpretation will depend on this fact. A **simple** plate will indicate a need for simplicity within our lives, whereas a more **ornate one** may suggest the need for celebration. If **we are holding the plate**, we are aware of what we have received from other people. If **someone else is giving us the plate** they are offering us something which belongs to them, but which we can now share.

② The plate as a container is an important image. If it is more **bowl-shaped**, it will represent what belongs to the feminine; **if flat** it will suggest some kind of group ownership. An **empty plate** signifies one's self-involved needs and appetites, whereas a **communal plate** highlights what there is to share. The pattern and colour of the plate may be important *(see Colour and also Shapes/Patterns).*

③ Formerly, plates were often only owned by the rich. Spiritually, to own a plate suggests that we have achieved a certain level of awareness.

Plateau

① Many dreams will hold images of climbing and of reaching a plateau – we reach a place which is even and not difficult to cross after a hard climb. Sometimes it can represent a period of peace and quiet, sometimes stasis where there is no energy left for change.

② If the **plateau is barren**, we may need some further stimulus to help us move on. If it seems to be **a place of safety**, we may not wish to move on and perhaps need to take time out to recuperate.

③ Spiritually a plateau offers choices. We can rest on our laurels and take time out to assess our progress, or we can use the plateau for calm and peace.

Play

① When in a dream we are **watching a play**, we need to decide whether it is a drama, a comedy or a tragedy. This is because we often are trying to view our own lives objectively. The **content of the play** may give us clues as to what our course of action should be in everyday life. If **people we know** are in the play we should be aware of the 'drama' we are playing out with them. To **be playing** in dreams suggests our ability to be lighthearted and carefree.

② In dreams, the play that takes place is a distillation of our experiences, knowledge and abilities. The creator in us directs the performance to enable us to get the best benefit of the information it contains. Images are put together to have the greatest impact and to make the interpretation as easy as possible. Sometimes, however, the unexpected occurs which means that we have to seek explanation elsewhere. It is said that we learn through play and such an approach allows us to experiment rather than sticking rigidly to rules. It is this freedom of expression which is important in dreams.

③ From a spiritual perspective, the life that we have creates a play which gives us the best opportunity to learn lessons through experience. Again there is the idea that we learn through practice. From a spiritual perspective practising ritual, for instance, allows for correct emphasis.

Ploughing

① As more people move away from working with the land, this symbol becomes less relevant in dreams. It does still mean, however, working at clearing oneself for new growth and being able to prepare for change.

② We may have a situation within our lives which needs 'turning over'. By looking at it from a different perspective we are able to make the situation more productive.

③ We are in process of creating new opportunities to develop spiritually.

Plumage
– also see Feather/Feathered Sun

① In a dream, plumage being drawn to our attention can often stand for a display of power and strength. It may also be a signal of defiance; we need to stand firm and show our colours, as it were.

② A bird's plumage is its protection, but it is also its power and strength. Used in this sense, it is alerting us to the fact that we can use our own strength and ability to achieve what we want to do in the future.

③ Spiritual triumph, success and an increase in knowledge is shown by a display of plumage.

Plumbing

① Dreaming about plumbing looks at the way we direct our emotions. It indicates how we make use of our emotions to bypass obstacles in order to create security for ourselves and to control the flow of emotions within. Another interpretation is that of the internal plumbing. Often, to dream of plumbing in this sense alerts us to something that is perhaps wrong with ourselves, with our bodies.

② Emotional security is important to almost everybody, and mostly these things are hidden from view. When we are looking at plumbing we are actually looking into our unconscious to where we have stored information and emotion. We need to be able to access these so that we can create clarity within our lives.

③ We are aware of the flow of spiritual energy within our lives. Learning how to control it is an important aspect of development.

Plunge

① To dream of **plunging into something** is to recognise that we are facing uncertainty. We are going into something unknown – something that we have perhaps not done before – and are taking a risk. That risk will very often take us into our emotional depths and we will learn new things about ourselves.

② When facing uncertainty in waking life we very often need reassurance that we have both the courage and the daring to go ahead with a particular activity. Very often, to dream of plunging is to recognise that we do have the ability to go forward. To dream of **a plunger** – as in something that clears a blockage – usually indicates that we need to use some force to enable us to deal with difficulty. Frequently, this can be because we have internalised a problem – we have either worked too hard and don't have the energy to move the difficulty away from us or we have created a problem for ourselves in that we have not acted appropriately.

③ We have reached a certain point on our spiritual journey. We must now 'take the plunge' into new areas if we are to progress further. We may think it risky, but the results should be worth it.

Pocket

① To dream of a pocket is to be dealing with one's personal secrets or thoughts – those things that we have deliberately chosen to hide rather than done so on impulse. They are perhaps secret thoughts that we do not want to share with anyone else. There may also be thoughts about our own abilities and the value that we have within our own personal community.

② A pocket in a dream can also indicate a sense of ownership and possession. **To have something in our pocket** means that we have appropriated it, that we have taken ownership. This can represent a situation in the everyday world, or it can represent emotions that we may have previously hidden and now need to own, in the sense of being able to make use of them.

③ A pocket suggests the Hidden, the Occult and as yet undiscovered Knowledge.

Point

① In dreams, to be aware of **the point of decision** is to come to a resolve that something has to be done about a situation. We must bring about change in one way or another. By tradition, anything pointed is said to suggest masculine sexuality, though it is probably more realistic to interpret it today as masculine drive or assertiveness.

② Psychologically and intellectually to have integrated ourselves means that we have reached our own centre. This is often symbolised in dreams by a point or dot.

③ Before there was number there was a beginning – a dot or a point – an intensification of energy which has now come to symbolise the Soul.

Pointing

① When we dream of **someone pointing**, normally we are having our attention drawn to a particular object, feeling or even place. We need to take note of both **who is pointing** it out to us *(see People)* and equally **what they are pointing at**. We may feel that we are at the receiving end – often pointing can be an aggressive act or accusation – and in dreams we may feel that we are being accused of wrong doing and need to look at the validity of our conduct.

② Pointing in a dream, particularly by one of our dream characters, indicates either that we are being given a sense of direction, or that we are being pointed away from a present action and should leave it behind.

③ A hand pointing in a particular direction is instructing us which way to go. Up suggests towards the spiritual, down towards the unconscious. A finger pointing towards us is accusatory.

Poison

① To be able to recognise poison in a dream means that we need to avoid an attitude, emotion or thought which will not be good for us. In our environment there is that which not only is not good for us now, but which could also cause unpleasantness for us in the future.

② Other people's attitudes and beliefs can contaminate the way we think and feel and this can sometimes be shown in dreams as poison. If **we are poisoning someone** in a dream, we are trying to force our beliefs and ways of thinking on them.

③ There may be a degree of contamination or ill-feeling around us as we continue on our spiritual journey. We should ensure that we are not making others uncomfortable or upsetting them as we progress.

Poker

① A poker obviously has links with masculinity, but also with rigidity. In dreams a poker can therefore suggest aggressive action, but also rigid attitudes and behaviour.

② Playing a **game of poker** in a dream suggests that one is taking a risk in everyday life. It may be important to note who we are playing with.

③ The poker in this instance suggests rigid and unbending discipline, which is necessary at one point in spiritual development.

Pole

① It will depend how the pole is being used in the dream as to the interpretation. It is seen as an expression of the life force – as in **a Maypole** *(see Maypole)* – but also as a stabilising force or rallying point, as in a **flagpole**. It can also be a support mechanism.

② In former times a pole was a standard measurement so in dreams can symbolise a measurement of personal standards of behaviour. The symbolism may be further extended to measure that which is in our reach. Interestingly, the pole was originally the measure from the ploughboy to the farthest oxen.

③ Pole position suggests the best position to start in the race of life and spiritually symbolises heroic and leadership qualities.

Police
– see Occupations

Pool/Pond
– also see Water

① Dreaming of a pool deals with our need for the understanding of our own emotions and inner feelings. A **pool in a wood**, for instance, would suggest the ability to understand our own need for peace and tranquillity. An **urban swimming pool** might signify our need for structure in our relationships with other people, whereas a **pool in the road** would suggest an emotional problem to be got through before carrying out our plans. A **pond** will have the same significance as a pool except that the former is usually man-made rather than a natural formation. The pond will often signify emotions brought about by external circumstances whereas a pool is our own innate emotion.

② In order to understand ourselves we may need to explore a pool by totally immersing ourselves in it, that is, to become involved in our own emotions. How we deal with what arises (in more senses than one) will teach us a lot about ourselves. The pool may suggest a form of cleansing, particularly of old traumas and emotions or of past misdeeds. The most potent image of that is baptism by immersion.

③ There is a meditation or guided imagery technique which can enhance our ability to dream. First, you picture yourselves walking in a field. Feel the grass beneath your feet and the wind on your face. Walk towards a slight dip in the ground which is to your left. At the bottom of this dip there is a pool which is surrounded by trees. Sit quietly by the pool, simply thinking about your life. When you are ready, stand up and walk into the pool very slowly. Feel the water rising slowly up your body until you are immersed completely. At that point let go of all the tensions of the everyday world and concentrate on the peace which is within. Then slowly emerge from the pool, and again sit quietly beside it. When you are ready, walk back to the point in the field where you started, and let the image fade. By practising this, gradually it will be found that dream images take on a deeper meaning.

Pope
– also see Occupations

① Often to meet the Pope in a dream is to meet the side of ourselves which has developed a code of behaviour based on our religious beliefs. He may appear benign or judgemental depending on how religion in general and the figure of the Pope in particular was presented in childhood.

② The Pope often appears in dreams as a substitute for the father or father figure, or perhaps as a personification of God.

③ Our spiritual mentor or Higher Self will sometimes appear in dreams as the Pope, since he is a recognisable figure of religious authority.

Poppy
– also see Flowers

① The poppy can appear in our dreams as either a symbol of sacrifice – **the remembrance poppy**, or as one of idleness and oblivion – **the opium poppy**.

② On a psychological level both significances can be united. We need to 'remember to forget'. By learning to forget past difficulties we give ourselves the opportunity to move on with clarity.

③ The poppy symbolises forgetfulness. In spiritual terms the soul must forget all it knows in order to reincarnate and rediscover its own awareness. The Great Mother *(see Great Mother/Mother Earth)* as the Goddess was, and is, responsible for that forgetting – hence the poppy signifies the Great Mother.

Position

① When a particular position is highlighted in a dream it usually signifies our moral standpoint, or our position in life. It can also give an indication of how we are handling situations in our lives. For instance, something in the *wrong position* means we are going about things in the wrong way.

② Our spirit, intellect, ideals and consciences are being brought to our attention when we dream of anything *higher* or *above* us. This applies also when dreaming of the *upper part* of anything (of a building or body, for example). Our altruism may be being brought into question. Anything *underneath, below or downstairs* signifies the anarchic or immoral side of our personalities. The sexual impulses can also be characterised in this way. Something appearing *upside down* emphasises the potential for chaos and difficulty. The 'ups and downs' of situations in life can be experienced in dreams as the actual movement of our position. The personality has a need to balance the heights and depths of its experience, and if this does not happen a warning will usually appear in dream form.

Back/Front Rejection and acceptance can be shown in a dream as seeing the back and front of something. *Backwards/Forwards* Having the attention drawn to a backward and/or forward movement is usually indicating the potential to adopt a regressive backward-looking tendency. There is a need to retire into the past, rather than tackling fears and moving ahead. Looking or moving forward suggests that we focus on the future.

Centre (also see Shapes/Patterns) To be conscious of the centre of any aspect of a dream is to be aware of a goal or objective, or perhaps even of our real Self *(see Self)*. There is a need to be the centre of attention whatever the circumstances.

Far/Near In dreams, space and time can become confused. Dreaming of something which is *far away*, may indicate that it is far away in time. This may be future or past, depending on the dream. A *long way in front* would be future, a *long way behind* would be past. *Near or close* would mean recently, or in the immediate.

Horizontal This usually symbolises the material world.

Left The left suggests the less dominant, more passive side. Often it is taken to represent all that is dark and sinister and those parts of our personality which we try to suppress. It is more to do with instinctive behaviour, what feels good inside and with personal behaviour without attention to moral codes. It is supportive in expression, and receptive by nature, so anything appearing in dreams *on the left side* can be accepted as a symbol of support. Any *pain experienced on the left side* is interpreted in terms of sensitivity. The left expresses the more feminine attributes and often the past. Feelings of being *left behind* suggest a sense of inadequacy, of disintegration and of having to leave the past behind. *Indecision over left and right* suggests an inability to decide whether to rely on drive or instinct.

Low In dreams, feeling 'low' can suggest a sense of inferiority or humility. Often we will give way to submissive behaviour, and put ourselves in a lower position than others.

Opposite Anything in a dream which is opposite us may suggest some difficulty in reconciling two paradoxes – good/bad, male/female, up/down, etc. This can sometimes suggest conflict. *One thing deliberately put opposite another* indicates there is a deliberate attempt to introduce discord. *Changing the position from opposite* shows that differences may be adjusted.

Right The right side represents the more dominant logical side. It is the consciously expressed, confident side which perceives the exterior world in perhaps a more objective sense. It is to do with 'rightness' – that is, correctness and moral and social behaviour. *Right and left conflicting* usually indicates a struggle between logic and intuition. Anything observed on *the right side* in dreams is usually significant as we progress spiritually. Any *pain experienced on the right side* can also be interpreted in terms of drive and energy. It also expresses the more masculine attributes. *Movement to the right* indicates that something is coming into conscious awareness.

Straight Being aware of anything being particularly straight suggests a direct approach, the shortest route between two objects, places, goals or ideas. It can also suggest the quickest route, 'as the crow files'.

Top To be *at the top* is to have succeeded. To be *on top* is to have assumed control. *Trying to reach the top* suggests more effort is needed.

Under/Underneath Being underneath something suggests either taking shelter or submitting to someone else's handling of us. It may also represent the part of us that we hide, or the part that is less capable. Occasionally, *to be below someone or something* can indicate a need to explore the underside or inherent negativity of a relationship or situation.

Up/Upper We have the capability of achieving a degree of supremacy. We are capable of getting the 'upper hand' in particular situations. We can move away from the mundane, ordinary everyday world.

Vertical The vertical in dreams tends to represent the spiritual realm, or our progress from the mundane to the more esoteric realms.

③ The points of the compass can be read spiritually. *The North* signifies the Unknown, and hence sometimes darkness. It is spirituality within the world. *The East* traditionally suggests birth and mystic religions. It also represents becoming 'conscious'. *The South* is representative of earthly passion and sensuality. *The West* can symbolise death, but more properly the state after death when there is increased spiritual awareness. Traditionally, it can also represent the more logical side of our natures.

Postures
– also see Yoga

① Body language is an important aspect in dreams. Our dream characters may develop exaggerated movements or postures to highlight certain information which we need to recognise.

② We often pick up information on a subliminal level without being able to understand why. The postures we, or others, adopt in dreams often give us the answers to those questions that need answering.

③ An exaggerated posture will indicate emotions. Living and being mean that we are capable of adopting certain recognisable stances and postures (as in yoga) in order to progress spiritually.

Poverty
– also see Debt, Finance, Money and Wealth

① To experience poverty in a dream highlights a sense of being deprived of the ability to satisfy our basic needs. We may feel inadequate, either emotionally or materially. Often we need to go right back to basics to discover what our real needs are.

② Poverty in a dream can be conveyed by **poor surroundings**. It may be that we need to deal with our surroundings rather than ourselves.

③ Spiritual poverty can be self-denial or denial of our right to progress.

Prayer
– also see Religious Iconology

① Prayer suggests the idea that we need to seek outside help for ourselves. We may need someone else's authority to succeed in what we are doing.

② Psychologically, the human being has always needed to feel that there is a greater power than himself available to him. To be praying in a dream reinforces this, since we need to use our own inner sense of self to access the Greater Power.

③ Supplication and Worship are two aspects of prayer, thus giving us access to the Divine.

Precipice

① The fear of failure is a very strong emotion. Often it can be represented in dreams by a precipice. To **step off a precipice** is taking risks, since we do not know the outcome of our action. To try to **climb a precipice** is to be making a tremendous effort to overcome obstacles which have arisen.

② The image of the Fool in the Tarot shows him at the beginning and the end of his journey. He is **unmindful of the precipice** and initially is not aware of the danger he is in. Conversely, he does not care because he is aware he is capable of stepping off the edge and taking flight. This type of dream often appears when we are in a position of great risk.

③ A precipice will indicate a perceived spiritual danger. We should ensure that we are not over-reaching ouselves on our spiritual journey.

Pregnancy

① Dreaming of pregnancy usually denotes a fairly protracted waiting period being necessary for something, possibly the completion of a project. A new area of our potential or personality is developing. Interestingly enough, to dream of pregnancy seldom actually means one's own pregnancy, although it can indicate pregnancy in someone around us.

② To dream of **someone else being pregnant** suggests that we are in a position to observe part of ourselves developing new skills or characteristics. We may be unaware of what the outcome of this process will be. To dream of a **man being pregnant**, particularly if it is **a woman's dream**, it can be a projection of her own wish for the man to take responsibility within her life.

③ There is always a gestation period in spiritual work. Dreaming of pregnancy shows we may have to be patient and wait for a natural process to take place so that we can fulfil a task. It is as though there is a hesitation before things can manifest properly.

Prehistoric
– also see Dinosaur and Fossil

① Being aware in a dream that something is prehistoric is to recognise that feelings and emotions we have arise literally from before the time we were able to understand ourselves. When we have not fully integrated and comprehended the basic urge for survival, it is possible for us to be self-destructive without necessarily appreciating why.

② Often in dreams the landscape or scenario appears to be prehistoric. This is a time 'before thought' and before we had the ability to record our impressions. If one believes that babies are conscious of the world they will enter before birth, then these impressions can appear in later life as prehistoric images. For instance, a barren landscape might indicate a lack of love.

③ Spiritual progression requires us to understand our physical, emotional, mental and spiritual urges. In this context, the prehistoric images which appear indicate the lack of ability to integrate either the various parts of ourselves successfully, or to integrate with society.

Present/Presents

① When a present appears in a dream, it can first of all be a play on words. We are being given a 'here and now'. We are being reminded to live in the moment, and not the past or future. A present can also indicate a talent or gift. If we are **receiving a present** we are being loved and recognised and are also gaining from the relationship. If we are **giving a present**, we appreciate that we have characteristics that we are able to offer other people. **A pile of presents** in a dream can signify as yet unrecognised talents and skills. If the presents give some indication of time – e.g. birthday presents – we may expect some success around that time.

② **To present something** in a dream (as in making a presentation) is offering work that we have done for approval and recognition. We appreciate that the work we have done is more important than we ourselves are. An idea is pre-sent in order to take root in the future.

③ One of the requirements of spiritual advancement is that we learn to live in the present. We need to be able to take advantage of anything that life presents – to use it for ourselves, but also to recognise that it has relevance to other people and can affect the way that they live.

Priest/Priestess
– see Archetypes and Occupations

Prince/Princess
– see People

Prison
– also see Key and Lock

① Prison, in dreams, stands for the traps we create for ourselves. We may feel that outside circumstances are making life difficult, but in actual fact we are creating those circumstances ourselves. This can be on an emotional, material or spiritual level.

② Often we create a prison for ourselves through a sense of duty or guilt and this can often be shown in dreams. The types of locks and bolts we perceive in our prison may show us how we are imprisoning ourselves. For example, **a lock with a key** would suggest that we know how to escape, whereas **a bolt** shows that we have to make a greater effort. **A barred window** would suggest that we are being prevented from using that which is external to us.

③ Often, when we feel trapped either by duty or guilt, which are are opposite sides of the same coin in a spiritual sense, we will dream of a prison. Duty can be a liability and therefore a trap, and guilt can prevent us from seeing a way forward. We must weigh up very carefully our necessary action.

Prize

① In dreams **to win a prize** is to have succeeded in overcoming our own obstacles. We are also being acknowledged by other people for having made the effort to succeed. **To be giving away prizes** suggests that we are giving public acknowledgement to efforts others have made.

② To prize an object (as in **a prize possession**) is to give it its proper value. This does not necessarily mean being materialistic, but being able to gain from an appreciation of its intrinsic value.

③ In spiritual terms, gaining a prize in a dream means we have used our instincts and intuition in harmony in order to be able to use inspiration.

Procession

① A procession means an orderly approach and often makes a statement of intent. In a dream, to see **a line of people** who all appear to have a similar goal or set of beliefs in mind, indicates that it is the intention behind the group which is important. Often a procession is hierarchical, with the most important people either first or last. This could be important in a dream in enabling us to adopt priorities for ourselves.

② A procession is often a way of marking a special occasion with pageantry and dignity. In dreams such an image can often represent our need to have our own successes and abilities recognised. To be **taking part in a procession** is acknowledging our need to belong to a like-minded group. To be **watching a procession** is to appreciate other people's single-mindedness.

③ Spiritually, a procession is indicative of a group of like-minded people but also of people who have great knowledge. In dreams we are recognising the importance of whatever system of belief or religion we belong to. We recognise that due respect and reverence must be paid.

Promote/Promotion
– also see Work

① Dreaming of promotion indicates that we feel we have reached a level of competence in waking life – if not in our employment – which deserves reward. To **lose a promotion** signifies a degree of disappointment in our own performance. To be **promoting a product or course of action** may signify a commitment to that idea or principle.

② In the same vein, promotion suggests that others have judged us to be competent and possibly capable of taking on more responsibility. We are expected to be proficient in certain tasks and may also be entitled to certain benefits. If we **promote someone else** in dreams we approve of them and their way of being.

③ Promotion in the spiritual sense can mean the same as initiation. We are privy to certain information which is not available to everyone.

Propeller

① A propeller acknowledges the drive and intent behind our progression. Recognising our needs, we also need to understand how we can best move forward. The action of a propeller is to give us 'lift', which suggests being able to use the intellect.

② When a propeller appears in a dream it will obviously depend on whether it is an old-fashioned areoplane propeller or one on a boat. The former suggests undertaking research into old ideas and ways of working, whilst the latter suggests learning how to use the force of our emtions to our best advantage.

③ As a motivating force the propeller symbolises the need to drive ourselves forward. It also highlights the idea of there being a degree of spiritual compulsion in what we do.

Prostitute

① Dreaming of a prostitute usually suggests a sexual need. **In a man's dream** it may signify his need for a relationship at any cost. **In a woman's dream** it can suggest her own need for sexual freedom. Often, dreaming of a prostitute forces us to look at our own sense of guilt or uncertainty about ourselves. **To be paying a prostitute** may suggest that we do not trust our own sexual abilities. **To be paid** for the sexual act may suggest that we feel relationships will cost us. In both these cases there may be some fear of loving relationships.

② In dreaming of prostitution, we may actually be connecting with a poor self-image. We are minimising our abilities and talents – this may be in a work situation as much as in our personal life. Very often, when we are expected to 'perform' in some way inadequacy or ego makes us feel that we are 'prostituting' our talents.

③ In Christian terms, just as Christ recognised the value of the prostitute as a person in her own right, we also spiritually need to accept other people's values. The temple prostitute was an important aspect of initiation.

Psychologist/Psychiatrist
– see Analyst/Therapist

Public House
– also see Bar/Barmaid/Barman

① To be in a pub in a dream and aware of our behaviour indicates how we relate to groups and what our feelings are about society. We may feel that it is appropriate to use a public space to create new relationships, or to come to terms with our own sense of loneliness. A public space where we can drop our inhibitions has links with the ancient Pagan need we all have for celebration and festivity.

② We all have social needs that can be met in convivial company, in a pub or bar. The origins of the public house were the old inns, which were stopping-off places for travellers. Any companionship was purely transitory. This symbolism is still present today in dreams. We are in a place where we can rest and relax and nothing more is expected of us.

③ As a public place where shared values are important, the public house can be a creative space. As a meeting place where few judgements are made, it becomes a place in which people can co-exist.

Puddle
– also see Pool/Pond and Water

① A puddle, being a smaller amount of liquid than either a pool or lake, can nevertheless have the same significance. We are becoming aware of our emotions and the way we handle them.

② How we deal with the puddle may be important. If we **mop it up**, we are trying to re-absorb emotion that we may feel to be inappropriate. If we **leave it**, we probably need other people to recognise either our, or their, emotions.

③ Esoterically, a puddle can be used for scrying – that is, looking into the future as though into a magic mirror. To be **looking into a puddle** may be trying to decide what future action needs to be taken.

Pulling

① Pulling suggests a positive action. We are being alerted to the fact that we can do something about a situation. In dreams, if **we are pulling** we are making the decisions within a project. If we are **being pulled** we may feel that we are having to give in to outside pressures. We may have to make extra effort to have something happen. **The object we are pulling**, and the means by which we are pulling it, *(for examples, see Bridle, Rope etc.)* may be important.

② In slang terms, pulling means picking up a potential partner. In dreams this can actually translate itself into a physical feeling. We may also in everyday life be being pulled by our emotions and feel that we are powerless to resist. This can translate into the dream image of being pulled. We may feel that we have to go along with something and do not have the ability to refuse.

③ At a certain stage of spiritual development, there is a feeling of being pulled in a particular direction. We may be compelled to do certain things without necessarily knowing where the impulse comes from.

Pulse

① A pulse is a rhythm which is essential to life. To be aware in sleep of one's pulse may indicate some kind of anxiety. In dreams this may translate itself into a rhythm which is external. There may also be health worries.

② To be **feeling one's own pulse** in a dream is to be trying to put oneself in touch with the processes of life. To be **feeling someone else's pulse** may indicate a concern about that part of our personality the other character represents. If we **cannot detect a pulse**, this may indicate the 'death' of part of ourselves or emotions.

③ It is said that, to the sensitive, a pulse is detectable in all things. Spiritually, the more we are in touch with internal rhythm the more whole (or holy) we can be.

Punishment

① When a child recognises that he or she is not conforming to what is expected, the threat of punishment is often present. In later life, when there is fear of retribution from an external source, we will often dream of being punished. Self-punishment occurs when we have not achieved the standards we expect of ourselves.

② When there is conflict in our lives, if we cannot resolve it we will often dream of being punished. This may be the only way out of our particular dilemma. We would rather suffer pain than resolve the difficulty.

③ The concept of Divine Retribution – that is, being punished by a force greater than ourselves – suggests a judgemental God. Spiritual punishment is much more, however, the idea of self-flagellation for not having achieved what is required of us.

Puppet

① When a puppet appears in a dream there is perhaps a sense of being able to manipulate circumstances or people around us. A puppet can also represent the more mechanical processes of our being, those activities which go on automatically in the background.

② If **someone else is working the puppet**, we may feel that we are being manipulated. It would be wise to look at how we are co-operating in everyday life in becoming a victim. If the **puppet is manipulating us** we have become aware that bureaucracy is causing us difficulty. What should be working for us has, in fact, turned into some kind of a manipulator.

③ At certain stages of development, we can become aware that we are powerless without a spiritually motivating force behind us. We are like puppets in the greater scheme of things.

Puppy

– see Baby Animals in Animals

Purse

– also see Bag and Money

① A purse is normally used to hold money, or something of value to us. In dreams it therefore becomes something of value it its own right. **To find a purse** would suggest that we have found something of value whereas **to lose a purse** suggests that we may be being careless.

② The material that a purse is made from can have an important significance. The old saying 'you cannot make a silk purse out of a sow's ear' has relevance in dreams. The mind often plays tricks and manifests an apparently inappropriate image which needs to be worked on.

③ One symbolism of a purse is the same as that of a bag: the feminine and the containing principle. We are often attempting to conserve our Spiritual energy or power.

Pushed/Pushing

① When in a dream we are being pushed, there is an energy around us that enables us to achieve what we want. If **we are pushing**, then we are usually exerting our will positively. **Pushing something uphill**, such as a car or snowball, suggests that we are trying to resist natural forces or overcome negative ones.

② When in everyday life we are aware of pressure this can be surface in dreams as being pushed and can sometimes indicate a fear of illness. In certain forms of mental illness, the patient experiences a feeling of being pushed around and made to do something he does not want to do. Occasionally, when experienced in dreams, this can actually be a form of healing.

③ When one is developing psychically, it is possible to become aware of the subtle forces and energy around. This can be experienced as being pushed.

Putrefaction

– also see Mould/Mouldy

① Putrefaction can represent disintegration. In real-life situations something may have gone wrong, and there is no longer any energy to sustain it. While on a conscious level we may not recognise this fact, dreams will often bring it to our attention.

② Decay – for example in a relationship – can be represented in dreams as putrefaction. When something is happening which will ultimately lead to a total collapse, we can often sense it as a bad smell – something is dying.

③ In spiritual terms there often has to be dissolution and disintegration before there is a new beginning. In dreams, if we have fear of this process it can manifest as putrefaction. Putrefaction can also mean death.

Pyjamas
– see Clothes

Pyramid
– also see Buildings, Egypt and Sphinx

① A pyramid is a very powerful image. On a physical level, it is a building of wonder. On a mental level, it is a structure of regeneration. On a spiritual level, it is a guardian of power. It will depend on our level of awareness as to which interpretation has most relevance.

② The pyramid always signifies a wider awareness of power and energy. There is a point inside the pyramid where all the planes intersect. This will regenerate any matter which is placed there; for instance, razor blades will become sharp again. In a larger pyramid, that particular spot can be used for enhancing mystical experiences. In dreams, to enter a pyramid is to be searching for the meaning of life.

③ Spiritually, the pyramid is a symbol of integration of the Self *(see Self)* and the Soul. In dreams it can represent death, but also indicates rebirth.

Quail
– see Birds

Quaker

① To dream of **somebody being a Quaker** indicates the recognition of the ability to maintain a religious belief, come what may. It indicates a tranquillity and peacefulness that is not necessarily available to us in the waking state.

② The human being has a need for a belief system that can support him or her in difficulty. To dream of **being a Quaker** allows us to link with our own inner self-sufficiency.

③ Religious beliefs and the acceptance of an ability to cope because of those beliefs is a great part of human development.

Qualification/Qualify
– also see Exams/Being Examined

① To dream that we are **qualified in some skill** suggests that we have accepted our right to carry out a set of actions in everyday life. We know what we are doing or have received approval. To be **receiving a qualification** indicates that we can be rewarded for having reached a degree of competence.

② A qualification is a seal of approval from an authority. In emotional terms receiving such an accolade in dreams indicates self esteem and the knowledge that we have attained a goal.

③ In the field of spiritual endeavour there is no qualification except the standard that we set ourselves. Receiving a qualification in dreams therefore is a kind of inner initiation.

Quarantine

① Dreaming of having to **put an animal into quarantine** signifies there is an inability to look after a vulnerable part of ourselves or others. It may also indicate our awareness of having to cut off the lower, more animal side of ourselves and create a no-go area.

② When in waking life we feel isolated, this may translate itself in dream language into being in quarantine. It would seem that 'authority' has taken over to manage this isolation.

③ Spiritually, quarantine means isolation, retreating from the world for a time.

Quarrel

① To dream that we are **quarrelling with someone** indicates an inner conflict. For a **man to be quarrelling with a woman**, or **vice versa**, signifies a conflict between drive and intuition. To be **quarrelling with authority**, e.g. police, indicates a conflict between right and wrong.

② Depending on the other aspects of the dream, quarrelling can suggest that there is conflict between what we have been taught and what we believe. Often, such a conflict can only be resolved through an outburst of emotion. Since an **argument** is usually based on thought-out ideas or principles, arguing in dreams rather than quarrelling will suggest that we need to consider our options carefully.

③ Spiritual conflict or a conflict between the spiritual self and the physical can appear in dreams as a quarrel.

Quartet
– also see Four in Numbers

① Dreaming of a quartet of any kind signifies a link with the material or practical aspects of other objects in the dream. It could be necessary to concentrate on pragmatic solutions to a problem.

② Anything repeated more than once emphasises the significance of that object to us. The dream object will be reproduced four times at the same moment, rather than being seen sequentially, in order to make the emphasis apparent.

③ Spiritually, the quartet links with the Quaternity, which signifies manifestation on the physical plane.

Quartz

① Quartz seen in dreams tends to represent the crystallisation of ideas and feelings. It touches into our deep internal processes, often enabling us to express that which we have found impossible before.

② The crystallisation process was seen by the Ancients as the trapping of light, and therefore power and, on a subliminal level, this is still recognised by many dreamers. To dream of quartz, therefore, signifies a recognition of developing power.

③ The quartz is recognised as both a receptor and transmittor of Spiritual energy.

Quarry

① Dreaming of a quarry means quarrying the depths of our personality, 'digging out' the positive knowledge and perceptions we may have. Often dream symbols are created which link with childhood or past experiences which we may have buried and which now need to be brought into conscious understanding.

② **Seeking a quarry** (that is, pursuing someone or something) in a dream can indicate that we, on some level, know what we are looking for, but that it is the action of finding it that is important.

③ We need to conduct a Spiritual search which may require the digging out of information so we can progress on our journey.

Quay
– also see Pier/Harbour

① **Standing on a quayside** in a dream can indicate either moving forward into a new phase of life or leaving an old one behind. If **looking forward** with a sense of anticipation, it is the new phase which needs understanding. If **looking back**, there may be something in the past which needs attention before we can move on.

② Because anything associated with water is connected with emotion and how we feel about things, being on a quay can indicate how we need to handle other people's emotions as we move into a new phase of life.

③ Spiritual progression can be suggested by a quay, since it is a recognised point of departure.

Queen
– see People

Quest

① The Hero's Quest is an archetypal image *(see Hero in People)* which can appear in many guises in dreams. To be searching for something usually indicates that we are aware that we must undertake a frightening task in order to progress. Many fairy stories and mythological tales have as their main theme the search for something rare or magical (e.g. Jason and the Argonauts). Such themes can be translated into dreams in a personally applicable way.

② Often, the trials and tribulations we have to go through in achieving something we feel to be important are translated in dreams into a quest or search. The way these events are faced is as important as the actual achievement itself.

③ The pursuit of the Spiritual and undertaking a spiritual quest is a way of developing oneself spiritually.

Question

① To be asking questions in a dream indicates a degree of self-doubt. To have **someone asking the dreamer questions** shows that we are aware that we have some knowledge to be shared. If the **question cannot be answered**, we may need to seek the answer for ourselves in waking life.

② If we have a question in waking life which needs answering, by keeping it in mind before going to sleep we may often find the answer through dreams.

③ Spiritual questioning and enquiry lead to greater knowledge. We have a huge repository of information at our fingertips.

Questionnaire/Quiz

① To be **answering a questionnaire or quiz** in a dream suggests we may be making an attempt to change our circumstances without being certain of what we should actually do to bring about the change. As there is a proliferation of quiz shows on television where either financial gain or celebrity status is possible if we have enough knowledge, it is this significance which has relevance in dreams.

② A questionnaire depicts the use of our mental faculties in a focused, decision-making way. Questionnaires may also appear in dreams when we are unsure about, or are questioning, our lifestyle or way of being.

③ Questioning the inevitable is a part of spiritual progression.

Queue
– also see Line

① A queue of people in dreams suggests that there is something worth waiting for, happening or about to happen.

② A queue signifies that some sort of prioritisation needs to occur in daily life. We need to decide what is important and then be prepared to be patient until we can put ourselves first.

③ Spiritually, we need to recognise that we are all equal. A queue symbolises the idea that 'All things come to he who waits', though inherent in that is the principle of patience being rewarded.

Quicksand

① Quicksand signifies a lack of security. In old-fashioned dream interpretation it represented business difficulties. Today it is more likely to signify taking a business risk.

② To find ourselves **trapped in quicksand** suggests that we have been put in a difficult situation that is not necessarily of our own making.

③ Spiritual quicksand suggests a situation where we may be on insecure ground insofar as our beliefs are concerned.

Quiet

① Becoming aware of **how quiet** it is in a dream shows that we need to cease being active for a while, perhaps in order to restore our emotional or spiritual balance.

② Experiencing **a need for quiet** in a dream suggests that we need to listen more carefully to either ourselves or others in waking life.

③ Peace and tranquillity give us the opportunity for contemplation.

Quilt

① The quilt or duvet can often represent our need for security, warmth and love. A particular quilt may have a special significance. For instance a **childhood quilt in an adult dream** would suggest the need for reassurance.

② If the colour or pattern (*see Colour and Shapes/Patterns*) of the quilt is particularly striking in a dream we may need to incorporate those meanings into our perception of our need for comfort. Yellow might suggest emotional security while blue might suggest healing.

③ Spiritual comfort and caring can be suggested by a quilt.

Quintessence

① 'Quintessence' literally means 'five beings', but is taken to mean 'supremely perfect'. To dream of this is to link with man's need to create, and to create as perfectly as he can.

② Perfection is one of those things that, the more man knows, the more he realises how far he is from perfect. So to dream of the quintessence is to recognise his own and others' potential.

③ The quintessence of creatures under the Supreme Deity is the Lion among beasts, the Ox among cattle, the Eagle among birds, the Dolphin among fish, Man among all.

Quip

① When we become aware of a joke or quip by someone else in a dream, we are alerted to the fact that we can allow ourselves to be affected by other people's actions and sense of humour.

② If we ourselves are the ones who are communicating through wit or sarcasm, we may often be surprised by our own abilities in everyday life.

③ Often if something spiritual needs to be remembered it can present itself in dreams as a joke or a phrase with a sting in its tail.

Quiver

① Quivering indicates a state of extreme emotion. Such a reaction in a dream would signify that we need to consider the emotion and deal with it in everyday life. For instance, an extreme fear reaction may be the residue of something that has happened to us previously and can only be dealt with in waking life.

② A physiological reaction can be translated into dreams as an action. To be quivering in a dream may simply be the effect of feeling cold.

③ As with shivering, a state of ecstasy can be induced, which is accompanied by quivering. This was initially how the Quakers got their name, as did the Shakers.

Quote/Quotation

① To be giving a quote – as in **a building estimate** – can signify the value that we put on our services or talents. We may have difficulty with the accuracy – or the acceptance – of the quote and therefore, in waking life, will need to reconsider not only our own self-image, but also how we think others see us.

② **To utter or hear a quote** – e.g. Shakespeare – indicates that we should consider the sentiment and power expressed within the quote. It may well have relevance for us in everyday life.

③ A quote in a spiritual sense signifies Truth. It cal also represent wisdom as understood by others.

Rabbit
– see Animals

Rack

① A rack in a dream suggests a need for us to store something or to keep it in order. **A wine rack**, for instance, may mean we have to pay close regard to our social life, while **a shoe rack** suggests a need to decide our best method of progress.

② To find oneself **on the rack**, in the sense of being tortured, would suggest we have either done something we are ashamed of or have put ourselves in the position of being someone else's victim.

③ We may have to put ourselves on the rack in a disciplinary sense. Spiritually we may find discipline a problem and need to produce order out of chaos.

Radar

① Radar in a dream represents our own personal intuitive faculty. It is our way of picking up subtle messages and signals which other people are giving out, often on a subliminal level.

② For many, radar will register in dreams as a sort of 'Big Brother is watching you' feeling. We are monitoring ourselves, perhaps as to whether our behaviour or thoughts are appropriate.

③ Radar can suggest a degree of clairvoyance is available to us.

Radiance

① When something appears as radiant in a dream it is being marked as having some kind of special quality which we may need to explore further.

② Radiance represents something out of the ordinary or supernatural. It also suggests purity of thought, wisdom and the transcendence of the mundane.

③ Radiance is a sign of pure spirituality. It will enlighten and dazzle us and at the same time draw us in.

Radio

① As a method of communication, a radio suggests information which is available to everyone and is widely understood. To dream of **hearing a radio playing** suggests a form of connection with the outside world. A **microphone** appearing in a dream indicates we have the opportunity to amplify our thoughts and ideas and to reach a wider audience. The context of the dream will give a wider explanation of the exact meaning.

② Often in dreams a radio can stand for the voice of authority, or of commonly held ideas and ideals. On a more mundane level, in the waking state, people with mental problems can sometimes think they are being given instructions via the radio.

③ A radio is symbolic of spiritual communication from other realms. We should be aware of all the senses and be open to any eventuality.

Raffle
– also see Games/Gambling

① In a dream, to be **taking part in a raffle** can indicate a need to win or come out on top. This is not necessarily, however, by our own efforts, but more by luck. To be **selling raffle tickets** would indicate our need to help others, whereas to be **setting up a raffle** suggests a group activity in which everyone can gain.

② Although gambling may not be acceptable in our normal code of behaviour, because a raffle is also a charitable act, it may, in dreams, be representative of quietening our conscience at having taken a risk.

③ Spiritually, a raffle can symbolise our need to be charitable. However, we are also recognising the various risks involved, such as vulnerability and reliance. There is an element of having to rely on fate.

Raft

① A raft is a place of safety, often amid turbulence. While it may not be overly secure, it has the ability to support us. This is the kind of dream which occurs when we are dealing with emotional difficulties.

② It can sometimes be meaningful to find out what the raft is made of. It can often appear in dreams as a symbol of transition, so the material can give us some idea of how to act.

③ The raft is an image connected with the spiritual transitions one must make in life. It is less secure than the idea of a boat, but more secure than doing it alone. If we are feeling 'lost' and can see no respite, then we may dream of a raft or other form of temporary structure.

Railway
– also see Train in Transport

① A railway in a dream signifies the way we wish to go in life. We can take a way forward and can make informed choices. A **single track** suggests that there is only one way to go, whereas a **multiple track** suggests many more opportunities.

② Psychologically, a railway suggests the idea of keeping to one goal (which may be a group one) and being single-minded about it. One early symbolism of the railway was the facility of being able to ignore obstacles, to go round, through or over anything which stood in the way.

③ Spiritually, the railway suggests a chosen direction or path which is usually fairly straightforward.

Rain
– also see Weather

① In its simplest meaning, rain stands for tears and emotional release. We may have been depressed with no way to release our feelings in everyday life. Rain in dreams often becomes the first realisation that we can let go.

② Rain in **a woman's dream** can suggest the sexual act. It can also have a more universal meaning, in that it is the realisation of potential on a group level. We should all be able to make use of the fruitfulness that it can bring.

③ Rain by virtue of its 'heavenly' origins symbolises divine blessing and revelation.

Rainbow
– also see Colours

① A rainbow appearing in a dream is the promise of something better to come. The old story of the pot of gold at the end of the rainbow is so firmly entrenched in folklore that this meaning often comes across in dreams.

② The raising of consciousness and appreciation of something as ethereal as a rainbow suggests the need for a heightened sense of awareness. More esoterically, a rainbow is said to represent the seven steps of awareness necessary for true spirituality.

③ A rainbow symbolises the spiritual glory that is available to us through understanding and learning. We may make a transition from the mundane to the spiritual world.

Ram
– see Animals

Ramp

① A ramp in dreams can have a dual meaning. It can suggest a smooth transition, often between two levels or areas, or it can mean the extra effort needed to make oneself understood. Ramping something up is improving its performance and in dreams a ramp gives tangibility to this idea.

② It will depend on how the ramp is being used as to the exact interpretation. Walking down or up a ramp will suggest the idea of using our own momentum to achieve a goal, whereas using some form of assistance will imply that help is needed to achieve a successful change. Such a dream might occur as we become accustomed to a growing disability or difficulty.

③ Returning to the idea of a smooth transition, a ramp can signify an easily accessed spiritual change in consciousness.

Rat
– see Animals

Raven
– see Birds

Razor
– also see Shave

① It will depend on the type of razor which interpretation is given. A **cut-throat razor** would have the same symbolism as a knife – that is, cutting through the unnecessary. A **safety razor** suggests a less risky method is needed to enable us to reveal the truth about ourselves. An **electric razor** suggests that we need to pay attention to the image we put across in everyday life.

② Psychologically, a razor is more of a tool than an aggressive implement. Thus, to be **using a razor on someone else** is to be carrying out a caring act unless our actions are deliberately violent. We may in this case be aware that part of our personality needs changing or sharpening up.

③ Dreaming of a razor may allow us to consider our spiritual image and decide how to make changes.

Reaching out

① Reaching out in a dream signifies our desire for something we do not have. This may be either emotional or material. We may be trying to manipulate circumstances in such a way that others become aware of our needs.

② We are attempting to grasp a concept, an idea or an opportunity, which appears to be beyond our reach or understanding. We may also be trying to control others by our own emotional neediness. This is particularly relevant when we become conscious of rejection or distaste in others.

③ There is a stage in development when there is a yearning for spirit or spirituality (*see Yearn*). It does allow us to sort out what we really need.

Reading
– also see Book, Library and Novel

① **Reading a book** in a dream suggests that we are seeking information. **Reading a letter** signifies receiving news. **Reading a list** (e.g. a shopping list) indicates a need to give some order to our lives. **Reading a Bible** or other holy book is attempting to understand a belief system or way of being.

② Until recently, the only way to record events was to write them down. Reading is an activity which assists us in recalling things from memory – our own, or joint, memories. To be aware that we are **reading a novel** is to begin to understand our own need for fantasy. A **psychic reading** often works with many basic dream images. To dream of having such a reading suggests a need to understand ourselves on a deeper level.

③ Reading, or being in a library, appears in dreams as a form of spiritual realisation.

Reaping

① In former times, the whole community took part in the reaping (gathering) of the harvest. This ensured that everybody gained in some way from this activity. Thus, to dream of reaping suggests a way of gaining from our activities.

② The saying 'as ye sow, so shall ye reap' can be interpreted as: if we do good deeds, then that good will be returned. When we dream of **reaping a reward** for something we have done, we approve of our own activities. More negatively, a harmful act will return to haunt us.

③ Perhaps the most recognisable image of reaping is the Grim Reaper – Death – who always pictured as carrying a scythe. The scythe is the association with reaping, or bringing in the harvest of our experience.

Recession
– see Unemployment and Work

Recluse
– see Hermit

Recycling
– see Garbage/Rubbish/Litter

Red
– see Colours

Reflection
– also see Mirror

① A reflection seen in a dream has a great deal to do with the way we see ourselves at that particular moment. Our self-image is important to us, as is the way other people see us. If the reflection is **in a mirror**, then our image will be perhaps more 'solid', whereas one seen **in water** will be more transient. The story of Narcissus and the way he fell in love with himself (or rather his own image) is a warning to all of us against self-worship.

② Often, to see a reflection in a dream is to try to be understanding the inner self and the way that we cope with the outside world. Our grasp of that outer reality is tempered by the inner self. If in a dream **the two images do not correspond**, we will need to make some kind of adjustment in order to live comfortably within the everyday world.

③ The Spiritual truth that is available to us is often shown to us as though in a reflection.

Refrigerator
– also see Larder

① The refrigerator is a symbol of preservation. In dreams this becomes self preservation and suggests we may be turning cold emotionally or sexually. To dream of **rotten food in a refrigerator** suggests we feel we may not be being sustained properly by those around us.

② To dream of **refrigerating leftover food** indicates we are storing up resentment. This, in turn, will 'cool down' our own responses to love and affection.

③ The very ordinary refrigerator stands as a symbol when we learn to treat things with dispassion and preserve our own integrity.

Refugee
– see Asylum/Asylum Seeker

Reindeer
– see Deer in Animals

Reins
– also see Bridle, Halter and Harness

① In dreams, reins, as a form of restraint, indicate the need to control the power and energy that we have.

② Psychologically, to be reined suggests some form of inhibition – either our own or other people's. To see **reins breaking** signifies freeing ourselves from constraint – that which was placed on us while we grew up.

③ Reins, as a symbol from the time when horses were the preferred means of transport, indicate intelligent control and will.

Relatives
– see Family

Religious Iconology

① Dreams have a way of introducing – or rather reintroducing – us to truths which we have long known to be. If spirituality is taken to be an inner truth, and religion as that which links us back to source, then it must be the case that religious imagery partly assists in that function of recognition. Using images that cannot be interpreted successfully in any other way reinforces the idea of spirituality being something separate in us. Because the images are so specific they may be really quite startling.

② When we, through deliberate or spontaneous neglect, deny ourselves access to the store of religious imagery in waking life, dreams will often react to this lack and try to compensate by jolting us back into an awareness of our inner spirit. In today's society it is very easy to fasten on the hypocritical aspects of religion and to accept that hypocrisy. It is also easy to make the assumption that the outward forms of religion often deny the existence of a true inner reality. This rejection can be valid, since it is not until the individual accepts responsibility for his own existence that true spirituality emerges.

If spirituality – the inner truth that we all hold – is neglected, it will not go away: it will simply reappear in its negative and terrifying form. In waking life the closest image we have to that is the Devil *(see Devil/Demon)*, or the more vengeful Indian gods. Our own personalised demons can indeed be more frightening than those.

③ If we are prepared to accept that each truth will have its own personal slant, and that we must get back to the basic truth, all dreams can be interpreted from a spiritual point of view. This is especially true of religious imagery. Most interpretations have had to be stated in general terms and are given here only as guidelines. When you can throw away the book and say that the interpretations are not valid, then you will have taken on true personal responsibility.

Angels (also see individual entry) In spiritual terms the angel symbolises pure being and freedom from earthly matters. It is vital that we as dreamers are able to differentiate between the personalised aspect of the Higher Self *(see Self)*, and the angelic form, since they are similar but different. Angels tend to be androgynous, and are generally not recognised either as male or female. Most religions, particularly the Abrahamic ones, have their own hierarchies of angels, each angel and each hierarchy having their own tasks. Perhaps the simplest to remember is this: 1. Angels – the realm closest to the physical; 2. Cherubim; 3. Seraphim. As more people become interested in, and seek knowledge about, spirituality there are those who have become more aware of the angel form, particularly in dreams. *Dark angels* are reputed to be those angelic beings who have not yet totally rejected the ego or earthly passions. When this image appears in a dream we are being alerted to a spiritual transgression, which often has already happened. *Warning angels* usually symbolise what should not be done.

Archangels These are a higher order of angels and traditionally are considered to be closest to God, particularly in the Judeo Christian systems of belief. The four best known are: Michael 'Who is like God', Raphael 'He who heals', Gabriel 'Strength of God', and Uriel 'God's light'. They seldom appear spontaneously in dreams but may be called upon to help us in our understanding.

Blessings These need a passionate concentration on bringing, for instance, peace of mind or healing to the recipient, and depending on your system of belief might be counted either as prayers or spells. They may be thought of in terms of a positive energy from beyond us being channelled towards a specific purpose. In dreams they usually signify a prayer of thankfulness. Saying grace before a meal would be one such act.

Buddha (also see individual entry) This figure appearing in dreams highlights the necessity to be aware of the Qualities of Being which Buddha taught. It links us to the power of renunciation and of suffering, but in the sense that experience of suffering is valid.

Ceremony/Ritual (also see individual entries) Ceremony and ritual are all part of the heightening of awareness which occurs on the path to spirituality. In dream ceremonies the imagery is extremely vivid; because they touch in on our own instinctive sense of being they can be very specific. While often based on known rituals they will have a personal touch.

Christ figure appearing in dreams epitomises the recognition of the ability to reconcile the physical and the spiritual, God and Man. He personifies Perfect Man, a state to which we all aspire. Appearing *on the cross* he signifies redemption through suffering. We do not need to be crucified physically to suffer. The *ideal Christ* is that part of ourselves which is prepared to take on our portion of the sufferings in the world by working within the world. The *anarchic Christ* is the part of us whose love and lust for life permit us to break through all known barriers. The *Cosmic Christ* is the part that is prepared to take on Cosmic Responsibility – that is, to be connected with the Universal Truth. While these aspects have been spoken of in Christian terms, obviously they are also present in all religious figures.

Church/Chapel/Synagogue/Temple (also see Church in Buildings and Church/Holy Buildings) We all are aware of our need for sanctuary from the batterings of the everyday world. Within the church or other sacred space we are free to form a relationship with our own personal God. In dreams we may also have the realisation that our body is our temple.

Cross Any cross stands for the realisation (in the sense of making real) of spirit into matter. Moving through the symbol of the sword to the *equal-armed cross*, from there to the cross of suffering and crucifixion, and finally to the *Tau* of perfection, the soul learns through experience to overcome the obstacles to spiritual progression. The *four arms pointing in opposite directions* signify conflict, anguish and distress, but ultimately going through these to reach perfection. The *hung cross with the figure of Christ* represents the sacrifice of self for others. The intersection signifies the reconciliation of opposites. The *three upper arms* are said to stand for God the Father, Son and Holy Ghost, but more properly they indicate any Divine Trinity.

Crucifixion (also see individual entry) This image in a dream links with the human being's need to sacrifice himself through passion and through pain. Any such act of sacrifice in any religion has the same connotation, such as the death of Buddha, who chose to die after eating a meal offered to him in good faith.

Devil/Demon (also see individual entry) In dreams the Devil represents temptation. This often arises from the repressed sexual drives which demand attention. It may also signify the Shadow *(see Shadow).*

Eye of God/Eye of Providence/Third Eye This is the all-seeing eye and is a representation which is found in most religions. It is the Third Eye of Buddha and symbolises unity and balance. It is also in dreams the developed clairvoyant perceptiveness that comes with spiritual development.

Father Christmas or other such cultural figure Appearing in dreams, such a figure represents munificence and kindliness. They represent the idea of good times and largesse, gifts of spirit which allow us to share good fortune.

Ghost (also see individual entry) Independent forces within, which are separate from the individual's will. It will largely depend on our own belief system as to whether we accept the appearance of ghosts as psychological or spiritual apparitions.

Gods/Goddesses (also see individual entries) We are each given the opportunity to make real our fullest potential. In doing so, iconic figures which represent the best and worst qualities will present themselves in dreams, frequently as gods and goddesses.

Halo The halo or nimbus in dreams as in religious pictures is a representation of a person's innate spirituality. In waking life, those with clairvoyance are able to perceive this. In dreams, when conscious restriction is removed, the halo can become observable.

Holy Books/Religious Texts (also see Bible/Religious Texts in B) A resource and a repository for knowledge is available to us. As our awareness of other systems of belief expands we may dream of reading and understanding such books as, for instance, the Koran or the Torah.

Heaven (also see individual entry) is a state of being where the energy is of such a high frequency that there is no suffering. In dreams the concept of heaven appears when the individual is transmuting his awareness into dimensions other than the purely physical or mundane. Also known as Nirvana and Samadhi, it is reputedly a place where bliss exists.

Hell (also see Heaven/Hell in H) is a state of being where nothing is ever as it seems and could be thought of as continually existing in a state of negative illusion. Normally pictured as a place of Fire, it is a state of Spiritual Agony where our worst dreams are fulfilled. As a place of punishment it is found in most systems of belief and known by various names – Gehenna or Purgatory, Jahannam or Naraka. In dreams it will tend to appear as we begin to appreciate that we can live life mindfully.

Holy Communion The belief that Christ's body was transmuted into heavenly food – symbolised by the Last Supper – appears in dreams as the intake of spiritual food. Holy Communion represents a sacred sharing.

Icon (also see individual entry) An icon is a representation of a religious figure or concept. It can, through usage, become revered as a holy object in its own right.

Incense (also see individual entry) Incense is an offering to the gods and a physical form of prayer through perfume and smoke.

Initiation takes place when some barrier is transcended in order to enable us to have access to other ways of being. In dreams it will often be accompanied by ceremony.

Mary, the Virgin Mother/Mother of God The symbolism of Mary, both as the maiden and as the mother, is a potent one. She epitomises all that is woman, and all that is holy.

Moses or other revered figure often appears in dreams as the one who will lead us out of difficulty. He has obvious connections to the Wise Old Man *(see Wise Old Man)*.

Priest/Prophet Such a figure appearing in dreams may be a version of the Wise Old Man but may also represent our ability to take control of our own destiny.

Religious Service This is an act of worship which is used to bring people together. It is recognised in dreams, perhaps as an act of integration of the whole self, and as an illustration that the whole is greater than the parts.

Religious Festivals and Celebrations (Also see Festivals) Dreaming of religious festivals such as Christmas, Diwali, Hannukah and Imbolc all signify the beginning of a new period of existence or a rededication of the Self *(see Self)*. Such festivals are usually associated with miracles or the provision of light, signifying a new-found spirituality. Other festivals, while today they have become secularised to a large extent, symbolise the gifts of the Creator to Mankind.

Sacred Music Whatever our system of belief, music dedicated to the perception of our God or Gods, is vibrations which lift the spirit and enhance our perception of Divinity. In dreams, because our senses are heightened, the effect of those vibrations is magnified.

Rent
– also see Tenant

① **Paying rent** in dreams is to undertake a personal responsibility. We are prepared to look after ourselves and to take responsibility for who we are. **Receiving rent** suggests that we have entered into a transaction which will benefit us.

② There comes a time when, if we wish to maximise our potential, we must find a space of our own. The concept of paying rent allows us to do this. In dreams this can be seen as an independent act. As times become more difficult, people are less able to afford to buy, and dreams of having to pay rent are often more to do with acquiring a safe space than the actual monetary value involved. **Buy to let** accommodation for the owner is more to do with monetary considerations and gain, whereas for the tenant it again will be about developing a safe space.

③ Often in spiritual terms we must relearn how to handle both money and value. The image of paying rent, of there being a cost, gives this concept a focus. Paying rent in dreams can also symbolise giving good value in our interrelationships with other people – we have a right to be there.

Reptiles
– also see Animals

① Reptiles in dreams link with our basic and instinctive reactions and responses. When there is a basic urge – such as a need for food, sex, etc. – we sometimes cannot face it full on, but will symbolise it as a reptile.

② When there is a need to understand why we do things, we first need to control our basic drives. Many reptilian dreams are about control or management. Control of a **crocodile** would suggest some fear of an aggressive nature. Feeding a **lizard** or stroking a **snake** can be very simply interpreted.

③ With understanding of the basic urges (represented in dreams by reptiles) and the way to manage them, we can create a firm foundation. From there we can progress spiritually.

Rescue

① **Being rescued** in dreams is a powerful image, since it leaves us indebted to our rescuer. **Rescuing someone else** often suggests that we wish to have a relationship with that person. **The knight rescuing the maiden** signifies the idea of the untouched feminine being rescued from her own passion.

② When we have put others in danger in dreams, we are required to rescue them. We are then able to show a degree of nobility and courage which allows us to have power over ourselves.

③ Spiritual rescue is generally accepted as help for 'lost souls', to enable them to achieve sanctuary.

Resign
– also see Work

① In dreams to resign is to give up. To dream of **resigning from work** means we are aware of major changes in our lives. We perhaps need to look at our lives and accustom ourselves to the idea that there are areas that we do not need to be in. **To be resigned to something** suggests that we have accepted the status quo in our lives.

② Resignation is a state of mind brought about through having to face difficulties in life. It is as though we come to a point where we are not capable of making any further effort or decision. Indeed, it may be better not to, but simply to resign ourselves to whatever may happen. In dreams this resignation is recognisable as not wanting to go on.

③ Spiritual resignation is the giving in to inevitability. We no longer have any need or wish to fight further.

Restaurant
– also see Eat/Eating and Food

① Dreaming of a restaurant or cafe suggests a need for company. We may be fearful of being alone, but equally be afraid of allowing someone to delve too far into our private space. This public space allows for contact but, at the same time, we can control our own level of intimacy.

② Any place connected with food is to do with our need for emotional sustenance. There is feedback to be received from eating in a public place. Our social needs our met. We may be conscious of the need for a 'relationship' with the place we are eating at, as much as with the person with whom we are eating.

③ Spiritually a restaurant symbolises our need to belong to a group of people who all have the same habits and perhaps a diversity of beliefs.

Ribbon
– See Bridle, Halter and Harness

Ring
– also see Wedding Ring

① A ring appearing in a dream usually signifies a relationship of some sort. A **wedding ring** suggests a union and a promise. **A ring belonging to the family** would represent old traditions and values, whereas **an engagement ring** suggests a more tentative promise of devotion. **An eternity ring** would be a long-term promise. **A signet ring** would indicate setting the seal on something. **A bull ring** suggests an element of cruelty.

② We all need some kind of continuity in our lives, something which gives a sense of long-term comfort. A ring holds this symbolism because it is never-ending and is self-perpetuating.

③ Like the circle, the ring signifies eternity and divinity.

Ritual
– also see Ceremony and Religious Iconology

① In dreams, repeated actions reinforce the intrinsic meaning of the action and allow us to consciously retain what changes we must make in waking life.

② Such rituals as getting up in the morning, because they are habits, simply have the purpose of getting us focused. **Religious** rituals have taken on a life of their own and help concentrate the power of the many. **Magical** rituals have become 'power centres' in their own right.

③ Spiritually we are able to focus our energies in such a way that we can work for the Greater Good.

River
– see Rivers/Streams in Water

Road
– see Journey

Robe

① Dreaming of a robe, such as a **bath robe** can have two meanings. One is that of covering up vulnerability and the other is of being relaxed and at ease. The dream will indicate the correct significance. To be **dressing someone else in a robe** is to protect them.

② A robe can suggest our attitude to sex and relationships. If it is **clean** we have a good self-image if **dirty**, the opposite. A dirty robe could also suggest unhappiness or depression.

③ In spiritual terms the **white robe** is innocence and the **seamless robe** represents holiness.

Rock
– also see Barrier/Barricade

① To dream of rock suggests stability in the real world. If we are on **firm ground** we can survive. We may also be aware that we must be firm and stand 'rock-like' and not be dissuaded from our purpose. **Seaside rock** can remind us of happier, more carefree times.

② On an intellectual level, all the images that one thinks of in relationship to rocks prevail. There is reliability, coldness, rigidity and so on. We need to recognise these qualities in order to handle ourselves properly. We can find ourselves between a 'rock and a hard place' – in a difficult situation in dreams.

③ Spiritually we will need, at some point, to go through a barrier from difficulty to sanctuary. This often presents itself as a rock barrier. Dual rocks through which we must pass suggest the same image as the passage between two pillars, that is, passing from one state of being to the next.

Rocket

① The rocket in basic terms has a connection with male sexuality. What is perhaps more important is the energy that is available to us in dreams. To be **given a rocket** suggests recognising that we are not functioning the way we should. To **take off like a rocket** means moving very fast in terms of some project we have.

② Nowadays any symbol of power connects with our ability to do, or be, better than before. The rocket in this sense will have much of the same symbolism as the aeroplane *(See Aeroplane)*, except the destinations will be further away. The explosive power and energy available is something to be carefully looked at, since we need this type of power in order to make radical changes in our lives.

③ Because of the spiritual symbolism of reaching heights to which none have been before, the rocket represents spiritual searching and adventure.

Rocking

① Rocking in dreams can be a comforting activity, a little like a child who will rock himself to sleep. It can also suggest infantile behaviour from the point of view that it puts us in touch with the natural rhythms of life.

② Particularly when we want to be soothed we like to be rocked. The gentle movement can allow us to be in touch with our own centre. So to be **rocking someone** is to be soothing them. Conversely, to be **being rocked** is to be soothed.

③ Rocking is a symbol of transition. To move to and fro suggests both hesitation and desire. Rocking is also a fertility symbol.

Rod
– see Staff

Roof

① To concentrate on, or be aware of, the roof of a building in a dream is to acknowledge the shelter and protection it affords. If **the roof leaks** then we are open to emotional attacks. If we are **on the roof** it shows we are not being protected.

② A roof is a basic requirement in man's need for comfort. Psychologically, it is important to be protected against the elements. Equally, he needs to know that he is capable of 'reaching for the sky'.

③ The sheltering aspect of the feminine as the guardian of the hearth is sometimes represented as a roof.

Rooms
– see Buildings and House

Root
– see Tree

Rope
– also see Hanging and Noose

① A rope can suggest strength and power, though the power can turn against us. A **rope and pulley** suggests using the forces of weight to help us. If the rope is made of an unusual substance, **such as hair or material**, there is a special bond or necessity which requires the qualities that that substance has.

② If we are **tied to the rope**, something is holding us back from expressing ourselves. **Being tied by a rope to something else** means we need to look at the relationship between us and what we are tied to. We should look at the limitations of that relationship.

③ A rope can offer security and freedom. As **a noose** it suggests despair.

Rosary
– see Necklace and Beads

Rose/Rosette

① The rose in dreams has a great deal of symbolism. It represents love and admiration; in a bouquet the number of roses and the colour will be significant *(see Numbers and Colour)*. It can also suggest fertility and virginity.

② As a psychological symbol the rose represents perfection. It contains within it the mystery of life and its grace and happiness. It also suggests the cycle of life, through the cycle of its own growth and decay.

③ Spiritually the rose has dual meanings. It suggests perfection and passion, life and death, Time and Eternity. It also represents the heart, the centre of life.

Round Table

① A round table in a dream is a symbol of wholeness. Partly because of the tales of King Arthur, there are various myths associated with a round table, but essentially it indicates that everyone is equal.

② The round table is a representation of the heavens, since the twelve knights are the signs of the Zodiac *(see Zodiac)*. In dreams we are continually trying to create perfection and this is one such dream.

③ Spiritually the table suggests a centre, but one from which all things can begin.

Rubbish
– see Garbage/Rubbish

Rucksack
– see Knapsack/Rucksack

Ruins

① When **something is in ruins** we have to discover if it is through neglect or vandalism. If the former, the suggestion is that we need to pull things together. If it is the latter, we need to look at whether we are making ourselves in some way vulnerable.

② If we have **deliberately ruined something** we need to clarify a self-destructive element in us. Sometimes by looking at the symbolism of what has ruined an object or an occasion will give us insight into our own processes.

③ Occasionally it is vital that there is an element of destructiveness in us in order that we can rebuild part of our lives on a better basis.

Running

– also see Exercise

① To be running in a dream suggests speed and flow. To be **running forwards** suggests confidence and ability. To be **running away** signifies fear and an inability to do something.

② Obviously in dreams of running, time and place are significant. Where we are going will perhaps indicate why speed is needed, although if we are being pursued this will also give some kind of reason. To be **running something** – as in **managing it** – is to be taking responsibility.

③ Running in dreams suggests the potential for anxiety or distress. Spiritually we may be trying to do something too quickly.

Rush

① To be in a rush suggests that we are having to contend with outside pressures. **To be rushing** suggests that we ourselves are putting the pressure on. The pressure would be on our time, and it is interesting that rushes or reeds actually do symbolise time.

② We need to learn how to manage time successfully, and to be rushing suggests that we have not done so.

③ In esoteric terms, time and space are interchangeable. In dreams therefore one can stand for the other. To be in a rush is to be conscious of the passage of time or of a change in our spatial awareness.

Rust

① Rust represents neglect and negligence. We have not looked after the quality of our lives properly and should look to address this oversight.

② To dream of **cleaning up rust** suggests that we recognise our own negligence. Dreaming of rust **appearing as we look at an object** signifies that a project has reached the end of its useful life.

③ Spiritually, we may have to remove evidence of contamination before we can progress. Rust may signify old outdated attitudes.

Sack

① At its simplest, to dream of a sack can link with word-play such as 'getting the sack'. It brings a period of our lives to an end, possibly in a rather negative way. Perhaps in an effort to move on, we have created circumstances within our lives which make us feel bad about ourselves for a time.

② The sack has the same significance as the bag, or any such receptacle. **In a woman's dream** it can therefore perhaps mean pregnancy, while interestingly enough **in a man's dream** it is more likely to mean some kind of womb experience or need for security. The womb is often symbolised in dreams as a bag or sack. Very often the sack as a utilitarian object has the significance of containing something for us – of giving us an opportunity to consider our belongings. We can empty the sack, as it were, and decide what is important to us and what we need to take forward.

③ In its starkest meaning the sack can indicate death. It can literally mean the death of a person, or it can indicate the liberation of part of our personality. We need to release a difficulty in order to continue within our own framework of life.

Sacrifices

① As a rule, sacrifice has two meanings. Firstly, it is to give something up and secondly to make something sacred or holy. So when those two things are possible within a dream scenario we are is prepared to give up our ego or individuality for the sake of something greater or more important than himself. Often a sacrifice is made because of passionately held beliefs, often religious in origin.

② There is usually some expectation of a forthcoming just reward (often spiritual), for having made sacrifices. There may be an element of deferred gratification in that we do not expect an immediate reward, except that of feeling good or knowing one has done the right thing. There is always an element also of giving up egotistic behaviour which is no longer appropriate, and going with the flow of life. **Sacrificing an animal** suggests that we are conscious of the fact that our lower, more basic instincts can be given up in favour of spiritual power. We have to be prepared to recognise our own human state, but to give up indulgence. There may be a sacrificial altar, or it may just be a question of killing and cooking an animal ritualistically. **If the animal is willing to be sacrificed**, then we are ready to transmute instinct into spiritual energy. If the animal is a hare or a rabbit, the symbolism is that of rebirth.

③ Sacrifice is an important aspect of spiritual growth and signifies the renunciation of the lesser for the rewards of the greater.

Saddle

① A saddle appearing in a dream will often indicate a need to exercise control over someone. Obviously this can suggest sexual control, particularly **in a woman's dream**. In a **man's dream** it is more likely to signify his need to control his own life in some way – perhaps the direction in which he is going or the circumstances of his own life. It will be more the sense of his own masculinity and drive which is highlighted.

② To some extent it will depend on what we are doing with the saddle, and also what kind of saddle it is. A **motorcycle saddle** – in that it is an integral part of the machine – will suggest a more rigid type of control than **a horse's saddle**, which is flexible and removable. If the **saddle is slipping** we are about to lose authority in a situation in our lives. If a **saddle does not fit in some way** – remembering that it is also designed for the comfort of the rider – we may be being made uncomfortable by external circumstances rather than by our own volition.

③ We have an opportunity to take control of our own lives from a spiritual perspective and should use that opportunity wisely.

Sailing
– also see Boat/Ship in Transport and Wind/Winding

① When we dream of sailing, we are highlighting how we feel we are handling our lives. We can either work with the currents or against them. If we are sailing **in a yacht** there is more of a sense of immediacy than if we were sailing **in a liner**. The first is more to do with one-to-one relationships, while the second suggests more of a group effort. **Sails** suggest the idea of making use of available power. Often the type of sail will be relevant. **Old fashioned sails** would suggest out-of-date methods, whereas **racing sails** might suggest the use of modern technology. The colour of the sails may also be important *(see Colour)*.

② To be tacking – **sailing against the wind** – suggests that we have created difficulties possibly by setting ourselves against public opinion. If we are **sailing with the wind** it means we are using opportunities to the best of our abilities. Because a boat or ship is usually thought of as feminine, the **sails** in dreams can represent pregnancy and fertility. By association, they can also signify how a woman will use her intellect.

③ Sailing suggests a sense of spiritual freedom and the ability to use our intellect. Sails represent the Spirit – as in a force that moves us.

Sailor

① Most people have a rather antiquated idea of the sailor. It is this image that usually appears in dreams. He represents freedom, both of movement and of spirit, and therefore is a representation of the Tramp *(see Archetypes)*. He suggests someone who is totally in control of his own destiny. A **modern-day sailor** would have the added benefit of being in control of his own environment.

② If a sailor does appear in a dream, particularly **in a woman's**, he is usually a somewhat romanticised figure and can represent the Hero *(see Archetypes)*. **In a man's dream** he represents the part of himself which seeks freedom, but that needs to be given permission or authority to take that freedom.

③ Spiritually, the sailor can signify communication. The aspect of freedom links with a quality of Mercury who, having been given a task, then forgets what it is.

Salary
– see Wages/Salary

Salmon

① The salmon signifies abundance and masculinity and is phallic. In its fight to mate by swimming upstream it can also symbolise the sperm. Often a salmon can appear **in a woman's dream** as a symbol of her sometimes subconscious wish for pregnancy.

② In common with most fish when they appear in dreams, the salmon signifies our basic urges – most often the need for survival. By being able to put in effort we reap the rewards of our actions.

③ In mythology the salmon signifies knowledge of other worlds (the lands beneath the sea) and of other-worldly things. This refers principally to the subconscious.

Salt

① In dreams, salt highlights the subtle qualities we bring to our lives, those things we do to enhance our lifestyle. It has been suggested that if the water was removed from the human body there would be enough minerals and salt left to cover a fifty pence piece. We run most of our lives through our emotions but the more subtle aspects are just as important.

② As a symbol of permanence and incorruptibility salt is important in dreams. As in the old days salt was paid as salary, so nowadays to be given salt is to be given one's correct worth. There are many customs associated with salt. It is **thrown over the shoulder**, supposedly in the face of the Devil. In Scotland, along with coal and bread, it is the first thing to pass over the threshold to greet the New Year.

③ As a distillation of everything we know, salt represents Spiritual Wisdom. It can also represent the emotional 'flavour' of our Spiritual beliefs.

Sanctuary
– also see Religious Iconology

① A sanctuary is a place of safety and therefore in mundane terms somewhere where we can relax. In dreams we may develop such a space which allows us to let the outside world go and be ourselves. One way of giving ourselves sanctuary is to develop a sacred space within our own environment.

② From an emotional perspective, by developing an inner sanctuary we are able to cope with most of life's idiosyncrasies. That sanctuary will present itself in dreams, perhaps as a religious building, a much loved remembered space or a strong sense of freedom.

③ A sense of spiritual sanctuary is an important aspect of growth. Initially that sense will be of an external space, only later being recognised as an inner tranquillity. Sanctuary is a space made sacred by the power with which it is invested.

Sand

① Sand in a dream suggests instability and lack of security. When **sand and sea are seen together** we are demonstrating a lack of emotional security. When the **sands are shifting** we are probably unable to decide what we require in life. If we are conscious of the **sand in an hourglass** we are conscious of time running out.

② Sand can represent impermanence. **Building sand castles** is something of a fantasy occupation since they will be washed away by the tide. To dream of doing this would indicate that the structure we are trying to give to our lives does not have permanence and may be an illusion.

③ Spiritually, sand represents the impermanence of the physical life and can suggest having to approach death or change in some way.

Sap

① The old adage that the sap rises in Spring is fully accepted by most people. In dream terms this means that we are maybe ready to undertake new work or perhaps a new relationship. We are aware of our own vitality and strength and prepared to take on new challenges.

② Sap is a derogatory term for a wimp or someone who had no moral backbone. In a negative sense we may become aware in dreams of inappropriate behaviour or ideas. These have the effect of sapping our inner vitality.

③ The life-force we use can often be perceived as the sap in plants.

Sarcophagus

① A sarcophagus is similar to a tomb, but is much more of a memorial, marking how important the occupant is or was. To dream of such an edifice is to recognise the importance of death and the rites of passage into the Everlasting associated with it.

② When we come to an important change in our lives we may wish to mark the passage or transition in some way. We have a need to have other people recognise or appreciate our efforts. A sarcophagus would indicate that there is a good deal of ego still to be dealt with within us.

③ Spiritually, death indicates both a change of state and a change of status and a sarcophagus is a symbol of such change.

Satan
– see Devil/Demon

Satellite

① Before satellites were invented, the stars were used as fixed points in communication. Nowadays a satellite would suggest efficient, effective contact. We are more globally aware of the effect we can have both on our environment and on other people around us. **Satellite television and receivers** mean that communication today is faster and more accurately targeted than in previous times and as a result we have become more globally aware. It is this meaning which is relevant if such images appear in dreams.

② A satellite can appear in a dream to indicate the dependency that one person can have upon another. Often in relationships one partner is more important than the other and either could therefore recognise the symbol of the satellite.

③ A satellite can represent spiritual communication from a discarnate source.

Satyr

① When man was less civilised than he is now, his animal nature was closer to the surface. It was possible for him to see and identify patterns of energy or spirits both in himself and in nature which then took on human or semi-human form. The satyr is one such form, and is a male spirit connected with nature at its rawest. While most of the time in the waking state we suppress such figures, in dreams – where there is no conscious control – they will sometimes appear.

② From a psychological standpoint the satyr is that part of nature which is out of control, and beyond restraint. It owes allegiance to no-one and is completely anarchic. If perceived as destructive then it will be so. If accepted as helpful then it will be equally obliging.

③ The satyr is a spirit of nature and of natural power. He is a woodland spirit similar to the god Pan and signifies ecstacy in the power of energy of Life.

Savings
– also see Bank/Banker, Money, Poverty and Wealth

① In dreams we often develop images which have dual meanings. Our savings may represent resources, either material or emotional, which we have hidden away until such times as they are needed. They can also represent our sense of security and independence. To dream of **savings we did not know we had** would suggest that we are able to summon up extra energy or time, perhaps by using material or information from the past. To dream of **making savings in the present** suggests we may need to give consideration to the wherewithal we have in the here and now in order to succeed in the future. If we are **aware of our goal in making savings** we should perhaps make long-term plans.

② When we dream of savings we are aware of the need for conservation. This may be on a personal level or in a more global sense. If there is a feeling of self-denial in our making savings we may not have managed our resources properly in the past and are having to suffer for it now. If **someone else gives us their savings** we are able to use their knowledge and expertise. Conversely, if we **give our savings away** we no longer have need of whatever those savings mean to us.

③ In the spiritual sense, savings suggests those talents and abilities which we have or have developed, but have not yet used, particularly those for the Greater Good.

Saw
– see Tools

Scaffold/Scaffolding

① A scaffold or scaffolding in a dream will usually indicate that there is some kind of temporary structure in our lives. **A hangman's scaffold** will suggest that a part of our lives must come to an end. We may, for instance, be aware that we have offended against some of society's laws and beliefs, and must be punished. We also may need to look at our propensity to be a victim. If **scaffolding** appears in dreams we should decide whether it is there to help us build something new or whether we must repair the old. We need a temporary structure to help us reach the height we wish in either case. If we are **building new**, that structure will support us while we build, whereas if we are **repairing the old** it will support the previous structure while we make the necessary changes.

② Sometimes in dreams a scaffold will indicate an enforced ending. This can be death, but is more likely to suggest the death of part of our personality. Rather than being able to achieve a successful integration, we actually actively have to stop the behaviour or activity which is causing a problem. We have to take the consequences of behaving in that way.

③ A scaffold suggests an enforced code of spiritual behaviour and the need for self-control. Scaffolding also reprsents spiritual support, a strengthening of the structure of our belief system.

Scales

① Scales in a dream suggest the necessity for balance and self-control. Without that balance we cannot make a sensible decision as to potential courses of action. We must 'weigh up' all the possibilities. Scales will also suggest standards – for instance, standards of behaviour – to which we are expected to adhere. We may be weighed and found wanting. If the **scales are unbalanced** in a dream we need to search our conscience and discover where we are not functioning properly.

② The type of scale we see in our dream will us give a more explicit interpretation. For example, **bathroom scales** would suggest a more personal assessment than a public machine, whereas a **weigh bridge** might suggest that we need to take our whole lives into consideration. If they were **doctor's scales** we may be alerting ourselves to a potential health problem.

③ The Scales of Justice represent balance and harmony, but also good judgement. By association, they also represent the astrological sign of Libra and sometimes the weighing of Life in the balance.

Scalp
– see Head in Body

Scapegoat

① The word scapegoat actually comes from the sacrificing of a goat to appease the gods, and in dreams this symbol can be highly relevant. If in our dream **we are the scapegoat** for someone else's action then we are being turned into a victim. Other people may be trying to make us pay for their misdemeanours. If **we are making another person a scapegoat** then this indicates a blame shift, and that we are not taking responsibility for our own actions.

② Often in families and teams one member takes the brunt of all the projections from the rest of the family or group. He (or she) is continually belittled or laughed at, and can be blamed for all sorts of things which are not their fault. They become the scapegoat. In dreams, however, there is recognition that there is an aspect of co-operation and collaboration withiin us. We need to do something to redress the balance, and often the solution can only come from us.

③ The scapegoat by tradition was an animal which took on the sins of the community yet was allowed to escape. Spiritually in dreams therefore the symbolism is of blame being apportioned and dealt with by higher authority, of a sacrifice being made.

Scar

① A scar in a dream suggests that there are old hurts which have not been fully dealt with. These may be mental and emotional as much as physical, and can remain unnoticed until we are reminded of them. Just as in physical injury there can be many kinds of scars, so there can also be in the other areas. We may, for instance, be left with a pattern of behaviour which is irritating to other people, but without the clear connection given by the dream image, we are unable to understand it.

② **It will often be significant which area of the body is scarred in the dream**. The nervous system can develop ways of giving information without us being conscious of it. This may give some indication of the area of life that is affected by the trauma. If **we see someone else who has been scarred** it may be necessary to discover if we are the ones who have hurt others in the past. If this is so, there are various techniques we can use in the waking state to help us release others either from the hurt we – or they – have inflicted. The healing may then be recorded in dreams by the loss of the scar.

③ Spiritually, a scar may suggest that something negative and harmful has occurred, which is an external force rather than internal. We may not have dealt with it as well as we might.

Sceptre

① The sceptre is representative of royal power and sovereignty. When it appears in dreams it is usually indicative of the fact that we have given someone authority over us. We have abdicated responsibility to the point that the inner self has to take over. The sceptre also has the same symbolism as most rods, which is, of course, phallic.

② **If we are holding the sceptre** we have the ability to transmit the life force. If **someone else is using the sceptre** and is bestowing honour or power on us, then we can accept that we have succeeded in our particular project.

③ The sceptre can represent the magic wand and in dreams can indicate our right to use such magic. Spiritually it also signifies the transmission of divine power from above rather than below. Thus it is masculine power.

School
– also see Education and Teacher

① School is an important part of everyone's life. In situations where we are learning new abilities or skills, the image of a school will often come up in dreams. It is also the place where we experience associations which do not belong to the family, and can therefore suggest new ways of learning about relationships. School may also be the place where we learn about competitiveness and how to belong to groups.

② When we are relearning how to deal with our own personalities, **the school or classroom** will often appear in dreams. They will often appear at times when we are attempting to get rid of old, outmoded ideas and concepts. Also, when we are learning different ways of dealing with authority and with feelings of inadequacy, our feelings about school will surface.

③ Spiritually it is often considered that life itself is a school. Life is an arena for learning and experiencing so that we can maximise our best potential. It is believed that this life is a testing-ground for the reality which comes afterwards.

Scissors

① Scissors in dreams suggest the idea of cutting the non-essential out of our lives. This may be feelings we do not think are appropriate, emotions that we cannot handle, or mental trauma which needs to be excised. The type of scissors may also be important. **Kitchen scissors** would, for instance, be more utilitarian than **surgical scissors** which would suggest the necessity to be more precise. Scissors can also suggest a sharp, hurtful tongue or cutting remarks.

② Dreaming of **sharpening scissors** suggests that we need to be more precise in our communication, whereas using **blunt scissors** suggests that we are likely to create a problem through speaking too bluntly. **To dream of a hairdresser using scissors** signifies our fear of losing strength and status.

③ Spiritually scissors can have an ambivalent meaning. They can cut the Thread of Life, but can also represent unity and the coming together of the spiritual and physical.

Screw

① It will depend on what society we belong to as to how we interpret 'screw'. To the criminal element a screw will mean a prison officer or jailer. To a younger element in society it is a slang word for the sexual act. So there could be word play, even if the object seen is a proper screw.

② Screws suggest tasks that are seen to be pointless, except in a wider context. To be **screwing two pieces of wood together** would presuppose that we intend to make something, so our action is a means to an end. Screws are reputed to give a better join than nails; therefore the implication is that we are building something to last. We need to take pride in our activities.

③ Spiritually we will be looking for satisfaction in a job well done. There is also a connection with the spiral *(see Shapes/Patterns)*.

Scroll

① Nowadays, a scroll will represent an acknowledgement of a learning process – i.e.

the scroll presented to graduating students. It will depend on the circumstances what the exact interpretation is. We are endorsing either our own knowledge or information which has been given to us, so that we can enhance our lives.

② A scroll can represent hidden knowledge, and also the passing of time. Thus, under certain circumstances, dreaming of a scroll signifies having to wait until the knowledge we have gained can be used at an appropriate time.

③ A scroll can signify the letter of the law and the respect that it deserves. If we are **given a scroll**, we are deemed responsible enough to use the information we have gained.

Scythe/Sickle

① The **scythe** is a cutting instrument, and therefore has the same significance as a knife *(See Weapons)*. In dreams it usually suggests that we need to cut out non-essential actions or beliefs. We need to be fairly ruthless in order to achieve a desired end. The **sickle** is no longer such an important image to man. Now that we have moved from an agricultural to a more technological society, we are left with the ancient symbol of the sickle representing mortality and death. As so often happens, this is not necessarily a physical death, but the death of part of ourselves.

② The scythe is a very old-fashioned symbol for the passage of time and can represent harvesting *(See Harvest)*. Its appearance in dreams shows we are linking with very deeply held concepts and ideas. We are becoming aware that something must end. It may be that part of us can no longer provide us with what we want.

③ The scythe, like the hour glass, is often held by the figure of Death and represents the ending of physical existence in some way.

Sea
– see Sea/Ocean in Water

Seal
– also see Animals

① Historically, a **wax seal** confirmed authority and power. It was also a symbol of identity. Nowadays in dreams, it is much more likely to signify legality or correct moral action. In dreams, **the possession of a seal** gives us the authority to take responsibility for our own actions.

② When we dream of legal documents, to become aware of the seal can indicate that a conclusion has been reached which is both binding and secret. **To be breaking a seal** indicates that we are possibly breaking a confidence or someone's trust in us. It has also been suggested that **a man breaking a seal in a woman's dream** suggests that she will lose her virginity or purity at some level.

③ Spiritually a seal suggests hidden knowledge. Not all esoteric and occult information is available to everyone. Such information is only entrusted to someone who has the courage to break the seal.

Searching
– also see Lose/Lost

① To be searching in a dream is an attempt to find an answer to a problem. If we are **searching for someone** we may be conscious of our loneliness. If we are **searching for something** we may be aware of an unfulfilled need.

② Searching in a dream for that which we have lost can suggest either that we need information from the past, or that we feel we have lost our identity in some way. Searching also suggests more of a commitment to actually finding than just simply looking.

③ The movement towards spirituality often begins from a feeling of searching for something.

Searchlight
– also see Light

① A searchlight in a dream denotes focused attention and concentration. If the **searchlight is trained on us**, it indicates we need to consider our actions and behaviour.

② A searchlight can suggest insight into matters which concern us. We have turned the searchlight on them in order to ascertain the real truth. A searchlight is used to light the way ahead.

③ A searchlight will allow us to fully comprehend spiritual matters so that we can reject the unnecessary. When matters are held to the light, they become clarified.

Seasons

① When we become conscious of the seasons of the year in dreams, we are also linking with the various periods of our lives (**Spring** signifies childhood, **Summer** – young adulthood, **Autumn** – middle age, **Winter** – old age).

② The need for us to be able to divide time into periods or phases arises initially from the necessity to co-operate with the seasons from a survival point of view. Given deadlines and limitations, the human being is able to survive through striving.

③ The division of the year into Spring, Summer, Autumn and Winter gives occasion for celebrations and festivals and follows a natural pattern of growth and decay. We make use of the Cycle of the Year.

Seed

(1) A seed in dreams stands for our potentiality. We may have an idea which is only just beginning, or a project which needs nurturing. **In a woman's dream** a seed may suggest pregnancy.

(2) Often in dreams a seed will suggest the validity of something we are planning. We need to know the right conditions in which to grow and mature.

(3) A seed carries great potential and latent power. It is this symbolism which is relevant spiritually.

Self

(1) The Self is the archetype or basic template of all the capabilities that we have and holds the secret of the integrated being; it is only gradually revealed. Because its latent possibilities beckon from the future, our first experience of it in dream form may be a figure encouraging us to move forward. Later it can develop into an ideal of perfection with which we can work in our waking lives to create a sustainable future.

(2) Our own experience and the uses we make of our awareness are unique although based on universal knowledge. The Self is an inner guidance which gives access to previously unknown information which must, with practice, be applied to everyday life. When images of this archetype, such as a guru *(see Guru)*, an animal with virtuous qualities, a cross or other geometric shape, begin to appear in dreams, you are ready to face the process of becoming wholly integrated.

(3) Often this aspect presents itself in dreams as a holy figure according to our perceived belief. Thus it may be recognised as Christ, Buddha, Krishna or some similar figure. As you become more efficient at dealing with – and understanding – the information you receive in your dreams, your perception of the image's energy changes and you are more likely to perceive it as light. You no longer have need of a personalised image on which to focus. When negative or destructive images – such as vengeful gods or threatening animals – occur you need to be aware that you are neglecting the power of the Self.

Serpent
– see Serpent/Snake in Animals

Sex

(1) One vital stage of growth in a baby's development is its fascination with its own body and the ability to be physical and sensual. This is as much to do with what feels comfortable and nice – how it feels to be in one's own skin, as it were. It is at this point that he or she learns about touch, whether it is nice to touch or be touched, and even if sensuality is appropriate. When there is difficulty in this

area, while the original trauma may be suppressed, it will often surface in dreams when the time is right for it to be dealt with. Real growth takes place when we are not afraid of the curiosity which allows an innocent exploration of our own bodies. Dreams will often allow us to explore this physicality in a safe way.

② Dreams highlight the whole range of our sexuality. Only if we ignores our own sexual nature and fail to appreciate our own life force do the negative aspects make themselves obvious in dreams. This is a perfectly natural attempt to balance the waking state which we may have over-intellectualised, or over-dramatised. We then need contact with others and often this will become apparent in dreams. Various aspects of sex and sexuality can be interpreted as follows:

Bisexuality Within ourselves we hold both masculine and feminine potentials (*See Archetypes*). One is always more overt than the other and there is often conflict between the inner and the outer expression. This can sometimes show itself in dreams as bisexuality and a need for some kind of union with members of both sexes.

Castration in a dream suggests fear of loss of masculinity and sexual power. To be *castrating someone* suggests an act of disempowerment.

Clothes in sexual dreams can have particular relevance often to do with our perception of ourselves: being fully clothed would suggest some feeling of guilt.

Contraception Dreaming of contraception can indicate a fear of pregnancy and birth, though interestingly it can equally indicate the choices we make when taking responsibility for our own bodies and actions.

Ejaculation/Emission The conflicts which arise in us because of our sexual desire for someone can be dealt with in the dream state through dreaming of emission, ejaculation or orgasm.

Hermaphrodite (also see individual entry) Dreaming of a hermaphrodite (someone who is both masculine and feminine) suggests either bisexuality, which is an erotic attraction to both sexes, or androgyny – the perfect balance within one person of the masculine and feminine qualities.

Intercourse or petting The wish or need to be able to communicate with someone on a very intimate level can translate itself into intercourse in a dream. If *intercourse is interrupted* in a dream we may have inhibitions of which we are not consciously aware. Often intercourse in a dream can mark the integration of a particular part of our own personality.

Kiss (also see individual entry) In dreams this can indicate either a mark of respect or an innate desire to arouse that part of us represented by the dream partner.

Masturbation Just as the child learns to comfort himself through masturbation, so dreaming of masturbation indicates a need for the comfort of a loving touch.

Penis/Phallus Any image either of, or to do with, the penis or phallus signifies everything that is creative, penetrative and masculine. It is vitality and creativity in both its simplest and most complex form. It is resurrection and the renewal of life.

Perversion Largely, when sexual perversion appears in dreams we are avoiding, or attempting to avoid, issues to do with closeness and bonding.

Semen is the sign of masculinity and of physical maturity and is often represented in dreams by a milky fluid. Dreams have an odd way of manifesting images of primitive rites and practices of which we may have no conscious knowledge. Many of these are representations of the sexual act or the spilling of seminal fluid.

Sexuality in a dream, in the sense of feeling desire for someone else – most often of the opposite sex – is a basic primeval urge for closeness and/or union with that person. We appear to be searching for a part of ourselves that we have lost. The other character in the dream represents the closest we can get to that part. If we were a fully integrated human being we would have no need for sexual union with someone else, but for most of us we have a desire to be united with everything which is not part of our own ego. Such a dream, which highlights the feelings we are capable of having, provides information to enable us to understand our own needs.

Transsexualism/Transvestism In dreams these signify a confusion so far as gender is concerned.

Venereal Disease In a dream this can suggest awareness of some kind of contamination. This need not necessarily be of a sexual nature, but could also be emotional.

③ Sexual activity is either the highest expression of love and spirituality, such as with Tantric union, or if purely physically based, is entirely selfish. In spiritual terms, each of us is searching for a Mystic Union, a conjoining of all aspects of our Selves.

Shadow
– also see Introduction

① A shadow in dreams may in mundane terms signify a potential difficulty of any sort of which we are being made aware. If however we are motivated to explore further it can represent a negativity in our own make-up. If we are chased by shadows we may need to confront our own fears and doubts.

② The Shadow as an archetype in dreams can be any forbidding, overbearing, frightening aspect which appears. It is those parts of our being that we most dislike (or are afraid of and are least able to face objectively. Initially, it will appear as a figure of the opposite gender to ourselves, only later revealing itself as the same gender when we have more understanding.

③ An extremely powerful part of the psyche, the energy of the Shadow once harnessed becomes a real force for transformation both within ourselves and within the world in which we live. We tend to lose our fear of the Unknown and can face our lives with courage.

Shampoo

① Shampoo in dreams has an obvious connection with cleansing and washing. On a practical level, we are trying to 'clear our heads' in order to think or see clearly. In the words of the popular song we may be trying to 'wash that man right out of my hair'.

② Because shampooing is connected with the head – which of itself represents intellect – there is a connection psychologically with needing to have clarity of thought. We may feel that our thought processes have been slowed down, or dirtied, by outside influences.

③ Spiritually shampoo – like soap – would suggest an attempt to get back to basics, to clear our wants, needs and requirements and to make a new connection with the Spiritual Self.

Shapes/Patterns

① The number of sides the shape has will be significant *(See Numbers)*, as will the colours *(See Colours)*. At a certain stage of development the geometric shapes which will give the individual a greater understanding of the abstract world begin to appear in dreams. It is as though the old perception of form is beginning to take on a new meaning and interpretation.

② We accept the nature of things as they are, and can look at the fundamental structure of our nature. We can appreciate the basic shape our life is taking without placing emotional inhibitions in the way.

③ Various shapes and patterns can be interpreted as:

Centre The centre symbolises the point from which everything starts. In relation to shape, it is the point from which the pattern grows.

Circle The circle represents the inner being or the Self *(see Self)*. It is also unity and perfection. *A circular object* – such as a ring – may have the same meaning as the circle. *A circle with a dot in the centre* can signify the soul in completion. It is sometimes taken to represent Woman.

Crescent (including the sickle and crescent moon) This signifies the feminine, mysterious power which is intuitive and non-rational.

Shapes/Patterns

Cross The cross is a known protective device against all forms of evil, especially the Devil, and is also thought to restore good health. It is one of the most common structures in Western cultures. The stem of the cross, the vertical line, stands for the heavenly or spiritual, while the transverse beam represents the material physical plane. The sunwheel – an equal armed cross surrounded by a circle – has been known since Bronze Age times. Hot cross buns carrying the same symbol originally marked the four quarters of the moon. As an Egyptian hieroglyph it means 'to divide into parts, to count.'

Cube – see individual entry

Diamond A diamond in a dream indicates that we have greater and lesser options available. By and large our choices will be between the physical mundane world and the more spiritual creative elements in our lives.

Hexagram A hexagram is a geometric figure which symbolises the harmonious development of the physical, social and spiritual elements of human life and its integration into a perfect whole.

Oval The oval is symbolic of the womb, and also of feminine life. Called the Vesica Piscis, it is the halo which completely encircles a sacred figure. It is also the intersection between two interlinking circles and therefore symbolises where the spiritual and physical worlds interlink – a very powerful energised space.

Patterns (in cloth, mosaic etc.) In dreams the patterns which appear as part of the scenario can categorise how we handle the patterns and perhaps repeated behaviours in our lives. In some patterns, the basic figure which is repeated over and over again draws our attention to the significance of numbers *(see Numbers)*.

Pentangle/Pentagram– see Star

Sphere The sphere has a similar meaning to the globe *(see Globe)*, and indicates perfection and completion of all possibilities.

Spiral (also see Labyrinth) The spiral is the perfect path to evolution. The principle is that everything is continually in motion, but also continually rising or raising its vibration. *If the spiral is towards the centre* we are approaching our own centre by an indirect route. *A clockwise outward movement to the right* is a movement towards consciousness and enlightenment. *If counter-clockwise* the movement is towards the unconscious, probably regressive behaviour. There is also a connection with the navel or solar plexus as the centre of power.

Square The square or signifies the manifestation of spirit into matter. It represents the earthly realm as opposed to the heavens. *A square within a circle* suggests the act of 'becoming'. *The human figure within the square* is the Self *(see Self)* or Perfect Man. *Any square object* signifies the enclosing and feminine principle. When a citadel or castle is square (as they are in many myths) it has a protective function.

Star The star, particularly if it is a bright one, indicates the individual's hopes, aspirations and ideals. It is those things we must reach for. *The five-pointed star or pentagram* evokes personal magic, and all matter in harmony. To be correct, the star should point upwards. In dreams it signifies our ownership of our own magical qualities and aspirations. If it is pointing downwards it symbolises wrongdoing and witchcraft. *The six-pointed star, or Star of David* is made up of one triangle pointing upward and another pointing downward: the physical and the spiritual are joined together in harmony to create wisdom. *Twelve stars* signify both the Twelve Tribes of Israel and the Apostles.

Swastika The swastika *with its arms moving clockwise* portrays Ideal Man and the power he has for good. In Eastern symbolism it signifies the movement of the sun. In this form it is a good luck symbol for many people in the East, and is considered particularly holy by the Hindu and Buddhist religions. Esoterically, *facing right* it symbolises the evolution of the universe, *facing left* it stands for the involution (descent into matter) of the universe. It signifies grounded stability since it points in all four directions (north, east, south and west).

Triangle The triangle represents Standing Man, with his three parts – body, mind and spirit (or being). Consciousness and love manifest through his physicality. There is potential still to be realised. If the triangle *points upwards* human nature moves towards the Divine. If it is *pointing down* it is spirit seeking expression through the physical. The triangle can also represent family relationships – that is, father, mother and child.

There is a game based on shapes in which you draw a square, a circle and a triangle, and then get someone else to elaborate each of the basic shapes into a drawing. Whatever he makes of the square is supposed to relate to his outlook on the world, the circle to his inner being and the triangle to his sex life. Meditating on such a drawing brings greater awareness.

Shark

① To dream of a shark may indicate that we are being attacked unfairly; someone is trying to take something that is rightfully ours. Being in **a sea of sharks** suggests that we are in a situation where we do not trust anyone. To be **pursued by a shark** may suggest that we have put ourselves in danger and created a situation by entering someone else's territory.

② Because a shark is a sea creature it has the significance of creating problems on an emotional level. We have no defences against the ferocity of others' attacks. It is as though our emotional capacity can be damaged and eroded by unscrupulous behaviour.

③ The shark is a symbol of the fear of death because of its connection with the Collective Unconscious. We are expected to go to the depths of our being and often lack the ability to confront these fears without help.

Shave

① The significance of shaving in a dream will obviously vary depending on whether the dreamer is a man or a woman. **If a man**, he is more likely to be shaving his face, which also suggests that he is trying to change his image. **If a woman**, she is likely to be shaving other parts of her body in order to create a more beautiful image. Both acts suggest removing an unwanted layer – that is, a facade which has been created.

② To dream that we have had 'a close shave' suggests that we have taken too many risks. We should be more aware of the difficulties we can have as well as the danger we put other people in.

③ In spiritual terms to be close-shaven suggests openness and honesty in our dealings with other people. For someone to have grown a beard when we would have least expected it indicates that they are trying to hide something from us.

Shawl
– see Coat/Cloak/Shawl in Clothes

Sheaf

① Previously a sheaf, particularly of corn, would signify a harvest or good husbandry. Now it is more likely to suggest old-fashioned ways and methods of operating. A **sheaf of papers** would suggest hard work.

② As a marker of time, the sheaf will suggest Autumn. It is often seen as a symbol of consolidation and of binding. We perhaps need to look at what needs to be gathered in, made into a coherent whole, and given boundaries.

③ As the symbol of Demeter *(see Goddess/Goddesses)*, the sheaf represents the nurturing mother. In can also suggest a dying world, in that Demeter refused to nurture 'her' humans when Persephone *(see Goddess/Goddesses)* was kidnapped by Pluto.

Shears
– see Scissors

Sheep
– see Animals

Shells
– also see Conch

① In dreams a shell represents the defences we use in order to prevent ourselves from being hurt. We can create a hard shell in response to previous hurt, or a soft shell which shows that we are still open to being hurt. Shells were also once a unit of currency, and in dreams can still be seen as this.

② A shell carries within it so much symbolism. It can be seen as a magical symbol which holds within it the power of transformation. The spiral of the shell suggests involution and evolution (going inwards and coming outwards). The ability to shelter is also symbolised, and being a receptacle it also links with the feminine, emotional side of nature.

③ Spiritually a shell is a miniature representation of the process of life and death.

Shelter

① Any shelter signifies protection. The human is aware of the need for a safe space, and this symbolism comes across in dreams quite strongly. The images used could be anything from a snail shell to an umbrella. Usually dreams about shelter highlight our needs or insecurities.

② The other image of shelter is protectiveness – that is, a more active participation in giving shelter or sanctuary. If we are **giving shelter** to someone in dreams, we may be protecting a part of ourselves from hurt or difficulty. If we are **being given shelter** we are conscious of the fact that there is protective power in our lives.

③ Shelter in the spiritual sense suggests sanctuary – a sacred space wherein we will not be harmed but can be ourselves.

Shield

① A shield is a symbol of preservation. It can appear in dreams as a **warrior's shield**, or as a barrier between us and the rest of the world. If we are **shielding someone else**, then we need to be sure our actions are appropriate and supportive. If we are **being shielded**, we need to be clear as to whether we are erecting the shield or whether it is being erected for us.

② In myths and legends the Amazonian woman is shown carrying a shield. This symbolises the sheltering, protective aspect of the feminine.

③ In spiritual development the shield appears as a symbol of a particular stage of awareness. It is at this point that the individual needs to appreciate that he has control over his own destiny. This symbol often first appears in dreams representing this stage of development.

Shirt
– see Clothes

Shiver

① To be conscious of shivering in dreams can represent either a fear of conflict, or of coldness of emotion. There is also a **shiver of excitement**. We may, in waking life, be reaching a conclusion or perhaps coming to a peak of experience.

② When we shiver in a dream we may be getting near to releasing unconscious behaviour.

③ The ecstatic experience results in a shiver as the energy on the physical level builds into an almost orgiastic experience. This can sometimes be experienced in dreams.

Shoe
– see Clothes

Shop/Shopping

① A shop in dreams signifies something we want or feel we need. If it is **a shop we know** then we are probably consciously aware of what we want from life. If it is an **unknown shop** then we may have to search our minds for information. A **supermarket** would suggest we have to make a choice.

② **To be shopping** is to be making a fair exchange for the satisfaction of our desires. We have the energy (money) which can be exchanged for something we want. What we are shopping for may have relevance. If we are **shopping for food** we need sustenance; if **for clothes** we may need protection.

③ In spiritual terms a shop has the same significance as a market *(see Market)*. Choices are being displayed for our consideration.

Shot/Shooting
– also see Gun and Weapons

① **To be shot** in a dream suggests an injury to one's feelings. In a **woman's dream** it can symbolise the sexual act – as much because her feelings are involved as for the masculine imagery. It could also indicate that we may feel that we are becoming victims or targets for other people's anger.

② If we are **shooting something** we may be having to deal with our own fears. We could be guarding against meeting parts of our personality we do not like. To be **on a shooting range** suggests needing to produce accuracy in our lives.

③ To be conscious of a shot or shooting in a spiritual sense is to be aware of a necessary directed explosion of energy. This may be the only way in which we can achieve a desired end.

Shovel/Spade

① A shovel in a dream will signify a need to dig into past experiences for information. We may need to uncover a past joy or trauma, or possibly even a learning experience. The type of spade or shovel will be of relevance. A **garden spade** would suggest being totally pragmatic, whereas a **fire shovel** would indicate a need to take care.

② Since a shovel can suggest a degree of introspection, of covering up, what is being shovelled is important. We are needing to be mindful of the content of our lives. **Shovelling compost**, for instance, would mean considering the sum total and most fertile aspects of our lives, whereas **shovelling sand** might suggest we need to be aware of the passage of time.

③ A shovel is an implement or tool which can be used to help us uncover what is spiritually correct. It may also suggest covering up what must remain hidden.

Shrink
– also see Analyst/Therapist

① In dreams, **to shrink** is to have a desire to return to childhood, or to a smaller space in order to be looked after. In everyday life we may be aware of losing face or of feeling small and this can be translated in dreams as shrinking. **To see something – or somebody – shrink** can indicate that it is losing its – or their – power over us.

② Psychologically we can learn to handle who we are by recognising both how necessary, and also how small, we are in the general scheme of things. The latter can be accompanied in dreaming by a feeling of shrinking. We therefore become less threatening to ourselves and others.

③ Following the psychological recognition of our smallness, we equally can become aware of the sense of belonging to a much greater cosmic whole. This can be represented in dreams by a feeling of shrinking.

Shroud

① In a dream a shroud can be a frightening image, since it is associated with death. If we recognise that by shrouding something it becomes hidden, then the image is less frightening.

② A shroud can signify a covering up of something we do not fully understand. We know that it is there, but we do not wish to have a look at it.

③ In spiritual terms a shroud is a mark of respect; dressing the body appropriately.

Sick
– also see Illness

① To **feel sick** in a dream is to be identifying a bad feeling which needs to be got rid of. To **be sick** is to be attempting to get rid of the bad feeling. We may in everyday life be 'sick' of a relationship or situation we have.

② Psychologically we are very much ruled by our emotions. Our stomach is a nerve centre which reacts to negative stimuli which can result in sickness in a dream.

③ When something is not right in our world spiritually, we need to eradicate it. Sickness is one way of doing this.

Sickle
– see Scythe/Sickle

Sieve

① The sieve in dreams is a symbol of the ability to make selections. This is in the sense of being able to sort out the large from the small, good from the bad etc.

② On a psychological level the sieve represents the ability to know oneself. We are able to make conscious choices which will enable us to extract the best from life.

③ Spiritually the sieve is said to represent fertility and rain clouds in the sense that pure rain, or water, permits proper growth.

Signature

① Our signature in a dream suggests that we have an appreciation of ourselves. We are prepared to recognise who we are and to make our mark in the world.

② At those times when we are arranging legal matters or agreements, but are actually not sure if we are doing the right thing, our signature can appear in dreams as obliterated or illegible.

③ Spiritually our signature is a reflection of ourselves. It is a representation of who we perceive ourselves to be.

Silence

① Silence in a dream can suggest uneasiness and expectancy. There is a waiting for something to happen (or not happen). If **someone else is silent** when we expect them to speak, we are unsure as to how that part of ourselves which is represented by the other person will react in waking life.

② When we are silent, we are unable to voice our feelings or opinions. We are either inhibited by our own selves or by outside influences.

③ Spiritually, silence is a space where there is no need for sound. Many religious orders are silent on the basis that there is then closer communication with God. In dreams it may be suggested that silence and withdrawal from the world is necessary.

Silver

① On a practical level, silver appearing in a dream suggests finance or money. Silver is something of value which can be held in reserve against difficulty.

② Silver on a more psychological level has been taken to represent the qualities of the moon. This is in the sense that something or someone is available, but is at the same time somewhat remote.

③ Spiritually, silver is said to represent the feminine aspect, gold being the masculine.

Sing/Singing

① To **hear singing** in a dream is to link with the self-expression we all have. We are in touch with the flowing, feeling side of ourselves and others. **To be singing** is to be expressing our joy and love of life. If we are **singing alone**, we have learnt to be skilled in our own right. To be **in a choir** suggests our ability to worship or express ourselves in a peer group. Obviously, if we are a singer in waking life, the interpretation will vary.

② Singing as an act of worship is a vital part of many systems of belief. A **football anthem**, for instance, will create a fellow feeling, whether it is a chant against the referee or a song of praise for the team. This has the effect of raising the vibration in a positive manner.

③ Spiritually when we sing we are capable of raising the vibration, either for ourselves or other people. We are in touch with the Higher Self. **Singing as chanting** has a valid place in religion – as in the Gregorian chant – where certain tones achieve a shift in consciousness. To hear this in dreams is to be in touch with a high vibration. Chanting of a mantra *(see Mantra)* also achieves the same end.

Sinking

① **To be sinking** in a dream suggests a loss of confidence. We may be in despair at something we have done, and feel hampered by the circumstances. What we are sinking into could be important. **To see someone else sinking** would suggest we are aware of a difficulty which perhaps needs our help. We may feel we are losing ground within a relationship or situation. To be **sinking in water** would suggest a particular emotion is threatening to engulf us. To be **sinking in sand or a bog** indicates that we feel there is no safe ground for us.

② A sinking feeling in dreams usually suggests worry or fear. Emotionally we are unable to maintain our usual happiness. We may feel that we are not in control, and that we cannot maintain forward movement. **To see an object sinking** may suggest that we are about to lose something we value.

③ Both spiritually and physically, to be sinking is to be getting into a situation where we are unable to see things clearly or to perceive the best course of action. For sensitives, this feeling may arise when the negativity of others is threatening to overwhelm us.

Siren
– also see Archetypes

① To hear a siren – as in an **ambulance or fire engine** – is to be warned of danger. For those old enough to remember, such a siren may well evoke memories of war and destruction. In particular, the 'all clear' will serve to relieve anxiety.

② Archetypally, the Siren suggests deception and distraction of man from his purpose. In dreams this is usually sexually oriented and difficult to handle. **In a woman's dream**, if she is not in touch with the siren within her, she can appear to be destructive. In psychological terms she is temptation and often appears in Greek or Roman attire, as if to enhance the erotic image. She can often be pictured in dreams sat by water, since she works with the emotions. In some cases she is a man's Anima *(see Anima/Animus)*.

③ It is only when it is understood spiritually that the Siren can ultimately restore man to himself, that the Siren becomes acceptable and can be worked with. After having rejected her enchantment, Man is free to become whole. When Woman understands her ability to use the Siren spiritually in order to heal, she understands her own enchantment.

Sister
– see Family

Size

① To be conscious of size in a dream highlights how we feel in relation to a person, project or object. **Big** might suggest important or threatening, whereas **small** might indicate vulnerability or something 'less than' ourselves. Thus a big house would be an awareness of the expansion of oneself, whereas a small house would indicate an intensity of feeling.

② A child learns very early on to make comparisons, and this is one of the things that we never lose. Something is bigger or smaller rather than simply big or small. In dreams size is relative. We might recognise somewhere we know, but find it is larger or smaller than we thought it to be. It is the size within the dream that is relevant.

③ Spiritually size is irrelevant. It is more the appreciation of feeling that becomes important. A 'big' feeling is something that consumes us, whereas a 'little' perception may be only part of what really exists.

Skeleton

① A skeleton in a dream suggests the 'bare bones' of something, perhaps an idea or concept. **A skeleton in a cupboard** represents a past action or shame we wish to hide. A **dancing skeleton** is an awareness of the life we have lived or are living. To **dig up a skeleton** is to resurrect something we have buried.

② Psychologically, we sometimes need to be aware of our feelings about death. Such an obvious image in dreams forces us to be aware of this. A skeleton can also suggest feelings or talents which we have forgotten and which therefore have 'died'.

③ A skeleton alerts us to our own feelings about death. We are aware that the physical must 'die', but that there is a framework which is left.

Skin
– see Body

Skull

① If a skull appears in a dream we may need to look at the rest of the dream in order to find out the symbolism. The **skull and crossbones** could represent either a romantic appreciation of a pirate, or a symbol of danger. Since the skull is a representation of the head it can also symbolise intellectual ability or rather, lack of it.

② To be conscious of **one's own skull** in dreams is to appreciate the structure that we have given our lives. To perceive a **skull where there should be a head** suggests that part of the person has 'died'. To be **talking to a skull** is recognising the need to communicate with those who are lost to us. When a **skull is talking to us**, a part of us which we have rejected or denied is beginning to come back to life. If we believe in life after death, we may feel that spirit is talking through the skull.

③ Spiritually the skull represents death and all its implications. When it appears in dreams, it is time for us to come to terms with physical death.

Sky

① In dreams the sky can represent the mind. It can also signify our potential. **Floating or flying** in the sky can be ambivalent, since it can either mean trying to avoid the mundane, or exploring a different potential. If the sky is **dark** it may reflect our mood of gloominess; if it is **bright**, our mood of joy.

② The sky signifies the unattainable. It appearance in dreams indicates we will need to make a great deal of effort to reach our goals.

③ The sky spiritually suggests infinity. It also signifies order – particularly that applied to the intuitive function.

Smell
– also see Perfume

① To be conscious of a smell, odour or perfume in a dream usually means that we are trying to identify an object or where the smell is coming from. Most other senses are sharpened in dreams, but the sense of smell is made available only if a specific interpretation is needed and particular note should be taken of what it is we smell.

② Childhood is a time when smell is very significant. Many smells which are associated with that time e.g. baking bread, burning oil, flowers, school dinners etc. can still be very evocative for us as adults. A **pleasant smell** could represent happy times or memories, whereas a **bad smell** can hold memories of particularly traumatic times.

③ As our spiritual senses develop, the ability to sense and recognise smells from the past on a clairvoyant level can be somewhat frightening. Provided this ability is recognised merely as a means of identifying a time, place or person there need be no problem and we need have no fear.

Smoke/Smoking
– also see Fire and Tobacco

① Smoke in dreams suggests that there is a feeling of danger around, especially if we cannot locate the fire. If **we are smoking**, we are trying to control anxiety. If we smoke in real life, but recognise in dreams that we no longer do so, we have overcome a difficulty. If smokers give it up in everyday life, they will often have many dreams focused around the issue of smoking. A **cigar** in dreams has obvious connections with masculinity and power, whereas **cigarettes** may suggest a degree of sophistication or, particularly for young people, a way of challenging the status quo.

② Smoke in dreams can represent passion, although it may not have 'flared' properly into being. Smoke can also represent either cleansing – as with incense – or contamination. As smoking bans become more widespread it may be seen in dreams either as a way of protecting the majority, as the imposition of control by a higher authority, or even a divisive device designed to attack our enjoyment of life.

③ Spiritually smoke signifies prayer rising to heaven, or the raising of the soul to escape from space and time.

Snail

① The snail appearing in dreams may engender a feeling of repulsion in some people. It does, however, also represent vulnerability and slowness.

② From a psychological point of view, the snail suggests steadiness and self-containment. To be **moving at snail's pace** suggests direct planned, careful movement.

③ Spiritually, because of the spiral shape of its shell, the snail is a natural symbol of the labyrinth (*see Labyrinth*).

Snake

– see Serpent/Snake in Animals

Snow

– also see Avalanche and Ice/Iceberg

① Snow is a crystallisation of water, and as such represents the crystallisation of an idea or project. **When melting**, it can represent the softening of the heart and emotions.

② Psychologically snow in dreams can suggest emotional coldness or frigidity. We need to consider whether we have frozen out other people from our lives and whether it has been appropriate to do so.

③ Spiritually, snow can represent pureness, beauty and the melting away of difficulties.

Soap

① Soap in dreams suggests the idea of being cleansed. We perhaps need to create an environment of cleanliness – both of physical cleanliness and appropriate behaviour. Often in emerging sexual dreams soap can appear as an image of ejaculated semen.

② Psychologically soap can indicate a need to clean up our act. We may feel a sense of having been made dirty by an experience and situation and our dream mind is alerting us to the fact that we need to deal with it.

③ Again, on a spiritual level, soap represents cleansing. There is a creative visualisation which can be carried out if we feel our space has been invaded. We should envisage ourselves scrubbing down the walls of a room three times in order to cleanse it (remembering to 'throw away' the water or let it drain away). Once is for the physical, once emotional, once spiritual. Following this there will be a feeling of lightness.

Son

– see Family

Soup

– see Eat/Eating, Food and Nourishment

South

– see Position

Sowing

① Sowing – in the sense of **planting seed** – is a symbol which has certain basic images attached to it. It can signify the sexual act, and as well as suggesting good husbandry. It is also representative of the beginning of a new project.

② The image of laying down a framework for success is implicit in sowing. The actions which have to be gone through – such as preparing the ground, tilling the soil and so on – are all evocative images even in today's technological society. When this image appears in dreams, we need to look at circumstances around us and decide what we can gain most.

③ Sowing in a spiritual sense suggests creating the correct environment in which growth can take place. It is, above all, the creative act.

Space

① In dreams, when we are aware of the space we occupy we are in touch with our own potential. We may be aware that our personal space is being, or has been, penetrated. To be **'spaced out'** is to have widened our personal boundaries artificially through the use of stimuli.

② Psychologically we often need space to make the best use of opportunities. We should be capable of going beyond our own concepts of limitation and ego states.

③ Space, in the sense of outer space, is a representation of a Cosmic Centre – a place that 'is, was and ever shall be'. This idea can widen our present view of the world.

Spade
– see Shovel/Spade

Spark
– also see Electricity

① A spark in a dream represents a beginning. Being aware of a spark is to be conscious of what is going to make things possible. From a physical perspective it is a small thing which gives rise to a greater one.

② The spark of an idea suggests the germ of a creative potential which, given the opportunity, will become much bigger. Since the spark also represents the basic life force, we need to appreciate our own lust for life.

③ The spark suggests fire and energy. It is the vital principle in life, without which we would not exist.

Spear

① The spear has many meanings. It represents the masculine in dreams and is phallic. It is the life-giving force. To see a **warrior with a spear** is to recognise the aggressive male. To **put a spear in the ground** is to mark one's territory. If we are **throwing a spear** we perhaps need to be aware of our more primitive aspects.

② The spear is psychologically that part of ourselves which is fertile and assertive.

Whether in a man's or a woman's dream, it allows us to be conscious of the need to cut out nonsense and get straight to the point.

③ Spiritually, the spear signifies directness and honour.

Spectacles
– see Glasses/Spectacles

Speed

① Speed in dreams identifies an intensity of feelings which is not usually available in waking life. Because everything is happening too quickly, it engenders anxiety in us which creates problems.

② **Travelling at speed** suggests trying to achieve a fast result. Speeding – as in a **traffic offence** – suggests being too focused on an end result, and not the method of getting there. To be **taking, or to be given, speed** (amphetamines) in a dream may have two meanings. If we use the substance in everyday life, we could be being alerted to a gift or talent we have which should be developed. If we do not normally use the drug, then we are putting ourselves in danger.

③ There is a point when, as we are developing spiritually, we lose our sense of time. Speeding things up may appear as slowing things down, and vice versa. This is all part of the growth process.

Sphinx
– also Egypt and Pyramid

① The sphinx for most people in dreams will represent Egypt, and all the mystery and knowledge it contains.

② Psychologically, and because even today so little is known about it, the sphinx stands for the enigmatic side of ourselves. In dreams it will highlight the mysterious strength which is available to us all, particularly in times of trouble.

③ Spiritually the sphinx stands for vigilance, power and wisdom as well as dignity.

Spider/Cobweb
– also see Web

① There is a great deal of ambivalence in the image of the **spider**. On a very mundane level it is disliked, perhaps because of its scuttling movement but also because of its association with dirt and unpleasantness. In dreams it can also suggest deviousness. The **cobweb** is the kind of image which has changed in symbolism over the years. Having a kind of delicacy about it meant that it signified the perfect pattern and nature's beauty. When dirty, however, it suggests horror and neglect – and is often used in this way in the media. It will tend to have this significance in dreams.

② In psychological terms the spider connects with the Mandala (see Mandala). It is the ability to create a perfect pattern which both nurtures and protects us at the same time. Picking up the symbolism of the spider, the cobweb can suggest industriousness on the one hand and a transitory existence on the other. Something beautiful can be easily destroyed.

③ Spiritually the spider represents the Great Mother (see Great Mother/Mother Earth) in her role as the Weaver. She weaves destiny from the body of her self, and is therefore the Creator. In coming to terms with this aspect, we become weavers of our own destiny. As a complex yet simple pattern the cobweb can symbolise the whole idea of a spiritual journey and the connections which must be made in order for us to have understanding.

Spine
– see Backbone in Body

Spirits
– also see Ghost

① At its very basic level, we all have fears and feelings about death, and the appearance of Spirit helps us to come to terms with these. It will depend on our own personal belief system as to whether we feel they are actual spirits or not.

② When spirits appear in dreams, their function may be to help us through various states of transition. While we cope with everyday fears, there are many unconscious memories and feelings which can surface unexpectedly. When we are conscious of a kindly or helpful spirit we are aware that we can move on. When we see the spirits of dead people it shows that we need reassurance.

③ During spiritual development, our perceptions widen from the ordinary everyday to other aspects and dimensions of knowledge that have become available to us. Whether these are aspects of our own personality or of the spirit realm is immaterial, since ultimately their function is to help us progress. The Spiritual Self has complete access to the Collective Unconscious.

Spiral
– see Labyrinth and Shapes/Patterns

Spire
– also see Church/Holy Buildings

① To see a spire in a dream is to recognise a landmark. In previous times, people oriented themselves by churches. Now a pub tends to be a marker, but in dreams the spire still persists.

② The spire can often be taken in dreams as a phallic symbol, particularly – and somewhat obviously – the erect one. It also represents ambition and striving. **A**

fallen spire would suggest the collapse of hopes. To be **building a tower or spire** has connotations with the Tower of Babel and shows a need for more, or improved, communication.

③ As a representation of our spiritual progression, the spire suggests the movement from the secular to the sacred.

Spit/Spittle

① Normally in dreams spittle will represent disgust. We would, in former times, 'spit venom', which is a very basic image as to how a hurt or threatened animal will react. If we are **spitting at someone**, we should consider whether we are acting appropriately in waking life. If we are **being spat at**, it shows others may disapprove of our action.

② More positively, spittle can indicate a sign of good faith. Some cultures still spit on their hands when completing a deal. There is a bonding through the exchange of bodily fluids.

③ Since Biblical times, spittle has been seen as a healing fluid. It was supposed to be an antidote against being cursed, particularly by the use of the Evil Eye. Spiritually it is perhaps symbolic of the flow of energy between healer and patient.

Splinter

① In dreams, a splinter can represent a minor irritation. It is something which has penetrated our defences and is now making us uncomfortable. Splinters may represent painful words or ideas. We may be holding on to ideas which cause negative feelings.

② To be part of **a splinter group** in a dream suggests feeling sufficiently strongly about something to break away from mainstream thought. To **hit something which splinters** is to recognise that we are all composed of parts which make a whole.

③ The sense of belonging to a group of spiritually like-minded people can often only come after we have recognised our isolation or, in some cases, fragmentation.

Sport
also see Arena and Games/Gambling

① As a well-loved physical activity, any sport can become part of a scenario in a dream to give the right atmosphere for information to be understood. In mundane terms for instance it can be used to either highlight solitary activity or perhaps the necessity for team work.

② Sport in dreams can suggest either a new or well-practiced activity. To be playing a sport we would not normally do suggests that we probably need to rethink our ways of working, whereas taking part in a much loved activity suggests confidence in our competence and power.

③ The rough and tumble of most sport is symbolic of a need for a spiritual activity which may test our endurance and stamina. It may be a warning of difficult but enjoyable times ahead.

Spring

① **Springtime** in a dream can suggest new growth or opportunities. Perhaps there is a fresh start in a relationship. A **spring of water** suggests fresh energy, whereas a **bed spring** or other type of coil would indicate upward spiralling.

② To walk with **a spring in one's step** is to be looking forward to something. The saying 'spring forward, fall back' is also applicable in psychological terms, since effort is required to progress.

③ Spiritually a spring is a symbol of progression, particularly insofar as emotion is concerned. We can now afford to make a new beginning.

Sprinkle/Sprinkling

① Sprinkling as a symbol in dreams suggests an attempt to make a little go a long way. Perhaps we need to get the best out of situations around us, by putting a little effort into many things.

② Sprinkling suggests the symbolism of impregnation, of conception and gestation. Psychologically we need to make a link with our creative side in order to function properly as human beings and can often do this through dreams about sprinkling.

③ Spiritually we are aware of basic concepts and abilities. In some cultures, semen is sprinkled on the ground to propitiate the Mother Goddess and ensure a good harvest. In many protective magical rituals herbs and salt are sprinkled.

Square
– See Shapes/Patterns

Squirrel
– see Animals

Stab
– also see Knife and Weapons

① **To be stabbed** in a dream indicates our ability to be hurt. **To stab someone** is, conversely, to be prepared to hurt. Since a stab wound is penetrative it obviously has connections with aggressive masculine sexuality, but also with the faculty of being able to get straight to the point.

② When we make ourselves vulnerable we are open to being hurt. Often a stab is a quick way of achieving a result. For instance, to be **stabbing at something rather than somebody** would suggest the need to break through some kind of shell or barrier in order to proceed.

③ When we realise that we can use particular skills, they can assume an almost ritualistic feeling. Fighting and stabbing can then be appreciated as a means of spiritual discipline (as in martial arts). We need to understand appropriate behaviour.

Staff

① A staff, in the sense of **a stick**, is a support mechanism, staff – as in **office staff** – a support system. Dreaming of either should clarify our attitude to the support we require in life. It is worthwhile noting that one is passive in its use (the stick) and one is active.

② The staff in dreams symbolises the journeying and pilgrimage that we must undertake. It also represents magical power in the form of a wand.

③ Spiritually the staff is a symbol of the support we have, or will need, on our spiritual journey. As we progress, we move from using it as a support to using it as a tool and finally as a sign of authority.

Stag
– see Deer in Animals

Stage
– also see Actor, Play/Playing and Theatre

① To be **on stage** in a dream is to be making oneself visible. An **open-air stage** suggests communication with the masses rather than a selected audience. A **moving stage** signifies the need to keep moving, even while performing a role. If we are **members of the audience** we need to be aware of the plot of the play and how it may be relevant to us.

② To be at a stage (of development, for instance) is to be cognisant of what one knows, but also what one does not. If a project or an idea reaches a certain stage, we can envisage the potential for success.

③ Spiritually a stage is a representation of our own life play. We are able to observe and be objective about what is going on. By externalising the 'play' into a framework we can manipulate our lives.

Stake

① To have **a stake in something** is to have made a commitment, either on a material or emotional level. To be **putting stakes in the ground** suggests marking out one's territory in some way.

② Psychologically we may experience a sense of being staked out. This can represent that we have been conned or forced into doing something we do not want to do.

③ Spiritually in previous times the stake would have represented a form of torture, sometimes necessary on our Life's Journey. However, it can also represent our point of contact with Earth's energies.

Stairs
– see Buildings and Steps

Star
– see Celebrity and Shapes/Patterns

Station
– see Arrival and Departing/Leaving in Journey

Statue

① Dreaming of a statue is to be linking with the unresponsive, cold side of human nature. We may be worshipping or loving someone and not getting any response.

② There is a basic side of nature which needs to look up to something and this can be represented in dreams by a statue. Sometimes this statue is representative of an idea or concept rather than a person. Much can be gained by identifying what the statue represents. What it is made of might also be important (*see Marble and Stone*).

③ Spiritually, as we progress, we come up against the knowledge that we have given value to something – for instance, a relationship – that no longer has significance. It is 'dead' and therefore solidified. If the statue comes to life again, it can be rescued.

Stealing
– also see Thief

① To dream of **stealing** suggests we are taking something without permission. This may be love, money or opportunities. If someone **steals from us** we may feel cheated. If it is by **someone we know**, then we need to work out how much we trust that person. If it is by **someone we don't know**, it is more likely to be a part of ourselves that we don't trust. If we are **in a gang of thieves**, then we should look at, and consider, the morals of the peer group we belong to.

② Stealing is a very emotive word for most people, and it will depend on our background as to how they feel about inappropriate behaviour. This image also comes up when dealing with the emotions. For instance, a 'needy' person may feel they are stealing affection.

③ Spiritually, stealing is using energy inappropriately. At each level of awareness we have certain power available to us which must be used wisely and well. For instance, 'black' magic could be interpreted as stealing. Psychic 'vampirism' is another form of stealing.

Steam

① Steam in dreams can suggest emotional pressure. We are passionate about something without necessarily knowing what it is.

② Because it is two substances uniting into one, steam suggests transformation. It also suggests a transitory experience, since steam also melts away.

③ We are looking at, and are aware of, the all encompassing power of the Spirit. Steam has the same connotations as mist *(see Mist)*.

Steeple
– see Spire

Steps
– also see Stairs in Buildings

① Steps in dreams almost invariably suggest an effort made to succeed. **Going up** steps suggests trying to make things better and improve them, whereas **going down** means going either into the past or the subconscious. The number of stairs which appear can also have relevance *(see Numbers)*.

② Steps represent changes in awareness within a project, quite literally the steps necessary. Steps also represent communication of a progressive kind.

③ There is still perceived to be a hierarchical structure in spiritual progression. We can achieve certain things at a certain level. We must extensively refine each level before moving on to the next.

Sterile/Sterilise

① To dream of **sterilising something** suggests a need for cleansing at a deep level. We wish to get rid of hurts or traumas and are prepared to put in the effort to do so. 'Sterilising' a situation may be taking the emotion out of it.

② For a **woman to dream of being sterile or being sterilised**, either by an operation or otherwise, may be connecting with her feeling of powerlessness. **In a man's dream** sterilisation may suggest either sexual dissatisfactions or doubts about his self-image.

③ Sterilisation in a spiritual sense is ambivalent. It can either suggest cleanliness of spirit, or an aspect of the Self *(see Self)* which is unable to grow at present. We need to accept the need for integration.

Stiffness
– also see Immobility

① Stiffness in dreams would suggest some anxiety or tension is present. There is a holding back of energy that is causing rigidity. In waking life this rigidity can manifest as difficulty with the joints.

② To be **stiff with someone** is to be reserved and withdrawn, probably through shyness but possibly through anger. A **stiff exterior** would suggest a judgemental attitude.

③ At certain stages of spiritual progression and development, discipline can appear as stiffness.

Stone
– also see Obelisk

① Dreaming of stone can suggest stability and durability, but also a loss of feeling. To be **carving stone** in a dream is to be attempting to create a lasting monument. A **deliberately formed stone circle** such as Stonehenge will have the significance of creating a lasting monument to a belief system.

② Stone has many connotations on an emotional level. For stone to be **broken up** signifies being badly hurt. Being **turned to stone** would suggest that we have had to harden up our attitudes. **Being stoned** could have two meanings. One is being punished for misdemeanours; the other is being under the influence of drugs.

③ Stone signifies the imperishability and the indestructibility of Supreme Reality. In ancient times stone circles would have the same significance as do churches and temples today.

Storm
– also see Lightning and Thunder/Thunderbolts

① In dreams a storm indicates a personal emotional outburst. We may feel we are being battered by events or emotions. It can also signify anger.

② When we are in difficulty, for instance, in a relationship, a storm can bring release. When an argument is not appropriate in everyday life, in dreams a storm can clear our 'emotional air'.

③ Spiritually a storm symbolises the creative power. Thunder and lightning are the tools of the storm gods such as Norse God Thor and Hindu Rudra.

Straightness
– *see Position*

Stranger
– *see People*

Strangle
– *also see Kill and Murder/Murderer*

① To dream of **strangling someone** is an attempt to stifle their emotions. To dream of **being strangled** is to be aware of our difficulty in voicing our emotions.

② Strangulation suggests a violent act of suppression. Emotionally, our more aggressive side may not allow us to act appropriately in certain situations.

③ Spiritually, wisdom arises out of learning how to hold back inappropriate speech, not strangle it.

Straw

① Straw in dreams highlights weakness and emptiness. Unless the image of straw appears in a countryside scene, we are probably aware of a passing phase which has little meaning. A **straw house** – being a temporary structure – would suggest a state of impermanence is present in our lives.

② When we say something is **built on straw**, we are aware that it does not have a proper foundation. We need to look at what we feel is impermanent in our lives and correctly manage it.

③ Straw appearing in a dream can often reveal that we feel there is a lack of support – or that the support we do have seems to be rather dry and brittle – when undertaking our Spiritual journey.

Stream
– *also see Swimming and Water*

① Dreaming of a stream suggests the awareness of the flow of our emotions. If it is **fast-flowing**, we should perhaps consider whether we are over-reacting to situations in waking life; if **slow** we perhaps should look at our levels of enthusiasm. To be **in a stream** suggests that we are in touch with our sensuality.

② Emotionally if we are to function properly we must feel loved and appreciated. To be **in the stream of things** suggests being part of a social group which will enable us to interact with people.

③ The image of a stream is often quoted as being blessed by Divine Power. Spiritual energy is often experienced as a stream of light.

String

① String appearing in dreams signifies some sort of binding, perhaps to make something secure. It may also represent trying to hold a situation together.

② In a psychological sense, string – like rope – can be seen as a link between two objects, concepts or ideas (*See Rope*).

③ Spiritually, anything that binds suggests a direct relationship with one's inner self, as in the Silver Cord.

Submarine

① A submarine in dreams indicates the depth of feeling that is accessible to us. Usually we are looking at the subconscious depths rather than the spiritual heights.

② If we are to be comfortable with ourselves we need to understand our subconscious urges. Since there can be some fear – and in some cases the need for protection – the submarine can be a good image to use.

③ Dreaming of a submarine indicates that we have a spiritual need to get underneath our emotions.

Sucking

① To be conscious of sucking in a dream suggests a return to infantile behaviour and emotional dependency. **Sucking a lollipop** alerts us to a need for oral satisfaction in the sense of comforting ourselves. **Sucking a finger** can suggest a physical need.

② Emotionally we all have needs which are left over from childhood. These may be unfulfilled desires or the need to be whole and complete. This need can surface in dreams as sucking something.

③ The snake which sucks its own tail is a potent image of spiritual completeness.

Suffocating

① When we feel **we are suffocating** in a dream, it may be that our own fears are threatening to overwhelm us. It can also indicate that we are not in control of our own environment. To be **suffocating someone** may mean we are overpowering them in real life.

② If we do not wish to have any sort of relationship with someone we may find that dreams of suffocation occur. Fears about sexuality may also surface in this way.

③ Suffocation may appear in dreams when negative energy is too strong for us to deal with.

Suicide

① Dreaming of suicide alerts us to a violent end to something, perhaps a project or relationship. It may also signify the end of a business or business relationship.

② Emotionally, when dreams of suicide occur, we may have come to the end of our ability to cope with a particular situation in our lives. It does not actually mean that we are suicidal. It simply marks the end of a phase.

③ Often on the path of spirituality we must let go of the old Self *(see Self)*. This letting go often appears in dreams as a kind of suicide. It is also a sign of anger against the Self.

Suitcase
– see Baggage and Luggage

Summer

① To be aware in a dream that it is summer suggests that it is a good time in our lives. We can look forward to success in projects we have around us. We have the ability to make the most of what we have done to date.

② The significance of summer on a psychological level is twofold. Because of its association with holidays and with fun and laughter, we are able to be more relaxed. We also have opportunities to meet with other people and to form new associations.

③ Esoterically, summer represents the mid-life. This is a time of spiritual success and of the ability also to plan for the rest of our lives. We have learnt by experience and can now put that experience into practice.

Sun
– also see Planets

① The sun in dreams suggests warmth and conscious awareness. A **sunny day** suggests happiness. To be **drawn to the sun** indicates we are looking for enlightenment. In turning towards the sun, the sunflower could be said to be a symbol of obsession, but also of worship. With its many seeds it also represents fertility.

② Because the sun is such a powerful image on its own as a life source, it can also appear in dreams as a symbol for other life energy. If dreaming of **a sun dance** we may be wishing to praise the sun for its all-encompassing power and energy. We are, in effect, using the energy of the sun for guidance and vitality.

③ The sun can symbolise spiritual enlightenment and radiance. We can 'soak up' and use the sun's power for further spiritual development.

Surgery
– also see Operation

① To find ourselves **in a surgery** in dreams would indicate that we should be looking at our health and health matters.

② Surgery indicates a fairly violent intrusion in our lives which may be necessary. Dreaming of having **surgery performed on us** shows we need to accustom ourselves to changes which may initially be difficult, but ultimately are healing.

③ Spiritually, we may feel that we have too much to deal with or that something needs altering. A dream about surgery can often indicate this.

Swallow
– see Birds

Swallowing

① Swallowing in a dream suggests we are taking something in. This could be knowledge or information. Dreaming of **swallowing one's pride** signifies the necessity for humility, whilst something being **hard to swallow** shows that we have a need to overcome an obstacle.

② When we are holding back on emotion, we physically need to swallow. Swallowing therefore becomes an act of suppression which can be harmful.

③ We may be taking in more spirituality than we can comfortably process. It would be advisable to slow down and 'digest' our spiritual teachings more methodically.

Swamp
– also see Marsh

① A swamp in a dream symbolises feelings which can undermine our confidence and well-being. To **be swamped** is to be overwhelmed by a feeling or emotion. To be **swamping someone else** in a dream may suggest that we are being too needy.

② Emotionally, when a swamp appears we are putting ourselves in touch with very basic feelings and emotions. A swamp is so-called primordial material, out of which everything emerges; at this stage we have no idea what our potential is.

③ A swamp can symbolise the vast amount of spiritual knowledge that there is to be taken in. The sheer vastness may leave us feeling utterly hopeless and out of our depth, but with some perseverance we can pull ourselves through and enjoy a much clearer outlook.

Swan
– see Birds

Swastika
– see Shapes/Patterns

Sweeping

① To dream of sweeping suggests being able to clear away outmoded attitudes and emotions. To be **sweeping up** suggests putting things in order.

② Sweeping is an old image which harks back to good management and clearing of the environment. In psychological terms it suggests an attention to detail and correctness, as much as to cleanliness. In modern day technological symbolism it could suggest searching for viruses.

③ We may have attained much spiritual knowledge on which we are now reflecting. There may be certain elements of confusion which we can take time to clear away.

Sweets
– see Food

Swimming
– also see Drowning and Water

① Dreaming of swimming has much the same symbolism as immersion *(see Immersion)*. To be **swimming upstream** in a dream would indicate that we are going against their own nature. **Swimming fish** can have the same symbolism as sperm, and therefore can indicate the desire for a child. Swimming in **clear water** indicates being cleansed, whereas **dark water** could symbolise the possibility of depression.

② Swimming in water will always be symbolic of the emotions, whereas **swimming through the air** connects with intellectual ability. To dream of being a **good swimmer** shows the ability to be able to handle emotional situations well, whereas being a **poor swimmer** in a dream could indicate the need to learn how to handle our emotions in a more positive way.

③ As swimming in water suggests moving a somewhat intangible obstacle out of the way in order to propel ourselves forward, so swimming in dreams can represent spiritual progression. We are moving forward in order to reach a particular goal.

Swine
– see Pig in Animals

Swing
– see Rocking

Sword

– also see Weapons

① The sword in dreams invariably suggests a weapon of power. We may have the ability to create power and use energy properly through our beliefs.

② The sword symbolises justice and courage as well as strength. For the image of a sword to appear in a dream indicates there is an element of the warrior in us, and that we are prepared to fight for our beliefs.

③ Spiritually the sword signifies the power of authority and protection. In dreams to be **given a sword** signifies that we have the protection of the sacred. We are able to make our own decisions.

Synagogue

– see Church/Holy Buildings

Syringe

– also see Injection and Vaccination/Vaccine

① To dream of a syringe suggests we have an awareness of the influence that other people can have over us in life. It will depend on whether the syringe is being used to take something out or to put something in as to the particular significance. A **garden syringe** (as in a fly spray) in dreams can suggest either masculine energy or decontamination.

② Dreaming of a syringe can indicate that when we are attempting to influence other people, we need to be conscious of the way we do it. We can be very specific and hit the right spot, or we can have a more 'scatter gun' approach. We need to be careful that we do not inflict hurt more than is necessary on others.

③ Penetrative awareness can suggest a particular way of approaching our own spiritual selves. Often, Spiritual Awareness appears in short, sharp bursts, but needs to be assimilated slowly.

Tabernacle

① A tabernacle is a place where a sacred object is kept for safety; it also represents a temple. To dream of one is therefore to be trying to understand our own need for sanctuary and safekeeping.

② Man has always required a way to make certain objects sacred. Psychologically, to acknowledge such sacredness gives him a sense of permanence. He can have some sense that the world will continue to exist without him.

③ A tabernacle, a repository for the divine presence, by being sacred becomes a world centre.

Table
– also see Altar and Furniture/Furnishings

① A table being **a focus for meeting,** whether socially or professionally, is usually recognised in dreams as a symbol of decision making. As **a place for a family rendezvous**, we may consider meals to be an important ritual. In business and professional terms, **the boardroom table** also has an element of ritual about it.

② To dream of dealing with **a table or list of objects**, or perhaps actions, instils a sense of order. It represents our ability to create order out of chaos.

③ A table can represent spiritual judgement and legislation.

Tablet
– also see Pill

① **Taking medicine in the form of tablets** signifies our recognition of our need to be healthy. We need to 'heal' something that is wrong. If we are **giving tablets to someone else** we may be aware that their needs are not being satisfied.

② In magical terms, a tablet presupposes knowledge greater than our own and therefore represents an element of trust. We trust our destiny to someone else.

③ As with the Tablets of Moses, there is access to esoteric and magical knowledge, particularly in the light of recent technological advances.

Tadpole

① Dreaming of tadpoles links to an awareness of the simplicity of life. We are aware that there is growth, but either we, or someone else, has not yet reached full maturity.

② **In a woman's dream** tadpoles may represent either her wish, or her ability, to become pregnant.

③ Spiritually, the tadpole represents the Germ of Life.

Tail

① To dream of a tail can signify some residue from the past, something we still carry with us. It can also indicate sexual excitement, or possibly, by association, the penis.

② The tail is necessary to the animal for balance, and thus in dreams can be recognised as a means of adjustment in difficult circumstances.

③ We have come to the end of, or completed, a spiritual action.

Tailor

① As with other occupations, it is perhaps more important to decide what significance the tailor has to us before attempting an interpretation. Any professional person develops certain talents and competencies, such as, in this case, the ability to do precise work and to 'fashion' something new. To dream of a tailor alerts us to these qualities within ourselves.

② The role that a character plays in our dream has relevance to how we think of our creativity and talents. Dreaming of a tailor may also have meaning in terms of word play. For example we may actually know someone called Taylor.

③ Creative Ability and the skills we need to reach our spiritual goals.

Talisman
– also see Charm/Amulet and Magic

① A talisman is a protection against evil or difficulty. When one turns up in a dream, we are often aware that our own mental powers are not sufficient to protect us from fear and doubt. We are in need of external help.

② Man has a deep connection with objects he believes to be sacred. In most Pagan religions, objects such as stones and drawings were given special powers. While consciously we may not believe, unconsciously we are capable of linking with ancient magic.

③ Objects bestowed with magical powers retain the ability to protect throughout time, but it is usually the technique used to empower the talisman which should be carefully considered.

Talking

① To be conscious of **people talking** in a dream gives a sense of being in contact with our own ability to communicate. We are able to express clearly what we feel and think, whereas in waking life we may not feel confident.

② We are perhaps afraid of **not being listened** to properly and this anxiety can express itself through hearing someone else talking. It is not necessarily the words that are important, more the sense of what is being said.

③ Psychic communication, needed Spiritual information.

Tambourine
– also see Musical Instruments

① As human beings we need rhythm in our lives. Dreaming of a tambourine, or any such musical instrument, allows us to be in contact with our own basic rhythms.

② The tambourine can indicate that we have some control over the rhythm and noise in our lives. Particularly if we are **playing the tambourine in a group**, we are accepting our ability to participate effectively in life.

③ Traditionally, noise was used to summon – or ward off – evil spirits. The tambourine is one such instrument.

Tame

① To dream of **taming an animal** indicates our ability to control or develop a relationship with the animal aspect of ourselves. To dream of **being tamed**, as though we ourselves were the animal, signifies the need for restraint in our lives.

② To find that something is extremely tame – in the sense of something **dull and boring** – suggests that we should reconsider the way we live our lives.

③ Self-control, or rather self discipline, which is spiritually necessary allows us understanding.

Tangled

① Sometimes when we are confused in everyday life, we may dream of an object being **entangled with something** else. Often the way that we untangle the object indicates action we should take in waking moments.

② When something like **hair is tangled**, we need to be aware that our self-image or projection is coming across to other people as distorted.

③ Cutting through a **tangle of trees or undergrowth** in a dream is part of the Hero's Journey (*see Hero/Heroic Figure in People*).

Tank

① Dreaming of **a water tank** is putting ourselves in touch with our inner feelings and emotions. Dreaming of **a military tank** connects us with our own need to defend ourselves, but to be aggressive at the same time. Such a dream would indicate that we are feeling threatened in some way.

② Often in dreams we become aware of our need to overcome objections and difficulties. Sometimes the only form of expression we have is to ride roughshod over those objections. The image of a war tank helps to highlight our ability to do this without being hurt.

③ We need to be a 'Spiritual Warrior'. With the help of a protective device, we can bring about success.

Tap

① The tap is an image of being able to make available universal resources. To dream of **not being able to turn a tap** either on or off highlights our ability – or inability – to control those things we consider to be rightfully ours.

② Water is considered to be a symbol of emotion, so a tap is representative of our ability to use or misuse emotion in some way. To be able to turn emotion on and off at will is indicative of great self-control.

③ Spiritual flow and access to regulated Spiritual energy. Power is available to us.

Tape

① Dreaming of **a measuring tape** indicates our need to 'measure' our lives in some way. Perhaps we may need to consider how we communicate with, or 'measure up' to, other people's expectations. Equally, **if we are doing the measuring** we may be trying to create order in our lives. Dreaming of **a recording tape** would suggest that we are aware that the way we express ourselves is worth remembering.

② **Masking or parcel tape** could be considered to be restraining – to create boundaries – within which movement becomes difficult. In dreams we become aware of the limitation we impose on ourselves in everyday life.

③ A way of recording life's processes, or of measuring spiritual progress would be signified either by a measuring or a recording tape.

Tapestry
– see Weaving

Tar

① Dreaming of **tar on the road** would suggest the potential to be trapped as we progress. Dreaming of **tar on a beach**, however, might suggest that we had allowed our emotions to become contaminated in some way.

② It would depend on the context of the dream whether the image of tar is appropriate or not. For instance to be **mending a road** might signify that we can be repairing wear and tear in our everyday lives. To be **tarring a fence** could mean we must protect ourselves. It will depend what is being done as to how we make the interpretation.

③ The symbolism of tar in a spiritual sense, because it is black and viscous, would suggest some kind of evil or negativity.

Target

① Aiming at a target in dreams would suggest we have a goal in mind. It would depend on the type of target what the goal is. To be **shooting at a bull's-eye** could be interpreted as a search for perfection. To be **aiming at a person** could suggest either hatred or sexual desire.

② Most of us need some kind of motivation in life, and a target as a symbol of our intellectual aspirations may not make much sense until we study the context of the dream. In a work sense **a sales target** might suggest our goals are imposed on us by others. On a more personal note if we were **setting someone else a target** in dreams, we would need to understand that the other person in the dream is a reflection of part of ourselves.

③ Spiritually a target can have the same significance as the mandala *(see Mandala)*, and represent the Self *(see Self)*.

Taste

① When something is not to our taste in a dream, it does not conform to our ideals and standards. To have a **bad taste** suggests that whatever is signified by what we are eating does not nourish us. To recognise that our **surroundings are in good taste** suggests an appreciation of beautiful things.

② In waking life we usually know what we like and what our personal standards are. In dreams those standards may be distorted in order to highlight a change. For instance, to discover that one likes a colour in a dream which would not normally be appreciated in real life could suggest that we need to study the new colour more fully in order to discover what it has to offer *(see Colour)*.

③ As we become more sensitive and aware, our taste becomes more refined. This is so in the spiritual realm, in that we appreciate finer, more beautiful things.

Tattoo

① On a physical level, a tattoo will stand for an aspect of individuality in us. We wish to be seen and appreciated as being different.

② A tattoo in dreams can also signify something which has left an indelible impression. This could be great hurt, but could also be a good memory. Sometimes, the **image which is tattooed** is worth interpreting if it can be seen clearly.

③ In spiritual terms a tattoo can suggest a group identity, belonging to a tribe or cult. It will be on a more intimate level than wearing a badge.

Tax

① In everyday life, a tax represents a sum of money exacted from us in return for the right to live a certain lifestyle. In dreams, therefore, having to **pay a tax** suggests some kind of a penalty or cost for living the way we choose.

② In real terms, a tax represents the extra amount of effort necessary to enable us to belong to society. Thus, dreaming of **car tax** would indicate that greater effort is needed to move forward. To be paying **income tax** suggests that we may feel we owe a debt to society. To be paying **council tax** may suggest that we feel we have to pay for the 'space' in which we exist. **Refusing to pay any taxes** suggests an unwillingness to conform.

③ Spiritually, any tax levied in a dream would indicate our attitude towards working for the greater, or communal, good. We need to take some responsibility for the universe we in which we live.

Taxi
– also see Car in Transport

① In a dream **calling a taxi** signifies recognising the need to progress – to get somewhere. We cannot be successful without help, for which there may be a price.

② A taxi is a public vehicle in the sense that it is usually driven by someone unknown to us. We therefore have to trust the driver's awareness and knowledge. In dreams, therefore, a taxi can suggest having the ability to get somewhere without knowing how.

③ A taxi can represent spiritual knowledge, coupled with practical know-how. This is an important attribute in personal development; allowing us the time for contemplation whilst still progressing.

Tea

① It will depend on whether the dream is about tea as **a commodity**, or a social occasion. On a practical level, tea as a commodity represents a unit of exchange, whereas the **social occasion** suggests inter-communication.

② The **Japanese tea ceremony** suggests a unique way of caring for and nurturing someone, as does **afternoon tea**. Dreaming of **tea cups** in particular links with the individual's need for divination (reading tea leaves). A **tea break in a work environment** suggests a need for rest and relaxation from concentration.

③ Tea as a symbol suggests spiritual refreshment and making an offering.

Teacher
– also see Education and School

① For many people, a teacher is the first figure of authority they meet outside the family. That person has a profound effect on the child and the teacher is often dreamt about in later years. Teachers can also generate conflict if their expressed views are very different to those learnt by the child at home. This may be something which has to be resolved through dreams in later years.

② When we are looking for guidance, our Anima or Animus *(see Anima/Animus)* can present itself in dreams as a teacher. Often the figure will be that of a **headmaster or headmistress** (someone who 'knows better').

③ A spiritual teacher usually appears either in dreams or in person when the individual is ready to progress. There is a saying 'when the *chela* (pupil) is ready, the teacher will come'. Often, that teacher will not appear as a Wise Old Man *(See Wise Old Man)* or woman, but as a person appropriate to the level of our understanding.

Teaching/Teachings
– also see Education, School and Teacher

① From a mundane perspective teaching is the passing on of information of things we need to know. Dreams are an efficient way of giving us such information and with practice can be used effectively to help ourselves and others.

② When we internalise information without necessarily being able to quantify it, it may come back in dreams in a teaching environment to enable us to bring it into conscious awareness.

③ The teachings of spiritual leaders and gurus tend to come to us in the form of holy books *(see Bible/Religious Texts)*. Those teachings which we receive intuitively and in dreams have the greatest relevance in our own search for spirituality. Often when we have received information in this way, with care we can validate the knowledge through other sources.

Tears

① Tears in dreams can indicate an emotional release and a cleansing. If **we are crying** we may not feel we are able to give way to emotion in everyday life, but can do so in the safe scenario of a dream. If we dream of **someone else in tears** we perhaps need to look at our own conduct to see if it is appropriate.

② To dream of **being in tears** and then to wake up and discover that we are actually crying, suggests that some hurt or trauma has come sufficiently close to the surface to enable us to deal with it on a conscious level.

③ Tears can represent hurt or compassion, and it is often this latter meaning which applies spiritually. Experiencing compassion in a dream can make us more aware of the necessity for it in waking life.

Teasing

① When we are **being teased** in a dream, we are becoming aware that our own behaviour may not be appropriate. If we are **teasing someone** and pointing out their idiosyncrasies, we may actually be highlighting our own discrepancies.

② Teasing can be a form of bullying, of becoming a victim. We need to understand our requirement to have power over someone, rather than helping them. Teasing will often arise from an insecurity and an awareness of our own doubts and fears. In archetypal terms it is an easy way to project our own difficulties onto other people around us.

③ Within spiritual development one becomes aware of others' faults of character. Teasing or being teased in dreams alerts us to an ego state which is not appropriate for further development.

Teeth
– see Body

Telegram
– also see Letter/Email

① Although now rather old-fashioned, **receiving a telegram** in a dream still highlights efficient communication. It indicates that a part of ourselves is attempting to give us information in a way that is going to be remembered. To be **sending a telegram** can suggest that we wish something to be known about ourselves that cannot be communicated verbally. Telegrams and other telegraphy services set the standard for electronic communication, so in dreams could be seen as a rather quaint method of communication.

② Previously, telegrams were messages of celebration or bad news. For many, that image is still retained in dreams. For instance, to receive **a telegram of wedding**

congratulations may link with our wish to be married. On the other hand, a **telegram bearing bad news** may be alerting us to something of which we are already aware on a subconscious level.

③ Any communication received in writing is to do with making knowledge, in this case spiritual knowledge, tangible.

Telephone

① **Using a telephone** in a dream suggests the ability to make contact with other people and to impart information we feel they may need. This could actually be communicating with someone in our ordinary everyday lives, or with a part of ourselves with which we are not totally in contact. **Being contacted by telephone** suggests there is information available which we do not already consciously know.

② When we are **aware of the telephone number we are ringing**, it may be the numbers that are important *(see Numbers)*. We also may be aware of the need to contact a specific person who we can help, or who can help us. If we are **searching for a telephone number** we are having difficulty in co-ordinating our thoughts about our future actions. Using the telephone suggests a direct one-to-one relationship. Using a **mobile phone** or one that is not fixed suggests a degree of freedom in our communication, though in dreams it can also represent the distractions of the mundane world.

③ Because communication via the telephone suggests that we are not able to see the recipient, using the telephone in a dream can signify communication with Spirit or with Guardian Angels.

Telescope

① Using a telescope in a dream suggests taking a closer look at something. A telescope enhances our view and makes it bigger and wider. We do need to make sure, however, that we are not taking a one-sided view of things.

② Using a telescope in a dream may mean that we should look at things with both a long- and short-term view. Without taking account of a long-term view, we may not be successful in the short term. Conversely, by looking at the long-term, we may be given information which will help us to 'navigate' our lives in the here and now.

③ Interestingly, a telescope in spiritual terms can signify the art of clairvoyance – the ability to perceive the future from an immediate perspective.

Television
– also see Celebrity, Fame and Media

① Like most modern forms of communication, television is so ubiquitous that it turns up frequently in dreams. It will represent information being brought to us,

427

though if we dream of appearing on television it suggests that we may have information which we feel is worth communicating to others.

② Entertainment is one way of communicating ideas and to dream of appearing on a reality or similar show suggests that we are prepared to stand up and be counted for our beliefs.

③ Communicating to a number of people either seen or unseen is very different to convincing other people on a one-to-one basis. A television can therefore symbolise such broadcasting to the masses, though interestingly it can also symbolise a message which is specifically designed for us.

Temple
– also see Church/Holy Buildings

① Often in dreams a temple can signify our own body. It is something to be treated with reverence and care. It has the same significance as a church since it is an object built to honour and pay respect to a god or gods.

② Psychologically, wherever there is a temple there is a sense of awe associated with creativity. Perhaps the biggest significance in dreams is the fact that it takes many to build one temple. This links with our awareness of the many facets of our personality which go to make a coherent whole.

③ Both as a sanctuary for human beings and as a place where the Divine resides, a temple reflects the beauty of Heaven. It is a microcosm (small picture) of what is, after all, infinite.

Temptation

① Temptation is a conflict between two different drives. For instance, in dreams we may experience a conflict between the need to go out into the world and the need to stay safe at home. Temptation is yielding to that which is easiest and not necessarily the best course of action.

② Intellectually, when presented with options of action we may tend to go for a result which gives short-term satisfaction, rather than long-term. The idea of giving in to temptation suggests that it is bigger or more powerful than we are. Often dreams can show us the course of action we should be taking.

③ Temptation is one of the biggest spiritual barriers we must overcome. Often it is a conflict between the Self *(see Self)* and the Ego *(See Introduction)*.

Tenant
– also see Rent

① To dream of **being a tenant when we are not so in waking life** suggests that at some level or another we do not want to take responsibility for the way we choose to live. We do not want to be burdened by having full responsibility. **To have a tenant** signifies that we are prepared to have someone live in our space. This may be the type of dream that occurs as we are preparing to become involved in a full-time relationship.

② If we follow up the idea of a tenant being someone with whom we have a commercial relationship, then we will have some insights into how we handle such transactions. **If the dreamer is a man and the tenant a woman** then the tenant is likely to represent his Anima *(see Anima/Animus)*. If **the situation is reversed** then the tenant will epitomise her Animus *(see Anima/Animus)*.

③ Dreaming of having a tenant in the spiritual sense can have two meanings. One would link with the idea that within us we have many personalities who must be synthesised into a holistic being. The other would suggest that tenants (inherited beliefs) can be evicted if they are inappropriate.

Tent

① A tent in a dream would suggest that we feel we are on the move, and not able to settle down and put down roots. Anywhere we settle is only going to be temporary. Actually **camping** suggests a fun activity which by its very nature is short-term.

② We perhaps need to get away from everyday responsibilities for a time, and rediscover our relationship with natural forces. There is benefit to be gained by being self-sufficient and not dependent on anyone.

③ The biblical and nomadic image of being able to pack up one's tent and steal away is the spiritual meaning here. We are not tied to any one place, but can be where we need to be at short notice.

Terror

① Terror in a dream is often the result of unresolved fears and doubts. It is only by experiencing such a profoundly disturbing emotion that are we likely to make an attempt to confront those fears. If **someone else is terrified** in our dream we are in a position to do something about it, and need to work out what course of action should be taken.

② Fear or terror dreams can be one of the triggers towards a deeper understanding of oneself. If we know we are fearful we can do something about it. Terror is more difficult to handle since in that state we will not know what the cause is. In the waking state it is possible to use a technique which will identify the terror. The statement which is made is 'I am terrified because...' followed by the immediate reason which comes to mind. Then work through each fresh statement until you come to a full stop. Thus:

'I am terrified because I have no money',

'I have no money because I spent it at the supermarket',

'I spent it at the supermarket because I have to eat',

'I have to eat because I'm afraid to die' and so on.

Gradually the meaning becomes clearer until there is a resolution.

③ Spiritual terror could be identified as a fear of evil, or a violation of our sacred space.

Terrorist
– also see Villain in Archetypes and Hijack

① From a mundane perspective, a terrorist is similar to the Archetypal Villain – that part of us that is totally self-involved and focused only on his own agenda. He does not care who he harms or hurts so long as his own needs are completely satisfied.

② Temperamentally the terrorist is that aspect of our own make-up which refuses to listen to reason and holds the more rational aspects to ransom. Selfish in make up his origins may be found in the child who would not conform to sensible constraints. Cold and calculating in dreams, he or she will manipulate circumstances until there is confrontation. We will sense treason when such acts threaten the fabric of society.

③ Spiritually a terrorist is the aspect of self belief which will not accept that there can be other ways of achieving a particular goal. Prepared to hijack any situation for his own beliefs he can also be perceived as the fanatic.

Tests
– also see Exams/Being Examined

① Dreaming of tests of any sort can indicate some form of self-assessment. **Medical tests** may be alerting us to the need to watch our health. **A driving test** would suggest a test of confidence or ability, whereas a **written test** would signify a test of knowledge.

② Testing something in a dream suggests that there has been some form of standard set, to which we feel we must adhere. This need not mean that we are setting ourselves against others, simply that we have resolved to maintain a certain standard.

③ A spiritual test is one that is created from the circumstances around us perhaps to test our resolve.

Text

① A text is taken to mean a collection of words which have a certain specific meaning. For a text such as this to appear in a dream would signify the need for encouragement and perhaps wisdom.

② **Text from a book** or a **text of a play** would indicate the need to carry out instructions in a particular way in order to achieve success. A **text message** as a quick, modern way of communication shows we need to be forward thinking in our actions.

③ A spiritual text is an encouraging message to enable us to progress. It may contain relevant wisdom.

Thaw
– also see Melt

① In dreams, to be conscious of a thaw is to note a change in our own emotional responses. We no longer have a need to be as emotionally distanced as we were previously.

② Psychologically we have the ability to 'warm up' a situation, and to melt coldness away. If we are aware of coldness within ourselves, on an emotional level we need to discover what the problem is or was, and work out why we have reacted as we did.

③ A spiritual thaw would suggest the ability to come to terms with old barriers and to become warm and loving.

Theatre
– also see Stage

① In dreams about the theatre it will depend which part of the theatre is highlighted. If it is **the stage**, then a situation that we are in at this particular moment is being highlighted. If it is **the auditorium**, then our ability to listen is significant. The play we create in our dreams as an aspect of our lives is particularly relevant. If we are **not involved in the action**, it indicates we are able to stand back and take an objective viewpoint.

② The theatre is a scenario which has meaning for many. Because it is a social venue, it has relevance in people's relationships with one another. It is this aspect which is being highlighted. To be **in the spotlight**, for instance, might signify our need to be noticed. To be up in **'the gods'** might suggest that we need to take a long-term view of a situation.

③ Spiritually the idea of a play in a dream highlights the idea of the microcosm within the macrocosm – the small within a larger framework.

Thermometer

① A thermometer in a dream will be representative of judging our warmth and feelings. We may be uncertain of how we come across to other people and need some kind of outside measurement. A **clinical thermometer** would portray our emotional warmth, whereas an **external thermometer** would suggest our intellectual abilities.

② Psychologically we sometimes need an external evaluation as to where we are coming from. A thermometer would be a reassurance device.

③ Just as a thermometer measures temperature, the way we handle situations around us will give indications of our spiritual health and ability and the passion we can generate.

Thief/Theft
– also see Burglar, Intruder and Stealing

① Dreaming of a thief links with our fear of losing things, or of having them taken away. We may be afraid of losing love or possessions.

② When a thief appears in dreams, we are aware of part of our personality which can waste our own time and energy on meaningless activity. It is quite literally stealing from us.

③ The thief in the spiritual sense is the Trickster *(see Trickster)*, the villain, who 'steals' our respects for Self and will not allow us the sanctuary of our own beliefs.

Thigh
– see Limbs in Body

Third Eye
– see Eye of God in Religious Iconology

Thirst

① Dreaming of **being thirsty** suggests we have an unsatisfied inner need; we may be emotionally at a low ebb and need something to give us a boost. Anything that gives us emotional satisfaction – whether short- or long-term – would suffice.

② To **satisfy a thirst** indicates we are capable of satisfying our own desires. By being prepared to take in what we need, we are able to experience life in the best way possible. If we are thirsty in a dream, we need to look very carefully at either what we are being denied, or what we are denying ourselves, in waking life.

③ Thirst is symbolic of our thirst for spiritual knowledge and enlightenment. It may well be an unquenchable thirst.

Thistle

① To be conscious of thistles in a dream is to be aware of some discomfort in waking life. **A field of thistles** would suggest a difficult road ahead. **A single thistle** would indicate minor difficulties.

② The thistle has a meaning of defiance and vindictiveness. When dreaming of a thistle we may be being made aware of those qualities, either in people around us or in ourselves. The colour of the thistles may be important *(see Colour)*.

③ The thistle can represent our spiritual defiance when faced with physical adversity.

Thorn

① To dream of **being pierced by a thorn or splinter** signifies that a minor difficulty has got through our defences. If the **thorn draws blood**, we need to look at what is happening in our lives which could make us vulnerable. In a woman's dream this could represent the sexual act, or rather, fear of intercourse.

② The thorn stands for physical suffering in dreams. In matters of health, it may indicate a vulnerability to infection.

③ The thorn may signify that we are dedicating ourselves to some element of our spiritual quest. The Christian emblem of the **crown of thorns** indicates suffering for our beliefs.

Thread

① Thread in dreams represents a line of thought, enquiry or communication. In terms of our ordinary everyday lives we perhaps need to follow that line to its end. **Threading a needle** has an obvious sexual reference. It can also, because of the perceived difficulty in threading a needle, suggest incompetence in ways other than sexual.

② To be aware of thread is to be aware of the way our lives are going. **A tangled thread** suggests a difficulty which needs unravelling. **A spool of thread** suggests an ordered existence. The colour of the thread is important *(see Colour)*. **A basket full of spools** suggests the various aspects of a woman's personality. This is because of its association with the Archetypal feminine.

③ The various lines of spiritual enquiry we have need to be interwoven in order to achieve wholeness.

Threshold

① Crossing the threshold in dreams indicates new experiences. To be being **lifted across a threshold** may suggest marriage, or in this day and age, a new relationship.

② When we are about to take on new responsibilities we can dream of **standing on the threshold**. We may be moving into a new life, or perhaps a new way of living. The threshold experience is a strong one in Masonic imagery and Initiation rites. Even in Parliament, permission must be asked to cross the threshold.

③ We may be standing on the threshold of a new spiritual dawn. We should be particularly astute at this time and be aware of all that is around us.

Throat
– see Body

Throne

① When we dream of **sitting on a throne**, we are acknowledging our right to take authority. When the **throne is empty**, we are not prepared to accept the responsibility for who we are. It may be that we are conscious of a lack of parenting. When **someone else is on the throne**, we may have passed over authority to others in our waking life.

② A throne is a seat of authority or power. In dreams it can represent our ability to belong to groups, or even to society. We may need to take the lead in a project or scheme. The throne usually suggests that we have attained control on all levels of existence, both spiritually and physically.

③ Spiritually we are now at a point where knowledge and understanding are finally within our grasp.

Thumb
– see Body

Thunder/Thunderbolts
– also see Lightning and Storm

① **Hearing thunder** in a dream can give a warning for the potential of an emotional outburst. We may be building up energy which eventually must reverberate. Hearing **thunder in the distance** signifies that there is still time to gain control of a potentially difficult situation.

② Thunder has always been a symbol of great power and energy. In conjunction with lightning, it was seen as a tool of the gods. It could bring doom and disaster, but also was cleansing.

③ Spiritually, the rumblings of thunder can demonstrate deep anger, or in extreme cases Divine anger. Thunder is one of the tools of the Norse God, Thor.

Tiara
– see Crown and Diadem

Ticket

① If we dream of tickets, it will depend on what type of ticket it is as to the interpretation. Generally, a ticket suggests that there is a price to pay for something. A **bus ticket** would indicate that there is a price for moving forward, as might a **train ticket**. A **ticket to a theatre or cinema** may suggest we need to take a back seat and be objective over a part of our lives. Tickets to **a football or rugby match** might mean that we will have to pay for some area of conflict in our lives.

② One interpretation of a ticket – in the form of a **certificate or voucher** – is that of us requiring recognition for the effort we have put in. To dream of **receiving such a ticket** indicates it is we who are being recompensed. If **we are giving someone else a ticket or voucher** we are recognising that we have received external help.

③ Spiritually a dream of a ticket will symbolise our recognition that all knowledge must be somehow paid for.

Tide
– also see Sea in Water

① Dreaming of a tide is attempting to go with the ebb and flow of life, or, rather more specifically, with the emotions. As a tide also removes debris, the symbolism of cleansing is relevant. A **high tide** may symbolise high energy, whereas a **low tide** would suggest a drain on our abilities or energy.

② In waking life there are two times in the year when there are very high tides – the Spring and the Autumn *(see Seasons)*. Thus, in dreams an exceptionally high tide might signify those times. **A moon over a moving tide** would, at a certain stage of development, suggest the powers of the feminine.

③ Spiritually, it may well be a simple image such as the tide turning which indicates that we are finding our way.

Tiger
– see Animals

Till
– also see Money

① There are two meanings of 'till'. One is to **till the ground**, and while that is a less potent images nowadays the image still appears in dreams in the sense of cultivating opportunities. The other meaning is as **a safe repository for money**. It is this symbolism of a commercial transaction which is the one most understood.

② When we put money in a till, it is being put there for safe keeping. However, it is also being put there to accumulate. It will increase and work for itself. This is where the more practical and psychological meanings coincide. We need to save or conserve what we have to get best benefit.

③ A till is symbolic of what we have accumulated spiritually being stored up, until such a time as we need to look at it more carefully.

Timber
– see Wood

Time

① For time to be significant in a dream there is usually the necessity to measure it in some way, or to use a period of time as a measurement. Usually we are only aware of the passage of time, or that a particular time is meaningful in the dream – it is part of the dream scenario. On consideration, the time in the dream may symbolise a particular time in one's life. **The daylight hours** will thus suggest our conscious waking life. **Where several days (or other long periods) pass**, some other activity which is not relevant to us has been going on. **The hours of the day** could refer to a time of our life or it may simply be the number which is important *(see Numbers)*. **Afternoon** This is a time of life when we can put our experience to good use. **Evening** The end of life highlights our ability to be more relaxed about our lives and activities. **Midday** When midday is suggested we are fully conscious and aware of our activities. **Morning** The first part of our life or our early experience is being highlighted. **Night** may be a period of depression or secrecy. We may be introspective or simply at rest. **Twilight** can indicate a period of uncertainty and possible ambivalence about our direction in life. It may also suggest a period of transition such as death.

② **To be early** for an appointment in a dream suggests having to wait for something to happen before we can carry on our lives. **Being late** shows our lack of attention to detail or the feeling that time is running out. **Watching the clock** indicates the necessity to make time work for us.

③ The passage of time is often represented by a clock or Father Time and thus in spiritual terms suggests change or death.

Titans
– see Giant

Toad
– see Animals

Tobacco
– also see Smoke/Smoking

① Tobacco appearing in dreams will have different meanings depending on whether we are a smoker or not. **If a smoker**, then tobacco, in the dream, is probably a comfort tool. **If not**, then the symbolism is probably more to do with the idea of using tobacco to achieve a particular state of mind. If we are **smoking a pipe**, there may be issues of masculinity to deal with.

② It is said that Native Americans use tobacco to drive away bad spirits, and it is true that initially tobacco will give the person a mood lift. In dreams it is this symbolism of change which is the meaningful one.

③ Tobacco as a giver of visions may be the symbolism here. We may be interested in the idea of spirituality and wish to explore it, but as yet have not found the right stimulation.

Toilet

① For many people the toilet has been until recently a symbol for dirt and lack of appreciation. There has also been the inevitable association with sexuality. Nowadays the symbolism is much more to do with notions of privacy, and the ability to reach a state where we can release our feelings in private.

② **Something wrong with the toilet** could suggest that we are emotionally blocked. Going to an **unfamiliar toilet** suggests we are in a position where we do not know what the outcome to a situation will be. **Cleaning a dirty toilet** suggests we are losing our 'prudish' attitude.

③ Spiritually, a toilet suggests we have the means at our disposal to cleanse away the negative. As an enclosed space it represents the ability to deal with our detritus.

Tomb
– also see Catacomb/Crypt

① **Going into a tomb** suggests going down into the darker parts of our own personality. We may be fearful to begin with, but later become more at ease. Finding ourselves **in a tomb** suggests we are ready to face our fears of death and dying.

② If we are **trapped in a tomb** in a dream we may be trapped by fear, pain or old outdated attitudes in our waking life. If there are **bodies in the tomb**, these are usually parts of ourselves we have either not developed or have killed off. If **one of those bodies comes alive**, the attention we have given to that aspect of our personality has been sufficient to resurrect it.

③ Spiritually we may feel that we have entered into a world that is all at once mysterious and dark – dark in the sense of wanting to see the light. Although we fear it, we are also excited. It is worth remembering that we are not trapped, but in a brief state of panic which can be overcome by belief.

Toner/Ink
– also see Pen/Pencil

① Since very few people now use fountain pens, the significance of ink on a physical level is no longer quite so valid. Formerly in dreams it suggested the ability to communicate in a lucid, clear and concise fashion. Today, toner ink may well have the same significance. Changing toner suggests looking at things from a different perspective.

② On a more intellectual level, ink signifies the ability to transcribe and understand knowledge in a more sophisticated way. Toner or ink cartridges in dreams can signify stored knowledge or the potential for understanding.

③ More spiritually, ink has significance, particularly in magical practices, when it was used to reflect powers which were outside the norm. In written magical spells it was necessary to use particular inks in order to achieve the required results. Often the colour will be significant *(See Colour)*.

Tongue
– see Body

Tools

① Tools appearing in dreams suggests there are practical methods at our disposal for enhancing our lifestyle and way of being.

② Each tool will have its own significance. **A drill** suggests working through emotions and fears as well as attitudes which have become hardened. **A hammer** provides the energy to break down old patterns of behaviour and resistances. **A saw** suggests being able to cut through all the rubbish we have accumulated in order to make something new. A **clamp** suggests tenacity whereas a **vehicle clamp** signifies some impediment to progress.

③ Spiritual tools which can be symbolised in a practical way are love, compassion and charity.

Top
– see Position

Torch

① In dreams, a torch can represent self-confidence. It can also suggest the need to be able to move forward, but at the same time carry our own light.

② A torch can be used not only for ourselves, but also for other people. Dreaming of a torch shows we can have the confidence to know that, because of our own knowledge, we have the ability to see the way forward.

③ We may feel that we need some spiritual guidance, and this can sometimes be symbolised as a torch.

Tornado

① A tornado appearing in a dream is a symbol of violent energy of one sort or another. Often it is emotions and feelings against which we feel powerless. It is a recognisable symbol of energy which has turned in on itself, and has therefore become destructive.

② While a tornado can be very destructive, interestingly, it can also be very cleansing and it is in this context that it is often met on a psychological level. It sweeps all in front of it, but after its passage there is the potential for new life.

③ Our early ventures into spirituality may make us feel powerless, and at the mercy of all the elements. This can be symbolised by the tornado. However, within the centre there is peace and tranquillity.

Torpedo

① The torpedo, because of its shape, has obvious connections with masculine aggressiveness. Its power in dreams can be destructive, but often is unconscious in origin.

② In terms of being able to home in on its target, the torpedo suggests directed energy. This may be the type of honest getting to the point which we can do with friends, or it may be a warning that such directness could be harmful.

③ A torpedo is symbolic of spiritual directness. We should be aware of taking the correct action for the circumstances in which we find ourselves.

Tortoise

① The tortoise for most people suggests slowness but also perhaps thoroughness. It also in dreams signifies a shell, that perhaps we – or others round us – have put up in order to protect or defend ourselves.

② The tortoise may of course simply be an image of a pet *(See Pet)* as an object which is loved. It may also however be a symbol for long life.

③ In Chinese lore the tortoise is a revered figure of wisdom and knowledge. He is said to carry the pattern of all existence on his back. He also represents Creation.

Torture

① Pain in any form can become magnified in a dream and be experienced as torture. This magnification is designed by the dreaming self to highlight a problem that needs dealing with immediately. Man's inhumanity to man through torture of the innocent can result in the spread of negativity and powerlessness.

② Since a component of torture is the mental agony that it inflicts, we will experience images of torture when the conscious mind cannot find a way to lessen the difficulty that it is experiencing. When we bring the dream images into full consciousness we can often find a way through.

③ Spiritual anguish is caused by our own reaction to extreme sorrow. We suffer for our own inability to overcome distress. Whilst we may be brave enough to accommodate any other kind of torture, anguish often has a positive outcome in that having come through it we have renewed inner strength.

Totem/Totem pole

① In a dream a totem pole links us back to a primitive need for protection. It is not the protection afforded by a father, but by those spirits whose energy is powerful enough to be used by us.

② When an object revered as a sacred article is given enough power by a joint belief, the thing itself is perceived as taking on a power of its own. One such object is the totem pole. When it appears in dreams we need to be looking at those parts of our lives which are based around our belief system to discover whether we are really living according to those beliefs.

③ Both in its symbolic meaning of a protector and as a representative of spiritual matters, the totem pole suggests strength and power.

Touch

① Touch in dreams suggests making contact in some way. We are linking up with other people, usually to our mutual advantage. We are perhaps becoming conscious of both our need for other people and of their need for us.

② Within relationships, touch can be an important act of appreciation. Often dreams will reveal our attitude to such concepts as touching and being touched.

③ The transference of power and Spiritual blessing can be signified by the simple act of touching.

Tourist/Tourism
– also see Journey

① A tourist in a dream is someone who does not have enough information to know his way around. If **we are the tourist** then we need to look at that aspect within ourselves. If **someone else is the tourist** then we need to be aware of what help we can give other people.

② To play the tourist in a dream is to be aware of the fact that we have the necessary information to do what we want, but that we are choosing not to. To be associated with the tourism industry in dreams suggests that we are able to take advantage of opportunities to enable us to get away from the mundane.

③ The tourist in a dream in spiritual terms represents the hermit, the willing traveller *(see Hermit)*. Tourism *per se* signifies our ability to help people to undertake their own spiritual journey of exploration.

Tower
– also see Buildings

① A tower in a dream usually represents a construction which we have developed in our lives. This may be an inner attitude or an outer life. To dream of **a tower with no door** suggests we are out of touch with our inner selves. **A tower with no windows** signifies that we are unable to see and appreciate either our external good points or our inner ones. An ivory tower suggests an innocent approach. A **square tower** signifies a practical approach to life, whereas a **round tower** is more spiritually geared. A **round tower at the end of a square building** is the combination of the practical and spiritual.

② Psychologically if we are to live life as fully as we can, we need to understand our own tower. In dreams it may appear initially as far away and later coming closer. How we get into the tower may be important. **Shallow steps** would indicate that to explore our inner self may be easy. More **difficult steps** may indicate that we are fairly private individuals. If the **door is barred** we are not ready to explore our unconscious self. If the **door is closed** we must make an effort to get in. If **inside the tower is dark**, we are still afraid of our subconscious. We, having been given these suggestions, should be able to interpret other symbolism. The **hidden room in the tower** would have the same significance as in a house *(see House)*.

③ The tower is rather ambivalent in the spiritual sense, since it can be feminine in the shelter it affords and masculine because of its shape. It suggests ascent to the spiritual realms, but also descent to the practical.

Town
– see City/Town

Toy

① When there are toys in a dream we may be aware of children around us, or of our more childlike selves. Toys will highlight the creative side of ourselves, and the more playful innocent part.

② Perhaps we need to look at the types of toys which appear. They often give some indication of what we are playing with. We may be mulling over new ideas or new ways of relating to others. Equally we need to 'play' more, to relax and have fun.

③ Toys appearing in a dream may be alerting us to our ability to create our own lives. Just as a child will imagine himself creating his own little world through his toys, so also can we as dreamers and creators.

Track
– see Path and also Train in Transport

Train
– see Transport

Traitor

① To dream of a traitor suggests that one is subconsciously aware of deviousness. This may be in someone else, or it could be a part of our personality which is letting us down. We may feel that our standards are not appreciated by others.

② When in a dream we are betrayed by others and believe them to have let us down, we are perhaps aware of the fact that it is with through shared belief in waking life that this has happened.

③ Spiritually, to be a traitor is to deny our basic belief.

Tramp
– also see Archetypes

① To dream of a tramp in the sense of a decrepit old wanderer links us back to the part of ourselves which is not expressed fully in real life. It is the 'drop-out' or gypsy within us. We may be becoming conscious of our need or desire for irresponsibility.

② The tramp personifies in us the wanderer, the freedom lover. In dreams he will often appear at a time when we need freedom, but can also show that that need can bring difficulty and sadness. He can also appear in dreams as the jester or fool. There is a part in all of us that is anarchical, and the tramp represents this side.

③ Spiritually, although this image starts out as negative, if we are prepared to work with it, it can have great positivity – since ultimately he is always in the right place at the right time for the right reasons, and often matures into the hermit *(see Hermit)*.

Transfiguration

① For something to be transfigured in dreams suggests that that image has a greater significance than just its symbolism. Transfiguration usually means being surrounded by light, and for this to happen suggests that it has some divine or special purpose. This dream can occur as we are working through stages of transition in our lives.

② Transfiguration is a phenomenon which can occur during altered states of consciousness. It is as though a light enters the personality and changes it. For transfiguration to occur in dreams indicates we are becoming conscious of a more permanent awareness of ourselves. In the waking state it is taken to suggest one is being used as a spiritual channel.

③ Spiritually, we are aware that we are all part of a greater whole, that we possess an inner core of spiritual.

Transformation

① Dreams where obvious changes occur and things are transformed into something else suggests a shift in awareness. A landscape may change from dark to light (negativity to positivity), a person may change from masculine to feminine or one image may change into another. Once we understand the change is for the better, we are able to accomplish changes in our own life.

② As the growth to maturity takes place, there are many transformations which occur. These are often depicted in dreams as immediate changes, like a speeded-up camera filming an opening flower.

③ Transformation takes place in spiritual terms when freedom of thought or action is indicated, or when the higher impulses are substituted for lower reactions.

Transparent

① When something is transparent in a dream we may be feeling vulnerable, but may also be aware of insights we would not normally have. **To be inside a transparent bubble**, for instance, would suggest visibility and vulnerability in our lives, perhaps taking on new responsibilities. For someone else to be **behind a transparent shield** suggests they are somewhat remote and unavailable to us.

② When we are aware in dreams that things around us are transparent, we recognise our ability to 'see through' things. We are able to be discerning in our judgement.

③ Transparency in the spiritual sense represents honesty and integrity – both for ourselves and others.

Transport

① The transport we are using in our dreams indicates how we are moving through this specific period of our lives. In old style dream interpretation the horse was used as an image to depict how we dealt with life. Nowadays the car, the aeroplane or other vehicles have come into prominence. If in our dreams we are with friends, we may wish to look at group goals. If we do not know the other people we may need to explore our ability to make social relationships, or there could be some fresh experiences coming our way.

② The vehicle or mode of transport which appears in our dreams often conforms with the view we hold of ourselves in our everyday lives. We may, for instance, be driving a very utilitarian car rather than a Rolls Royce, or driving a sports car or little runaround. Such images may represent either our physical body or the facade we present to the world. The most frequently appearing dream images are:

Aeroplane An aeroplane suggests a swift easy journey with some attention to detail being necessary. Interestingly, the aeroplane can symbolise a new awareness of spiritual matters, or more mundanely a new intimate relationship. An *airport* signifies a state of transition.

Ambulance Dreaming of an ambulance has much the same significance as a lorry. However, it also suggests that professional assistance offered in a timely fashion is available when we are having difficulties in waking life.

Bicycle As a representation of duality, the bicycle represents achieving a balance between the physical and the spiritual. It also signifies using the correct energy to propel us forward in order to succeed. In today's society, the bicycle may also stand for the principles of correct conservation and proper management of resources.

Boats/Ships It will depend on what kind of boat is depicted as to the interpretation, thus a small *rowing boat* would suggest an emotional journey, which requires a great deal of effort. A *yacht* might suggest a similar sort of journey, but one done with style, whereas a large ship such as a *cruise liner* would suggest creating new horizons but in the company of others. On the other hand, a *speedboat* might represent an adventurous spirit, and a *canoe* a different personally challenging way of working. A *ferry* holds all the symbolism of the ancient myth of the journey across the River Styx after death. It symbolizes the giving up of selfish desires. After such a journey we may be 'reborn' into a better life, or way of life. A ferry journey may also represent a transition in our lives. If we *miss the boat* we either not have enough information or not paid enough attention to detail in a project in our waking lives. Interestingly, it is thought that ships are referred to as 'she' through respect and love. A boat of any sort may therefore in dreams be taken to represent the feminine.

Bus (also see individual entry) A bus journey in dreams has a great deal to do with our public image in waking life. It signifies the impetus which enables us to be with other people with whom we share the need to be making progress. It is a shared journey with a common aim. *Getting on the wrong bus* or perhaps *going in the wrong direction* shows that there are conflicting needs and desires within us. This is usually a warning of a wrong action and we need to be aware of our own inner intuition. *Trouble with timetables* – missing the bus, arriving too early, missing a connection etc. – indicate that we are having difficulty prioritising things in our waking lives. We should perhaps take time to re-evaluate the way we are living and how we want to live our lives in the future. Dreaming of *not being able to pay the fare* shows that we do not have enough resources to set out on a particular course of action.

Car The car in dreams epitomises our sense of self. It is a reflection of how we handle life, and the image we wish to project to other people. It also mirrors the physical body, so anything wrong with the car can help alert us to a problem or difficulty. If the *starting motor is not working* this would suggest that we need help to start a project, or that we lack motivation. The way that an *engine* runs represents our instinctive drives, life force or basic motivation. If it runs *too fast* we may be expending unnecessary effort, whereas *too slow* suggests we have not enough power to achieve our objectives. If the *engine* of our particular car is not working properly we are literally feeling 'run down'. When we perceive that *something is wrong* with the engine it also may indicate the beginning of a health problem of which we are not consciously aware. It should be relatively easy to decipher the symbolism of dreams about cars with relevance to our own lives. The *back tyres* might suggest our 'rear end', the *steering wheel* the way we control our lives. If the *brakes are not working* we are probably not exerting proper control over our lives. Perceiving that there are *too many people in the car* would suggest that we feel overloaded by responsibility.

Lorry/Commercial vehicle It will depend on the type of vehicle as to its correct interpretation. A *lorry* in a dream will generally have much the same meaning a car, except that the drives and ambitions will be linked more with work and how we relate on a business basis to the outside world. A *commercial van* for instance suggests shorter, more intensive periods of activity, whereas something like a *flatbed truck* may represent similar activities of longer duration.

Motorbike/Motorcycle Imaging independent behaviour, blatant masculinity and daring, the motorbike can also be a symbol of freedom. If in dreams the rider is a woman the motorcycle can suggest an independence of spirit and the ability to blend logic (a masculine quality) and intuition (a feminine one) in order to be ahead of the pack. A *group of motorcyclists* will symbolise camaraderie with like-minded individuals. If however the riders are *Hell's Angels*, this would tend to suggest a degree of anarchical behaviour.

Train A train, being a method of public transport, brings our attitude to relationships and how we react with others into prominence and clarifies our behaviour in public. A *modern-day train* might suggest a degree of speed and efficiency, while a *steam train* would denote a romanticised, perhaps outdated way of working. An *underground train* may indicate exploring the unconscious. We dream of actually *catching the train* we have successfully achieved a particular goal and circumstances have gone our way. If we *miss the train*, however, we may be missing an opportunity and do not have the resources immediately available to enable us to succeed. Equally we may feel that external circumstances are imposing an element of unwanted control over us. Often dreams of *missing a train and then – in the same dream – catching either it or a later train*, suggest that we are managing our inner resources more successfully. Dreams of *missing a train alternating with dreams of catching one* show that we are trying to sort out our motivation. *Getting off the train before it starts* suggests we have changed our minds about a situation in waking life. *Getting off the train before it reaches our destination* means that we have doubts about our ability to succeed at a particular project. *Railway lines and tracks* will have relevance as ways of getting us to our destination or final goal. *Being conscious of the way the track is laid*, for instance whether it turns right or left ahead, may give us an inkling as to which way we should be proceeding. *Turning right* generally suggests acting appropriately, whereas *turning left* indicates that there may be difficulties ahead. *Coming off the rails* might suggest acting in an inappropriate way, or that something has gone wrong. *Not wanting to be on the train* might suggest we feel we are being unduly affected by external circumstances or are being forced into some kind of action. *Arriving at the station by train* indicates we have completed a particular stage of our life journey. It may be that we now feel ready for new relationships and experiences. The *carriages* on a train suggest the various facets of our lives and the way we feel about them. For example, if a carriage is *untidy or dirty*, we should be aware that we need to 'clean up' an aspect of our lives.

Trams combine the best of several types of transport, although are seen by some as out-dated. They run on rails, as do trains, and are motivated by an external source of energy. In dreams, therefore, they will indicate controlled efficient movement as well as an often predetermined destination. They also represent an efficient use of resources.

Walk If in our dreams we are conscious of walking as opposed to using a mechanised form of transport, it usually suggests that we are capable of achieving results at that particular time on our own. In dreams, deliberately going for a walk (a symbol of a short journey) shows that we can enjoy the process of recharging our batteries and clearing our minds.

③ From a spiritual perspective, transport and how we use such resources symbolise those inner aspects of our personalities. In dreams, it is an indication of how we can either make life easier or more problematic for ourselves.

Transvestism
– see Sex

Trap/Trapped

① To be **in a trap** in a dream signifies that we feel we are trapped by outside circumstances. To be aware of **trapping something or someone** is attempting to hold onto them. To be **trapping a butterfly** is to be trying to capture the inner self.

② When we feel trapped in dreams, we are not usually able to break free of old patterns of thought and behaviour. We need outside help to enable us to break though emotional difficulties.

③ Spiritually we are holding ourselves back. We may also be aware of being trapped by the restrictions of the physical body. When this happens it is worth exploring the Eastern disciplines and martial arts.

Travelling
– see Journey

Treason
– see Betray/Betrayal and Terrorist

Treasure

① Treasure in dreams always represents something which is of value to us. It is the result of personal achievement and effort. To **find buried treasure** is to find something we have lost, perhaps a part of our personality. To be **burying treasure** is to be trying to guard against the future and potential problems.

② To **find a box which has treasure in it** is to have some understanding of the fact that we must break through limitations before we find what we are looking for. The **search for treasure** suggests the finding of earthly goods or material gain which will not necessarily be good.

③ To search for treasure symbolises Man's search for enlightenment, his search for the Holy Grail (see Holy Grail).

Tree
– also see Forest and Wood

① The tree is symbolic in dreams of the basic structure of our inner lives. When one appears in our dreams it is best to work with the image fairly extensively. A tree with **wide branches** would suggest a warm loving personality, whereas a **small close-leafed** tree would suggest an uptight personality. A **well-shaped** tree would suggest a well-ordered personality, while a **large, messy tree** would suggest a chaotic personality. There is a game which can be played in waking life if one dares. Ask a friend a) what sort of tree does he or she think you are, and b) what sort of tree they think they are. The results are interesting. An oak for instance would represent strength.

② The roots of a tree are said to show our connection with ourselves and the earth. It could be more accurate to suggest that they signify our ability to belong to the practical side of life, to enjoy being here. **Spreading roots** would indicate an ability to relate well to the physical, and, conversely, **deep-rootedness** would suggest a more self-contained attitude. The trunk of the tree gives an indication of how we use the energies available to us, and also what exterior we present to the world. A **rough trunk** suggests obviously a rough and ready personality, whereas a **smoother trunk** would indicate more sophistication. **Branches** signify the stages of growth we go through, and leaves suggest the way we communicate to the rest of the world. To be **climbing the tree** suggests we are looking at our hopes and abilities, in order to succeed.

③ Spiritually the tree symbolises the Tree of Life and represents the union of heaven, earth and water. When we learn and understand our own Tree we are able to live life successfully on all levels.

Trespassing

① When we find **ourselves trespassing** in a dream, we are perhaps intruding on someone's personal space in waking life. This may also suggest that there is a part of ourselves which is private and feels vulnerable. We should learn to respect those boundaries.

② If it is **our space or area which is being trespassed upon**, then we need to look at our own boundaries. Sometimes it is interesting when interpreting the dream to find out whether the trespasser is there voluntarily or involuntarily. We can then work out whether we are the victim or not.

③ Spiritually we are approaching areas of knowledge where we cannot go without spiritual permission.

Trial
– see Judgement and Jury

Triangle
– see Shapes/Patterns

Trickster
– also see Villian in Archetypes

① In dreams, the trickster is literally that part of ourselves which can create havoc in our lives. When under stress this personage can present himself in dreams as the character who points one in the wrong direction, answers questions with the wrong answers etc.

② Psychologically, if we have been too rigid in our attitude to life – for instance, struggling to be good the whole time or continually taking a moral stance, the trickster can appear in dreams as a counter-balance.

③ This is the spiritually irresponsible part of our nature. We have not yet put ourselves on the correct spiritual path and need to do so.

Trophy

① Dreaming of a trophy is to recognise that we have done something for which we can be rewarded. It depends on what the trophy is for as to its significance. The trophy will take on the significance of the object being presented. A **cup** would suggest receptivity *(see Cup)* and a **shield** *(see Shield)*, protection. A common dream that men have is the presentation of a football cup or trophy of some sort. They are the 'first among men'.

② Formerly trophies such as animal heads were much sought after. This is no longer so, but the symbolism of overcoming one's basic fears in order to achieve still remains.

③ A trophy would signify a Peak Experience (having moved into an expanded state of awareness) in order to achieve a spiritual goal.

Trumpet

① A trumpet in a dream will most often suggest either a warning or a 'call to arms'. From a practical point of view it will be alerting us to some danger we have put ourselves in or are facing. When there is conflict around us we may need some kind of warning to be ready for action and a trumpet can be one such symbol.

② Representations of angels are often shown blowing trumpets. This represents the call to maximise one's potential. We reach for the best within ourselves in order to have the maximum effect in our lives.

③ The trumpet sounds a spiritual vibration which requires awareness.

Trunk

① In previous times to dream of a trunk was supposed to foretell a long journey. Nowadays, as people tend to travel light, it is much more likely to represent a repository for old things and hence signify old out-dated ideas.

② We have the ability to store all sorts of rubbish – both physically and mentally. When a trunk appears in a dream it is time to 'open the box' and have the courage to sort out what is there. Often, when one is ready to do this but does not do so, the image of the trunk will appear over and over again. To find a **jewel in a trunk** indicates the good that can be found in doing a personal spring-clean.

③ Dreaming of a trunk indicates that spiritually we need to explore our hidden depths to get the best out of ourselves.

Tug of War

① To dream of a tug of war suggests some sort of conflict between good and bad, male and female, positive and negative.

② A tug of war may indicate the need to maintain balance through tension between opposites. To be on the **winning side** suggests that what we wish to achieve can be achieved with help. To be on **the losing side** requires us to identify the parallel situation in ordinary everyday life and decide whether to continue.

③ A spiritual tug of war suggests the need to resolve the conflict between whatever two opposites are presenting themselves.

Tumble
– see Fall

Tunnel

① A tunnel in a dream usually represents the need to explore our own unconscious and those things we have left untouched.

② A tunnel in dreams is supposed at times to represent the birth canal and therefore the process of birth. If there is a **light at the end of the tunnel**, it indicates we are reaching the final stages of our exploration. If **something is blocking the tunnel**, then some past fear or experience is stopping us from progressing.

③ Spiritually, the image of a tunnel both helps us to escape from the unconscious into the light and also to go down into the depths.

Turf
– also see Arena

① To dream of being on 'sacred' turf – ground that is revered because of its association, perhaps a sportsground or arena – is to wish for supreme success in our endeavours.

② Dreaming of our association with a particular piece of ground can activate memories and feelings connected with happy times. This may, by recollection, help to clarify a particular problem or situation.

③ Sacred or hallowed ground of any sort would be represented by turf in a dream.

Turkey
– see Birds

Tutorial
– also see Education, Teacher, Teaching/Teachings and School

① A tutorial implies one-to-one or small group teaching, so in the mundane sense will signify a need for us to understand particular ideas and concepts. If we are **teaching a tutorial** then we have specific knowledge which is useful to others. If we are **taking part in a tutorial** in dreams we are being given explicit information we need in the waking world.

② As tutorials generally concentrate on one particular aspect of knowledge, in dreams it is the specialness of the subject, the individuality of the participants and the ability of the teacher which will be of note. Equally, such a dream may highlight how we relate to groups and to group dynamics.

③ The learning of spiritual concepts is specific to each of us as individuals and the image of a tutorial and one to one teaching allows us access to the Higher Self or Inner Guru.

Tweezers

① Dreaming of tweezers suggests that we need to look at a situation in minute detail. By grasping this detail properly much good can be achieved.

② In the sense that tweezers are tools, such a dream might suggest that we need to develop the correct tools for the job. To be **using other implements as tweezers** and vice versa would suggest confusion as to exactly what our purpose is.

③ Tweezers signify attention to detailed examination of a spiritual concept.

Twins
– also see People

① In dreams twins may, if **known to us**, simply be themselves. If they are **not known to us** then they may represent two sides of one idea.

② Often in everyday life we come up against conflicts between two opposites. Twins in dreams can actually represent two sides of our personality acting in harmony.

③ Duality must eventually re-unite into unity. Twins illustrate the idea that while separate at the moment, that unity can be achieved.

Typhoon
– see Storm and Wind

Ulcer

① An ulcer is a sore that is only cured with great difficulty. Thus, to dream of one makes us aware of work which needs to be done to heal a great hurt. It will depend on where the ulcer is as to what needs healing. To dream of a **stomach ulcer**, for instance, would suggest an emotional difficulty, while a **mouth ulcer** would suggest some problem with speech or making ourselves understood to those around us.

② If we are dealing with **someone else's ulcer** we are aware that that person is not dealing with a dilemma in which we are involved.

③ An ulcer is something which erodes matter. Spiritually it suggests some soreness of Spirit or a spiritual dilemma.

Umbilical Cord

① Often in life we can develop an emotional dependency on others, and the umbilical cord in dreams can signify that dependency. We have perhaps not yet learnt to take care of our own needs in a mature way.

② The umbilical cord particularly represents the life-giving force and the connection between mother and child. **Severing the umbilical cord** often appears in teenage dreams as the child grows into adulthood.

③ The Silver Cord as the spiritual connection is an image seen psychically as the connection between body and soul.

Umbrella

① An umbrella is a shelter and a sanctuary, and it is this symbolism that comes across in dreams. Often in a work situation we need to work under someone's teaching, and this feeling of safety can be recognised in dreams.

② As we mature we need to develop certain coping skills. In dreams these can be seen as a protective covering, hence the image of the umbrella.

③ As a sunshade conferred status and power, so does the umbrella.

Unattractive

① Often in dreams we uncover feelings which we will not acknowledge in everyday life. Thus, **to find ourselves unattractive** means we have little self-appreciation. It is also possible however that we are being too hard on ourselves and judging ourselves too harshly.

② When an emotion comes up in dreams which we find unattractive or hard to handle, it may be the very aspect of our personality which we need to understand and come to terms with. To be angry when we are not usually so in everyday life suggests that we may be suppressing a perfectly valid response to a difficulty. To **to find someone else unattractive** signifies that we need to understand our own ability to make judgements.

③ When we are learning to understand our own Shadow (*see Shadow*) we will find that many aspects of our dream content strike us as unattractive or indeed ugly until we have contemplated our own spiritual make up.

Uncle
– see Extended Family in Family

Under/Underneath
– see Position

Undercover

① To be **working undercover** in dreams can have two meanings. First we have something to hide and second we are aware that there is something not operating correctly in our lives. We should investigate how we can best resolve the difficulty.

② Any aspect of a dream which appears to be undercover signifies the unconscious side of Self (*see Self*) which may need consideration before we can move on.

③ In spiritual terms, transformation can only take place when matters that we have chosen to store undercover are revealed.

Underground

① Just as Alice dreamt of falling down the rabbit hole in 'Alice in Wonderland', so we all have opportunities to explore our own hidden depths through dreams. We cannot usually access the unconscious in waking life, and to dream of being underground will often allow us to come to terms with that side in a very easy way.

② **To be on the underground or subway** usually signifies the journeys we are prepared (or forced) to take towards understanding who we are. They are necessary expeditions into the Unconscious.

③ The subconscious or the unconscious is often perceived in dreams as a cave or place underground.

Undertaker
– also see Ceremony, Death and Ritual

① The undertaker in dreams is what might be called a transitional figure. In waking life he is present to take care of necessary arrangements at a difficult time. He may appear in dreams as we become aware of an aspect of our personality which no longer serves us well and make a transition into a different way of thinking.

② Emotionally, as we mature and grow, certain things must come to an end and we must 'bury' the past. Ceremony and ritual help us to achieve this, and the undertaker symbolises the organisational aspect of our personality which allows this to happen.

③ From a spiritual perspective, the undertaker in dreams signifies that part of us which can be of service to others. Literally, he undertakes those tasks that consciously we may feel we are not competent to deal with.

Undress
– also see Clothes

① When we find ourselves undressing in a dream, we may be putting ourselves in touch with our own sexual feelings. We may also be needing to reveal our true feelings about a situation around us, and to have the freedom to be totally open about those feelings.

② **To be watching someone else undressing** often indicates that we should be aware of that person's sensitivity. **To be undressing someone else** suggests that we are attempting to understand either ourselves or others on a very deep level.

③ To be undressing suggests a need for Spiritual openness and honesty.

Unearth

① When we are trying to unearth an unknown object in a dream, we are attempting to reveal a side of ourselves which we do not yet understand. When we know what we are searching for, we are trying to uncover aspects of our personality which we have consciously buried.

② Occasionally, we may be aware of knowledge and potential within ourselves or others which requires hard work to realise. It has to be unearthed.

③ Spiritually, when we are prepared to move on we are able to confront the hidden Self *(see Self)*.

Unemployment
– also see Career and Work

① Dreaming of being unemployed suggests that we are not making the best use of our talents, or that we feel our talents are not being recognised properly in waking life. Unemployment in everyday life can cause much stress and result in nightmares and bad dreams as we attempt to work through the various issues associated with it.

② Unemployment is a fear that almost everyone has. When an event connected with unemployment occurs, e.g. redundancy, benefit payments etc. in a dream, our feelings of inadequacy are being highlighted. We need to experience that fear in order to deal with, and overcome, it.

③ A sense of spiritual inadequacy and inability can translate itself into the image of unemployment. This is more to do with not being motivated enough to accept a spiritual task.

Unicorn
– see Animals and Fabulous Beasts

① Traditionally, the only people who were allowed to tend unicorns were virgins. Therefore, when a unicorn appears in a dream, we are linking with the innocent, pure part of ourselves. This is the mostly instinctive, receptive feminine principle.

② There is a story that unicorns missed being taken into Noah's Ark because they were too busy playing. We need to be mindful of what is going on in the real world if we are to survive.

③ The unicorn signifies unconditional love, the single horn signifies perception.

Uniform
– also see Clothes

① Dreaming of uniforms is all to do with our identification with a particular role or type of authority. However rebellious we may be, a part of us needs to conform to the ideas and beliefs of the social group to which we belong. Seeing ourselves in uniform confirms that belonging.

② Often, in collective groups, the right to wear a uniform has to be earned. Dreaming of being **in a group of uniformed people** indicates that we have acheived the right to be recognised.

③ Identification of a common spiritual goal and an agreement as to 'uniform' behaviour is an important aspect in spiritual development. Ceremony and ritual *(see Ceremony and Ritual)* are an integral part of this behaviour.

Union

① Union indicates a joining together, and this can be of pairs or of multiples. **Union in pairs** suggests the reconciliation of opposites and the added power and energy that this brings. A union, in the sense of a **trade union**, suggests collective action which is for the good of all.

② We all attempt to achieve unity from duality – to create a relationship between two parts or opposites. Dreaming of achieving union depicts this relationship. Psychologically, the human being is consistently looking for a partner and this appears in dreams as any form of joining together – union.

③ Unity in a spiritual sense is usually perceived as a return to Source.

University
– also see Education

① Dreaming of being in a university highlights our own individual potential and learning ability. We may not be particularly academic in waking life, but may be subconsciously aware of our ability to connect together with people of like minds. However, we perhaps are not using our expertise and knowledge as well as we should.

② Since a university is a place of 'higher' learning, we are being made aware of the breadth of experience and increase in knowledge available to us. We need to move away from the mundane and ordinary into specific areas of knowledge and awareness. We also need to be aware of our ability to share the knowledge and experience we have with others.

③ Spiritual Knowledge and the ability to use it can only be achieved in 'The University of Life'.

Unknown

① The unknown in dreams is that which has been hidden from us, or that which we have deliberately made secret. This may be the 'occult' – that is, knowledge which is only available to initiates. It may also be information that we do not normally need, except in times of stress.

② When we are conscious of the unknown in dreams, we should try to decide whether it is threatening or whether it is something we need to know and understand. It is the way we handle the information – rather than the information itself – which is important.

③ The hidden or the Occult remains both unknown and unknowable unless we have the courage to face, and explore, it. This we can often first do within the safety of our dreams.

Unload
– also see Baggage, Luggage and Journey

① In dreams, to be unloading a vehicle, for instance, will signify deciding what we need to carry with us on our life journey and what we can leave behind. Unloading shopping bags suggests deciding what we need to sustain us in the immediate future.

② Unloading anything in the emotional sense may signify the end of a particular project or period of activity. We need to get rid of emotional baggage we no longer need and clear the ground for the future.

③ By unloading we make ourselves lighter, so the spiritual implication is that we are opening ourselves up to different perspectives. We are creating space for new ideas and concepts.

Unpopular

① To dream of being unpopular highlights our feelings of lack of self esteem. How we relate to other people has a great deal to do with our self-confidence and as we make adjustments in waking life or go into new situations, our fears may come to the fore.

② Being unpopular in dreams may signify that we are aware on some level that a decision we have to make will not be accepted by, or popular with, our friends and family.

③ As we mature spiritually we must sometimes undertake tasks and actions which are not always understood by others. If we find ourselves unpopular in dreams we must decide whether our own code of conduct is right or whether we are acting for the Greater Good.

Unravel
– also see Knitting and Tangled

① To be unravelling a tangle of wool or other material in dreams suggests that we are attempting to simplify what at first glance appears complicated. In practical terms this may mean taking into account other people's needs and desires before we can reach a satisfactory conclusion.

② When in dreams we find ourselves unravelling an article which has been carefully crafted, the symbolism is that we need to get back to the basic emotional state which has led to a particular situation. While one solution may be eminently reasonable, there are others which may result in an equally successful outcome.

③ In understanding systems of belief and spirituality, concepts can become unnecessarily complicated. By finding and being prepared to follow the single strand which runs throughout such thought, we move closer to the ideal of unity.

Up/Upper
– see Position

Upset

① Any upset is a disturbance of order, and in dreams such disturbance needs clarification. If a group of articles is upset and thus creates mess and chaos we perhaps should decide if we need a different arrangement of the important aspects of our lives. If on further consideration we do nothing to put matters right, this image is indicative of potential difficulty or difficulties.

② An emotional difficulty can be upsetting and dreams will often highlight this in chaotic images, emotional states, nightmares and so on. When consideration is given to the theme of the dreams and some kind of order imposed we are able to begin to a process of healing.

③ In learning about spirituality there are often challenges and small upsets which occur along the way. Sometimes these test our resolve and sometimes our awareness. Our dream content or perhaps even a series of dreams will frequently show us the way forward.

Urine
– see Body

Urn
– also see Vase

① For many people **the tea urn** is a symbol of community life. To dream of one suggests our ability to belong to a community and act for the greater good.

② Just as all receptacles signify the feminine principle, so does the urn, although in a more ornate form. In earlier times, **a draped urn** signified death. That symbolism is still carried on today in the urn used in crematoriums. Thus, to dream of an urn may alert us to our feelings about death.

③ The urn represents the feminine receptive principle.

Vaccination/Vaccine

– also see Injection and Syringe

① In normal everyday life, vaccination is an action which initially hurts but is ultimately good for us. To dream that we are **being vaccinated** therefore suggests that we are likely to be hurt by someone (perhaps emotionally). What they are trying to do to us will in the end, however, be helpful.

② It is very easy for us to be influenced by other people. Vaccination indicates that we can be affected by other people's ideas and feelings. The substance being used in vaccination – the vaccine itself – may be of some concern if we are required in the dream simply to accept it unquestioningly. With the knowledge we acquire, we actually need to know more.

③ Vaccination in dreams suggests Spiritual indoctrination.

Valley

① Dreaming of **going down into a valley** can have the same significance as going downstairs – that is, going down into the subconscious or unknown parts of ourselves. The result of this can be either depression and gloominess or finding new areas of productiveness within us.

② **Being in a valley** can represent the sheltering, feminine side of our nature and also being down-to-earth. **Leaving a valley** suggests coming out of a period of introversion in order to function properly in the everyday world.

③ Fears of death and dying are often translated in dreams as entering into a valley – the valley of death. It is worth remembering that entry into the Valley of Death is often said to be a conscious act, and we should recognise that it is our own subconscious fear at work.

Vampire

① When heavy demands are made on us which we do not feel capable of meeting, a vampire can appear in a dream. We are figuratively being 'sucked dry'. The vampire or blood sucker is such a fearful figure that it is accepted as an embodiment of evil.

② Often the fear of emotional and sexual relationships can be represented in dreams as a vampire. Because the human being still has a fear of the unknown, ancient symbols that have represented this fear can still appear in dreams. The succubus and incubus preying on young people's vital energy is often pictured as a vampire. As media treatment of such figures increases, and is perhaps more sympathetic than before, they will appear more often in dreams, particularly of young people.

③ Life-threatening evil is represented by the vampire in dreams. However, it may be that we have a rather fantastical outlook on the realms of evil and some reservation could be applied to our thoughts.

Van
– see Lorry in Transport

Vandal/Vandalism

① Vandals or vandalism in dreams highlights destructiveness in ourselves or others. To have our belongings vandalised brings our vulnerability into prominence. To be committing an act of vandalism suggests an anger or distress which is becoming out of control.

② Wanton destruction such as vandalism in dreams represents resentment and a violent nature which has not been harnessed correctly. A vandal appearing in dreams is that part of our personality which has not been properly integrated successfully and has become alienated.

③ Spiritually a vandal in dreams is destructive of beauty and all that is fine.

Varnish

① Varnish is a protective outer covering which is designed to enhance the appearance of an object. Dreaming of varnish can therefore signify either of the following meanings. We may be covering something up in order to hide imperfections or we may be protecting ourselves and attempting to present a better self image.

② **To be varnishing something** suggests that we are not happy with our original creation. It may need further work to preserve what we have already done, or it may need enhancing in order that others can understand.

③ Having achieved a spiritual goal, we may wish to preserve the secret and hold it sacred. Dreaming of varnish would confirm this.

Vase

① As a holder of beautiful things, any receptacle – such as a vase, water pot, pitcher or urn – tends to represent the feminine within a dream. Such an object can also signify creativity.

② The accepting and receptive nature of the feminine, intuitive side is often suggested by a hollow object such as a vase. It can also represent the womb and the emotion associated with it

③ A vase, particularly a beautifully decorated or colourful one, represents the Great Mother (*see Great Mother/Mother Earth*) in all her glory.

Vault

① In dreams any dark, hidden place suggests sexual potency or the unconscious. It can also represent our store of personal resources, those things we learn as we grow and mature. To be **going down into a vault** represents our need to explore those areas of ourselves that have become hidden. We may also need to explore our attitude to death.

② Collective wisdom (or the Collective Unconscious – information available to all of us) often remains hidden until a real effort is made to uncover the knowledge available. While a vault can represent a tomb, it also represents the 'archives' or records to which we all have access, and will also have this meaning when the image is a bank vault. Such a place will also signify the retaining of rightful resources.

③ A vault represents the meeting place of the spiritual and physical. Consequently a vault can also symbolise death, or death of a belief. It is also that which remains after a belief has outlived its usefulness.

VD
– see Sex

Vegetables
– see Food and Harvest

Vegetation

① Vegetation in a dream can often represent the obstacles that we put in front of ourselves in order to grow. For instance, **a patch of brambles** can suggest irritating snags to our movement forwards, whereas **nettles** might represent people actually trying to prevent progress. The image of vegetation also links with the forest (*See Forest*).

② While the obstacles we create may cause difficulty, there is also an underlying abundance and fertility that is available to us. In dreams, a pictorial image can help us to understand this. **To be clearing vegetation**, for instance in a vegetable garden, can suggest clearing away that which is no longer of use to us.

③ Vegetation in a dream symbolises abundance and the capacity for growth on a spiritual level.

Veil

– also see Clothes

① When an object is veiled in a dream, there is some kind of secret which needs to be revealed. We may, as dreamers, be concealing something from ourselves, but we could also be being kept in ignorance by others.

② The mind has different ways of indicating hidden thoughts in dreams. The veil is one of these symbols. It can also represent modesty.

③ A veil can represent all that is hidden and mysterious – and this translates into aspects of the Occult i.e. Hidden Knowledge and Mystery. In spiritual terms the idea of veiling a woman's head out of modesty is from choice and for her protection. Most religions in former times instructed women to cover their heads and men to bare theirs in the presence of the divine. Dreaming of a veil with this purpose indicates a recognition, not of subservience but of connection.

Velvet

① It is usually the texture and quality that is relevant when a material appears in a dream. The sensuousness and softness of velvet is significant here.

② In old-style dream interpretation, to dream of velvet was to dream of discord. In modern day interpretation it is more likely to mean the opposite i.e. harmony.

③ Spiritually velvet can depict richness and giftedness. The colour may also be important *(see Colour)*.

Vermin

– see Animals

Vertical

– see Position

Vesica Piscis

– see Aura and Religious Iconology

Vicar

– also see Priest in Archetypes and Monks/Priests/Ministers in Occupations

① Just as the priest was given spiritual authority over many, and was often a figure to be feared, so the vicar is also given this authority. He is perhaps less feared than the priest. In dreams he is often the authority figure to whom we have given control.

② When a vicar appears in a dream, we are usually aware of the more spiritual, knowledgeable side of ourselves.

③ A vicar is a man of God and we may need to acknowledge that there is much to learn about the management of spirituality.

Vice

① There are obviously two meanings to the word vice. **One is a tool** which clamps and the other **a wrong action**. Dreaming of a vice in its first sense may suggest that we are being constrained in some way. The second indicates that we are aware of the side of ourselves which is rebellious and out of step with society. We may in both cases need to make adjustments in our behaviour.

② Often dreams allow us to behave in ways which are not those we would normally try in waking life. Being conscious of a particular vice, e.g. sloth, envy, apathy, etc. in one of our dream characters may enable us to handle that tendency within ourselves.

③ Unacceptable behaviour may manifest in the form of vice. Vice is somewhat subjective and dependent on our own individual sense of right or wrong. Dreams will often highlight what needs to be dealt with in order to improve spiritually.

Victim

① In dreams we are often aware of something happening to us over which we have no control. We are the victim – in the sense that we are passive or powerless within the situation. Sometimes we are aware that we are treating others incorrectly. We are making them victims of our own internal aggression, and not handling ourselves properly in waking life.

② When we are continually creating 'no-win' situations this tendency is highlighted in dreams, but may be done so somewhat dramatically. In dreams we may find we are victims of burglary, rape or murder, for instance. It is highly unlikely these will be precognitive dreams, but do indicate we need to properly identify our own ability to victimise ourselves. The nature of the difficulty may reveal itself through the dream content.

③ If we are repressing our own ability to develop spiritual potential, we will appear in a dream as a victim – a victim of our own making.

Victor/Victory

① There are many ways to achieve victory in dreams. The dream scenario may be a conflict between two aspects of ourselves or require us to overcome some difficulty. The sense of achievement we feel in dreams can be a feeling we can reproduce in waking life. It gives us confidence in our own abilities.

② Victory in a psychological sense is the overcoming of obstacles which we have set up for ourselves. In dreams we often need a 'dry-run' and a pictorial representation of our abilities in order to achieve success. To be the victor in any conflict is actually to have overcome our own lack of confidence in our own abilities.

③ If we have achieved a degree of spiritual success, it can show itself as a victory of some kind.

Vigil/Vigilant

① As technology and machinery becomes more expensive and complex we may find that we dream of watching them as if we were undertaking a vigil – that is, being watchful. In dreams this highlights how mechanisation has overtaken other concerns.

② Being vigilant in dreams is warning us to be aware of what might go wrong. Often the watchful part of us becomes aware of problems before our conscious mind registers them.

③ A vigil in the spiritual sense is a devotional exercise or service held at night. It is also a wake, held over a deceased person. In dreams it signifies our care and concern over our loved ones.

Village

① A village appearing in a dream suggests a fairly tightly knit community. It may also illustrate our ability to form supportive relationships and foster a community spirit.

② A village can present certain problems. For instance, everybody knows everybody else's business – which can become trying. In this case we may be highlighting the oppression felt in close relationships. Because the pace of life is slower and more measured, we may find that the village in a dream is a symbol of relaxation.

③ Often village life was centred around the church and the pub, providing many contrasts. Spiritually, we often have to look at balancing two parts of our lives.

Villain
– see Archetypes

Vine/Vineyard
– also see Grapes

① The vine in dreams can suggest growth and fruitfulness. This can be of our whole self, or the various parts of our personality.

② When we dream of the vine we are often referring to the various members of our family, including our ancestors. It is a sort of visual representation of the family tree. We are linking also with the more spiritual side of ourselves which has grown through shared, rather than individual, experience.

③ A vine or vineyard can symbolise growth of a spiritual nature. It can also represent fertility of concepts or ideals.

Vinegar

① Vinegar, because it is sour, is a representation of all that is problematic in taking in information. It can thus signify knowledge which is unpalatable.

② Oddly enough vinegar is a symbol of life, both because it preserves, and also because it is something which is left after a change of its original state. In dreams this symbolism can come across very strongly.

③ The preservation of spiritual life and all that we hold dear to us is symbolised by vinegar because of its preservative qualities.

Violence

① Any violence in dreams is a reflection of our own inner feeling, sometimes about ourselves, sometimes about the situations around us. Often the type of violence is worthy of notice if we are fully to understand ourselves.

② When we are unable because of social pressures or circumstance to express ourselves properly, we can find ourselves behaving violently in dreams. If **others are behaving violently** towards us we may need to take care in waking life not to upset others.

③ A sense of spiritual injustice or unequality may be represented by scenes or acts of violence in a dream.

Viper
– see Serpent/Snake in Animals

Virgin

① To dream of **being a virgin** suggests a state of innocence and purity. To dream that **someone else is a virgin** highlights the ideals of integrity and honesty.

② The virginal mind – that is, a mind that is free from deception and guile – is perhaps more important than physically being a virgin, and it is this aspect which often becomes evident in dreams. **In a woman's dream** such a figure suggests she is in touch with her own psyche.

③ Spiritually there is a kind of innocence and purity, which can often be dedicated to service. This was the origin of the virgin priestesses.

Virgin Mother
– see Religious Iconology

Virus

① In mundane terms a virus indicates some form of contamination and will have this connotation whether we dream of a physical illness or of a computer. Traditionally a virus is difficult to eradicate so will in dreams represent some kind of complex problem or difficulty with which we need to deal in our everyday lives.

② A virus is insidious in its contamination, in that once in position it grows rapidly. In dreams therefore it will signify something similar such as a bad thought, unchallenged gossip or other type of negativity. It may need careful thought before we can locate the source in waking life.

③ A spiritual virus is an evil which is allowed to multiply unchecked.

Visit

① To be **visited by someone** in a dream can suggest that there is information, warmth or love available to us. If it is **someone we know** then this may apply in a real-life situation. If it is not, then there may be a facet of our personality which is trying to make itself apparent.

② To be **paying someone else a visit** in a dream signifies that we may need to widen our horizons in some way. This may be physically, emotionally or spiritually.

③ Our spiritual guides *(see Guardian Spirits)* often first makes themselves available by a visit in the dream state, as do loved ones.

Visions

① The mind, once it is free of conscious restraint, appears to work on several different levels. Thus, it is possible to be aware of three separate parts of a dream. These are the 'I' of the dream, the content, and finally – usually pictorially – information and knowledge. These are the visions of dreams. Many dreamers have suggested that this type of dream has a different 'feel' to it from other more mundane dreams.

② In the half-awake, half-asleep state just before and just after sleep many people experience very strong images which are remembered in a way that dream images are not. These could also be called visions.

③ Spiritual manifestations, or rather, manifestations of Spirit, are accepted as visions. As we grow in awareness, we develop the ability to envision – to see matters not of this world.

Vitamin

– also see Pill

① Dreaming of taking vitamins indicates a concern about health. We may be aware that we are not nurturing ourselves properly and require additional help.

② On a slightly more esoteric level, we are aware that we are not doing the best for ourselves and need more out of life in order to function according to our true potential. There could be a situation in our lives which needs a particular type of assistance.

③ We have reached the point on our spiritual journey where we need to achieve a higher vibration in order to progress.

Voice

① The voice is a tool that we use to express ourselves. We all have inner awareness of our own state which is sometimes difficult to disclose. Often in dreams we are able to use our voices in more appropriate ways. Often we are **spoken to** in dreams so that we remember the information given.

② A voice that speaks through, or to, one has two areas of significance. If one believes in the spirit realm, this is communication from a discarnate spirit. More psychologically, when we suppress certain parts of our personalities they may surface in dreams as disembodied voices.

③ The Voice of God is a term which is used to describe the energy of a spiritual summons.

Void

– see Abyss

Volcano

① The image of a volcano in dreams is a very telling one, partly because of its unpredictability. To dream of a **volcano being extinct** can indicate either that we have 'killed off' our passions, or that a difficult situation has come to an end. This may be one that has been around for some time.

② An **erupting volcano** usually signifies that we are not in control of a situation or of our emotions – of which there may be a hurtful release. If the **lava is more prominent** feelings will run very deep. **If the lava has cooled** there has been a deep passion which has now cooled off. If the **explosiveness is more noticeable**, anger may be more prominent.

③ A volcano is representative of spiritual deeply held passion. This can sometimes erupt with frightening results.

Vomit

① To dream of **vomiting** suggests a discharge of disagreeable feelings and emotions. It would be a clearing of something from within that makes us extremely uncomfortable. To dream of **watching someone else vomit** indicates that we may have upset them and need to have compassion and understanding.

② Intuitively, we can often be aware of problems around us and be affected by them. When we become overloaded, we may need to 'throw up' (or away) the distress it is causing us. To **wake up feeling sick** intimates that we have been affected on an emotional level by the release that occurred in the dreams that we have had.

③ Vomiting is a symbol of a discharge of evil. We may have held on to bad feeling for so long that it has caused our spiritual system some difficulty.

Voodoo

– also see Ceremony, Ritual and Shadow

① As a shamanic system of belief Voodoo suffers from a degree of media hype and will often manifest in dreams as frightening and scary. The various rituals and ceremonies, however, are a rich source of imagery. If contemplated carefully they allow us to overcome fears and doubts in a way which cannot be accomplished in any other conscious fashion.

② Just as Voodoo arose among oppressed slaves out of a need for protection, so in dreams the images of Trickster (*see Trickster*) and vengeful gods allow us to come to an understanding of our inner 'demons' and the Shadow side of our personality.

③ We learn to understand the need for simplicity in our relationship with those things which are beyond our comprehension. The personalisation of Forces of Nature and of the Divine becomes an effective way of managing those relationships from a spiritual perspective.

Vortex

– see Whirlwind

Vote

– also see Election

① Dreaming of voting in an election, whether general or within the workplace, highlights our wish and ability to belong to groups. If we are conscious we are **voting with the group** we are happy to accept group practice. **Voting against the group** indicates a need to rebel.

② While the process of voting is supposed to be fair and just, when we dream of this we may be questioning that whole process. To dream of **being elected** to a position is to seek power.

③ Spiritually when we have given unconditional acceptance to something, we have placed our trust in it. A votive offering is a spiritual request.

Voucher

① A voucher – in the sense of a **promissory note** – can be taken in dreams to suggest our ability to give ourselves permission to do something. If, for instance, it is a **money off voucher** we may not be valuing ourselves properly, or alternatively we could be looking for an easy option.

② A voucher opens up our opportunities. Because it is usually an exchange between two people, it can indicate the help that others can give us.

③ A timely invitation to the Unconscious, in the sense that we are attempting to bargain with ourselves in some way, would tend to show itself in dreams as a voucher.

Vow

① A vow is a pact or agreement between two people or oneself and God. To dream of **making such a vow** is to be recognising responsibility for one's own life. It is more solemn than a simple promise and the results are consequently more far-reaching.

② Because a vow is made in front of witnesses, we need to be aware of the effect that it will have on other people. In dreams we are expecting others to help us honour our promise. To be **listening to or making marriage vows** indicates our commitment to totality.

③ A vow is a spiritual promise made between us and our universe.

Voyage
– see Journey

Vulture
– see Birds

Wading

① Dreaming of wading puts us in the position of recognising what our emotions can do to us. If we are **impeded by the water** *(see Water)*, then we need to appreciate how our emotions can prevent us from moving forward. If we are **enjoying our wading experience,** then we may expect our connection with life to bring contentment. Sometimes the depths to which our bodies are immersed gives us information as to how we are able to cope with external circumstances.

② Often the feeling associated with wading can be more relevant than the action of wading itself. For instance, to recognise that we are not actually in water – for example, we are **wading through treacle** can give us a clue to how we feel about ourselves or our circumstances.

③ Spiritually, wading suggests a cleansing process which ties in with baptism. Many meditations use the symbolism of walking through water.

Wadding
– also see Packing

① In dreams our need for security can become more noticeable than we allow it to be in ordinary, everyday life. Because wadding is normally a protective material, we may need to become aware that we should take action to *protect* ourselves rather than *defend* ourselves.

② Sometimes bodily changes can be reflected in the images that we produce in dreams. Wadding in this sense can represent a fear of getting fat or becoming ungainly.

③ Wadding in spiritual and psychic terms suggests security. It is an image which arises when we are looking for security.

Wafer

① A wafer is a thin layer of matter which is usually very fragile. In dreams it can represent something which is easily broken and which we need to treat with care.

② **A wafer biscuit** is constructed in many layers. It thus becomes a symbol for diversity. We may need to understand the various 'layers' of our lives in order to manage our lives successfully.

③ The Bread of Life, or spiritual sustenance for whatever belief system we subscribe to. In Christianity, the wafer symbolises Christ's body.

Wager
– see Games/Gambling

Wages/Salary

① Wages or salary are normally paid in exchange for work done. In dreams, to be **receiving such payment** signifies that we have done a good job. To be **paying somebody in that way** implies that we owe that person something. To **receive a wage packet or notification of salary** suggests that our value is tied up with other things such as loyalty and duty.

② Most actions we take have a result. Often when we are doing something that we do not want to do – or which we do not enjoy – the only pay-off is in the financial payment we receive. To have a dream about wages may signify that we should not expect anything else in a situation in everyday life.

③ Spiritually, wages can represent recompense for our actions and that the reward we so deserve is coming our way. Salary signifies that we must wait for that reward.

Wail

① Wailing is a long, protracted way of releasing emotions. When we hear **someone wailing** in a dream, we become conscious of someone else's sadness. When we **ourselves are wailing**, we may be allowing ourselves an emotional release which would not be seen to be appropriate in everyday life.

② Wailing is reputed to be a method of summoning the spirits. In dreams, therefore, it can suggest that we are trying to get in touch with a power that is greater than ourselves.

③ Grieving and the making of sounds is used spiritually to banish bad spirits. We should look at what we feel needs 'banishing' from our life.

Waiting

① **To be waiting** for somebody, or something, in a dream implies a need to recognise a sense of anticipation. We may be looking to other people, or outside circumstances, to help us move forward or make decisions. If **we are impatient**, it may be that our expectations are too high. If we are **waiting patiently**, there is the understanding that events will happen in their own good time.

② When we become aware that something is expected from us, and **other people are waiting for appropriate action**, we may need to consider our own leadership qualities.

③ In developing spiritually we must often learn to wait until the time is right. We have to wait for the passage of time.

Waiter/Waitress
– also see Occupations

① The interpretation of this dream depends on whether we ourselves are waiting at table, or whether we are being waited upon. If we are **in the role of waiter**, we are aware of our ability to care for other people. If **we are being waited on**, we perhaps need to be nurtured and made to feel special.

② When such a person appears in a dream, there may be a play on words. Part of us needs to be conscious that for complete fulfilment in any task or responsibility we need to wait.

③ Spiritually we must learn two lessons – service and patience. This must be learnt before we can really progress.

Wake

① A wake, in the sense of a funeral service, gives us an opportunity to grieve properly. When in dreams we find ourselves attending such an occasion, we need to be aware that there may be some reason in our lives for us to go through a period of grieving. We need to let go that which we hold dear.

② In most religions, there is a period around a death when it is appropriate to express our feelings. Sometimes it is easier to do this in company and with the support of other people. In a dream the symbolism of a wake such as this is that we may need support to overcome a disappointment.

③ Spiritually, a wake signifies appropriate grief, but is also a period when the living literally stay awake to ensure the dead a safe passage into the next realm.

Waking Up

① There is a condition in sleeping where we become alert to the fact that we are dreaming and that we can wake up. This appears partly as a way of forcing us into taking note of a particular action or circumstance, and partly to enable us to use the therapeutic tool of being able to wake up and make an adjustment to a dream which might have a happier ending.

② To **wake up in a dream** can indicate that we have come out of a period of mourning and withdrawal.

③ Spiritually, to wake up signifies becoming aware. The dream state alerts us to various ideas and concepts we should be looking at, although it may take us a little time to 'wake up' to them.

Walking

① In a dream, walking indicates the way in which we should be moving forward. To be **walking purposefully** suggests we know where we are going. To be **wandering aimlessly** suggests we need to create goals for ourselves. To take **pleasure in the act of walking** is to return to the innocence of the child. To be **using a walking stick** is to recognise our need for support and assistance from others.

② Walking may be used as a relaxation from stress, and it is this significance which often comes up in dreams. If we **are alone** then our walk can be silent and contemplative. If it is **in company**, then we can communicate and converse without fear of interruption.

③ A spiritual walk is a journey of exploration into realms we do not know.

Wall
– also see Buildings

① In dreams, walls usually indicate the boundaries we have set ourselves. These may be created as defence mechanisms or support structures, and it is sometimes helpful in the interpretation to decide whether the walls have been created in order to keep ourselves in, or other people out.

② A wall also has the symbolism of a dividing line – a marker between the inner and the outer, privacy and open trust. **A hole in a wall** suggests a breach of trust or privacy. It can also mean we can access hidden resources. **If the wall is imprisoning us** we are being held prisoner by our own fears, doubts and difficulties **If the wall appears and disappears**, we have only partly dealt with our problem.

③ A wall symbolises the boundaries of a sacred space. We need to be aware of what our limits are.

Wallet
– also see Money

① In dreams, the wallet is a representation of where we keep our resources safe. These need not simply be financial resources, but can be of any kind. Many dreams can suggest our attitude to money and finance, and to dream of a wallet is one of those dreams.

② Interestingly, because the wallet can also suggest the feminine aspects of care and containment, it can highlight our attitude to intuition and awareness.

③ In ancient times, the wallet would hold the wherewithal to sustain the traveller until his next destination. Spiritually in dreams it still retains that connotation.

Wallpaper

① **To be stripping wallpaper** in dreams suggests stripping away the old facade in order to create a new image. **To be putting up wallpaper** signifies covering up the old self (possibly superficially), particularly if the old wallpaper is not removed.

② Wallpaper in a dream can have the same significance as clothes on a character. We may be wanting to make changes in our lives but need to experiment – and get a proper fit – first.

③ Because wallpaper often symbolises an outer facade of some kind, its appearance in dreams indicates we should consider whether we are acting appropriately or are being true to ourselves and our beliefs as we progress spiritually.

Walnut
– see Nut

Waltz
– see Dance/Dancing

Wand
– also see Magic

① As more people begin to understand the principles of the raising of consciousness, old ideas about magical tools begin to make sense. A wand is a device to concentrate power in one direction and will often have this significance in dreams. When we dream of **using a wand** we are aware of our influence over others. Conversely, if **someone else uses a wand** we are aware of the power of suggestion, either for negative or for positive within the situation around us.

② Conventionally the wand is an instrument of supernatural forces, and it is often this image which is the most important. By learning how to concentrate the power of the mind we learn to have control of both internal emotions and external forces; this skill can first manifest in dreams through the use of magical tools.

③ Obviously a wand works in tandem with magic, so to dream of a wand can symbolise 'magical' powers which may influence us. Wands are often made from wood and other substances which have special attributes. They can symbolise such special spiritual skills in dreams.

Wanderer/Wandering
– see Tramp in Archetypes

Want

① To be conscious of a want in a dream is perhaps to link with our basic nature. We may have suppressed those wants in waking life only to have them surface in dreams.

② When in dreams we find we want to do – or be – something different, we are aware of the potential within us either to achieve success or to change our lives. For instance, to dream of wanting to be a poet instead of an actor can suggest exploration of our creativity in a different format.

③ Desire in its fullest sense – although we should take care – as want is sometimes considered a form of sin.

War
– also see Fight and Weapons

① In dreams war always denotes conflict. It has a more global effect than one-to-one combat, and would suggest that we need to be more conscious of the effect our actions will have on others. We also need to be aware that we are taking part in conflict which is deliberately engineered rather than spontaneous.

② War is ultimately a way of dealing with distress and disorder. The outcome should be the establishment of order, although sometimes this can only happen through the passage of time. To dream of war, therefore, indicates that this natural process is taking place on an inner level.

③ War is a symbol of spiritual disintegration. We need to be aware of what could potentially disintegrate within our lives to understand the full symbolism. We should also be aware of the effect that our actions and behaviour can have on others around us.

Warden

① A warden in a dream is often a manifestation of the guardian or the keeper. We may have a part of our personality which acts as monitor or attempts to suppress other parts of our personality, and this appears as a warden.

② In working with dream images we will often recognise aspects of the Spiritual Self which protect us from outside influence and this also can appear as a warden.

③ 'The Guardian of the Threshold' between the physical and the spiritual is reprsented by the warden.

Warehouse
– see Buildings

Warmth
– also see Hot

① Warmth or heat in a dream touches our 'feel good' factor and enhances our sense of comfort and well being.

② Psychologically, feelings of cheerfulness and hopefulness can create an awareness of warmth and the meaning can be interchangeable.

③ A feeling of warmth or heat in a dream can symbolise that most sought-after prize – unconditional love. We can afford to move positively in search of this.

Warning
– also see Alarm

① To receive a warning in a dream suggests that we are aware that either internally or externally something needs attention. We may be putting ourselves in danger.

② To be **warning someone** highlights our ability to be aware of difficulty and danger, either to others or to hidden parts of our personality. To receive **a written warning** indicates we may be behaving badly.

③ A warning in this case can actually be showing us the way toward being a more intuitive person. Our intuition can be trusted – we should use it accordingly.

Warrant

① A warrant represents permission from a higher authority, either spiritual or physical. It will depend on the type of warrant as to what action we need to take. For instance, **a search warrant** suggests looking at our motives, whereas **a warrant for arrest** indicates we need to stop carrying out a particular action.

② When we are unable to make decisions, dream images can often help us. A warrant appearing in a dream shows there are possibilities opening up of which we may not have been aware.

③ We may be seeking spiritual permission for some reason, and this can be symbolised by a warrant.

Warts

① Any blemish which comes to the attention in dreams can be accepted as evidence of there being a distortion in our view of the world.

② We are often distressed by anything which is out of the ordinary or wrong. A great deal of folklore has grown up around warts and how to get rid of them. Dreaming of warts links with that part of ourselves which remains superstitious.

③ Just as warts are a distortion or blemish which sometimes cannot be shifted, a distortion of a spiritual kind may be affording us little insight at this time. We should bide our time and allow the difficulty to run its course.

Washing
— also see Water

① Dreaming of **washing either oneself, or for instance, clothes,** suggests getting rid of negative feelings. We may need to change our attitude, either internally or externally. **Washing other people** touches on our need to care for others.

② Since water is a symbol for emotion and the unconscious, washing stands for achieving a relationship with our emotional selves and dealing successfully with the results.

③ A spiritual cleansing may be necessary in order to preserve our integrity.

Wasp
— see Insects

Waste
— also see Ecology and Garbage/Rubbish

① Waste in dreams signifies matter or information we no longer need. It can now be thrown away. Often the colour will have significance *(see Colour)*. Waste can also suggest a misuse of resources – we may, initially, be using too much energy on a particular project.

② If we are being wasteful in dreams we need to reassess how we are running our lives. We may be giving too much in relationships, or trying to make things happen.

③ There may be an energy crisis for us which we cannot fathom. We therefore need to look to where there is most likely to be an 'energy leak'.

Watch
— see Time

Watching

① To be aware of **someone watching us** in a dream suggests that we feel threatened by someone's close interest in us. This may be in a work situation, but could also be in personal relationships.

② In dreams, we are often conscious of the Self *(see Self)* which is watching and participating in the dream. We need to be aware of all parts of the dream in order to achieve the best results.

③ There is a need for us to monitor our own actions, particularly if new forms of spiritual discipline have recently been taken on.

Water

① A frequent theme in dreams is that of water and images connected with it. Water is usually taken in dreams to symbolise all that is emotional and feminine. Water can represent our hidden potential and, in response to deep-felt need for change, our ability to create a new life for ourselves. It also represents cleansing of any sort and being able to 'wash away' the things which deeply affect us in everyday life.

② Water appears in dreams, in so many guises and with so many different symbolic meanings, that it is possible only to suggest some of the more common ones:

Coming up out of the water indicates a fresh start. *Deep water* suggests the unconscious and the possibility of being out of our depth. *Flowing water* signifies either peace and comfort or going with the grand scheme of events. While *rushing water* denotes passion, *shallow water* reveals a lack of essential energy, our get-up-and-go. *Walking into water* indicates a need to renew our inner strength, while being *immersed in water* can suggest sometimes pregnancy and birth, more often an excess of emotion around us *(also see Immersion)*. To be *on the water* (as in a boat) can represent indecision or a lack of emotional commitment, while to be *in the water but not moving* signifies a degree of inertia at that particular time in our waking lives.

Other significant images and symbolisms associated with water are:

Bathing is associated with purification of body, mind and spirit. This also may be the cleansing of old feelings and perhaps the need to seek forgiveness.

Canals often symbolise the process of birth, and can also suggest attempts to regulate our emotions in some way – to keep them under control.

Dams, islands and driftwood Anything which forms an obstacle to the flow of water in dreams suggests some kind of intentional obstruction in our emotions. These may be self-inflicted, or difficulties that other people put in our way. A *dam* may be a self-inflicted difficulty, whereas *driftwood* suggests force of circumstance. An *island* which we may well see first as an obstacle may later become a place of sanctuary *(see Sanctuary)*.

Diving into water can be interpreted as trying to find the parts of ourselves which we have suppressed. It can also suggest taking unusual risks.

Drowning indicates that we are pushing ourselves to our limit, whether physical or emotional. We may not be in control of our emotions properly and may be in a situation where we can be overcome by them. To *see someone else drowning* suggests that we are aware of, and sympathetic to, another person's emotional state.

Floods, being by their nature chaotic and destructive, symbolise the uncontrollable 'welling up' of emotion which can destroy our known way of life. That destruction can have a positive outcome due to the cleansing process that must take place.

Fountains To dream of a fountain means that we are aware of the process of life and 'flow' of our own consciousness. It can also represent the surge of our emotions. The fountain can also represent an element of play in our lives and the need to be free-flowing and untroubled. Fountains may also be taken as symbols of womanhood, in particular the Great Mother *(see Great Mother/Mother Earth)* in her most giving sense. They can also suggest the Fountain of Immortality.

Lake A lake, like a pool, can signify a stage of transition between the conscious and the spiritual Self. To come across a lake unexpectedly in a dream shows the need to consider our emotional responses very carefully. To see our image reflected in water suggests that we need to come to terms with our inner self or the Shadow. We have to understand that there is a part of ourselves that we do not appreciate but which, when harnessed, can give much energy for change.

Rivers or streams, like roads, denote our lives and the way we are living at that moment. It will depend on our general attitude or state of mind as to whether we see life as a large river or a small stream. If the water in the river in our dream appears to be *dirty or contaminated* in any way we are perhaps not deciding for ourselves on the best course of action. We may be letting others affect our judgement inappropriately. *Crossing a river* indicates there will be great changes in our waking lives. Such an image can sometimes suggest death, as in the ancient myth of crossing the River Styx, though this can be also be the relinquishing of our old life in favour of the new. It may mean venturing into the unknown. If the river is *very deep* we should perhaps be paying attention to our deeper feelings and how we relate to the rest of the world. If the *river is rushing* by we may feel that life is moving along at too fast a pace. If we can see the *sea as well as the river*, we have to accept that a great change must occur. This may mean that there will be an expansion of consciousness, or a deeper awareness of our unconscious motives. If the *river frightens us*, it shows that we are creating an unnecessary difficulty for ourselves in waking life by not understanding the flow of our emotions.

Sea/Ocean The original chaotic state from which all life emerges is often pictured as a sea. It usually depicts Cosmic Consciousness – that is, a state of total knowledge. This knowledge may be obscured by our fear of 'the deep'. We need not fear that which we understand. A *shallow sea* suggests insincere emotion. To be able to *see the seabed* indicates that there may be an end to some emotional distress. The *waves* in the sea characterise emotion and yearning. Waves on any body of water signify the ups and downs of everyday life. A *calm sea* suggests a peaceful existence, whereas a *stormy sea* signifies passion of any kind. To be conscious of the *rise and fall of the tides* is to be aware of both the passage of time and of the ebb and flow of our own emotions.

Waterfalls in dreams often suggest some kind of spiritual cleansing. Sometimes previously taken to represent an orgasm, today such an image is more properly principally representative of any display of emotion that is powerful and yet under control.

③ Spiritually, water is used in baptism as a symbol of the cleansing of previously held so-called sins. Seen also as a force of nature, sweeping away all before it, the power of water symbolises the cleansing away of all blockages, impediments and obstacles to growth. In order to grow and progress we often need to eliminate old habits, beliefs and concepts which have been inherited from the family. To dream of a *baptism* therefore may suggest that it is time to let go of these family inheritances.

Wave/Waving
– also see Hand in Body and Water

① If in dreams a character is either waving generally or waving specifically at us we may assume that we need to give something our particular attention. We are being alerted to what that character represents or plays in the dream scenario. If a direction is indicated – e.g. forward or backward – we can interpret that in the light of the circumstances around us.

② A wave in the sea represents the movement of emotion often emerging from the depths of our personality. Interestingly, the so-called Mexican Wave beloved of sports fans has the same connotation but with the accent on group emotion. Seen in dreams, it indicates our ability to be part of a joint effort.

③ If we are waving we have a need to communicate. If someone else is waving, our attention is being focused on a particular spiritual issue.

Wax

① Dreaming of wax is a great deal to do with the pliability that we are able to achieve in our lives. We need to be able to be malleable, to be moulded, perhaps by external events. We should be prepared to give way, but also to be firm when necessary.

② Wax can also to be taken to represent insincerity. Additionally is something that is consumed by the flame – for instance, of a candle – and therefore can be moved and changed into something else with qualities that it did not initially have.

③ Wax is symbolic of the need for spiritual pliability, and the desire to move away from rigidity.

Wealth

– also see Debt, Finance, Money, Poverty and Savings

① Dreaming of **being wealthy** is to dream of having in abundance those things that we need. We may have possibly come though a period where we have put in a lot of effort and to dream of having **a great deal of wealth** indicates that we have achieved what we have set out to do.

② Wealth and status usually go naturally together, so often when we are having problems in dealing with our own status in life we will have dreams about wealth. It can also often indicate the resources that we have or that we can use from other people. We have the ability to draw on our experiences or feelings and to achieve a great deal within the framework of our lives.

③ There is a 'wealth' of spiritual knowledge to be gained, and to dream of wealth of any kind indicates that it is within our grasp.

Weapons

– also see Gun and Knife

① To have a **weapon used against us** means that we have to look at how we are party to people being aggressive around us. It may be that we have done something to upset the other person which results in some form of aggression, or alternatively that we have put ourselves in a position of becoming the victim of circumstance.

② To dream of weapons usually suggests our desire to hurt someone or something. We have internalised our aggression and it is marginally more acceptable to dream of weapons and of using them against people, than actually having to deal with such circumstances in everyday life. The weapon which appears can often give us an idea of our difficulty in waking life. An **arrow** indicates being pierced by some kind of powerful emotion, of being hurt by someone else through words or actions. We need to turn our attention inwards in order to make ourselves feel better. A **cannon**, being an old-fashioned weapon which is highly destructive, will signify old-fashioned attitudes which are capable of breaching our defences. A **cannon ball** may have the same significance as a bullet – a targeted hurt designed to cause the maximum distress. The **gun or pistol** traditionally represents male sexuality and for **a woman to dream of being shot** often indicates her wish for, or fear of, sexual aggression. If **we are shooting the gun** ourselves we may be using our masculine abilities in quite an aggressive way, in order to defend ourselves. A **knife** represents the ability to cut through debris, to 'cut into' whatever is bothering us and to cut out the hypocrisy that perhaps is prevailing in a situation.

③ Various weapons can suggest varying degrees of spiritual power. We should use this power with relevant caution. The **sword** has more than one meaning. Because of its hilt – which is a cross shape – it often represents a system of belief which is used in a powerful way. Equally it can be used to suggest spiritual strength, creating an ability to cut away the unnecessary more powerfully than the knife. The **sword when sheathed** is the soul or the Self *(see Self)* in the body.

Weasel
– see Animals

Weather
– also see Lightning, Storm and Thunder/Thunderbolts

① Weather, as being part of the environment of the dream, usually indicates our moods and emotions. We are very much aware of changing external situations and have to be careful to adjust our conduct in response to these.

② Weather also can indicate our internal responses to situations. If, for instance, there was **a storm** in our dream our emotions would be stormy, perhaps angry and aggressive. If we are watching **a very blue, unclouded sky**, we may be recognising that we have the ability to keep the situations that we are in under control. We do possess the ability to control internal moods and emotions which may not have been possible in the past. Being aware of the weather would indicate that we need to recognise that we are part of a greater whole rather than just individuals in our own right.

③ Different types of weather may be symbolic of a spiritual response. For example, if we require the answer to a question we may well dream of wind of some sort *(see Wind/Winding)*.

Weaving
– also see Loom

① Weaving is a very basic symbol and suggests the need to take responsibility for our own lives. To be doing any handicraft shows that we have situations in hand.

② Weaving signifies life itself and our attitude to the way we run our lives. The warp and weft of weaving was a recognisable ancient symbol of the 'fabric' of life.

③ Weaving is one of the strongest spiritual images there is. In most cultures there is an image of our fate being woven in a particular pattern. We are not supposed to be in control of that pattern, but must accept that the gods or God know what is best.

Web
– also see Computer, Internet and Spider/Cobweb

① In everyday life, we may well be caught up in a situation that could trap us. We could be in a 'sticky' situation and not quite know which direction to move. This can result in the symbol of a web appearing in the dream. We are 'caught in the middle' or we are trapped. Because the situation is extremely complex we have no idea which way is going to be most advantageous for us.

② From an emotional perspective, we can become very caught up in our own feelings to the exclusion of everything else. A spider's web in dreams can highlight the patterns that we use in such a process. A broken web suggests that we have lost an aspect of manoeuvrability in our thinking.

③ The spider's web is the Cosmic Plan. When we dream of a web of any sort we are linking into one of the most basic of spiritual symbols. It is within the 'web of life' that the divine powers have interwoven fate and time in order to create a reality in which we can exist. We are the spiritual entrapped within the physical and not able to escape back to our own spiritual realm.

Wedding/Wedding Dress

① To be **attending a wedding** may indicate that there is cause for celebration, and a willingness to have others recognise our involvement with others – to someone or something other than family concerns. To be dreaming of **wearing a wedding dress** is to be trying to sort out our feelings and hopes about relationships and weddings *(see Bride)*. To be **dressing someone else in a wedding dress** can indicate our feelings of inferiority – 'always the bridesmaid, never the bride'.

② To be at a wedding in dreams, whether as participant or observer, suggests that we are part of a wider celebration in tune with the cycles of nature and fertility. We, for a short time, are focused on future happiness, mutual support and a coming together of two families. Just as in waking life weddings bring forth a great deal of emotion, in dreams they may give us the opportunity to express emotion in an appropriate fashion.

③ In pagan lore, handfastings or weddings generally took place at Beltane (1 May) in tune with the coming together of the God and Goddess to initiate the new Cycle of the Year. In spiritual terms a wedding symbolises a new cycle or stage of consciousness.

Wedding Ring
– also see Ring

① Traditionally, the wedding ring was a symbol of total encircling love. Because it is in the shape of a circle, it is complete with no beginning and no end. So to dream of this symbol is to link in with that basic concept of eternity. To dream of **losing one's wedding ring** would very often symbolise a problem within a marriage. To dream of **finding a wedding ring** might well indicate that a relationship is being formed which could result in marriage or commitment.

② Within the human being there is the innate need to make vows, to give promises and above all to symbolise the making of those promises. The wedding ring, worn on the finger which represents the heart – the fourth finger of the left hand – therefore suggests that we have made that type of promise. To dream of **a wedding ring being on any other finger** than that particular finger may indicate that the promise is not valid or we feel the wedding ring to be a constriction or an entrapment in some way.

③ A wedding ring symbolises the binding sacrifice which is eternal love.

Wedge

① Dreaming of a wedge often indicates that we need to open up situations around us. We need to put something in position which means that we can be open and truthful at all times. Since the wedge is also a symbol of support, it may be that we need to be aware that in situations around us we might need increasing assistance. We would also need to guard against becoming too dependent on that kind of support.

② The triangle symbolises the ability to manifest matter within the physical. The wedge esoterically indicates the passage of time which allows something to become real in our lives – for a dream to become reality.

③ If we are feeling somewhat isolated, a wedge will symbolise the spiritual support that we have been seeking.

Weeds
– also see Plants

① Weeds are generally **plants which grow on waste ground** and their symbolism in dreams reflects this. They may indicate misplaced trust, misplaced energy or even misplaced attempts at success. They do not contribute a tremendous amount to our lives and if allowed to run riot or to overgrow can stop our own positive growth. To be **digging up weeds** would show that we are aware that by freeing our life of the non-essential we are creating space for new growth and new abilities.

② Mental attitudes and old patterns of behaviour which clog us up and do not allow us to move forward can very often be shown in dreams as weeds. We may need to decide which of these weeds are helpful to us (that is which could be composted, transferred into something else and made use of to help positive growth) or which need to be thrown away. Often plants growing wild have healing properties. By using these properties we can enhance our lives. For instance, dandelion tea is a natural diuretic, and dreams can often tell us what we need.

③ Weeds, by courtesy of their irritating qualities and refusal to be quickly eradicated, symbolise spiritual difficulties.

Weeping
– also see Mourning

① Weeping suggests uncontrollable emotion or grief, so to experience either **ourselves or someone else weeping** is to show that there needs to be a discharge of such emotion. Crying, while less heart-rending, will have the same significance. We may be sad over past events or fearful of moving into the future. It is worthwhile exploring the quality of weeping. Are we sobbing and therefore not able to express ourselves fully? We may simply be creating difficulty within ourselves which enables us to express the feelings we have bottled up.

② Something exuding moisture so that it seems to be weeping is often deemed to be miraculous, and this dream can appear quite often in stages of transition as we are moving from one state of awareness to another. The excess energy can be shown as a weeping plant, tree or some such image.

③ Weeping suggests mourning for some spiritual quality we have lost, or are perhaps yet to find.

Weighing

① To be **weighing something** in dreams is to be assessing its worth. This image connects with the calculation of our needs and what is of value to us, whether materially or spiritually.

② **Weighing something up** is to be trying to make a decision accurately to assess what the risks are. If we are trying to **balance the scales** we are looking for justice and natural balance within our knowledge.

③ We are weighing up our spiritual options. We could also be trying to work out our spiritual worth and value.

Weight

① Experiencing a weight in a dream is to be conscious of our responsibilities in everyday life. It may also suggest that we should assess the importance and seriousness of what we are doing.

② Weight in a dream may well indicate the need to be practical and down to earth in waking life. We need to keep our feet on the ground.

③ Weight in a dream indicates gravitas and seriousness. We perhaps need to be taking our spiritual journey a little more seriously.

Welcome

① **To receive a welcome** in a dream suggests that we are accepting of our own selves. We are beginning to like who we are. If the welcome is from **a member of our family** we are being accepted by, and accepting, a better relationship with the family.

② To be **welcoming someone into our own house** suggests we are learning to trust ourselves. Being in a **welcoming party** signifies our ability to belong to a social group with common beliefs.

③ We are being accepted, or indeed welcomed, on the first steps to spiritual fulfilment.

Well
– also see Water

① A well is a way of assessing the deepest resources of feeling and emotion that we have. Unless we have such access we are not going to be whole. If there is something wrong with the well, e.g. we **cannot reach the water**, we are not able to get in touch with our best talents.

② The image of a well in a dream suggests our ability to be 'well'. We have the ability to be healed and to fulfil our dearest wish, if we so desire. By putting ourselves in touch with our intuitive, aware selves we open up the potential and possibilities for healing and success.

③ A well can symbolise a form of contact with the depths – possibly the depths of emotion.

Werewolf

① The werewolf or part-man part-beast has long been an image in mythology. Wolves have also at various times been thought of as both sacred and something to be feared. The werewolf in dreams can thus represent the dichotomy between man's animal nature and his spiritual self.

② As media coverage of the strange and bizarre increases, our minds are able to accept weird images created by others. The imagery behind the idea that sensitive individuals can be affected by changes in the lunar cycle gave rise to a mythology of its own. The werewolf, whose destructive self emerges according to pre-set triggers, in dreams mirrors a psychological state.

③ Interestingly, there is thought to be some confusion between the Greek word *lycos* for wolf from which we get lycanthropy and *lyke* meaning light. A werewolf highlights the idea of spiritual clarity opposed to spiritual darkness.

West
– see Position

Wet
– see Water

Whale
– see Animals

Wheat
– see Grain

Wheel
– also see Circle in Shapes/Patterns

① A wheel in a dream indicates the ability and need to make changes – to move forward into the future without being thrown off course.

② To **lose a wheel** from a vehicle is to lose motivation or direction – to be thrown off balance. A **large wheel**, such as the Ferris Wheel in a fairground, suggests an awareness of life's ups and downs.

③ The wheel has several spiritual meanings. It represents the Wheel of Life, and how we see ourselves fitting in and also the Pagan Wheel of the Year of growth and decay.

Whip/Lash

① The whip is an instrument of torture. For this to appear indicates we have either the need to control others or to be controlled by them. We may be trying to control by using pain – either physical or emotional.

② Because the whip is an instrument of punishment we need to be aware that in trying to force things to happen, we may also be creating problems for ourselves.

③ A whip suggests corrective punishment and self-flagellation. Whiplash suggests the recoil before a positive action which may be painful.

Whirlpool/Whirlwind

① Both these images are symbols of the vortex, a representation of life and natural energy. There are usually conflicting energies in both. When they appear in dreams we are aware of the quality of power we have within. The **whirlpool** will more properly represent emotional energy, while the **whirlwind** will suggest intellectual power.

② Intellectually we may know that we have control over our lives, but are caught up in an endless round of activity which appears to be unproductive, if not destructive, but in fact contains a tremendous amount of energy.

③ A whirl of creativity lies ahead. We must 'go with the flow' and fully take advantage. It should be seen as cleansing.

Whisky
– see Alcohol

Whispering
– also see Gossip

① To **hear whispering** in a dream suggests that we need to listen to someone or something very carefully. It may also mean that we do not have the full information available to us about a situation in our waking lives.

② Sound in dreams can often manifest as the opposite quality to that which is required. Thus, whispering could be interpreted as a shout for attention. A whisper can also suggest the need for privacy and caution.

③ Hidden Information and Occult Knowledge are often first heard as a whisper or whispering.

Whistle/Whistling

① A whistle being blown in a dream can mark the end of a particular phase of time. It can also sound as a warning to alert us to a particular event. Whistling in the ear suggests in dreams the need to pay attention to what is to come.

② A whistle may be heard and recognised in dreams about games *(See Games/Gambling)*. As a means of controlling and training, it may be relevant as to how it is blown. For instance if it is **blown harshly**, we may be being made aware that we have transgressed a known code of conduct.

③ A Spiritual summons. A whistle can also represent the development of our psychic powers.

White
– see Colours

Widow

① Dreaming of being a widow can suggest loss and sadness. Sometimes such a dream can mark the change in a woman's awareness as she moves towards the 'Crone' or Wise Woman. For a **woman to dream of a widow** highlights her ability to be free and use her own innate wisdom.

② In **a man's dream** a widow may signify a deeper understanding of a woman's needs. He may recognise that all women do not necessarily become dependent on him. This will, of course, be mediated by his relationship with his mother.

③ Feminine Spiritual Wisdom, although sometimes in its negative sense.

Wife
– see Family

Wig

1. In previous times, covering the head was considered to be a way of hiding the intellect, of giving a false impression or of indicating wisdom and authority. A **judge's wig** can suggest all of these. To become conscious of a **hairpiece or toupée** highlights false ideas or an unnatural attitude.

2. Sometimes a wig highlights the fact that we have something to hide. We are perhaps not as competent, as youthful or as able as we would like others to believe.

3. A symbol of Spiritual authority and judgement, that conferred by Knowledge.

Wild

1. In dreams anything wild always represents the untamed. Within each of us there is a part that dislikes being controlled in any way. It is the part of ourselves which needs to be free, and is creative and independent. A **wild animal** will stand for that aspect of our personality which has not yet committed itself to using rational thought. If the dreamer is male, a wild woman will represent the Anima *(see Anima/Animus)*, if feminine the Shadow *(see Shadow)*.

2. Anything which grows wild is not subject to the same constraints which normal society puts upon us, so in this context wildness may signify anarchy and lack of stability. In its more positive sense there is profusion and promise in whatever we are trying to do.

3. In a dream to be, or feel, wild often suggests a lack of spiritual control. It is passion without restraint.

Will

1. To dream of a will or any legal document is connected with the way in which our unconscious side can push us into taking notice of our inner needs. To be **making a will** is to be making a promise to ourselves over future action. It may also have overtones of attempting to look after those we love and care about. To **inherit from a will** means that we need to look at the habits, characteristics and morals that we have inherited from our ancestors.

2. We may dream of a will at a time when we need everything to be done properly and with certain levels of correctness. There is the obvious play on words where a will would indicate the will to do or to be – the determination to take action, for instance. Because for many making a will is a very final action, in dreams it can indicate a recognition that we are entering a new phase of life. We are moving on from the old.

3. Determination in spiritual matters is represented here. This can also suggest the resolution of a problem with which we have been dealing.

Willow
– see Trees

Wind/Winding
– also see Gale and Hurricane

① In dreams, the wind symbolises the intellect. It will depend on the force of the wind how we interpret the dream. For instance, **a breeze** would suggest gentleness and pleasure. An idea or concept we have is beginning to move us. In another sense, to be **winding something up** such as thread or a screw can suggest creating a necessary tension which enables matters to be brought to a conclusion.

② On a slightly more psychological level, wind in a dream can suggest the beginning of a new, much deeper awareness of ourselves. **A gale** might indicate a principle we feel passionately about, whereas a **north wind** might suggest a threat to our security. **Winding up proceedings** such as in a court case indicates that we need to take all opinions into account before making any sort of decision. **Winding someone up** in dreams may highlight our need to prove ourselves superior. **Being wound up** by someone else suggests we are not fully in control of our own emotions.

③ The Power of the Spirit and the movement of Life. Just as the Holy Spirit in Christianity was said to be 'a mighty rushing wind', so such a dream can represent a Divine revelation of some sort.

Windmill

① The image of a windmill in dreams can often suggest the correct use of resources. Because wind often suggests intellect, it is therefore the use of intellectual assets. Most people's image of a windmill is of the old fashioned type with wooden sails. To dream about the rotary blades used in **wind farms** suggests we need to be more aware of ecological *(see Ecology)* and technological issues.

② A windmill has significance as an image of the harvesting of our efforts – in this case, of material resources – available to us. As a storehouse of fertility, in dreams it can sometimes represent the feminine or the mother.

③ The windmill is symbolic of the many facets of the Spiritual Intellect, which in turn is stimulated by our own spiritual powers and abilities.

Window
– see Buildings

Wine
– also see Alcohol

① In dreams, wine can suggest a happy occasion. As a substance it has an influence on our awareness and appreciation of our environment. A **wine cellar**, therefore, can represent the sum of our past experiences, both good and bad.

② As a symbol of 'the liquid of life', wine highlights our ability to draw the best out of our experiences and to make use of what is gleaned to provide fun, happiness and enjoyment. The **wine glass** can have two meanings. Firstly, it stands for the container of our happiness and secondly it can stand for pregnancy, or our thoughts about pregnancy. A **broken wine glass** can depict sorrow or missed opportunities. In old-fashioned dream interpretation in **a woman's dream** it could suggest miscarriage.

③ Wine can represent potential spiritual abundance (as in the parable of turning water into wine). It can also signify the taking in of spiritual power.

Wings
– also see Flight and Flying

① Because wings make us think of flight, to dream of, for instance, **birds' wings** would suggest attention is being drawn to our need for freedom. A **broken wing** indicates that a previous trauma is preventing us from 'taking off'.

② Wings can also be protective, and this symbolism often appears in dreams. An **angel's wings** would depict the power to transcend our difficulties, as also would the wings of a bird of prey.

③ The protecting, all-pervading power of God, as seen in the wings of the Seraphim.

Winter

① In dreams, winter can represent a time in our lives which is unfruitful. It can also represent old age, a time when our energy is running down.

② At a period in our lives when we are emotionally cold, images associated with winter – such as ice and snow *(see Ice/Iceberg and Snow)* – can highlight the appropriateness, or otherwise, of the way we feel. In clairvoyance, the seasons can also indicate a time of year when something may happen.

③ Within the cycle of nature, winter can represent a time of lying fallow before rebirth; hence winter can represent death or great change.

Wireless
– see Radio

Wisdom

① Wisdom is a quality that is developed, often by being able to interpret our own and others' dreams. To dream that we are wise indicates the potential we have to run our lives successfully and to relate meaningfully to other people.

② Any figure of wisdom appearing in dreams usually refers to the Self *(see Self)*.

③ Confirmation of our spiritual integrity is represented by the presence of wisdom in a dream. It may often appear in the guise of a Wise Old Man *(see Wise Old Man)*.

Wise Old Man

① When a person understands that the best guidance arises from deep within himself, the Wise Old Man puts in an appearance in dreams, sometimes as an authority figure, sometimes as a magical one, but always epitomising the wisdom of experience.

② As the Great Mother is with the feminine, the Wise Old Man is the synthesised figure of all masculine characteristics. When they are recognised equally for their power and integrated into the personality, we achieve gravitas and dignity in our experiences in everyday life.

③ Only when we have learnt to access the deeper recesses of our unconscious do we become able to consult this personalisation of a mentor, friend and source of inspiration. Sometimes he appears in times of deep trouble, offering help and solace when all other forms of help have disappeared.

Witch
– see Archetypes

Witness

① When we find ourselves in the position of **being a witness** to, for instance, an accident, it may be that our powers of observation are being highlighted. We need to take very careful note of what is going on around about us. Our interaction with authority may also be being called into question.

② **Testifying as a witness** suggests that we feel we are being called to account for our actions or beliefs. We may feel somewhat insecure until we have been accepted by our peers.

③ We are acknowledging a degree of objectivity and 'Spiritual Testament'. We bear witness to, or take responsibility for, our own conduct.

Wolf
– see Animals

Woman
– see People

Womb

– see Body

Wood

– also see Forest, Plank and Trees

① Dreaming of wood, in the sense of timber, suggests our ability to appreciate the past and to build on what has gone before. We are capable of building a structure, which may or may not be permanent. Dreaming of **a wooden toy** highlights our connection with the more natural childlike side of ourselves.

② When our behaviour becomes rigid or wooden, dreams will often attempt to make us aware of this and of the necessity to balance our feelings.

③ The wood is often a manifestation of the Spirit. If it is a wild wood, we need to show some control of our own spirit. We need to explore the wildness of our nature.

Woodpecker

– see Birds

Wool

① How we interpret wool depends on whether the image we have is of lamb's wool or of knitting wool *(see Knitting)*. **Lamb's wool** may stand for blurred thoughts and feelings. We have not really sorted our thoughts out.

② Wool has, from earliest times, represented warmth and protectiveness. Nowadays it particularly represents gentleness and mothering.

③ Wool is symbolic of Spiritual Protection. 'Pulling the wool' over someone's eyes, though generally considered to be devious, can also be a protective act. There may be things which we do not wish, or need, to see spiritually at the present time.

Word

① When in dreams we are conscious of a word being repeated, it can be either the sound that is significant or the meaning. Either way, we are being altered to its intrinsic importance.

② Certain words have esoteric meanings, such as the Hebrew word JHVH (Jehovah) and are more likely to appear in the dream state than in ordinary everyday life. We are more open to such information while we are asleep.

③ The vibrational sound of words can turn them into Words of Power. This is the Logos, or Sacred Sound.

Work
– also see Career and Unemployment

① Dreaming of being at work highlights issues, concerns or difficulties we may have within the work situation. We could be actively trying to make changes in our lives in our lives, or be having changes forced upon us through unemployment or global recession. Since we spend a great deal of time in our waking lives at work, that environment will often be found in dreams. Changes occurring in the dream scenario can highlight and give focus to the need to accept necessary change.

② Often what we do as a job bears no relation to what we consider to be our real work. Dreams can very often help us to change our situation by giving information as to our real talents and gifts. When we dream of working at something which does not have a place in our ordinary everyday lives it may be worth exploring the potential within that line of work.

③ There may be some degree of activity of the spirit ahead. We could be being moved towards the beginning of new spiritual work. Often as we are forced through changes in the material world to reconsider options we are enabled to move closer to our spiritual goals.

Workshop
– also see Garage

① A workshop is a place that is productive. In dreams it symbolises the part of ourselves which creates projects which then become profitable for us, though not necessarily financially.

② A workshop may often be where we meet others of like mind, people who are creative in the same way as we are. It therefore represents group interaction and talent.

③ A workshop often holds within it creative outlets – this creativity can be used for our spiritual progression.

World
– also see Globe

① The world represents the area of experience in which one lives, and our everyday activities. Often to dream of a world beyond our sphere of influence suggests the necessity to take a wider viewpoint in a situation around us.

② To dream of **other worlds and dimensions** suggests different ways of experiencing our own lives. We perhaps need to be less rigid in our opinions.

③ As we progress spiritually we become conscious that, just as on an individual level we belong to the family, so the world belongs to the Cosmos. Being aware of the world in this sense means we must take responsibility for the way the world functions in order to create a sustainable future.

Worm

① At its very basic interpretation, the worm can suggest the penis. Depending on our attitude to sexuality and gender, there may be a sense of threat. The worm is not necessarily seen to be particularly clean.

② The worm in dreams can also highlight our feelings of ineffectiveness and insignificance (whether this is about ourselves or others). **If the worm is bigger than we are** then this would suggest that our own sense of inferiority is a problem. If we are particularly conscious of a **wormcast** – that is, the earth the worm has passed through its body, then this is a transformation image and indicates we are capable of changing our lives into something more productive and fertile.

③ Being given to the worms is a metaphor for death, so we need to be aware that on a spiritual level changes may shortly be taking place.

Worship
– also see Religious Iconology

① Dreaming of being in a situation where we are **worshipping something** such as an idea, a person, a concept or an object is to be opening ourselves up to its influence. If we are not particularly religious but find ourselves in the middle of **an act of worship** we may need to look at how we deal with a common belief system or set of principles.

② Sometimes, as we move towards a greater sense of Self, dream images materialise which indicate that we are in a position to be **worshipped**. This may mean we need to take a careful look at whether we are developing an inflated idea of our own importance, or whether we are actually learning to accept that part of ourselves which is of value to other people. **To be worshipping an object which is not a religious image** may suggest that we are paying too much attention to whatever that object represents. For instance, we may be too materialistic, be paying too much attention to sex and so on.

③ An Act of Worship is an acknowledgement of the power that belief has.

Wound
– also see Fight and Weapon

① Any wound or trauma in dreams will signify hurt feelings or emotions. **If we are inflicting the wounds** our own aggression and mistrust are being highlighted, **if the wounds are being inflicted on us** we may be making ourselves into, or being, the victim.

② The type of wound will be important in interpreting the dream. A **large ugly wound** will suggest more violence, whereas a **small one** may indicate a more focused attack.

③ A wound symbolises an experience – which may have been unpleasant – that we should take note of and learn from.

Wreath

① A wreath in a dream can suggest honour. The shape, often circular, will be important as thus signifying continuity and completeness, as well as everlasting life. **Dreaming of being given a wreath** suggests being singled out, perhaps for some honour. It formerly warned of the potential for one's own death. **Dreaming of giving someone else a wreath** validates our relationship with that person.

② A wreath in dreams can have the same significance as any of the binding symbols such as harnesses and halters. It forms a bond which cannot be broken, or a sacrifice which must be accepted.

③ A wreath has triple spiritual significance – dedication, sacrifice or death (significant change). We will need to decide which is the most appropriate meaning.

Wreck

① Dreaming of a wreck – such as a **car or shipwreck** – indicates that our plans may be thwarted in some way. It is necessary to decide whether we are at fault for the failure of our plans or someone else's.

② Since a wreck can happen due to circumstances beyond our control, such a dream can indicate a greater need for control, or management of resources.

③ A wreck of some kind symbolises a defeat. We, though frustrated on this occasion, should continue to 'battle' through to reach our intended goal.

Writing
– also see Toner/Ink and Pen/Pencil

① To dream of writing is an attempt to communicate information that one has. Sometimes **the instrument we are writing** with is important. For instance, **a pencil** would suggest that the information is less permanent than with **a pen**, whereas a **typewriter or word processor** would tend to suggest business communication rather than personal. As computers and other forms of communication become more sophisticated our dreams will contain more images of such instruments.

② Writing as a creative art is meaningful, and as a form of self-expression it perhaps allows us to communicate when spoken words are inadequate. In dreams we may learn how to communicate with ourselves in differing ways. It is thought that when man began to describe in pictures and in symbols what he saw around him he took huge steps forward in developing his intelligence. To be writing by whatever means in dreams signals the need to understand more and to communicate what we do understand.

③ We may not be consciously aware of our spiritual progression. Dreaming of writing suggests a subconscious record is being kept. From the time of hieroglyphics to modern-day computers, there has been a need to record and communicate the progress of man's development. In spiritual terms writing may signify our need to chart and quantify our own progress mentally, emotionally and spiritually.

X

① If an X appears in a dream, we are usually 'marking the spot'. It can also represent an error, a misjudgement or possibly something which we particularly need to note in waking life.

② If a cross appears in the shape of an X, this usually represents the idea of sacrifice or perhaps of torture (*see Cross in Religious Iconology*).

③ Man within the Cosmos.

Xenophobia
– also see Asylum/Asylum Seeker

① Xenophobia is not the same as racism, but is more a fear of strangers, so in dreams can highlight fear of change. This necessitates identifying exactly what we are afraid of in waking life. It might be fear of authority, or perhaps a loss of control.

② Fear of the unknown or the unexplained is often suppressed in waking life but may surface in dreams as hatred of strangers.

③ True spirituality is inclusive in its ideals – that is, accepting of everyone's right to their own beliefs. Since xenophobia is exclusive, shutting out those unlike us, such a dream will highlight our inner struggle to be accepting of others.

X-rays

① Dreaming of X-rays can be significant in a number of ways. There may be something influencing our life on an unconscious level which needs to be revealed. **If we are carrying out the X-ray** it may be necessary to look more deeply into a situation. There may also be a fear of illness, either in oneself or others.

② Within waking life, it may be that there is something we need to see through. This can be a play on words, in that we need to finish something off, or we may need to have a very clear view of a situation around us.

③ Spiritually, an X-ray can symbolise a new visual clarity that we are about to experience. This clear-sightedness should enable us to move ahead confidently.

Y

① The Y is said to represent the human form with outstretched arms. It is reaching towards spirituality.

② In Spiritual terms, the Y represents duality becoming unity. Two forces uniting to reach a single goal.

③ Spiritual searching, worship or supplication.

Yacht
– see Boat/Ship in Transport

Yardstick

① Formerly, as a measuring tool, the yardstick represented correctness and rigidity. Since metrication and the changes that are taking place in the everyday world, it has less significance. Today, it still however represents good judgement.

② The yardstick represents the measurement of acceptable standards. In dreams this may represent standards of behaviour, belief or conformity.

③ Spiritually a yardstick symbolises the standards that we have set ourselves. We may wish to be re-assured that we are maintaining these standards fully.

Yarn
– also see Knitting, Loom and Weaving

① Yarn in the sense of **knitting yarn or twine** often signifies our ability to create order out of chaos. In olden times it suggested spinning, an archetypal symbol for life, and often in dreams it is this image that is portrayed. We fashion our lives out of what we are given.

② A yarn – as in a tale or story – is most often to do with our sense of history or of continuity. To be **being told a yarn or story** links with our need for heroes and heroines, and perhaps our need for a mentor.

③ The myths and stories of the old heroes who undertook their own spiritual journey can help us identify a strategy for life. Yarn may also represent guidance through a difficult situation.

Yawn

① If we become conscious of yawning in a dream it can indicate boredom and tiredness. We may also be attempting to articulate something, but have not yet thought through properly what we wish to say.

② In the animal kingdom a yawn often is a warning against aggression, and a yawn in dreams may be a way of controlling our own or other's abusive behaviour.

③ In the physical world a yawn is a way of taking in more oxygen. In the spiritual sense it suggests our inner selves are attempting to assimilate more knowledge.

Year
– see Time

Yearn

① Feelings in dreams are often heightened in intensity. A need which may be perfectly manageable in ordinary everyday life becomes a yearning and seeking in dreams. Such a dream would highlight an emotion which we may need to look at in order to understand.

② If we have suppressed our needs through long habit or self-denial, an urgency may emerge in dreams for the very thing we have consciously denied.

③ We may have become somewhat impatient in our seemingly never-ending search for our spiritual self. This is often symbolised by a yearning feeling in a dream.

Yeast

① Yeast is accepted as a substance which both lightens food and makes it palatable. At the same time it changes the substance and texture. In dreams it represents ideas or influences which can irrevocably change our lives or situations, often for the better.

② As a leavening agent – something which brings lightness – yeast symbolises light, love and laughter all components of *joie de vivre*.

③ Yeast can be symbolic of the steady growth towards the realisation and beauty of natural love.

Yell

① A yell, as a loud sudden shout, epitomises either approval or an excess of emotion caused through pain or passion. In dreams it will represent some sort of shock to the system, thus making us aware of what we need to know or alerting us to danger.

② If in dreams we are ourselves yelling, we may need to have due regard in waking life to how we express ourselves. If such expression is not our usual *modus operandi* it would be wise to look at what we have been suppressing and what needs expressing with passion. If someone is yelling at us in dreams we need to identify the emotion behind the yell – fear, anger, surprise or enthusiasm.

③ A yell in dreams can be an expression of a jointly held enthusiasm, belief or ideal, as with a football or protest chant. Such sound has an impact far beyond that created solely by the individual, manifesting a particular resonance. This could be said to be spiritually relevant – in that it represents something greater than the sum of its parts.

Yes

① Occasionally in dreams we become aware that we have 'said' yes. This is an instinctive acceptance or acknowledgement of the validity of whatever has been happening.

② Often, before we are able to make changes in our ordinary everyday lives, we need to give ourselves permission on an unconscious level. Recognising this in the dream state can be an important part of our growth process.

③ We are being given permission to spiritually grow and flourish. With this permission, we can look towards a more directed lifestyle.

Yew
– also see Tree

① In former times the yew tree symbolised mourning and sadness. While few people would necessarily recognise a yew tree, there is, on an unconscious level, awareness of such knowledge in everyone. Such a symbol can surface as instinctive awareness in dreams.

② There can be an aspect of word-play here in that the 'yew' is in fact 'you' in the sense of someone other than us as the dreamer. This wordplay is a way of focusing the our attention away from us.

③ A yew tree, which is said to outlive many other trees, may symbolise spiritual immortality.

Yield

① To yield in a dream is to be aware of the futility of confrontation. There may be situations in our waking life in which it would be wise to take a back seat and avoid difficulties.

② Yielding is one of the more feminine attributes and signifies our need to let go and simply 'go with the flow'. We perhaps need to be more open to change.

③ We may have been contemplating the idea of a more spiritual existence for some time, and has now finally yielded, or submitted, to the notion.

Yin-Yang

① This symbol has become much better known in the last fifty years in the West as the balance of two complementary opposites. In dreams it indicates the balance between the instinctive, intuitive nature of the feminine and the active, rational nature of the masculine.

② We are continuously searching for balance, but not necessarily a state of inertia. The yin-yang symbol signifies a state of dynamic potential.

③ Perfect Balance is achieved by the energy created between two complementary opposites, yet each containing the potential of the other.

Yoga
– also see Meditation

① For those people who practise yoga disciplines it is possible that their practice will come into dreams as a guiding force, and certain postures will improve after dreams of correct posture. The inner guru has been released.

② Because it is a mental discipline as much as a physical, in yoga certain concepts and awareness will surface in dreams initially in order that they can be consciously considered.

③ Yoga is union with the spiritual and as one learns to manipulate the dream state it becomes easier to enter a meditative state where that sense of completeness can be experienced.

Yogi
– see Guru

Yoke
– see Harness and Halter

Yolk
– also see Egg

① If in dreams our attention is drawn to the yolk of an egg, we must concentrate on which aspects of our everyday life need nurturing. It might be a new idea or way of thinking which has not yet properly taken shape. A broken yolk may suggest that time is of the essence in a particular project.

② Emotionally, the yolk of an egg seen in dreams as separate from the white and shell can signify that we are making the mistake of isolating our emotions and not allowing ourselves the luxury of emotional maturity.

③ As nutritive material, the yolk will represent the raw material, the urge for growth and the natural awareness we must have before we begin our spiritual journey.

Young/Youth
– also see Archetypes

① To experience oneself as being young in a dream can signify an innocence that is necessary in a particular situation in waking life. If we recognise someone in dreams as being younger than they actually are either they, or what they represent, may be acting in an immature fashion in waking life.

② From an emotional perspective the youth, or youthfulness in dreams suggests an honest, full-on approach – what you see is what you get.

③ Spiritually, youth as a theme in dreams suggests an attitude of simplicity before ideas have been contaminated by learned behaviour. If there is a world-weary attitude we would be wise to consider our own ability to question the status quo.

Yule log
– also see Fire

① In Pagan times a log was decorated and burnt in order to clear away the Old Year. In dreams it will be seen as a symbol of light and new life.

② In modern times, the Yule log is symbolised as a celebration cake. Therefore in dream language it tends to suggest the New Year and new beginnings.

③ A Yule log represents a spiritual offering or sacrifice, particularly at the time of a spiritual or religious celebration when we pay homage to the gods.

Zebra
– see Animals

Zen

① Zen is a system of enlightenment through meditation and being aware of it in dreams may mean that we should look to take the most direct route possible to success.

② Psychologically, a Zen moment can be a sudden flash of insight or inspiration – something which is achievable in dreams while in a state of relaxation.

③ The deliberate practice of Zen – focussed meditation –allows dreams to access more and more subtle realms of spiritual knowledge, of which we need to be aware as we progress on our life journey.

Zenith

① Technically, the zenith is the highest point in the celestial sphere immediately above us. In dreams therefore it signifies success in reaching for all we need and desire.

② Peak performance in our activities is the overcoming of our own doubts and fears. Reaching the high point of personal achievement is attaining the zenith and can be symbolised as such in dreams.

③ As the culmination of a spiritual journey the zenith represents realization and the attainment of our goals.

Zero
– also see Numbers

① In many ways in dreams, zero signifies the point of balance between negative and positive. If we have an interest in numbers or mathematics, zero can also suggest a cipher or symbol as well as an absence of quantity.

② Zero denotes no-thing and is a symbol of the void when perhaps the mind cannot totally accept the ideas inherent in the absence of everything.

③ In dreams zero signifies completeness as shown by its symbol, 0, when it has the same connotation as the circle. It is the starting point from which everything begins.

Zigzag

① When we see a zigzag in dreams we are looking at the potential to be hit by disaster, such as in a bolt of lightning. An event will occur which brings about a discharge of energy. Circumstances will then be brought back into balance.

② In a psychological sense, we will achieve a new level of awareness, perhaps even a revelation. Such a symbol in dreams can also suggest a flash of insight in everyday life. Since the writing of the Harry Potter books, young people may find the idea of being magically gifted attractive.

③ New potential and growth. The zigzag of a lightning flash in dreams signifies the act of creation or manifestation as the energy travels through the various dimensions to take form in the material world.

Zip

① A zip appearing in a dream may indicate our ability – or difficulty – in maintaining relationships with other people. A **stuck zip** suggests a difficulty in keeping our dignity in an awkward situation.

② Psychologically, we are capable of being either open or closed to our friends and family. Often a zip can highlight this in a dream.

③ Spiritual connections. It also represents fastening onto an idea or concept.

Zodiac

① Everyone has a fascination for horoscopes, without necessarily understanding the significance of the zodiac wheel. It is often only when we begin the journey of self-discovery that images and symbols from the zodiac will appear in dreams. Frequently, the animal or creature associated with our own star sign will appear, almost as a reminder of basic principles. The way we deal with that image will give us insight into how we really feel about ourselves.

② The zodiac wheel is symbolic of our relationship with the universe. Sometimes the signs of the zodiac are used in dreams to demonstrate time or time passing, and also suggest courses of action we might take. For instance, if we dreamt of a girl riding a goat we might have to seek perfection (Virgo) through tenacity (Capricorn). Each sign also rules a particular part of the body, and often a dream alerts us to a possible imbalance.

③ The spheres of influence of the various signs as described below are:

Aries The symbol is the Ram and it governs the head. The colour associated with the sign is red; its specific gemstones are amethyst and diamond.

Taurus The symbol is the Bull and it governs the throat. The colours associated with the sign are blue and pink; its specific gemstones are moss agate and emerald.

Gemini The symbol is the Twins (often shown as masculine and feminine) and it governs the shoulders, arms and hands. The colour associated with the sign is yellow; its specific gemstones are agate and beryl.

Cancer The symbol is the Crab and it governs the stomach and higher organs of digestion. The colours associated with the sign are either violet or emerald green; its specific gemstones are moonstones and pearls.

Leo The symbol is the Lion and it governs the heart, lungs and liver. The colours associated with the sign are gold and orange; its specific gemstones are topaz and tourmaline.

Virgo The symbol is the Virgin and it governs the abdomen and intestines. The colours associated with the sign are grey and navy blue; its specific gemstones are pink jasper and jade.

Libra The symbol is the Scales and it governs the lumbar region, kidneys and skin. The colours associated with the sign are blue and violet; its specific gemstones are opal and lapis lazuli.

Scorpio The symbol is the Scorpion and it governs the genitals. The colours associated with the sign are deep red and purple; its specific gemstones are turquoise and ruby.

Sagittarius The symbol is the Archer and it governs the hips, thighs and nervous system. The colours associated with the sign are light blue and orange; its specific gemstones are carbuncle and amethyst.

Capricorn The symbol is the Goat and it governs the knees. The colours associated with the sign are violet and green; its specific gemstones are jet and black onyx.

Aquarius The symbol is the Water-Bearer and it governs the circulation and ankles. The colour associated with the sign is electric blue; its specific gemstones are garnet and zircon.

Pisces The symbol is the Fishes and it governs the feet and toes. The colour associated with the sign are sea-green and mauve; its specific gemstones are coral and chrysolite.

Zoo
– also see Animals

(1) Dreaming of being in a zoo suggests the need to understand some of our natural urges and instincts. We perhaps need to be more objective in our appraisal than subjective.

(2) There may be an urge to return to simpler, more basic modes of behaviour. Some people are natural observers, and we may be being alerted to the fact that we also need to be capable of participating in conduct appropriate to the group to which we belong. We also, of course, may be conscious that we ourselves are being observed, perhaps in the work situation.

(3) Dreaming of a zoo can alert us to the necessary and appropriate customs and behaviour in an impending situation.

Remembering your Dreams

To be able to remember all your dreams you need to train yourself to do so. Good-quality sleep is the first prerequisite since, while you are learning, you may well be waking yourself up fairly frequently. Later you will remember creative dreams particularly, but first of all you must get into a particular routine.

① Decide which sleep periods you are going to monitor. A good idea is to give yourself an approximate four-hour period to have a proper sleep, then to monitor everything after that in chunks of waking yourself up every hour or so.

② If you have an illness or are taking medication, please check with your doctor or medical practitioner before undertaking this exercise.

③ Set your alarm or wake-up device – soft light or soothing music – for the time you wish to wake. Don't allow yourself to be 'shocked' into wakefulness, for example, by very loud music. It is counter-productive because it is most likely to chase away the dream.

④ When you have woken up, lie perfectly still. Do not move until you have recalled your dream with as much detail as you can remember.

⑤ Write down your dream and analyse it. Make note of any particularly memorable or unusual features you can recall.

⑥ It is here that your dream journal will come in useful, because in it you will also be able to record fragments of dreams which at the time may not seem to have relevance but, later on, may do so.

⑦ Dreams are remembered best from periods of REM sleep, so with practice, you should begin to discover when these periods are. Don't be too worried if at first your dream recall is deficient. You will get better with practice.

⑧ Try not to let the day get in the way when you first awake – begin to consider it when you have looked at your mind's night time activity.

Day's Residue

Use this space to analyse how the activities and experiences of your waking hours have influenced the content of your dreams.

Dream

I dreamt like this because in the last 48 hours I have

① *Seen:*

② *Heard:*

③ *Recognised:*

Keeping a Dream Journal

Below are some easy-to-follow instructions to help you develop good practice when trying to recall, and record, your dreams accurately.

① *Any paper and writing implements can be used – whatever is most pleasing to you.*

② *Always keep your recording implements at hand.*

③ *Write the account of the dream as soon as possible after waking.*

④ *Use as much detail as possible.*

⑤ *Be consistent in the way that you record your dreams. By way of example, one simple format is suggested on the page opposite.*